Some issues in human sexuality

Some issues in human sexuality

A guide to the debate

A discussion document from the House of
Bishops' Group on *Issues in Human Sexuality*

CHURCH HOUSE
PUBLISHING

Church House Publishing
Church House
Great Smith Street
London
SW1P 3NZ

ISBN 0 7151 3868 5

GS 1519

Cover design by Church House Publishing
Typeset in 10.5 pt Sabon
Printed in England by
The Cromwell Press Ltd,
Trowbridge, Wiltshire

Published 2003 for the House of Bishops
of the General Synod of the Church of
England by Church House Publishing.

Copyright © The Archbishops' Council
2003

Unless otherwise indicated, the Scripture
quotations contained herein are from the
New Revised Standard Version Bible,
copyright © 1989, by the Division of
Christian Education of the National Council
of the Churches of Christ in the USA, and
are used by permission. All rights reserved.

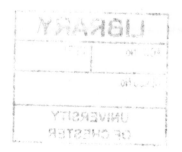

Contents

Membership of the Working Group on *Issues in Human Sexuality*

The Right Revd Dr Richard Harries (Chairman), *Bishop of Oxford*
The Right Revd Dr Peter Forster, *Bishop of Chester*
The Right Revd John Gladwin, *Bishop of Guildford*
The Right Revd Michael Scott-Joynt, *Bishop of Winchester*

Consultant
The Revd Dr Jane Shaw, *Fellow, Chaplain and Dean of Divinity, New College, Oxford*

Staff
Dr Martin Davie, *Theological Consultant to the House of Bishops*
Mr Jonathan Neil-Smith, *Secretary to the House of Bishops*
Mr David Skidmore, *Secretary to the Board for Social Responsibility*
Miss Jane Melrose, *Assistant Secretary to the House of Bishops*

Preface

This document is published under the authority of the House of Bishops and is commended by the House to the Church for study.

On behalf of the House of Bishops
✠ Rowan Cantuar
✠ David Ebor

November 2003

Foreword

The title of this study exactly defines its purpose. It is a guide to the theological debate on questions that have arisen in response to the 1991 House of Bishops report *Issues in Human Sexuality*. It works within the parameters of this earlier statement and does not seek to change the position of the House of Bishops from the one expressed there.

In the eleven years since *Issues in Human Sexuality* was published there has been much debate in the churches, not least the Anglican Communion and the Church of England, on the issue of sexuality, particularly homosexuality. This document is intended to help people to enter into that debate, especially into issues connected with Scripture and its interpretation. Our hope is that readers may find here the resources to engage with the questions in an informed way, enabling all of us to enter more deeply into the outlook and theology both of those with whom we agree and those with whom we disagree.

Above all, this guide is intended to bring about greater levels of mutual understanding, encouraging us not only to be better informed but to listen to one another with genuine hearing and imaginative insight. A philosopher once said that that 'All ethics is training in sympathy'. That sympathy, that is, the attempt to enter into both the mind and feelings of the other person, is crucial to this debate because sexuality is an integral part of being human. When Christians argue for their position in a forthright manner, which of course they are entitled to do, this can be painful to others, especially to lesbian, gay, bisexual and transsexual Christians. For them, this debate is a debate about their personal sexual identity and practice, and all too often they experience rejection by other members of the Church.

At the same time, those who believe that the Church's traditional teaching on sexual morality embodies the God-given teaching of Holy Scripture itself can also feel pained by those who interpret Scripture differently or who appear to set aside the teaching of Scripture entirely. This is why the words from the final report from The International Anglican Conversations of Human Sexuality are particularly pertinent.

We discovered in our own experience the importance of 'Interpretive charity': imputing the best intentions to our colleagues and other members of our communion, telling the better stories about them, checking (if possible at first hand) before drawing conclusions.

The report came from a group of twelve Anglican leaders meeting for three years after the 1998 Lambeth Conference. In commending it to the Anglican Communion Archbishop George Carey noted that:

We use dialogue in order to *clarify* where misunderstandings may lie; to *probe* deeper into the motives for adopting this or that position in regard to certain issues; and to *appreciate* better (even though we may not agree with them) the reasons why some people's views differ so radically from our own. In this way our deeper search for truth will not be divorced from the fellowship we need for truth to emerge.[1]

That, we hope, has been the model followed by our own working group and will be the model for continuing discussions throughout the Church on the basis of this guide.

As we have already explained, this guide is intended to inform the current debate about human sexuality in the Church of England. It is hoped that it will be a useful resource for both individual and group study. No previous knowledge of the debate about human sexuality is assumed, and it is hoped that the material will be accessible to anyone within the Church who is prepared to invest the necessary time to think through the issues involved. (A study guide to help people work through the material is also available from Church House Publishing.)

A note about terminology: the terms 'heterosexual', 'homosexual', 'bisexual', 'gay', 'lesbian' and 'transsexual' are all inventions of the nineteenth and twentieth centuries and their use tends to reflect the widely held modern beliefs that we each have a specific sexual orientation and that this can be distinguished from our actual sexual activity. These beliefs cannot be assumed to underlie earlier discussions of human sexuality and it is, therefore, strictly speaking, anachronistic to use the modern terminology when referring to these earlier discussions. For ease of reference, however, this guide does use these modern terms throughout, though wherever possible it refers to same-sex or homosexual activity, rather than homosexuality, when referring to the premodern era.

Bishop Richard Harries
Chairman of the Working Party

chapter 1

The current debate on sexuality

A. The background to the current debate

1.1 Changes in society

1.1.1 If one were to choose one word with which to sum up the current state of play in regard to human sexuality within British society then that word would have to be 'diversity'. There is currently in British society a great variety of sexual practice and diversity of attitudes to sexual morality.

1.1.2 Looking first of all at sexual practice, it has to be acknowledged from the outset that there has always been a wide variety of sexual practice within British society. Research by social historians has made clear that there never was a 'golden age' in which sexual behaviour was limited to consensual sex between heterosexual married couples. Sexual activity outside marriage is something that has been known throughout recorded history.

1.1.3 Lack of information from the past makes it extremely difficult to say with confidence whether there is a greater variety of sexual expression today than there has been in the past. For example, although it seems probable that homosexual relationships and premarital sex are more common today than they have been in the recent past, it is not clear whether the same is true for prostitution, which was extremely widespread in both the eighteenth and nineteenth centuries. Then again, with regard to paedophilia, it is not clear whether there is more sexual abuse of children today than there was in the past or whether people are simply more willing to admit that it is taking place.

1.1.4 However, what seems unarguable is that there is now a greater diversity of attitudes to sexual morality than was the case in the past.

1.1.5 In the middle of the twentieth century there was a widespread consensus that the proper context for human sexual relationships was marriage and the begetting of children and deviations from this norm were regarded as morally wrong. The particular form of family life that this consensus presupposed – a father, a mother, and their children as opposed to an extended family or household – may be a product of the modern era and industrialized society (although the changing structure of the 'family' or 'household' throughout Western history has been much debated by historians in recent decades), but, as we shall see, the view of sexual morality underlying this consensus was one that had been accepted throughout Christian history.

1.1.6 Today, there are still very many people who would continue to hold to this traditional position, but there is also a growing number of people who would argue that some forms of sexual relationship outside marriage are to be accepted.

1.1.7 Surveys of social attitudes make it clear that most people would regard violent or exploitative sexual activity as wrong and would, therefore, be opposed to rape or paedophilia. In addition, most people believe that fidelity in marriage is important and would, therefore, be opposed to adultery. However, the *British Social Attitudes Survey* for 1998, for example, indicates that two thirds of those surveyed did not believe that sex before marriage was wrong and, indeed, thought that it was a good idea for people to live together before marriage. Furthermore, a small majority of those surveyed rejected the idea that same-sex sexual relationships were always wrong, with young people in particular taking this approach.

1.1.8 Evidence from those working with young people indicates that there is a growing trend for many of them to have sexual relationships with partners from both sexes. This does not necessarily mean that they are bisexual, if this term is understood to refer to some form of fixed sexual orientation. What it does mean is that they feel sexual attraction to members of both sexes and see no moral objection to having a sexual relationship with them as part of a journey of sexual exploration and discovery that may very well end up with their entering into a long-term relationship with a partner from one particular sex.

1.1.9 If we ask what has caused this shift to a greater diversity of approaches to sexual morality, the first thing to note is that it is part of a much wider cultural shift to a greater variety of lifestyles and beliefs than we have ever seen before.

1.1.10   In the words of the Christian social commentator Os Guinness:

> Life is a now a smorgasbord with an endless array of options. Whether it is a hobby, holiday, lifestyle, world view or religion, there's something for everybody – and every taste, age, sex, class and interest.[1]

1.1.11   The result of this multiplication of choice is a vast diversity of lifestyles. There was recently an advertisement for an Internet search engine, which exhorted people to 'define your own universe' and people are increasingly attempting to do just that, not simply through their choice of Internet search engine, but through the way they choose to decorate their homes, the clothes they choose to wear, the music they choose to listen to, the TV channels they choose to subscribe to and so forth. People, that is to say, are increasingly attempting to construct the world that immediately surrounds them, 'their world', by the selection they make from the huge variety of choices that are available to them and, because the choices they make are different, a diversity of lifestyles is the inevitable result.

1.1.12   It is, of course, true that human beings have been making choices since the dawn of time and there has always been a diversity in the way that people have lived their lives but, until very recently, the range of choices available to individuals within particular cultures has been very limited. There have been two main reasons for this limitation of choice.

1.1.13   The first reason has been a scarcity of material goods. That is to say, in pre-industrial societies most people were dependent on what could be caught, grown or manufactured in their particular local area and this limited their range of choices. If you were an English peasant in the Middle Ages, for example, it would have been no good wanting to wear cashmere and eat pineapple. You had no choice in the matter. It is only since the industrial revolution and the growth of efficient systems of communication associated with it that people in the Western world have had access to a vast range of material goods and have, therefore, been able to make a choice between them.

1.1.14   The second reason for lack of choice in the past was that most traditional societies were marked by strong systems of social control that shaped the way that people behaved in most areas of their lives. In Western Europe during the Middle Ages, for instance, the way people lived their lives was heavily determined by the popular local manifestations of the teachings of the Catholic Church and the traditions of feudal society. This would have meant that the choices open to an English peasant would have been further limited. What they could eat and when, what they could wear, where they could live, the jobs they could do, and the religion they could follow would all be limited both by strong social custom and by civil and ecclesiastical law. The Reformation and the other social, economic and political changes of the sixteenth and seventeenth centuries broke the Roman Catholic Church's monopoly of ecclesiastical power in much of Western Europe. However, for the most part, this simply meant than one form of social control was replaced by another, otherwise the situation for most people remained unchanged until the last two hundred years.

1.1.15   It is only during the last two centuries that the idea that there can be a variety of equally legitimate ways of living from which an individual is free to choose has become widely accepted. This has been due to three key changes in Western society.

1.1.16   The first of these has been the breakdown of the traditional social patterns of pre-industrial society as a result of industrialization and the urbanization that has accompanied it. This, in turn, resulted in the breakdown of traditional forms of socially imposed morality.

1.1.17   The second has been the combined influence of Enlightenment philosophy and the growing prestige of the natural sciences. In the eighteenth and nineteenth centuries, many countries saw a reaction to the Enlightenment that led to increased intellectual and social conservatism. However, in the long term, the Enlightenment and the development of the natural sciences can be seen to have resulted in a widespread unwillingness to conform to accepted patterns of thought and behaviour because of:

> a.   a growing belief that personal choice rather than the acceptance of given moral norms is the proper basis for moral commitment.[2]

> b.   a growing belief that accepted patterns of thought and behaviour have been inimical to the growth of human knowledge and happiness and based on a view of the nature of human existence that science has shown to be mistaken.

1.1.18   The third, and in many ways the most important, factor has been the twentieth-century emphasis upon personal fulfilment and emotional happiness as the proper goal of human existence. This emphasis has been connected with a decline in religious belief in much of Western society, particularly a decline in the belief that this life is a preparation for the hereafter, and that the character of our existence in the hereafter will be determined by our obedience or disobedience to God. When people cease to hope for heaven or fear hell they naturally seek their happiness in this life and, for many people, traditional forms of Christian morality have come to be seen as barriers to the achievement of this happiness.

1.1.19   The multiplication of choices that has emerged from the technological and social changes just outlined has inevitably spilled over into the area of sexual relationships. In traditional Western society the range of choice in sexual behaviour was severely constrained by two factors.

1.1.20   The first of these, which has already been alluded to at the beginning of this chapter, was the widespread social acceptance of the traditional Christian belief that the only form of legitimate sexual activity was that which took place between a man and a woman who were married to each other. As was previously noted, other forms of sexual activity were met with strong social disapproval and were often subject to punishment under the laws of both Church and State.

1.1.21   This was not only because they were believed to be theologically wrong but also because they threatened the orderly transmission of wealth and property from one generation to the next and were seen as bringing dishonour on the families of the people involved.

1.1.22   The second factor was the absence of reliable forms of contraception and the comparatively unsophisticated state of medicine in general. This state of affairs meant that sexual activity was perceived as a more risky business than it is today since, in its heterosexual form, it was likely to result in pregnancy for the woman involved, and because all forms of sexual activity carried the risk of sexually transmitted diseases for which there was no effective treatment.

1.1.23   Studies such as Angus McLaren's *Twentieth-Century Sexuality: A History*[3] show that the history behind the changes in sexual behaviour and attitudes that have taken place has been a complicated one, but a number of factors seem to stand out, including the ones alluded to above.

1. The widening of choice in all areas of life has made people increasingly unwilling to accept external restrictions in their choice of sexual activity. If people now have greater freedom than ever before to choose what to believe and how to behave in all other areas of life, why should this not also be true of their sex lives, providing that what they do does not cause harm to others?

2. The existence of an unprecedentedly high standard of living in a market-dominated society where the consumer is supreme has also affected sexual conduct. Throughout history the rich have always been able to buy the sexual activity they wanted and to use their wealth to defy religious and social norms. In recent times the spread of wealth in Western society has meant that many more people have been able to do the same.

3. The development of reliable forms of contraception and increasing confidence in the effectiveness of medicine in general has meant that, in spite of the AIDS scare of the early 1980s, people are much less concerned than they once were about the medical consequences of sexual activity. Furthermore, the work of 'sex experts' such as Havelock Ellis, Marie Stopes and Alfred Kinsey has led people to believe that sexual fulfilment is a key to emotional and psychological well-being. These two facts together have led increasing numbers of people to feel neither the need nor the inclination to accept the traditional restrictions on sexual activity because such activity is felt unlikely to do serious harm and likely to give much pleasure. Furthermore, reliable contraception has broken the link between sexual activity and having children, with the result that increasing numbers of people link sex with pleasure rather than the possibility of procreation.

4. Marriage has come under increasing pressure. Arguments rage over why this is the case,[4] but the explanation that seems most plausible is that people are now entering into marriage with higher expectations than ever before in terms of personal fulfilment but, paradoxically, these expectations are harder than ever to meet because of the current confusion about what such fulfilment might mean and how it might be achieved, and because of conflict between men and women caused by the changing pattern of gender roles in British society. Because people

have high expectations and these are often not being met, and because there is no longer the social and legal pressure to remain married that there once was, more people than ever before are choosing to end marriages that they find unfulfilling in order to try to find a better life either on their own or with someone new. In addition, people who are aware of the pressures on marriage and the harm that marital conflict can cause are choosing to remain unmarried and either to cohabit or lead a single life.

Because the decline in the number of marriages and the increasingly diverse pattern of relationships have not been accompanied by a corresponding decline in the desire to engage in sexual activity, more and more people are engaging in sexual relationships outside marriage. People still seek happiness and fulfilment in intimate sexual relationships but increasingly they do not see marriage as the only or even the best context for such relationships.

5. It is also arguable that the increase in the variety of sexual activity in Western society is not purely driven by people's exercise of personal choice, but is heavily influenced by a new form of social conformity. The great proliferation of the print and electronic media and the continuing reduction in censorship, combined with the fact that there is always money to be made from sexual titillation, have meant that there have been increasingly widespread and graphic descriptions and depictions of sexual activity of all kinds in books, newspapers, magazines, the cinema, television and now the Internet. This has in turn led to ever-increasing acceptance that varied sexual activity is a normal state of affairs. British society is being increasingly shaped by the influence of the media, and the message that is coming across is not in favour of traditional sexual morality.

6. All the factors mentioned so far have meant that most people know people among their friends or family who engage in a variety of sexual activities that differ from the traditional moral norm. This makes moral condemnation of such activity much more difficult since it is much more difficult to condemn people you know and of whom you are fond. It is easy to condemn moral stereotypes but much more difficult and painful to disapprove of the behaviour of your own friends and family.

1.1.24 All these factors taken together have meant that across the Western world people have simply not been willing to restrict their sexual activity to marriage, and there has been less and less social pressure for them to do so. It has also meant that restrictions on gay, lesbian and bisexual activity have come to be seen as increasingly outmoded and hypocritical. If heterosexual people can freely engage in sexual activity that is purely for pleasure and is not aimed at the production of children, then why should not gay, lesbian and bisexual people do the same? Why should heterosexual people deny others the emotional and physical pleasure of sexual activity that they allow themselves? As the American writer David Greenberg puts it:

> The acceptance of some forms of sexual experience whose sole purpose is pleasure, sociability, or the expression of love makes it hard, in the absence of rational grounds, to reject others that are equally harmless and consensual.[5]

1.1.25   Similar issues concerning personal choice and the search for personal fulfilment, allied to advances in medical technology, also apply in the case of people suffering from 'transsexualism' or 'gender dysphoria' who are seeking to achieve a greater degree of self-acceptance and personal fulfilment by changing their bodies to conform to what they believe to be their true sex. Why should they be trapped in what they believe to be the wrong body and thus be unable to achieve emotional and sexual fulfilment? Why should they not use medical technology to give them the same chance of fulfilment as everyone else?

1.1.26   All these changes have, of course, had an impact on thinking within the Churches and the practices of individual Christians and Christian communities. The Christian ethicist Mark D. Jordan has called this 'the undoing of Christendom's sexual compact'.[6] It is this development that we will now explore.

1.2 Changes in the Church

a. The traditional Christian view of sexual ethics
1.2.1   When C. S. Lewis wrote in his classic work of Christian apologetics *Mere Christianity*: 'There is no getting away from it; the Christian rule is, "Either marriage, with complete faithfulness to your partner, or else total abstinence",'[7] he was expressing what has always been the mainstream Christian approach to sexual ethics.

1.2.2   As Derrick Sherwin Bailey shows very clearly in his study *The Man-Woman Relation in Christian Thought*[8] there has been a variety of approaches to this subject among Christian authors down the centuries.

1.2.3   This variety has been caused by a number of influences, among the most important of which have been:

• Differing views of the place of the human body in our relationship with God.
• Differing views of the place of sexual abstinence in Christian discipleship.
• Differing understandings of the relationship between human sexuality, the fall of humanity recorded in Genesis 3, and the subsequent transmission of original sin.
• Widespread male fear of women and their sexuality as sources of temptation and impurity.

1.2.4   However, alongside this variety there has also been a core of commonly held beliefs about human sexuality that together have led to an acceptance of the conclusion expressed by Lewis.

1.2.5   The first belief is that God's intention for human sexual activity has been made known to us primarily in Holy Scripture.

1.2.6   Furthermore, there are three passages of Scripture that have been seen as especially significant for understanding God's intention. These are the creation narratives in Genesis 1–2, the teaching on marriage by Christ himself in Matthew 19.1-12 and the teaching on marriage by St Paul in 1 Corinthians 7.1-40.

1.2.7   Corinthians 7.1-40 has had a particularly important history, having been used by the patristic writers to argue for celibacy as the greater good, and by the Protestant reformers to argue for the equal importance of marriage and celibacy as forms of Christian discipleship. It therefore provides an interesting instance of a biblical passage that has been interpreted in two opposing ways.

1.2.8   The importance of philosophical reflection on human existence has been widely acknowledged, particularly by those in the Catholic tradition, but its conclusions have been seen as subordinate to, and supportive of, the teaching of the Bible.

1.2.9   The second belief, based on the teaching of Genesis 1.26-27 and 2.18-24, is that the division of humankind into two distinct but complementary sexes is not something accidental or evil but is, on the contrary, something good established by God himself when he first created the human race.[9] By complementary what is meant is that the differences between men and women were intended for the mutual good of each.

1.2.10   The sixteenth-century Protestant reformer, John Calvin, for example, while acknowledging the dissension between men and women caused by sin, writes in his commentary on Genesis 2.18:

> If the integrity of man had remained to this day such as it was from the beginning, that divine institution would be clearly discerned, and the sweetest harmony would reign in marriage; because the husband would look up with reverence to God; the woman in this would be a faithful assistant to him; and both, with one consent, would cultivate a holy, as well as a friendly and peaceful intercourse.[10]

1.2.11   What Calvin's comments also indicate, however, is that until recent times this belief in the complementary nature of the differences between men and women was also combined with a strong belief in a hierarchical relationship between them, in which men were destined to rule and women to assist and obey. Only since the Enlightenment has a belief in equality between men and women found widespread acceptance, although it was held earlier by radical Christian groups such as the Quakers and by some of the earliest Christian churches.

1.2.12   The third belief is that God ordained that men and women should relate to each other in marriage for the three reasons classically expressed in the marriage service of the *Book of Common Prayer*: 'for the procreation of children ... for a remedy against sin and to avoid fornication ... for the mutual society, help, and comfort, that the one ought to have of the other, both in prosperity and adversity.'

1.2.13   This is the belief set out, for example, by St Augustine in his treatise *On the Good of Marriage* in which he argues that the three 'goods' of marriage are *fides* (the sexual fidelity that prevents sexual activity being fornication or adultery), *proles* (the begetting of children) and *sacramentum* (the lifelong union of man and wife that meets the human need for love and companionship).[11] Furthermore, as Augustine's teaching about *sacramentum* indicates, it has been universally accepted that marriage is meant to be for life, although both the Orthodox and Protestant traditions have allowed for divorce in certain circumstances.

1.2.14   The fourth belief is that sexual union has a legitimate place in the context of marriage.

1.2.15   The patristic tradition held that sexual activity was good in the context of marriage in so far as it acted as a remedy against lust outside marriage, and led to the production of children, although St Augustine argued that sexual pleasure was a venial sin because, in our fallen state, it represented the triumph of lust over reason.[12]

1.2.16   However, from St Thomas Aquinas onwards, it came to be seen that sexual pleasure within marriage was good in itself providing that it did not unduly dominate the marital relationship, and that sexual activity was engaged in appropriately and with due moderation. In his discussion of the matter in the *Summa Theologiae*, St Thomas responds to the Augustinian argument that sexual activity within marriage is sinful because it involves immoderate passion. St Thomas' response is as follows:

> The excess of passion that amounts to a sin does not refer to the passion's quantitative intensity, but to its proportion to reason; wherefore it is only when a passion goes beyond the bounds of reason that it is reckoned to be immoderate. Now the pleasure attaching to the married act, while it is most intense in point of quantity, does not go beyond the bounds previously appointed by reason before the commencement of the act, although reason is unable to regulate this during the pleasure itself.[13]

1.2.17   This is a somewhat difficult argument for us to follow today, but what St Thomas is saying is that sexual pleasure within marriage is not sinful because, although the pleasure itself is not governed by moral reason, the act itself takes place within a virtuous context that has been established by the exercise of moral reason. As Lisa Cahill explains, what this means is that:

> Although Aquinas retains the Augustinian teaching that sex for pleasure's sake is a sin, he does not see the enjoyment of pleasure itself as wrong, as long as it is properly contained within the marital and procreative union. Aquinas has achieved a link between sexual

intimacy, even sexual pleasure, and the intense love of spouses; his definition of marriage as a sacramental vehicle of Christ's presence in the church is not achieved over against or apart from sexual love or sexual pleasure.[14]

1.2.18   Where St Thomas led, the Christian tradition has subsequently followed, so now it is generally accepted that the enjoyment of sex within marriage is something that is God-given. As the 1994 *Catechism of the Catholic Church* puts it, quoting the Papal encyclical *Gaudium et Spes*:

> The acts in marriage by which the intimate and chaste union of the spouses takes place are noble and honourable; the truly human performance of these acts fosters the self-giving they signify, and enriches the spouse in joy and gratitude.[15]

1.2.19   The fifth and last belief is that because sexual activity has its proper setting within marriage it followed that those who were not married should not engage in any sexual activity at all and that those who were should engage in it only with their spouse. The alternative to marriage was, therefore, abstinence or celibacy; abstinence for those who might get married at some point in the future, and celibacy for those called to this vocation.[16]

1.2.20   There has been a classic division of opinion at this point between the Catholic and Orthodox traditions on the one hand and Protestantism on the other, a division of opinion that reflects the difference of opinion about the importance of sexual abstinence referred to earlier.

1.2.21   The Catholic and Orthodox traditions, while accepting the goodness of marriage, and of sexual relations within marriage, have followed patristic precedent in seeing celibacy as a higher form of Christian discipleship than matrimony.[17] The Protestant tradition, however, has seen marriage and celibacy as having equal spiritual value (though in practice it has tended to see marriage as the vocation to which most Christians are called).

1.2.22   Because of the high estimate of the value of celibacy in the Christian Church prior to the Reformation, it has sometimes been suggested that a positive view of marriage only developed at the Reformation.

1.2.23   It is true that the understanding of marriage developed after the Reformation, and Protestant theologians generally placed a greater emphasis on the relational rather than the procreative aspects of matrimony. However, the relational aspects of marriage had always had a place in Christian thinking about this subject and it would certainly not be true to say that pre-Reformation Christianity took a negative view of marriage as such.

1.2.24   There are three pieces of evidence that indicate a positive view of marriage in the pre-Reformation period:

1. Those groups such as the Gnostics, the Manichees and the Cathars, who did teach that marriage and sexual intercourse were evil, were condemned as heretical by the Church. Thus, in his treatise entitled *To his Wife*, Tertullian argues that Christians should become celibate after the death of their husband or wife. His argument might seem to us to imply a depreciation of marriage but, in this very work, Tertullian rejects as heretical the ideas that marriage should be abolished or that it was not given by God:

> But let it not be thought that my reason for premising this much concerning the liberty granted to the old, and the restraint imposed on the later time, is that I may lay a foundation for teaching that Christ's advent was intended to dissolve wedlock, [and] to abolish marriage unions; as if from this period onward I were prescribing an end to marrying. Let them see to that, who, among the rest of their perversities, teach the disjoining of the 'one flesh in twain;' denying Him who, after borrowing the female from the male, re-combined between themselves, in the matrimonial computation, the two bodies taken out of the consortship of the self-same material substance. In short, there is no place at all where we read that nuptials are prohibited; of course on the ground that they are a 'good thing.'[18]

2. On the basis of Ephesians 5.32, the Western Medieval Church developed a sacramental view of marriage. That is to say, it came to be believed that, far from being something negative, or simply a remedy against lust, marriage was an instrument of divine grace.[19]

3. The very reason why voluntary celibacy, also referred to as holy virginity, was given such a high spiritual value was precisely because it meant the renunciation of something that was in itself good, for the sake of the kingdom of God.

This point is made very clearly by St John Chrysostom in his work *On Virginity*:

> Whoever denigrates marriage also diminishes the glory of virginity. Whoever praises it makes virginity more admirable and resplendent. What appears good only in comparison with evil would not be truly good. The most excellent good is something even better than what is admitted to be good.[20]

1.2.25 Because of the five core beliefs about human sexuality previously mentioned, and because it has been believed that it has been specifically condemned by a number of biblical texts (Genesis 19.1-14, Leviticus 18.22; 20.13, Deuteronomy 23.17-18, Romans 1.26-27, 1 Corinthians 6.9-10, 1 Timothy 1.9-10), homosexual activity has been consistently condemned within the Christian tradition. The Yale historian John Boswell argued that homosexual relationships have been tolerated in some periods of Church history and that provision was even made for the blessing of same-sex unions,[21] but his controversial claim has been not been widely accepted by historians.[22]

1.2.26 The *Catechism of the Catholic Church*, although not representing the range of contemporary Roman Catholic thinking on the matter, gives clear expression to the traditional Christian position on homosexuality when it declares that:

> Basing itself on Sacred Scripture, which presents homosexual acts as acts of grave depravity, Tradition has always declared that 'homosexual acts are intrinsically disordered.' They are contrary to the natural law. They close the sexual act to the gift of life. They do not proceed from a genuine affective and sexual complementarity. Under no circumstances can they be approved.[23]

1.2.27 Bisexuality has not received separate treatment in the Christian tradition but, if bisexual activity involved same-sex relations, it would have come under the condemnation of homosexuality and, if it involved heterosexual relations outside marriage, it would have been seen as either adultery or fornication. Transsexualism has also not featured in the tradition for the simple reason that the medical techniques that have made it possible to try to change the sex of people's bodies did not exist until very recent times. However, the Christian tradition has rejected transvestitism on the grounds that cross-dressing is forbidden in the book of Deuteronomy (Deuteronomy 22.5) and, more widely, on the basis of the belief that the distinction between male and female instituted by God at creation is a boundary that must not be transgressed.

b. The development of Anglican thinking

1.2.28 In the centuries since the Reformation, the Church of England and the Anglican tradition in general have continued to adhere to the mainstream Christian position on human sexuality, affirming that marriage, understood as a lifelong exclusive relationship between one man and one woman, was the context created by God for the proper expression of human sexuality.

1.2.29 This Anglican consensus is reflected in the following words from the report of the subsection on Human Sexuality at the 1998 Lambeth Conference – a report that was, however, produced in the midst of a fierce debate about whether this Anglican consensus should hold or whether our thinking should shift after dialogue with those gay and lesbian Christians who have found themselves excluded from the churches by this very consensus:

> Human sexuality is the gift of a loving God. It is a gift to be honoured and cherished by all people. As a means for the expression of the deepest human love and intimacy, sexuality has great power.
>
> The Holy Scriptures and Christian tradition teach that human sexuality is intended by God to find its full expression between a man and a woman in the covenant of marriage, established by God in creation, and affirmed by our Lord Jesus Christ. Holy Matrimony is, by intention and divine purpose, to be a life-long, monogamous and unconditional commitment between a woman and a man.[24]

1.2.30 Within the Church of England this consensus has been reflected in the two recent House of Bishops teaching documents, *Issues in Human Sexuality* and *Marriage*.

Issues in Human Sexuality declares that there is, in Scripture, 'an evolving convergence on the ideal of lifelong, monogamous, heterosexual union as the setting intended by God for the proper development of men and women as sexual beings'[25] and holds that: 'God's perfect will for married people is chastity before marriage, and then a lifelong relationship of fidelity and mutual sharing at all levels.'[26]

In similar fashion, the document on *Marriage* maintains that: 'Sexual intercourse, as an expression of faithful intimacy, properly belongs within marriage exclusively'[27] and declares that 'marriage is indissoluble in the sense that the promises are made unconditionally for life'.[28]

1.2.31 However, neither the Church of England nor the Anglican tradition as a whole has been static in its thinking about issues connected with human sexuality and human sexual relationships.

1.2.32 There has been a development of thinking on these issues that has been reflected in a change of attitude and approach in a number of areas, and which has both influenced and been influenced by changes in society as a whole.

1. The purpose of marriage

1.2.33 First, in line with development of thinking about marriage in the Christian Church as a whole, and secular thinking as well, the Church of England has moved away from an emphasis on the avoidance of sin and the production of children as reasons for marriage, in favour of an emphasis on marriage being a context for an intimate, pleasurable and mutually supportive relationship.

1.2.34 This movement of thought can be seen very clearly if one compares the reasons for matrimony given in the *Book of Common Prayer* with those given in the *Common Worship* marriage service. As was noted earlier, in the Prayer Book the first two reasons given for marriage are the procreation of children and to provide a remedy against sin and fornication, only then is there mention of marriage as a source of 'mutual society, help and comfort'. In *Common Worship*, marriage as a remedy against sin drops out entirely, and the birth and upbringing of children are only mentioned after material emphasizing the relational and sexual aspects of marriage:

> Marriage is a gift of God in creation through which husband and wife may know the grace of God. It is given that as a man and woman may grow together in love and trust, they shall be united with one another in heart, body, and mind, as Christ is with his bride the Church. The gift of marriage brings husband and wife together in the delight and tenderness of sexual union and joyful commitment to the end of their lives. It is given as the foundation of family life in which children are [born and] nurtured and in which every member of the family, in good times and in bad, may find strength, companionship and comfort, and grow to maturity in love.[29]

2. Divorce and remarriage

1.2.35 At the time of the Reformation, Archbishop Cranmer had proposed a revision of English canon law, the so-called *Reformatio Legum Ecclesiasticarum*. This set out several grounds on which divorce might be allowed, including not only adultery, but also insanity, desertion and leprosy. He also proposed allowing people divorced on such grounds to remarry during the lifetime of their previous spouse. His proposals never became part of canon law and, in 1602, Archbishop Bancroft ruled that marriage was indissoluble.

1.2.36 However, the memory of Cranmer's approach remained and, as late as 1912, it was still being quoted as an authority by those who did not take the indissolubilist point of view.[30] Overall it may be said that, until the beginning of the twentieth century, the Church of England does not appear to have had a unanimous policy on the issue of whether remarriage after divorce should be permitted.

1.2.37 From the early years of the twentieth century the attitude of the Church of England became more definite. Stress came to be laid on the indissoluble nature of marriage and, as a result, it came to be seen as theologically unacceptable for someone who had been divorced to marry in Church while their former partner was still alive.

1.2.38 However, as Owen Chadwick notes in his biography of Archbishop Michael Ramsey, by the beginning of the 1960s both English society and the Church of England had found it impossible to maintain a simple rejection of all divorce.

> In the conditions which prevailed in European society then, it had to be accepted that sometimes a first marriage was a calamity and a second marriage was made in heaven. Social right, and the interests of children, were often made safer by recognizing this fact than by asserting still that it was wrong. But this could only be done in such a way that the Church preserved the ideal of a permanent marriage between two people. By the time Ramsey became Archbishop of Canterbury it was well established as general custom that the Church refused to marry in church a person who had a previous partner still living – thus maintaining the ideal – but soon accepted back into its bosom the remarried couple – thus not depriving them or their children of the pastoral care which they might need.[31]

1.2.39   The development of the Church of England's thinking moved the Church on from this position in two ways.

1.2.40   First of all, in 1966, a report entitled *Putting Asunder*[32] was produced by a Commission on Divorce Law Reform chaired by the Bishop of Exeter, Robert Mortimer. This Commission, which had been set up by the Archbishop of Canterbury to consider the question of whether civil divorce law needed reform, argued that the grounds on which a divorce could be obtained needed to be changed

1.2.41   At the time, the Commission reported the grounds for obtaining a divorce were that one of the parties involved had committed a grave matrimonial offence (adultery, cruelty, three years' desertion, five years' continuous insanity, or bestiality). In the words of Chadwick, what the Mortimer Commission recommended was that: 'the idea of an offence against marriage be dropped at last and that the sole ground for divorce should be that marriage had broken down irretrievably and despite efforts at reconciliation could not be repaired'.[33]

Together with the report of the Law Commission, which appeared at the same time and took a similar line, the Mortimer Commission report was the basis of the Divorce Reform Bill, which became law in 1969, although the Bill departed from the proposals of the Mortimer Commission by shortening the period of separation necessary for a divorce with the consent of both parties from three years to two, and by introducing divorce with the consent of only one party after five years' separation.

1.2.42   As Chadwick further explains, the changes in contemporary society that had led to a change in the civil law on divorce also raised questions about the Church's own practice.

> If it was once accepted that in the conditions of modern society some first marriages were born to fail and some second marriages were made in heaven was it right of the Church to keep to its rule of refusing to remarry divorced persons in Church? And was it not pastorally better for the Church to do what it could to accept the higher ideals of couples who came to them even if one of the pair had been married before? Some thought that the old rule of no marriage in church while a former partner lived maintained the sanctity of marriage while it caused no serious hardship. But others in parishes were faced with heart rending pleas. Some clergymen began to marry in church couples who had a partner still alive.[34]

1.2.43   Clergy who acted in this way could legally do so because of the conscience clauses in the 1937 and 1965 Matrimonial Causes Acts, which left the final decision with the member of the clergy concerned, but their actions were contrary both to the Church's general teaching on divorce and to resolutions passed in the Convocations of Canterbury and York in 1938 and 1957, which declared that the Church's marriage service should not be used for the remarriage of someone whose former partner was still living.

1.2.44   This tension between precept and practice led to the production of a series of reports that looked at the issue of the remarriage of divorced people in church.[35] All of these reports recommended, though on one occasion by a majority rather than unanimously, that the Church should make official provision for the remarriage of such people in church.

1.2.45   The principle that remarriage of divorced people should be permitted was accepted by General Synod in 1981. A private member's motion was passed declaring that the Synod considered that: 'there are circumstances in which a divorced person may be married in church during the lifetime of a former partner'. In addition, in July 1985, the House of Bishops approved a service of prayer and dedication after civil marriage that could be used in the case of people who had been divorced and, in 1990, the bar on people who had remarried during the lifetime of a former partner, or who were married to someone who had done so, being ordained was removed.

1.2.46   Partly because of continuing opposition to the principle of remarrying divorced people in church, but mostly because of disagreement about how such a change of policy should be implemented in practice, it has proved difficult to reach agreement on officially permitting such marriages to take place, even though increasing numbers of clergy have been exercising their legal right to officiate at such weddings.[36] However, the meeting of General Synod in July 2002 accepted in principle the recommendation of the 2000 report *Marriage in Church after Divorce*[37] that there are exceptional circumstances in which divorced people should be allowed to marry in church in the lifetime of their former partner.

1.2.47   Synod then followed this up in November 2002 by formally rescinding the marriage resolutions of the Canterbury and York

Convocations. By so doing it removed any inconsistency between the cleric's right in civil law to solemnize further marriages in cases where the former partner is still living – which remains unaffected – and the Church's official exhortations against such marriages.

1.2.48 The Church's official position is, therefore, that, while God's intention is that marriage should be for life, this fact should not be seen as an automatic bar on remarriage in church in the lifetime of a former spouse because there are circumstances in which this is the best Christian response to a less than ideal situation.

3. Contraception

1.2.49 Because the procreation of children was traditionally regarded as one of the key reasons for sexual activity within marriage, the idea of a married couple restricting the number of their children or even deciding not to have children at all was traditionally regarded within the Christian Church as a rejection of the purposes of God as laid down in Genesis 1.27-28.

1.2.50 During the twentieth century, however, Anglican thinking on this issue changed and Church of England thinking changed with it. A clear indication of this change can be seen in the resolutions on this subject passed by the Lambeth Conferences between 1908 and 1968.

1.2.51 Reflecting a concern about falling birth rates as well as the theological concerns just outlined, the 1908 Conference declared that it:

> ... records with alarm the growing practice of the artificial restriction of the family and earnestly calls upon all Christian people to discountenance the use of all artificial means of restriction as demoralising to character and hostile to national welfare.[38]

1.2.52 By the 1920s, an increasing number of Anglicans had come to believe that a sexual relationship between a husband and wife might be good in itself even if it was not intended to lead to the procreation of children, and that it might be legitimate to limit the number of children in order to give those children who were born a better chance in life.

1.2.53 The 1930 resolution, which had a mixed reaction, marked this beginning of a change in attitude, a change that was rooted in theological reflection on the experience of Anglican married couples.

The view was still held that procreation was a necessary part of the purpose of marriage, and the resolution still advocated sexual abstinence rather than artificial birth control: 'Where there is a clearly felt moral obligation to limit or avoid parenthood, complete abstinence is the primary and obvious method.'[39] However, the resolution also declared that:

> ... in those cases where there is ... a clearly felt moral obligation to limit or avoid parenthood, and where there is a morally sound reason for avoiding complete abstinence, the Conference agrees that other methods may be used, provided that this is done in the light of the same Christian principles.[40]

1.2.54 By 1958, contraception had become widely accepted among Anglicans and the resolution of the 1958 Lambeth Conference on the issue said that that the responsibility for deciding on the number and frequency of children was to be decided: 'in such ways as are acceptable to husband and wife in Christian conscience'.[41] Finally, the 1968 Lambeth Conference rejected the ban on artificial contraception contained in the Papal Encyclical *Humanae Vitae* published that year.[42]

1.2.55 It needs to be noted, however, that Anglican thinking would be sympathetic to much that is said in *Humanae Vitae* both about marriage in general and about the importance of procreation as a fundamental part of what marriage is about. Where Anglican thinking would part company with the teaching in *Humanae Vitae* is over the specific issue of whether the use of artificial as opposed to 'natural' methods of birth control is always wrong.

4. Abortion

1.2.56 It has been argued that the issue of abortion should not be considered in connection with issues to do with sexuality and marriage because it is really an issue to do with the sanctity of human life. As noted below, Anglican thinking about this issue has acknowledged that it is an issue that involves respect for the sanctity of life. However, it also an issue that is connected with sexuality and family life because, like the issue of contraception, it involves the question of whether it is right in certain circumstances to try to prevent sexual activity resulting in the birth of a baby.

1.2.57 During most of the history of the Christian Church, abortion, except as a side effect of an attempt to save the life of a mother, was rejected as a form of infanticide, and this position was also taken by the Church of England. Until the 1960s, abortion was also illegal under British law.

1.2.58 As Chadwick explains, in the years after the Second World War, pressure began to mount for a change in the law:

> In an urbanized world this ancient law and moral code produced as a side-effect 'back-street abortions'; illegal operations performed for fees by criminal surgeons with dirty tools. After the Second World War there were widespread demands for the legalization of abortion under proper conditions; to prevent the criminal trade; to help the health of girls endangered by the incompetence of criminal surgeons; and to recognize that there might be reasons, other than the immediate peril to the mother's life which justified the performance of the operation.[43]

1.2.59 The Church of England had to think how to respond to this change in public attitude and in 1964 a report was published by the Church's Board for Social Responsibility, which argued that there were circumstances in which abortion could be justified:

> After surveying the matter afresh in the light both of traditional discussions and of present proposals, our broad conclusion is that in certain circumstances abortion can be justified. This would be when, at the request of the mother and after the kind of consultation which we have envisaged in the report, it could be reasonably established that there was a threat to the mother's life or well-being, and hence inescapably to her health, if she were obliged to carry the child to term and give it birth. And our view is that, in reaching this conclusion, her life and well-being must be seen as integrally connected with the life and well-being of her family.[44]

1.2.60 This report was welcomed by the Church Assembly (the forerunner of General Synod) in 1966 and helped to influence the Abortion Act of 1967, which legalized abortion in this country. Although many Anglicans felt at the time that the 1967 Act went too far in the direction of abortion on demand and have continued to feel this ever since, the majority opinion in the Church of England has been that abortion could be justified in exceptional circumstances.

1.2.61 The resolution passed by General Synod in July 1983 reflects the tensions that have continued to be felt over this issue. It declared that: 'all human life, including life developing in the womb, is created by God in His own image, and is, therefore, to be nurtured, supported and protected'.[45]

On this basis it expressed serious concern about the rising number of abortions and called for the amendment of the 1967 Act. On the other hand, it also recognized that: 'in situations where the continuance of a pregnancy threatens the life of the mother a termination of pregnancy may be justified and that there must be adequate and safe provision in our society for such situations'.[46]

c. The pattern reflected in these developments

1.2.62　If we look at these developments in Anglican and Church of England thinking, what we find is a consistent pattern in the developing Anglican approach to sexual ethics. This pattern has two key elements.

1.2.63　The first of these is a reassertion of traditional Christian principles such as the lifelong nature of marriage, the production of children as one of the purposes of marriage, and the sacredness of human life, including that of the life of the unborn child.

1.2.64　The second is a willingness to allow the outworking of these principles in practice to be shaped by pastoral realities and dilemmas such as the realities of marital breakdown and the need and desire of couples to limit the number of their children, and the dilemmas posed by backstreet abortions and the threat that could be posed by an unborn child to the life of the mother.

1.2.65　As we shall see, the development of Anglican thinking about homosexuality has reflected a desire to uphold both of these two key elements in Anglican sexual ethics in this area as well.

1.3 The development of Anglican thinking on homosexuality

1.3.1　As we have already noted, the Christian Church as a whole has traditionally rejected homosexual activity as sinful. However, from the 1950s onwards there has been a growing debate about whether this traditional teaching should continue to be upheld.

1.3.2　As we shall see in more detail in Chapter 9, this debate has taken place in all the major Protestant Churches in the Western world, and in the Roman Catholic Church as well. Although some Churches, such as the Church of Christ in the USA and the United Church of Canada, have moved to an official acceptance of homosexual relationships and a willingness to ordain those in such relationships, most have not been willing to go this far. In most Churches there has been a division of opinion on the matter, and Churches have seen both the blessing of same-sex relationships and the ordination of openly practising homosexuals even where this has been contrary to official policy.

1.3.3   This debate has also affected both the Church of England and the Anglican Communion as a whole.

The debate in the Church of England

1.3.4   The modern debate in the Church of England can be seen to have begun with the publication of an article by Sherwin Bailey on 'The problem of sexual inversion' in the edition of the journal *Theology* for February 1952.

1.3.5   In this article, Bailey discussed the moral issues raised by what he called sexual 'inverts', by which he meant those who are by nature sexually attracted to members of their own sex. He rejected the idea that the Church should recognize homosexual relationships as a form of marriage, but he did argue very strongly that the Church ought to campaign against the law that then existed against male homosexual relationships:

> It is, without doubt, a Christian duty to press for the removal of this anomalous and shameful injustice, which has done untold harm, and has achieved no good whatever, and it is to be hoped that those who looked to the Church for a lead will not be disappointed.[47]

1.3.6   The discussion provoked by Bailey's article led to a report on the subject being produced in 1954 by the Church of England's Moral Welfare Council, of which Bailey was a member. This report, entitled *The Problem of Homosexuality – An Interim Report*, did not accept the ethical legitimacy of homosexual activity. It declared that a man who was a sexual invert was not responsible for his inversion, but:

> Where such a person expresses his condition in overt acts of a sexual nature, thus deflecting the activity of the sexual organ from its proper end, we rightly hold him responsible as we would hold a heterosexual man responsible for immoral sexual acts with girls and women. In

neither case does the fact that he is of a certain nature (homo- or hetero-sexual) excuse the immoral expression of his sexual urges.[48]

1.3.7   Like Bailey's original article, however, the report held that the law against male homosexual activity ought to be abolished. It was unjust because the law did not also punish heterosexual fornication and adultery, it encouraged blackmail, and it discouraged the homosexual from seeking help for fear of prosecution.

1.3.8   It recommended a male homosexual age of consent of 21 in order to protect young National Servicemen from the particular risks associated with living in a predominantly male service community.

1.3.9   The Moral Welfare Council Report was significant because it was one of the major influences that led to the setting up of an official government committee under the Anglican layman Sir John Wolfenden, which reported in 1957 and argued for the same position taken by the Moral Welfare Council – the abolition of the law against male homosexual activity and the setting of the homosexual age of consent at 21.

1.3.10   The Wolfenden recommendations received strong support from members of the Church of England, including the Archbishop of Canterbury, Michael Ramsey, and after much debate eventually became law in 1967.

1.3.11   The fact that members of the Church of England were in favour of a change in the criminal law regarding homosexuality did not mean that they were in favour of changing the Church's traditional rejection of homosexual activity. For example, Archbishop Ramsey was asked in 1971 whether the Church could ever bless a marriage between two people of the same sex and his reply was:

> I don't see the Christian Church ever giving its blessing to that. Because the Christian Church gives its blessing to the best and perfect use of sex, which is the union of a man and a woman in marriage. We confine our blessing to that.[49]

1.3.12   The combination of beliefs that we find in the case of Archbishop Ramsey – a belief that homosexual activity between consenting adults should not result in criminal prosecution[50] combined with a belief that the Church could not rightly bless homosexual relationships – remains the official position of the Church of England.

1.3.13   Three reports on the issue of homosexuality were produced by Church of England working parties between 1970 and 1989 in response to the need for guidance about the selection and training of homosexual ordinands.[51] All three revealed the extent to which the Church was divided on the matter, but all three were prepared to consider the possibility that homosexual activity might be regarded as morally justifiable in certain circumstances.

1.3.14   The 1979 report declared, for example, that while it would not be right for the Church to view 'homosexual erotic love as an alternative and authentic development of the living Christian tradition' nonetheless:

> we do not think it possible to deny that there are circumstances in which individuals may justifiably choose to enter into a homosexual relationship with the hope of enjoying a companionship and physical expression of sexual love similar to that which is to be found in marriage.[52]

1.3.15   However, while these reports were regarded as valuable contributions to a continuing debate, their teaching was never endorsed by the Church.

1.3.16   The mind of the Church came to be expressed instead in two other ways.

1.3.17   The first way it was expressed was through a debate in General Synod in November 1987 initiated by the Revd Tony Higton. This debate reflected the fact that the failure of the 1979 report to receive synodical endorsement meant that the Church lacked any kind of official guidance on the matter, and that many people in the Church, particularly on its evangelical wing, wanted a clear restatement of traditional principles.

1.3.18   At the end of the debate the following motion was passed by 403 votes to 8:

> This Synod affirms that the biblical and traditional teaching on chastity and fidelity in personal relationships is a response to, and expression of, God's love for each one of us, and in particular affirms;

1. that sexual intercourse is an act of total commitment which belongs properly within a permanent married relationship.

2. that fornication and adultery are sins against this ideal, and are to be met by a call to repentance and the exercise of compassion.

3. that homosexual genital acts also fall short of this ideal, and are likewise to be met with a call to repentance and the exercise of compassion.

4. that all Christians are called to be exemplary in all spheres of morality, and that holiness of life is particularly required of Christian leaders.[53]

1.3.19 The second was the publication in December 1991 of *Issues in Human Sexuality*, which was produced by the House of Bishops after it had decided not to publish the 1989 'Osborne' report. As has already been noted, this statement endorsed the traditional Christian belief that the teaching of the Bible is that heterosexual marriage is the proper context for human sexual activity. This in turn led the statement to declare that what it called 'homophile' orientation and activity (it preferred the term 'homophile' to 'homosexual') could not be endorsed by the Church as:

> ... a parallel and alternative form of human sexuality as complete within the terms of the created order as the heterosexual. The convergence of Scripture, Tradition and reasoned reflection on experience, even including the newly sympathetic and perceptive thinking of our own day, make it impossible for the Church to come with integrity to any other conclusion. Heterosexuality and homosexuality are not equally congruous with the observed order of creation or with the insights of revelation as the Church engages with these in the light of her pastoral ministry.[54]

1.3.20 It also argued, however, that the conscientious decision of those who enter into such relationships must be respected, and that the Church must not 'reject those who sincerely believe it is God's call to them'.[55]

Nevertheless, because of 'the distinctive nature of their calling, status, and consecration' the clergy 'cannot claim the liberty to enter into sexually active homophile relationships'.[56]

1.3.21 The 1987 Synod motion and *Issues in Human Sexuality* are currently the two most authoritative Church of England statements on the issue of homosexuality, and they take a more traditional line than the three reports that were not accepted by the Church. While stressing the need for pastoral compassion for homosexual people, they follow the Christian tradition in holding that homosexual sexual activity cannot be endorsed by the Church.

1.3.22   In 1997 *Issues in Human Sexuality* was debated in General Synod and at the end of the debate Synod voted to accept the following motion moved by the then Archdeacon of Wandsworth, the Venerable David Gerrard:

> That this Synod
>
> (a)   commend for discussion in dioceses the House of Bishop's report *Issues in Human Sexuality* and acknowledge it is not the last word on the subject;
>
> (b)   in particular, urge deanery synods, clergy chapters and congregations to find time for prayerful study and reflection on the issues addressed by the report.'[57]

The purpose of the present guide is to contribute to this process of prayerful study and reflection.

1.3.23   The fact that the person who proposed the 1987 General Synod motion was a leading member of the evangelical group in Synod is significant. It is significant because it indicates that, if a part of the context of the debate about homosexuality has been the rise of liberal attitudes to sexuality within the Church of England, another part of the context has been the resurgence of conservative evangelicalism in the years since the Second World War.

1.3.24   In the first half of the twentieth century traditional conservative evangelicalism remained strong at a parochial level but, at the national level, the most prominent evangelicals were liberal evangelicals such as Vernon Storr and Max Warren, who sought to combine an evangelical emphasis on a personal relationship with God through Jesus Christ with a liberal commitment to reinterpreting Christian belief in the light of contemporary thought.

1.3.25   From the 1940s onwards, however, there was a conservative evangelical renaissance and the leadership of the evangelical movement in the Church of England passed to men like John Stott and J. I. Packer, who pioneered a return to a theological position rooted in the teaching of the Bible as interpreted by some of the English reformers, the Puritans and the evangelical leaders of the eighteenth and early nineteenth centuries (although it should be noted that the modern evangelicals' interpretation and use of those English reformers and other earlier English thinkers has been much debated within Anglicanism). Under their leadership, evangelicals became a much more influential tradition in the Church of England. Following the National Evangelical Anglican Congress held at Keele in 1967, evangelicals became increasingly committed to playing a full part in the national life of the Church of England, and in this context they have led the opposition to an acceptance of same-sex relationships by the Church.

1.3.26 Although their critics have accused them of a naïve fundamentalism,[58] evangelicals have become increasingly aware of the importance of engaging with biblical criticism and issues of biblical interpretation[59] and have sought to engage constructively with the ethical issues raised by contemporary culture.[60]

However, generally speaking, this has not led evangelicals, any more than it has led many other more Catholic Anglicans, to depart from the traditional Christian rejection of homosexual practice. As we shall explain in more detail later on in this guide, this is because most evangelicals and many others remain convinced that, even when looked at in the light of the most up-to-date interpretative techniques, the Bible still seems clear in its rejection of same-sex sexual activity, and for them this necessarily settles the matter.

The debate in the Anglican Communion

1.3.27 Debate about homosexuality has also taken place in other parts of the Anglican Communion, particularly in North America and Australia, and this wider Anglican debate has been reflected in resolutions produced by the Lambeth Conferences in 1978, 1988, and 1998.

1.3.28 The first two resolutions refrained from making a judgement about the moral status of homosexuality, calling instead for more study of the subject and for dialogue with homosexual people.

The 1978 resolution declared:

> While we reaffirm heterosexuality as the scriptural norm, we recognise the need for deep and dispassionate study of the question of homosexuality, which would take seriously both the teaching of Scripture and results of scientific and medical research. The Church, recognising the need for pastoral concern for those who are homosexual, encourages dialogue with them . . . .[61]

The 1988 resolution reaffirmed the call for further study issued in 1978 and went on to say that the Lambeth Conference:

> Urges such study and reflection to take account of biological, genetic and psychological research being undertaken by other agencies, and the socio-cultural factors that lead to the different attitudes in the provinces or our Communion[62]

and that it

> Calls each province to reassess, in the light of such study and because of our concern for human rights, its care for and attitude towards persons of homosexual disposition.[63]

1.3.29　At the 1998 Lambeth Conference the subgroup studying human sexuality was unable to reach a 'common mind' on the 'scriptural, theological, historical, and scientific' issues raised by a study of homosexuality.[64] As the subgroup report noted:

> Our variety of understanding encompasses:
>
> • Those who believe that homosexual orientation is a disorder, but that through the grace of Christ people can be changed, although not without pain or struggle;
>
> • Those who believe that relationships between people of the same gender should not include genital expression, that this is the clear teaching of the Bible and of the Church universal, and that such activity (if unrepented of) is a barrier to the kingdom of God;
>
> • Those who believe that committed homosexual relationships fall short of the biblical norm, but are to be preferred to relationships that are anonymous and transient;
>
> • Those who believe that the Church should accept and support or bless monogamous covenant relationships between homosexual people and that they may be ordained.[65]

1.3.30   In spite of these differences of approach, the subgroup did reach agreement on a general approach to the ethics of human sexuality, which the Conference as a whole then built on in its resolution on the subject (Resolution 1.10). This resolution, which was more conservative than those produced in 1978 or 1988, recognized:

> ... that there are among us those who experience themselves as having a homosexual orientation. Many of these are members of the Church and are seeking the pastoral care, moral direction of the Church, and God's transforming power for the living of their lives and the ordering of their relationships.[66]

1.3.31   It also stated that the bishops committed themselves 'to listen to the experience of homosexual persons' and wished to assure them that 'they are loved by God and that all baptized, believing and faithful persons, regardless of sexual orientation, are all full members of the Body of Christ,'[67] and called on all Anglicans to 'minister pastorally and sensitively to all irrespective of sexual orientation and to condemn irrational fear of homosexuals, violence within marriage and any trivialisation and commercialisation of sex'.[68]

1.3.32   However, it rejected homosexual practice as 'incompatible with scripture', declared that 'abstinence is right for those not called to marriage' and refused to advise 'the legitimising or blessing of same sex unions' or 'ordaining those involved in same gender unions'.[69]

1.3.33   Although this resolution was passed by 526 to 70 with 45 abstentions there are Anglicans who have refused to accept it on the grounds that it does not adequately reflect the development of contemporary scientific and theological understandings of homosexuality. Nevertheless, it remains the nearest thing there is to an official statement by the Anglican Communion on the subject, though it needs to be remembered that resolutions of the Lambeth Conference have not been seen as binding upon the Anglican Communion.

B. The nature of the current debate

1.4 Introduction
1.4.1   Overall then it can be said that the official teaching about homosexuality in both the Church of England and the Anglican Communion in general has remained more conservative than it has on

other subjects connected with sexual morality. However, the debate continues, as it does also on the subjects of bisexuality and transsexuality, on which there has as yet been no official Church of England or Anglican teaching.

1.4.2   The second part of the chapter will go on to look at the nature of the continuing debate on these subjects.

a. The debate on homosexuality

1.4.3   As Elizabeth Stuart and Adrian Thatcher note in their book on sexual ethics entitled *People of Passion*,[70] the issues raised for the Churches by the issue of homosexuality are both theoretical issues concerning theological method and practical issues about how both individuals and the Church as a whole should act.

1.4.4   As they indicate, the theoretical issue is to do with the authority of Scripture and tradition and, more generally, how God makes his will known to us. In specific terms the questions under discussion in the current debate are the following:

• Where do we find the authoritative revelation of God's will for his people in this area?

• How should we interpret those biblical texts that have traditionally been seen as condemning homosexuality, in the light of our current understanding of the original meaning of the texts themselves and the cultural context in which they were written, contemporary research in the natural and human sciences, and the experience of gay and lesbian people?

• How do we relate what the Bible has to say about homosexuality with its wider teaching about the nature and expression of human sexuality, and the need for us to treat all people with justice and compassion?

1.4.5   In terms of practical issues the debate focuses on five issues:

• Do homosexual people simply have to come to terms with their orientation or should they be encouraged to change it through some form of therapy? The discussion here includes both the question of whether it is right that someone should seek to change their orientation and the question of whether such therapy is ever effective or simply causes psychological harm.

- Is it right for those who feel they are homosexual in orientation to respond to that deeply held self-identification and desire by expressing it in genital sex, or does obedience to God mean abstaining from same-sex sexual activity?

- Should homosexual people be encouraged to enter into permanent same-sex partnerships or is continence considered to be impossible, in distinction to single heterosexual experience?

- Is it right for people who are in same-sex sexual relationships to be ordained?

- What is the right way to respond pastorally to the needs of homosexual people?

1.4.6   The debate around these issues is as complex as the debate around sexual ethics in general, but it is nevertheless possible to identify three broad approaches within this complexity.

1.4.7   Tradition holds that same-sex sexual activity is wrong in all circumstances and that those of a homosexual orientation should either seek to change their orientation or accept a life of permanent chastity.

1.4.8   Others would argue that, while homosexual sexual activity cannot be regarded as being as consonant with the will of God as heterosexual activity within marriage, nevertheless those who are homosexual by orientation and have not received the gift of celibacy should enter into a permanent faithful same-sex relationship as a better alternative than a life of sexual promiscuity.

1.4.9   Still others would argue that same-sex sexual activity has exactly the same status as heterosexual sexual activity, that the Church should regard permanent same-sex relationships in exactly the same light as marriage and bless them accordingly, and that same-sex sexual activity should be no bar to ordination.

b. The debate on bisexuality
1.4.10   There has not been nearly so much discussion of bisexuality as there has been of homosexuality. There is, for example, almost no literature devoted to the issue and it receives very little attention in official Church documents on sexuality. When it is mentioned it tends to be subsumed within the wider debate about homosexuality. However, it is not a subject that can be ignored, because it raises important

theological issues in its own right. As Stuart and Thatcher note, potentially, 'bisexuals undermine the whole sexual system, the neat classification of people into homosexual and heterosexual, the pathologizing of homosexuality as a heterosexual disorder and so on'.[71]

1.4.11   The point they are making is that the existence of overtly bisexual people draws attention to the theory put forward by Sigmund Freud and endorsed by students of sexuality such as Kinsey, that human beings cannot be divided neatly into a large majority of heterosexuals and a small minority of homosexuals. Instead, it is bisexuality that is the norm. Most people have both heterosexual and homosexual tendencies and it is only social pressure that stops more people from accepting or expressing their homosexual ones.

If accepted, this theory means that any argument advanced against homosexuality on the basis that heterosexuality is the norm, loses credibility, and it becomes much more difficult to maintain that God's creative intention was that people should be heterosexual.

1.4.12   The suggestion made by Stuart, Thatcher and others may or may not be correct, but it is certainly something that Christians need to consider and discuss.

c. The debate on transsexualism
1.4.13   There has also been comparatively little attention given to the subject of transsexualism, the condition in which people feel that they are a member of the opposite sex from that of their present body, although theological literature on the subject has now begun to appear[72] and it has recently become the subject of attention in the media.

1.4.14   Christian discussion of this topic has focused on the issue of whether those who feel that their existing bodies do not express their true sexual identity should nevertheless accept that their birth sex is that given to them by God and seek help in overcoming their rejection of it, or whether it is possible that someone's God-given sex is not identical with their physiology, and that it is therefore legitimate to allow people to change their bodies to allow this true sexual identity to be expressed.

1.4.15   In addition, there has also been discussion of the relevance of the prohibition of castration in texts such as Leviticus 21.16-23 and Deuteronomy 23.1, and of cross-dressing in Deuteronomy 22.5, and about whether it is right for those who have gone through gender reassignment surgery to be married in their new identity, to have their birth certificate altered to reflect this identity, or to exercise ordained ministry.

1.5 The importance of the continuing debate

1.5.1   The debate about human sexuality that we have looked at in this chapter is not one that is going to go away. Furthermore, it is not a debate that should go away. Real people really do have homosexual and bisexual desires and do feel that their current bodies do not represent their true identity, and the Christian Church, therefore, has a duty to think carefully about the status of these desires and feelings before God, and how people who have them can be given appropriate pastoral care, taking into account the pressures and expectations of a highly sexualized social culture.

1.5.2   The Anglican tradition, which we have considered in this chapter, is instructive. It has sought to combine long-held principles with a response to changes in society in a mature and responsible pastoral manner. On some issues, for example the need for faithfulness within and abstinence outside marriage, its beliefs have not changed. On others, for example contraception and divorce, the Church of England, in a relatively short period of time, accepted what had previously been regarded as morally unacceptable. What this means is that we have to accept that the Church of England could in principle change its current approach in the case of the particular issues under consideration in this report providing that (a) it had sufficient theological grounds for so doing and (b) that such a change did not entail a change to its core ethical beliefs. Much of the current debate, for example on homosexuality, turns on whether (a) and (b) apply.

1.5.3   On the issue of abortion, however, there is a different lesson to be learnt. Although the Church of England accepted that abortion might be legitimate under certain exceptional circumstances, there is now widespread unease at the way it is possible to obtain an abortion for reasons that were not originally envisaged. So those who say that the Church can change its mind even on crucial moral issues must face the fact that mistakes can be made in ways that were not originally predicted. The fact that there is widespread acceptance of homosexual relationships in the wider culture does not necessarily mean that the Church of England should reflect this change in the way that it did over contraception and divorce. The issue of gay and lesbian relationships may be one in which the Church should hold fast to its original teaching, even though in other areas it has changed, and the same may also be true in the case of bisexuality and transsexualism.[73]

1.5.4   This current report is intended to help those in the Church of England to think more deeply and more theologically about the issues we have explored in this chapter. It is an attempt to encourage the kind of learning commended by Professor Oliver O'Donovan in his contribution to the 1997 symposium on Christianity and homosexuality *The Way Forward?*:

> Our first and last duty in this sphere is to discern the light the Gospel sheds on the Gay movement of our time. The Church must learn to attest its faith in the Gospel before this cultural phenomenon. The gay Christian must learn to attest the truth of the gay self-consciousness in the light of the Gospel. What we commit ourselves to, when we commit ourselves to true debate is no more and no less than this learning.[74]

1.5.5   In order to begin to provide a framework for such learning to take place the next chapter will go on to look at how we should use the Bible in the debate about sexual ethics.

chapter 2

The use of the Bible in sexual ethics

2.1 Introduction

2.1.1   In the first chapter of this report it was noted that one of the key factors in the development of the traditional Christian view of sexual ethics was the use made of a number of biblical texts. This has been as true for Anglicans as it has been for Christians of other traditions and raises the question as to why Anglicans have seen the Bible as providing normative guidance for their sexual conduct

2.1.2   The answer to this question lies in the status that Anglicans have given, and continue to give, to the Bible as a whole as pointing to Christ, through whom God has revealed to his people what he is like, what he has done for them, and how they should respond to him.

2.1.3   This status was classically expressed by Archbishop Thomas Cranmer in his 1547 homily *A Fruitful Exhortation to the Reading and Knowledge of Holy Scripture*:

> In these books we shall find the Father from whom, the Son by whom, and the Holy Ghost in whom, all things have their being and keeping up; and these three persons to be but one God, and one substance. In these books we may learn to know ourselves, how vile and miserable we be, and also to know God, how good he is of himself, and how he maketh us and all creatures partakers of his goodness. We may learn also in these books to know God's will and pleasure, as much as, for this present time, is convenient for us to know. And as the great clerk and godly preacher, St John Chrysostom saith, whatsoever is required to the salvation of man is fully contained.[1]

2.1.4   It has also been reaffirmed in recent Anglican statements about the Bible. Thus the 1998 *Virginia Report* of the Inter-Anglican Theological and Doctrinal Commission, which was commissioned in the wake of the 1988 Lambeth Conference to consider questions of authority within the Anglican Communion, states that:

Anglicans affirm the sovereign authority of the Holy Scriptures as the medium through which God by the Spirit communicates his word in the Church and thus enables people to respond with understanding and faith. The Scriptures are the 'uniquely inspired witness to divine revelation' and 'the primary norm for Christian faith and life'.[2]

2.1.5 Likewise the *Porvoo Common Statement* of 1993 agreed by the Church of England, the other Anglican Churches of the British Isles and most of the Nordic and Baltic Lutheran Churches, declares that:

We accept the canonical scriptures of the Old and the New Testaments to be the sufficient, inspired and authoritative record and witness, prophetic and apostolic, to God's revelation in Jesus Christ. We read the Scriptures as part of public worship in the language of the people believing that in the Scriptures – as the Word of God and testifying to the gospel – eternal life is offered to all humanity, and that they contain everything necessary to salvation.[3]

2.1.6 What these statements about the status of the Bible make clear is that it is regarded by Anglicans not simply as a static source of abstract theological information, but as the living word of God by means of which we may learn about the salvation that God offers to us and how we should live in the light of that salvation. They would agree with the statement contained in the Second Vatican Council's Dogmatic Constitution on Divine Revelation *Dei Verbum* that:

... in the sacred books, the Father who is in heaven meets His children with great love and speaks with them; and the force and power in the word of God is so great that it stands as the support and energy of the Church, the strength and faith for her sons, the food of the soul, the pure and everlasting source of spiritual life. Consequently these words are perfectly applicable to Sacred Scripture: 'For the word of God is living and active' (Hebrews 4.12) and 'it has power to build you up and give you your heritage among all those who are sanctified' (Acts 20.32 see 1 Thessalonians 2.13).[4]

2.1.7 As we shall go on to explain later in this chapter, viewing the Bible in this way means reading it as a witness to the grace of God through which salvation is offered to us in fulfilment of God's covenant promises, and as guide to the path of Christian discipleship by which we may live appropriately in response to that grace. In terms of the specific issue of human sexuality it means reading the Bible in such a way as to discover how God's will for human sexual conduct gives expression to his grace, and what it means to respond rightly to him in this area of our lives.

2.2 The nature of biblical interpretation

2.2.1   Reading the Bible as a witness to the grace of God and a guide to the path of Christian discipleship means engaging in biblical interpretation. If we want to make sense of what the Bible says to us about God and how we should respond to God, then this means learning how to interpret the Bible properly so as to understand what it tells us about these matters.

2.2.2   It should be noted at this point that an acknowledgement of the importance of proper biblical interpretation is not at odds with the Reformation emphasis on the perspicuity of Scripture. What the Reformers meant by the perspicuity of Scripture was that the ordinary reader could learn from the Bible the way of salvation and how to live in obedience to God. It did not entail a denial that there are things in Scripture that are difficult to understand or that the Bible requires proper interpretation if it is to be properly understood.[5]

2.2.3   It is important to remember, too, that Anglicans, like other Christians, have always emphasized the importance of biblical interpretation within a *community* over and above individual biblical interpretation. God has placed his people in community for their mutual benefit and this is as true for biblical interpretation as it is for any other aspect of the Christian life.

2.2.4   The question of how we interpret the Bible properly is one that has engaged Christian theologians throughout the history of the Church and they have come up with a number of different proposals.[6] Each of these proposals has been a response to the questions that have been raised by a particular historical context, and in our particular context the key question that is being explored by those looking at the issue of biblical interpretation is what it means to interpret the Bible rightly in the kind of pluralist society that we described in Chapter 1.

2.2.5   This is a point made forcefully by the American Old Testament scholar Walter Brueggemann in his recent Old Testament theology. Brueggemann begins this work by reflecting on the nature of biblical interpretation and notes that biblical interpretation has ceased to be the preserve of Western academic theologians:

The great new fact of interpretation is that we live in a pluralistic context, in which many different interpreters in many different specific contexts representing many different interests are at work on textual (theological) interpretation. The old consensus about limits and possibilities of interpretation no longer holds. Thus interpretation is no longer done by a small, tenured elite, but interpretive voices and their very different readings of the texts come from many cultures in all parts of the globe, and from many subcultures even in Western culture.[7]

2.2.6   If we accept Brueggemann's description of the context in which interpretation now takes place, and what he says seems to be undeniable, the question that arises is how we should respond to this context.

2.2.7   In contemporary discussion about biblical interpretation two answers are being given to this question.

2.2.8   The first answer is that, in spite of the variety of interpretations of the biblical texts now on offer, we must stick to the belief that these texts do have specific meanings expressed by the words of their human authors but, as biblical texts, bearing the inspiration and authority of God. It is the task of the interpreter to discover their meanings and to discern their significance for the world in which we live.

2.2.9   The second answer is that the variety of differing interpretations of the biblical texts now on offer should lead us to realize that the meaning of a text is created as a particular group of people reads the text in the light of its own particular traditions and beliefs and in its own particular context. That is to say, the 'meaning' of a text is relative to the people who interpret it.

2.2.10   It might seem that this is a rather abstruse argument, but it is one that has very important consequences in the area of human sexuality. If the first view is taken then interpreting the Bible in order to discover what it says about human sexuality means attempting to discover the meaning(s) that are present in the biblical texts that are under discussion. Thus we can ask what the teaching of Romans 1.26-27 about homosexuality means and reply that it means this and not that. If the second view is taken, however, then the meaning of the text is the way we choose to read it, and we are free to read Romans 1.26-27 in such a way as to reflect what we believe about God's attitude to homosexuality.

2.2.11   How should we respond to these two differing approaches to biblical interpretation?

2.2.12   A helpful approach is offered by Trevor Hart in his essay 'Tradition, Authority, and a Christian Approach to the Bible as Scripture'. In this essay, Hart argues that both those who believe that they can uncover a final fixed 'determinate' meaning in the biblical text through the use of the right interpretative tools, and those who hold that the meaning of the text is one created by its readers, nullify the authority of the Bible by refusing to allow it to challenge their own interpretations of it.

2.2.13   Those who believe that they can establish the 'true' meaning of the text:

> ... effectively render themselves immune to any alternative readings of it. They 'have' the text. They are no longer open, therefore, to fresh considerations of it, or to hear it speaking in any other voice than the one they have trapped, tamed and packaged for observation. Thus they allow their own readings to have a finality bestowed upon them, a sufficiency that lifts them above the level of the text itself and out of reach of its criticism. Far from establishing the text's 'authority', therefore, this is a strategy that effectively subverts it and enthrones our 'objective' readings in its place.[8]

2.2.14   On the other hand, those who believe that meaning is bestowed upon the text by those who read it mistake the 'elusiveness' of the text's meaning for its 'absence':

> Thus they set about the task of creating meaning to fill the void. For such approaches there is nothing whatever in or attaching to the text which might constrain our reading. Such constraints as bear upon us come from the community to which we belong, or from our own particular perspective as readers. Unable to transcend this particularity, we are incapable of hearing any strange or uncomfortable voice speaking through the text. We are protected from doing so. The meanings we retrieve are those which our context authorises.[9]

2.2.15   In such a situation, says Hart:

> ... the text means what we will allow it to mean – no more, and no less. Here too, then, there is an effective relocation of authority from

the text to the reader. The possibility of the text challenging us or speaking with a strange voice is undercut.

2.2.16 Hart's suggestion is that in place of both these unsatisfactory approaches we should acknowledge that there is some truth in both of them.

On the one hand we need to acknowledge that:

> ... the abiding objective form of the text, taken together with the context within which it was fashioned, constitutes some form of 'given' to which our reading has a moral obligation ... The text stands over against and over us, and calls us first to hear it speak. In this role it may judge us, as well as encourage and confirm our insights and understanding.[10]

On the other hand we also need to acknowledge that:

> ... the inherent instability of texts bestows upon the task of reading a freshness and vividness, and again a responsibility to submit our readings ever afresh to the constraints and guidelines laid down by a text the resources of which to provoke new resonances of association and response are nonetheless as endless as the differently attuned perspectives with which we come to it.[11]

2.2.17 According to Hart, what this dual acknowledgement entails is that:

> A properly Christian approach to Scripture ... will be one that seeks to submit to the text, presuming on the presence of communicative intent mediated through the text, seeking to be constrained in its initial approaches and subsequent responses by a discipline of hearing what the text is saying, so far as it is possible, and recognizing the partial and provisional nature of all its readings, thereby being open and committed to a continuing process of disciplined listening and hearing.[12]

2.2.18 If we are to engage in the sort of interpretative process that Hart outlines, this means our interpretation of the Bible needs to be marked by the virtues of humility and charity.

2.2.19 Awareness that our particular reading of the Bible will at best be provisional and partial means that we need the kind of humility described by St Augustine:

... the knowledge of holy scripture is a great, large, and a high place; but the door is very low so that the high and arrogant man cannot run in; but he must stoop low, and humble himself, that shall enter into it. Presumption and arrogancy is the mother of all error; and humility needeth to fear no error. For humility will only search to know the truth; it will search, and will bring together one place with another, and where it cannot find out the meaning it will pray, it will ask of others that know, and will not presumptuously and rashly define any thing which it knoweth not.[13]

2.2.20 This kind of humility will then lead to the exercise of charity towards others who are seeking to interpret Scripture, on the presumption that they too are seeking to learn from God, and may have heard from him what we have not. This means taking others, including those with whose interpretation we differ, seriously, and listening as attentively as possible to what they have to say, presuming what they have to say is a possible Christian interpretation even if we cannot at first see how it can be.

2.2.21 It also means that, when describing their views to others, or explaining why we disagree with them, we must put the best possible construction on what they have to say. Stephen Fowl helpfully describes this approach in terms of being a 'charitable interpreter' of the thoughts of others:

> To be a charitable interpreter one must develop the dispositions, habits, and abilities which enable one to show how a sensible person could hold views with which one differs without being considered irrational. In other words, the charitable interpreter presumes that those who differ hold their differing views for good reasons and tries to display what these are or were.[14]

It may in fact be the case that either we ourselves, or the person from whom we differ, do not hold our views for good reasons but are wilfully refusing to recognize what a particular text is saying. We need to take this possibility seriously but, just as we would not wish others to assume this of us, so we should not assume it of others without good reason.

2.2.22 At its best, the Anglican tradition, with its willingness to tolerate a broad spectrum of theological opinion, and its encouragement of biblical scholarship, has allowed the space for precisely the kind of serious, but humble, charitable and provisional reading of Scripture that we have just described.

2.2.23 Awareness that our reading of Scripture is provisional might seem to call into question the effective authority of the Bible. If we cannot be sure that we have fully understood the meaning of the biblical text how can we confidently build our Christian lives upon it? Anthony Thiselton responds to this question by arguing that Christian faith means trusting that God is at work in the process of interpretation, leading us to an understanding of his will for our lives that he will ratify at the last judgement. In his words:

> I entrust my daily life to the consequences and commitments entailed in acts of promise, commission, appointment, address, directive and pledge of love spoken in the name of God or God in Christ in Scripture, even though the definitive corroboration of these linguistic acts awaits final confirmation at the last judgment. Just as sanctification entails a process of transformation into the image of Christ, although through justification I am already 'in Christ', clothed in his righteousness, even so interpretation and understanding of Scripture entails a process of grasping more fully the implications, entailments, nuances, and perhaps further commitments and promises that develop what has been appropriated in faith.[15]

2.2.24 In this context, says Thiselton:

> ... we need not regard conflicts of interpretation with dismay. For they belong to a broad process of testing, correcting, and initiating readiness for fresh advance, even if from time to time they also enter blind alleys. But such is the nature of appropriating the gifts and grace of God which is both fallible and bold, touched by sin, yet empowered and directed by the Holy Spirit.[16]

2.2.25 In relation to the specific issue of human sexuality, reading the Bible in the way that has just been described means, on the one hand, rejecting the idea that any reading of what the Bible says about human sexuality will do. The texts that are relevant to this issue do constitute a 'given' by which our readings must be constrained. On the other hand, it also means accepting the idea that our particular reading of these texts is a provisional and partial one, with the corollary that we must be open to the possibility of revising our reading in the light of our own study of the text in new contexts or on the basis of fresh insights provided by other readers.

2.3 **Four issues in reading biblical texts**

2.3.1   So far we have argued that a responsible reading of the Bible means a reading that is marked by provisionality, humility and charity, and which is constrained by the given form of the biblical texts themselves.

2.3.2   According to the orthodox Christian belief about the nature of the Bible that Anglicans have traditionally accepted, these texts have a dual nature. On the one hand, they are the 'word of God', texts inspired by God through his Spirit to be the medium of his self-communication to us. On the other hand, they are also human artefacts, created by specific human beings in specific historical circumstances.

2.3.3   As Max Turner argues in his essay 'Historical Criticism and Theological Hermeneutics of the New Testament',[17] a responsible reading of Scripture that takes seriously both the human origins and the theological significance of the biblical text as the 'word of God' will need to address three kinds of issue.

2.3.4   First of all there are what he calls 'behind the text' issues. These are issues that are to do with the linguistic, cultural and religious assumptions that the human authors of the Bible shared with their readers and which made communication with them possible. In order to explore these issues the interpreter of the Bible will need to know about the languages in which the Bible was originally written, and about the historical, cultural and religious background out of which the various biblical books emerged.

2.3.5   In the case of texts that deal with sexual issues, this means that we will need to know what the words used to describe various kinds of sexual activity signified at the time when they were written, and what cultural and religious understanding of sexuality lies behind what the biblical writer is saying.

2.3.6   Secondly, there are what he calls 'in the text' issues. These issues have to do with how a particular text functions as a text. They are concerned with how the particular words chosen by the author fit together to make up the text as a whole. When looking at John's Gospel, for example, we need to ask how the miracle stories and the discourses fit together to constitute St John's apologia for the belief that 'Jesus is the Christ, the Son of God', and how his use of key terms such as 'love', 'glory' and 'world' fits into this wider picture.

2.3.7   In the case of texts that deal with sexual issues, this means that we will need to know how the texts that deal with such issues fit into the larger texts of which they are a part and how their being part of these larger texts should shape our understanding of their meaning.

2.3.8   Thirdly, there are what he calls 'in front of the text' issues. These are issues that are concerned with how particular biblical texts, such as John's Gospel, relate to the biblical canon as a whole, how they have spoken to Christians down the centuries, and how they might speak to us today.

2.3.9   This means considering how a particular text relates to God's communicative intention revealed through the whole of the canon, to supplement our own listening to the text by hearing what others have heard it say. It also means thinking seriously about what it says to us in our particular situation, bearing in mind Hart's point about the ability of the text to speak in fresh ways in new contexts.

2.3.10   The second and third issues we have just highlighted raise a further issue, which is how we deal with the tensions that appear to exist between different parts of the biblical canon, tensions that the critical approach to the Bible has increasingly highlighted.

2.3.11   As Oliver O'Donovan points out in his book *On the Thirty Nine Articles* this is a serious issue because the belief that the Bible is internally inconsistent calls into question its ability to function as a doctrinal authority in a way in which the Christian tradition, the Anglican tradition included, has insisted that it does:

> Unless we can think that Scripture is readable as a whole, that it communicates a unified outlook and perspective, we cannot attribute doctrinal authority to it, but only to some part of it at the cost of some other part. The authority of Scripture, then, presupposes the possibility of a harmonious reading; correspondingly, a church which presumes to offer an unharmonious or diversifying reading may be supposed to have in mind an indirect challenge to the authority of Scripture itself.[18]

2.3.12   He suggests that the way to understand the tensions that so many people have discerned in Scripture is to read the Bible in terms of the dialectic of God's historical self-revelation in which God's further self-revelation through his activity in history relativizes that which went before.

2.3.13   To take an obvious example, the sacrificial system set out in the book of Leviticus (Leviticus 1.1 – 7.38; 16.1 – 17.15) was, for its time and place, an expression of God's will for his people. However, it has to be understood in the light of the later prophetic critique of the sacrificial system in texts such as Isaiah 1.11-13, Hosea 6.6, and Amos 5.21-27, and the argument of the letter to the Hebrews (Hebrews 9.1 – 10.25) that, once Christ had offered the sacrifice of himself once for all on the cross, the sacrificial system ceased to have its original significance and took on a new significance as a testimony to Christ.

2.3.14   As we shall argue in more detail later, the implication of this is that reading the Bible responsibly in connection with human sexuality means reading what it has to say about the issue in this kind of dialectical fashion, understanding how the relevant texts fit into the overall pattern of God's unfolding self-revelation in salvation history.

2.4 The use of reason and tradition

2.4.1   Addressing these issues in the way that has just been described will also take into account the classic Anglican concern that we should take reason and tradition seriously in the formation of our theological understanding.

Reason

2.4.2   To take reason first of all, it needs to be noted that, while 'reason' is often appealed to as an essential component of Anglican theology, the word is in fact used in two distinct senses.

2.4.3   One way it is used is to refer to the exercise of the human capacity for rational thought. Thus, when it is said that theology should involve the use of reason, what is meant is that theology ought to be a rational enterprise in which the decisions that are arrived at result from a proper and responsible use of the intellect rather than from prejudice or emotion. It was in relation to this sense of the term reason that Richard Hooker argued against the Puritans that they themselves believed in the exercise of human reason when it came to the interpretation of Scripture. The approach to the interpretation of Scripture outlined above certainly gives full place to reason in the sense that it proposes a rational approach to discerning the Bible's meaning.

2.4.4   The term reason is also used in a second way, however. In this second sense it is used to refer to the moral awareness that human beings have because of their being created in the image and likeness of God. The argument developed by a long line of theologians from the second-century apologists onwards, and by Anglican theologians from the time of Richard Hooker, is that the revelation given to us in Holy Scripture supplements that basic awareness that all human beings have of what God requires of them in terms of service to him and to their neighbours.

2.4.5   As Bishop Robert Sanderson put it in his 1647 *Lectures on Conscience and Human Law*:

> The proper end and design of the Holy Scripture, is to make us wise unto salvation through faith which is in Christ Jesus; for since the light of natural reason is insufficient to bring us to a supernatural end, as well because of the obscurity it contracted by the fall of Adam, as also because a supernatural end must be attained by supernatural means, it pleased Almighty God, in pity to our weakness, to reveal such a measure of his Will to us in the Holy Scripture as he thought fit; so that by this gracious and saving dispensation we are not only instructed in matters of faith, but are informed to more advantage of what was naturally known to us; insomuch that those duties of morality, which we know by the dictates of nature, we discharge now from a nobler principle, the love of God, and for nobler ends, which are his glory, and our own salvation.[19]

2.4.6   If the biblical revelation does thus, in the famous phrase of St Thomas Aquinas, 'perfect and not overthrow nature', it follows that, in outlining how the Bible can speak to us today, a responsible biblical interpreter will seek to show the connections between biblical teaching and the existing moral norms of contemporary culture. Part of the reason C. S. Lewis's apologetic works were so successful in the 1940s and 50s, for example, was because of his skill in making precisely these kinds of connection.

2.4.7   A problem arises, however, when the moral values of a particular culture appear to clash with biblical teaching, as many would say is happening today over issues of sexual morality. As we have seen, our culture seems increasingly unwilling to accept that biblical teaching on sexual morality as this has been traditionally understood is morally justifiable. It questions it on moral grounds, and this raises the question of how we should respond to what David Brown has called: '... the challenge of the secular conscience'.[20]

2.4.8   One proper response would be to see whether the traditional understanding of what the Bible says is in fact a correct interpretation of it. If, however, after proper examination this still seems to be the case, the question arises 'what then'? The classic Christian and Anglican answer has been that what the Bible has to say has to take priority because human intuition may be faulty and clouded by sin, whereas the biblical revelation carries the direct authority of God. To quote Sanderson again:

> Holy Scripture is the adequate rule of faith, and of things supernaturally to be believed, and of moral actions likewise, so far as they are spiritual, and conduce to a supernatural end. It is also the law of the conscience, and the principal and supreme rule of what we are to practise; so that where the Scripture determines absolutely either by precept or prohibition, no other law has a right to interfere and stand in competition with it.[21]

2.4.9   The Christian theologian therefore has to take a middle path, neither denying the existence of genuine moral insight outside the Christian tradition, nor affirming uncritically the moral insights of any particular culture. Oliver O'Donovan makes the point well:

> The Christian moral thinker ... has no need to proceed in a totalitarian way, denying the importance and relevance of all that he finds valued as moral conviction in the various cultures and traditions of the world (whether these be 'Christian', 'non-Christian' or 'post-Christian'). He has no need to prove that anything worth while in them has arisen historically from Christian influence. But neither can he simply embrace the perspectives of any such culture, not even – which is the most difficult to resist – the one in which he happens to belong and which therefore claims him as an active participant. He cannot set about building a theological ethic upon the moral *a priori* of a liberal culture, a revolutionary culture or any other kind of culture; for that is to make of theology an ideological justification for the cultural constructs of human misknowledge. He can only approach these phenomena critically, evaluating them and interpreting their significance from the place where true knowledge of moral order is given, under the authority of the gospel. From that position alone can be discerned what there is to be found in these various moral traditions that may be of interest or value.[22]

2.4.10   It also needs to be acknowledged, however, that there is a two-way relationship between our understanding of the gospel and the moral convictions of the surrounding culture. It is not simply a question of Christians making a critique of society's moral convictions. The moral convictions of society may also lead Christians to understand the gospel more deeply by offering a critique of what are set forth as Christian teachings. A clear contemporary example of this is the way in which secular criticisms of the concepts of hierarchy and patriarchy have led Christians to reconsider traditional Christian teaching about these matters and to ask afresh what the gospel has to say about these matters.

2.4.11   Taking reason seriously has become more complicated in recent years because of the pluralist context that we now inhabit. The *Virginia Report* states that 'reason': 'refers to what can be called the "mind of a particular culture", with its characteristic ways of seeing things, asking about them and explaining them'.[23] In contemporary Western society there is no general agreement about such matters, and as a result taking reason seriously means that the ways in which we read the Bible have to address the varied intellectual concerns and moral intuitions of the different groups of people with whom we are in conversation.

Tradition
2.4.12   To move on to the question of tradition, it has to be admitted that some Anglicans of a Protestant persuasion have been dismissive of what Cranmer called: 'the stinking puddles of men's traditions'.[24] However, Anglicanism as a whole, the Reformers included, has insisted on the importance of taking note of the tradition of Christian theology, the theology of the patristic period in particular, as a vital resource for interpreting Scripture correctly. That is why, for instance, Canon A 5 declares that the doctrine of the Church of England is grounded not only in: 'the Holy Scriptures' but also: 'in such teachings of the ancient Fathers and Councils of the Church as are agreeable to the said Scriptures'.

2.4.13   Seeing tradition in terms of inherited teaching might lead to the idea that it is something static, simply a storehouse of ecclesiastical decisions handed down from the past. However this would be a misleading view of tradition since, as the recent Anglican Roman Catholic International Commission statement *The Gift of Authority* puts it, tradition is in reality 'a dynamic process, communicating to each generation what was delivered once for all to the apostolic community'.[25]

2.4.14 To quote the *Virginia Report* again:

> Tradition refers to the ongoing Spirit-guided life of the Church which receives, and in receiving interprets afresh God's abiding message. The living tradition embraces the ecumenical creeds and the classical eucharistic prayers, which belong with the Scriptures as forming their essential message. Tradition is not to be understood as an accumulation of formulae and texts, but as the living mind, the nerve centre of the Church. Anglican appeal to tradition is the appeal to this mind of the Church carried by the worship, teaching and the Spirit-filled life of the Church.[26]

2.4.15 Tradition does not, therefore, constitute a second and separate source of revelation alongside Scripture. Rather, it is the way in which the Holy Spirit brings the truth about our relationship with God in Christ to which the Scriptures testify alive in a fresh way for the Church of today. And if we believe that the Holy Spirit speaks to us today then we should also be ready to listen to what he has been saying in the historical traditions of the Church.

2.4.16 Furthermore, where a particular way of reading Scripture has received the general assent of God's people down the centuries, as in the case of the traditional teaching of the Christian Church concerning human sexuality, this must cause us to consider especially seriously whether it is not, in fact, a reading to which people have been guided by the Spirit, and which we should therefore accept.

2.4.17 Conversely, however, we also need to be discerning, since people can, and have, been deceived about hearing the voice of the Spirit, or the Spirit may be saying something fresh in our day. This means that we need to test tradition against the Scriptures themselves and against the moral convictions of contemporary society, and remember that even the most venerable traditions can be wrong or inappropriate for today.

2.4.18 To sum up, while accepting the classical Anglican acceptance of the patristic and reformed position we can echo the words of the *Virginia Report* and say that:

> The characteristic Anglican way of living with a constant dynamic interplay of Scripture, tradition and reason means that the mind of God has constantly to be discerned afresh, not only in every age, but in each and every context.[27]

In short, Christian tradition is dynamic and not static. This is as true for our thinking about human sexuality as it is for any other area of our Christian lives.[28]

2.5 Reading the Bible as a witness to the grace of God

2.5.1   If we are to read the Bible in order to hear what God has to say to us about how we should live before him, it is important that we do not simply reduce its teaching to a series of discrete ethical commands, a list of 'dos' and 'don'ts' supported by divine authority.

2.5.2   As O'Donovan puts it:

> Not only is it insufficient to quote and requote the great commands of the Decalogue and the Sermon on the Mount (and there are still many who need persuading of this, in practice if not in theory); but it would be insufficient even if we added to them, if we could compile a complete list of things commanded or prohibited; it would be insufficient even if we included in such a list, with a shrewd awareness of the relativity of semantic forms, principles derived from other modes of moral teaching in the Bible, such as stories, parables or laments. We will read the Bible seriously only when we use it to guide our thought towards a *comprehensive* moral viewpoint, and not merely to articulate disconnected moral claims. We must look within it not only for moral bricks, but for indications of the order in which the bricks belong together.[29]

2.5.3   In other words, as we have indicated earlier on in this chapter, we have to look at how the commands and prohibitions that the Bible contains relate to an overall understanding of God and his purposes. It is only in relation to this larger perspective that these specific commands and prohibitions can be rightly understood, and it is only a grasp of this larger perspective that will enable us to make informed decisions about ethical issues and situations that the Bible does not directly address.

2.5.4   The question then arises as to what this 'big picture' of God and his purposes looks like. Over the centuries, as Christians have pondered the Bible, they have consistently come up with a picture of God and his engagement with his creation that is summarized in the Creeds and to which the Anglican tradition has also subscribed.

2.5.5   This is the familiar account that sees God as existing as Father,

Son and Holy Spirit and relating to creation in the 'salvation history' that the biblical narrative describes.

2.5.6 This 'salvation history' is usefully summarized by *Issues in Human Sexuality* as follows:

> ... the world is created good but then distorted as a result of the decision of free beings to go against the will of God. Chiefly responsible is humankind, made in God's image and likeness, and given power over other creatures as God's steward or viceroy in the world. This human disobedience affects the whole natural order but especially men and women themselves, whose own nature is thereby corrupted and placed in need of liberation from evil. However, the same infinite love which created is also active to rescue and restore. God has been constantly at work to guide history and to support those he loves, and finally in Jesus comes to live in his world in the undistorted image of a perfect humanity perfectly identified with the divine will. In this true humanity he endures all that sin and evil can inflict, and breaks their power by the undefeated love and holiness which pass through the Cross to the resurrection and Ascension. For those who acknowledge this victorious love revealed in Jesus Christ there is forgiveness of sins and access to new and eternal life, in which the transforming presence of God's own Spirit can make every human being Christlike in the way appropriate to each, and ultimately restore the whole creation.[30]

2.5.7 At one level this story is about a series of covenants between God and his creation. There is the 'covenant of works' in the garden of Eden in which God declares to Adam and Eve that their enjoyment of the garden is conditional upon their refraining from eating the fruit of the tree of the knowledge of good and evil (Genesis 2.15-17). There is the covenant after the flood in which God promises never again to destroy what he has made (Genesis 9.8-17). There is the covenant of universal blessing, which is made initially with Abraham (Genesis 12.3) and then developed in the covenant with Israel at Sinai (Exodus 19.4-6) and the covenant with David (2 Samuel 7.4-16). Finally, there is the new covenant prophesied by Jeremiah (Jeremiah 31.31-34) and enacted in Christ (Hebrews 8.8-12) in which all the previous covenants are both focused and fulfilled.

2.5.8 If we then dig deeper and ask what gives coherence to the story of these successive covenants, what we find is that the biblical story is a story about grace. That is to say, it is a story about God's undeserved love towards his creation. Existence itself is a gift and, when creation falls into sin, God gives to it the gift of new and eternal life through the incarnation, death and resurrection of his Son, and through the work of the Spirit, a gift that is foreshadowed in the Old Testament and bestowed in the New.

2.5.9   To put it another way, it is a story about the freedom of God, and how he exercises this freedom to be for humanity. As Karl Barth writes, what is at the heart of the biblical message is the good news that:

> In His free grace, God is for man in every respect; He surrounds man from all sides. He is man's Lord who is before him, above him, after him, and thence also with him in history, the locus of man's existence. Despite man's insignificance, God is with him as his Creator who intended and made mankind to be very good. Despite man's sin, God is with him, the One who was in Jesus Christ reconciling the world, drawing man unto Himself in merciful judgment. Man's evil past is not merely crossed out because of its irrelevancy. Rather, it is in the good care of God. Despite man's life in the flesh, corrupt and ephemeral, God is with him. The victory in Christ is here and now present through his Spirit, man's strength, companion and comfort. Despite man's death God is with him, meeting him as redeemer and perfecter at the threshold of the future to show him the totality of existence in the true light in which the eyes of God beheld it from the beginning and will behold it evermore. In what He is for man and does for man, God ushers in the history leading to the ultimate salvation of man.[31]

2.5.10   If this story of God's free grace is the reality that lies at the heart of the biblical witness, then reading the Bible as a coherent canonical whole means asking how each of the component parts of the Bible, including the laws that it contains, relates to this history.

2.5.11   In looking at the laws and regulations that the Bible contains we also have to ask how the contingent and particular character of many of the biblical commands relates to the universal will of God for the human race to which they gave expression in their own time and place. Down the centuries Christians have wanted to insist that the Bible is a trans-cultural document in the sense that it does not simply address the particular cultural contexts out of which the biblical material arose but speaks God's word into all other cultural contexts as well. If this claim is to be justified, however, the question of the relationship between the universal and the particular has to be addressed.

2.5.12 The Thirty Nine Articles begin to address this problem in what they say about the Old Testament law in Article 7. This declares:

> Although the Law given from God by Moses, as touching Ceremonies and Rites, do not bind Christian men, nor the Civil precepts thereof ought of necessity to be received in any commonwealth; yet notwithstanding, no Christian man whatsoever is free from the obedience of the Commandments that are called Moral.

2.5.13 As O'Donovan explains, in this Article:

> ... a division is set between the Christian era and the society to which the Old Testament (as law) bears witness. The dialectic of historical development is acknowledged. The order by which the social good was mediated in ancient Israel cannot claim us directly, but is part of the historical dialectic through which the gospel of Christ was revealed. Yet this contingent social order was *also* a mediation of the universal good; to understand it, it is not enough to understand its contingency, but we must understand its relation to the universal good as well. Hence we detect also within this law a revelation of created order and the good to which all men are called, a 'moral law' by which every human being is claimed and which belongs fundamentally to men's welfare. The theologian's task in expounding the Old Testament is to allow the contingent and the universal to emerge distinctly. If the *universal* does not shine through the contingent, then what is done is not theology, but only history: if the universal does not shine *through the contingent*, then what is done is bad theology, not founded in the narration of God's mighty deeds in saving-history, and so inadequately Christian.[32]

2.5.14 The principle that one has to ask about how specific commands relate to God's universal will and intention is one that does not, however, simply apply to the Old Testament.

2.5.15 Unlike the Old Testament, the New Testament can never be relativized by any further stage in God's self-revelation since the revelation given to us in Christ to which the New Testament bears witness was both full and final. This is the point that is made, for example, by the author of Hebrews in Hebrews 1.1-3.

2.5.16   However, where the New Testament is like the Old is in the fact that much of what it has to say about Christian conduct also relates to specific circumstances of its own time. One can think, for example, of Our Lord's teaching about non-resistance in Matthew 5.38-41, which relates to the situation of occupation in the Palestine of his day, or of the commands not to eat food that is strangled, or blood, in Acts 15.20, and not to participate in meals associated with idolatry in 1 Corinthians 10.14-22.

All three examples relate to specific cultural and historical circumstances that have no direct parallels in this country today, even though the teaching about non-resistance in Matthew 5 is still extremely relevant to Christians suffering under oppressive regimes in other parts of the world, and the question of eating food sacrificed to idols is still a live issue for Christians in south-east Asia.

2.5.17   As in the case of the Old Testament, we have to ask how these texts can speak to us through their contingency about the universal will of God, which we are called upon to obey.

2.5.18   In the specific case of what the Bible has to say about sexual relationships, the same principle applies. We have to look carefully at what it says about such relationships and seek to discover how this points us to God's overall will for human sexual conduct as a subset of his overall will for human conduct as a whole, and how this is best expressed by us in our time and place.

2.6 Reading the Bible as a guide to Christian discipleship

2.6.1   This brings us to the penultimate point we need to consider in this chapter, which is how to read the Bible as a guide to Christian discipleship.

2.6.2   If reading the Bible as a witness to the grace of God means seeking to discern the overall moral framework that God has established by his mighty acts in salvation history, then reading the Bible as a guide to Christian discipleship means seeking guidance concerning what it means to live appropriately within this framework, both as individuals and as Christian communities.

2.6.3   As David Atkinson explains in his book *Pastoral Ethics in Practice,* when seeking this guidance, we need to remember that ethics cannot be separated from theology and spirituality:

There is in fact no 'biblical ethics' which stands apart from theology and spirituality. For the people of God in the Bible, morality and spirituality are two sides of the same coin. 'Biblical' ethics are primarily the ethics of allegiance to God. In Old Testament terms this can best be expressed as allegiance to the covenant God. In New Testament language, it may be described as 'following Christ', or 'living as a member of God's kingdom'. Christian ethics involves surrender to the Lordship of God in Christ, in loving obedience to his will and in the power of his Spirit.

So the question as to the use of the Bible then becomes: what role does the Bible play in helping us in our allegiance to God? Our use of the Bible in ethics is closely related to its use in doctrine and in spirituality. It is part of the resource we need by which our 'faculties [are] trained by practice to distinguish good from evil' (Hebrews 5.14).[33]

2.6.4 Atkinson also reminds us of a point that we have already noted, which is that we should not fall into the trap of using the Bible as a quarry for a series of discrete proof texts that give us direct guidance for every situation in which we find ourselves:

We misuse it and we get things wrong if we try to use the Bible simply as a moral text-book, and by seeking out proof texts (as though 'Thou shalt not kill' settled all the moral problems of life and death).

The harder, but necessary task is to ask of any biblical passage: 'what is it telling me about God, and his will, which was expressed in that way then, which I need to know for my life and decisions now?' We thus seek out theological guide-lines, not proof texts. The Bible simply does not have a ready answer to all our moral questions, but it can serve as a way of deepening our knowledge of God and his will. It shows us through law, through parable, through poetry, through history, and especially through the life and teaching, death and resurrection of Jesus Christ what we need to know to make us into more mature Christian disciples. With the biblical theological minds and attitudes we so develop, we then make our moral judgements in allegiance to the God we are coming to know.[34]

2.6.5 The final point we need to note is that we cannot simply reduce the Bible's ethical instruction to the command to love. Love for God and our neighbour is fundamental to Christian discipleship since it is the summary of what God requires of us (Mark 12.28-34). However, if we are to love rightly, we need further instruction. As was noted above, we need to let the Bible itself teach us what love for God and neighbour means.

2.6.6   As O'Donovan argues, while 'Love is the overall shape of Christian ethics, the form of Christian participation in the created order', love is itself 'ordered and shaped in accordance with the order that it discovers in its object, and this ordering of love it is the task of substantive Christian ethics to trace'.[35]

2.6.7   We are called to express our love for God through our love for the rest of creation, both human and non-human, but to act lovingly towards creation, the human creation included, we need to know what God's purpose is for it, since we will only be acting lovingly if our actions enable it to flourish in accordance with that purpose. That is why, in the Old Testament, the Torah is seen as an expression of God's love for Israel, because it is given as a means by which Israel can flourish (see, for example Psalm 119.89-106).

2.6.8   That is also why, as O'Donovan further notes:

> ... classical Christian descriptions of love are often found invoking two other terms which expound its sense: the first is 'wisdom', which is the intellectual apprehension of the order of things which discloses how each being stands in relation to each other; the second is 'delight' which is affective attention to something simply for what it is and for the fact that it is. Such love is the fruit of God's presence within us, uniting us to the humanity of God in Christ, who cherishes and defends all that God the Father has thought and made.[36]

2.6.9   In a fallen world, the order intended by God is not always easy to discern, and the darkness of mind from which we suffer as a result of our sinful condition (Romans 1.18-22) makes this task doubly difficult. Therefore, if we are to love rightly, we need to be instructed by God through his word as to the nature of this order and how we can behave so as to enable its flourishing.

2.6.10   In the following chapters we shall go on to consider how this principle of encouraging people to flourish in accordance with God's purposes for them should guide us in terms of the specific dilemmas about sexual morality facing the Church today, seeking instruction from the Bible in accordance with the principles of interpretation explored in this chapter.

2.7 Ethics, virtue and biblical interpretation

2.7.1 The last matter we need to consider in this chapter is the relationship between ethical beliefs, the practice of a Christian way of life, and the interpretation of the Bible.

2.7.2 The traditional Christian method of using the Bible in relation to human sexuality has been to determine what the Bible says about the subject using the approaches outlined above and then seek to apply it. In his essay 'Is the Bible Good News for Human Sexuality? Reflections on Method in Biblical Interpretation' Stephen Barton rejects this approach. Instead, he asks:

> What if the Bible is more like the text of a Shakespearean play or the score of a Beethoven symphony, where true interpretation involves corporate performance and practical enactment, and where the meaning of the text or score will vary to some degree from one performance to another depending on the identity of the performers and the circumstances of the performance? A number of writers have begun to explore this alternative model of interpreting the Bible. Its advantage is that it brings the reading of the Bible back into the process of community formation, celebration and mission, and places responsibility on the community to read the text in ways which are transforming and life-giving.[37]

2.7.3 According to Barton, what his alternative approach means is that:

> ... individual groups and communities will have to accept responsibility for the way they interpret and 'perform' what the Bible says about gender and sexuality. This will involve making decisions (either explicitly or implicitly, consciously or unconsciously) of a theological and ethical kind – questions about who Christ is for us, who we are in the light of Christ, and what kind of people we want to be in relation to God-in-Christ and to our neighbours. Here, it will undoubtedly be the case that the communities who do this most wisely will be the ones whose members are trained in the Christian virtues and who therefore have the traditions, skills and practice necessary to the task.
>
> The question 'Is the Bible good news for human sexuality?' is, in other words, not best taken as a question first and foremost to put to the Bible. Rather, it constitutes a challenge to the church at the fundamental level of practical spirituality. It is those who know of what just and loving Christian practice consists who will be best equipped to read the Bible in a life-giving and liberating way. It is

those who are themselves transformed and being transformed according to the image of Christ who will be best able to perform the scriptures in ways which bring life and Christ-like transformation to human sexuality.[38]

2.7.4 Barton is suggesting that, rather than biblical interpretation preceding and shaping Christian ethics and practice, it is the ethics and practice of the Christian community that needs to (and in reality does) precede and shape its biblical interpretation. It is the knowledge of 'what just and loving Christian practice consists' that enables Christians to perform the text in a life-giving and transforming fashion. Barton places the emphasis on this order of things – of our practice informing our reading – but we should not think of this in too rigid a way, for he also gives a realistic sense of the ways in which a symphony of voices and concerns necessarily shapes our reading.

2.7.5 Building on Barton's argument that ethical issues precede hermeneutical ones, Stuart and Thatcher argue in *People of Passion* that what is required for a fruitful reading of the Bible is 'a hermeneutical key which will enable us to read scripture in such a way that encourages us to have a deeper love of God and others' and that their own reading of Scripture:

> ... can only be judged by the behaviour it encourages. The fact that many lesbian, gay and bisexual people (and indeed many others) do not feel loved, included, cared for, or supported by many of the churches is the greatest indictment of those churches' hermeneutics. Only by standing in solidarity with those on the margins will those who are responsible for writing church documents on sexuality be able to read the Bible in a way that does help to establish an inclusive, just and justice-seeking Church (which is what they all claim to want).[39]

2.7.6 The proposal that the Bible needs to be read in such a way as to encourage virtuous behaviour is laudable. Any approach to reading the Bible that prevents the Bible from being useful in this way is clearly flawed. After all, 2 Timothy 3.16-17, traditionally seen as the key verses explaining the purpose for which the Bible was given to us, insist that the Bible is useful because of its role in the formation of a Christian character:

> All scripture is inspired by God and is useful for teaching, for reproof, for correction, and for training in righteousness, so that everyone who belongs to God may be proficient, equipped for every good work.

2.7.7 It is also obviously the case that the attitude with which we approach the Bible and the questions that we bring to it will determine the way that we read it, and we are more likely to be receptive to allowing the Bible to shape our lives as individuals and as a Christian community if we are already people who have sufficient openness to God and his ways to be willing for this to happen. As Luke 8.18 indicates, *how* we hear God speaking to us through the Bible is vitally important because it is the way in which we hear that will determine whether our hearing is fruitful or not:

> Then pay attention to how you hear; for to those who have, more will be given; and from those who do not have, even what they seem to have will be taken away.

2.7.8 Nevertheless, if this proposal leads to a belief that our reading of Scripture should be primarily or entirely shaped by a desired ethical outcome, this can raise two particular difficulties, and it is well to be aware of these.

2.7.9 The first difficulty can arise if the proposal is based too much on the belief that the readers of a text have the freedom to determine its meaning by the way in which they choose to read it. As suggested above, this belief can fail to do justice to the fact that the given form of a text places constraints on our reading of it and, therefore, we are not at liberty simply to read the text in any way that we find proper. To return to Barton's Shakespearean analogy, there is a variety of ways we can read a play by Shakespeare, but some readings (for example, seeing *Hamlet* as comedy or *As you like it* as tragedy) are simply not true to the text we are reading, and what is true of Shakespeare here is true also of the Bible.

2.7.10 The second difficulty arises if we make our pastoral concerns the sole guide to reading Scripture. As Stuart and Thatcher point out, we must be deeply concerned if those seeking recognition within the range of identities represented by the lesbian, gay and bisexual spectrum do not feel loved or cared for by the Christian Church. Their feelings of hurt and rejection must lead us to reconsider our reading of the biblical text in order to see if it is indeed the way we read the text that is causing the problem.

2.7.11 However, while our concerns about what would be pastorally helpful for lesbian, gay, or bisexual people are an important resource in our reading of Scripture, it would not be true to the Anglican tradition to allow those concerns to become the *sole* hermeneutical key that determines our reading of the biblical text. Obviously, we all bring the issues raised by our own experience and our pastoral experience to the biblical text and, equally obviously, these, consciously or unconsciously, shape the way that we read it. However, if we insist that the Bible can only speak to these issues in a certain specific way, then we are constraining the freedom of the text to challenge our existing assumptions and look at things in a new light.

2.7.12 Furthermore, if we insist that the Bible can only speak to these issues in a certain way, we run the risk of failing to allow God to be God. It is only as we respect the freedom of the text that we respect the freedom of God to speak to us through his word and to declare what is the best for us as God's people. This is, of course, true of any reading of Scripture, from any point of view in the spectrum of Christian views on human sexuality in which a particular reading is forced onto a text.

2.7.13 A point made by John Webster in his essay 'Hermeneutics in Modern Theology' may be helpful here. He notes that the distinctive feature of a Christian reading of the Bible is an openness to being addressed by God through the words of Scripture, and that this openness necessarily involves the mortification of our desire to read the text in the way that we want.[40] As an example of the kind of approach he is advocating, Webster points to a classic passage from Calvin's *Institutes* in which Calvin stresses that the fact that a Christian belongs to God means submitting his or her intellect and will to God's leading:

> But if we are not our own, but the Lord's, it is plain both what error is to be shunned, and to what end the actions of our lives ought to be directed. We are not our own; therefore neither is our own reason or our will to rule our acts and counsels. We are not our own; therefore, let us not make it our end to seek what may be agreeable to our carnal nature. We are not our own; therefore as far as possible, let us forget ourselves and the things that are ours. On the other hand we are God's; let us therefore, live and die to him (Romans 14.8). We are God's; therefore let his wisdom and will preside over all our actions. We are God's; to him, therefore, as the only legitimate end, let every part of our life be directed. O how great the proficiency of him who, taught that he is not his own, has withdrawn the dominion and government of himself from his own reason that he may give them

to God! For as the surest source of destruction to men is to obey themselves, so the only haven of safety is to have no other will, no other wisdom than to follow the Lord wherever he leads.[41]

2.7.14   In this passage, Calvin is outlining an approach to the Christian life as a whole rather than addressing the specific issue of how to read Scripture, but as Webster comments:

> If reading is part of what Calvin calls 'service' of God which involves a 'departure from self', then a Christian anthropology of reading will give high profile to *faith*, in its broadest sense of the shape which human life takes in response to the prevenient, gracious Word of God. The 'faithful' reader is the reader whose being and acts are grounded *extra se*, and who corresponds, exists in analogy, to God's creative and redemptive action. Faithful reading is not so much constructive or constitutive of what is heard, but *consent* – consent to the text as an instrument for the speaking of God, and therefore the self-presentation of God's will to save. Reading is an exercise in *conscientia*, not in the modern sense of reflexive moral awareness, but in the much larger sense of 'the response of the human consciousness to the divine judgment', in which we are stripped of our efforts to impose a shape on the text and made capable of free and attentive listening.[42]

2.7.15   This means that, when reading the text, we have to try, as honestly as we can, to bring our preconceptions about sexual ethics, *be they traditionalist or radical*, to the bar of the text and allow them to be challenged, modified or confirmed by the voice of God addressing us through the 'givenness' of the text itself. We must also be aware of being trapped by wooden secular categories and labels, taking note especially of the debate between those who see a homosexual identity as an essential characteristic given to someone by nature, and those who see it as a construct resulting from psychological and/or social influences on the individual concerned.

2.7.16   In the next five chapters of the report we shall attempt this kind of engagement, looking first of all at the overall teaching of the Bible about human sexuality as this has been understood within the Christian tradition, and then going on to consider how this teaching relates to the specific issues raised by homosexual, bisexual and transsexual people.

chapter 3

The theology of sexuality

3.1 The search for fulfilment

3.1.1 During the course of human history there have been many different accounts of what it means to be a human person. Within the Christian tradition, however, the declaration in Genesis 1.27, 'So God created humankind in his image, in the image of God he created them; male and female he created them', has been seen as providing us with the key to a correct understanding of what it means to be human. To be a human being is to be someone who has been created in God's image and likeness.

3.1.2 Over the centuries, many theologians have identified the 'image of God' in human beings with some aspect of their created nature such as their ability to stand upright, or their capacity for morality or rational thought. The problem with this approach is that it lacks biblical support. The biblical text nowhere identifies the image of God with some inherent human capacity to be or to do certain things.

3.1.3 As David Atkinson notes in his commentary on Genesis 1–11, in view of this:

> ... many Old Testament specialists would disagree with this approach. They would argue that the image is not a question of a quality in people, but of the fact that God has created people as his counterpart and that human beings can have a history with God. Westermann argues that 'human beings are created in such a way that their very existence is intended to be their relationship with God'. The image, on this view, is not about something we have, or something we can do: it is about a relationship.
>
> First and foremost it is about the particular relationship in which God places himself with human beings, a relationship in which we become God's counterpart, his representative and his glory on the earth.[1]

3.1.4 On this understanding of Genesis 1.27, to be human means being made for relationship with God. Human beings exist in order to be in this relationship. Seeing things in this way sheds fresh light on the question of what it means for human beings to find true fulfilment.

3.1.5　In the first chapter of this report it was noted that the changes in sexual attitudes and behaviour that have taken place in recent decades have been driven in large measure by a search for personal fulfilment. Increasing numbers of people have sought fulfilment in the achievement of personal happiness, and they have sought to find happiness through personal relationships. It is, of course, also recognized that social and economic factors have affected the shape of household and family structures

3.1.6　It was also noted that this search for personal fulfilment has been linked to a belief in the freedom of individuals to determine their own lifestyle as they see fit without external control from either religion or society.

3.1.7　As the 1995 Church of England Doctrine Commission report *The Mystery of Salvation* notes:

> In our postmodern culture self-fulfilment has become a matter of individually self-chosen goals. Freedom – in the sense of the absolute autonomy of the individual – has become the single, overarching ideal to which all other goals are subordinated. I must be free to be whoever I choose to be and to pursue whatever good I define for myself.[2]

3.1.8　There is much in the contemporary search for self-fulfilment that coheres with traditional Christian belief. The Christian faith has traditionally held that the human search for fulfilment is in principle correct since it is based on the fact that human beings have been created by God precisely in order that they might find fulfilment.

3.1.9　However, there is one fundamental difference between the major features of the contemporary search for fulfilment and a Christian understanding of the matter. The difference is that, from a Christian perspective, the ideal of absolute human autonomy is a misleading one, because, having been created in God's image, human beings cannot find fulfilment along any route they choose, but only along the route of a relationship with God, the ground of our being and the goal of our longing.

3.1.10 This is a point that the *Mystery of Salvation* makes very clearly by drawing a contrast between the secular understanding of fulfilment and the Christian understanding of fulfilment in terms of salvation:

> ... many of the particular things in which people seek self-fulfilment – self-integration, healing of relationships, finding a purpose in life, and so on – are also aspects of Christian salvation. The point is that, beyond all such correspondences between secular fulfilment and Christian salvation, God makes all the difference. Fulfilment is sought axiomatically without God, whereas salvation is nothing at all without God. From one point of view the various aspects of salvation which can be sought and even attained by secular people without reference to God are good things. Their value should certainly not be denigrated. Christians themselves are constantly, rightly, engaged in pointing people to them and helping people to find them. But nevertheless from the point of view of the Christian desire to see human life attain its fullest meaning and destiny, consciously integrated into its ultimate source and goal, these good things, had without reference to God, lack the one thing necessary. They are Hamlet without the Prince.[3]

3.1.11 Furthermore, as well as this fundamental difference between the secular and the Christian understandings of human fulfilment, there is also another difference, and that is the difference in the timescale involved. The secular understanding of human fulfilment is based on the belief that this life is all there is, so we need to attain happiness now because, once we are dead, the chance of happiness has gone for ever. The Christian faith, however, has traditionally taught that true happiness, the full and final flowering of our relationship with God, will only happen when we die and indeed because we die.

3.1.12 This is a truth that is emphasized by the great Anglican theologian and preacher Austin Farrer in his sermon 'The end of Man'. In this sermon Farrer explains that the true end of human beings, the purpose for which they exist, is to come to know and love God. He then goes on to explain that this end cannot be fully achieved without death because it is only by dying that we can fulfil the condition necessary to attain it.

> We cannot, in this life, wholly possess the end we pursue; for man cannot reach his end, until there is an end of man – until we cease from self, and turn outwards on God and on the children of God. And such self-forgetfulness is not attained in a mortal body. Flesh

and blood, says Christ's apostle, cannot attain the kingdom of God.[4]

3.1.13   What all this means is that, from a Christian perspective, the search for fulfilment through sexual relationships has to be seen in a wider context. This context is a right relationship to God and the Christian hope that this life is not all there is. For our desire for fulfilment finds its consummation beyond time and space.

3.1.14   In this chapter we shall be exploring what can be said concerning human sexuality in this wider context.

3.2 God the Holy Trinity

3.2.1   In our contemporary pluralist and multi-faith society, the Christian claim that human beings can only find true fulfilment in relationship with God raises the question 'what do you mean by the term "God"?'. The answer to this question from a Christian viewpoint is that the term 'God' is to be understood with reference to that 'salvation history' referred to in the last chapter. 'God' means the principal author and actor in that history, the creator and saviour who began that history, has sustained that history, and will bring that history to its completion at the end of time.

3.2.2   Reflection on this story has led the Christian Church down the centuries to be still more specific about the God made known to us in this history. It has come to see that, in order to do justice to the biblical narrative, it is necessary to see God not as a simple unity, but as a complex unity in which the one God exists simultaneously as God the Father, God the Son, and God the Holy Spirit.

3.2.3   That is why, for example, the first of the Church of England's *Thirty Nine Articles* states:

> There is but one living and true God, everlasting, without body, parts, or passions; of infinite power, wisdom and goodness; the Maker, and Preserver of all things both visible and invisible. And in the unity of this Godhead there be three Persons, of one substance, power, and eternity; the Father, the Son, and the Holy Ghost.

3.2.4   It is because God exists as Father, Son and Holy Spirit that God is able to be the God of salvation history, the God of the covenants, the God who in Jesus Christ shares his life with creation. Once again this is a point that is well made in *The Mystery of Salvation*. It notes that the Christian understanding of God as Trinity affirms:

> ... that God in his own divine self really is such that God *can share himself* with his creation. God is not only the utterly other, who infinitely transcends creation; God can also be deeply and intimately present within creation, as the Spirit, and God can also be one of us, a genuinely human person, as Jesus Christ the Son. Therefore God can and does open his own life for his creation to share. Moreover, because He is Trinity God can share his life even with those created beings, ourselves, who are alienated from God and opposed to God. As incarnate Son and indwelling Spirit, God enters our situation of evil, suffering and mortality, shares with us the pain of our alienation, bears for us the pain of overcoming our enmity and healing our estrangement, sustains us in the struggle to be truly human, redirects our lives towards the Father as the source and goal of our being.[5]

3.3 The Trinity and the Christian life

3.3.1   Thus far in this chapter it has been argued that, from a Christian perspective, human beings can only find the fulfilment for which they were made through a relationship with God, and that 'God' means God the Holy Trinity, the God who as Father, Son and Holy Spirit has shared his life with us. The question to which we now turn is what it means to be related to this God.

3.3.2   The answer to this question has already been anticipated in the quotation from Austin Farrer given above. To be rightly related to God means living a life of obedience that involves self-forgetfulness to the point of death. In order to explain this point in more detail we shall look in turn at what it means to relate to God as Father, Son, and Holy Spirit.

God the Father

3.3.3   One of the distinctive features of the ministry of Jesus was the way in which he taught his disciples to call God 'Abba', 'Father' (Matthew 6.6-13). This is a point that is emphasized by the Doctrine Commission's 1987 report *We believe in God*. It notes that, whereas contemporary Jewish spirituality was focused on relating to God through the Jewish law:

> ... the most notable feature of Jesus's spirituality was that, without in any way denying the Law, he did not relate to God through the Law but directly as 'Father' and invited his hearers to share in the same

relationship. Though God was indeed known and addressed as 'Father' in Judaism, the image was not a prevalent one, and as far as we know the Aramaic word 'Abba' was not used to address God in prayer in contemporary Judaism. It was the family word, implying both affection and respect, used not only by children, but also by the disciples of a rabbi. It thus suggests an attitude of humility, obedience and reverence, as well as one of dependence, security and confidence.[6]

3.3.4   As the report also notes, because Jesus related to God in this way:

There is thus a new richness of content in Jesus's concept of God. Fatherly attributes come to the fore in his teaching. God is one who loves, cares, gives, listens, welcomes, seeks, accepts, forgives, provides. The concept is positive, and there is little hint of the darker father-image associated with the idea of an angry God.[7]

3.3.5   However, it says, the fatherly love of God that Jesus revealed:

... extends also to expectations and demands. It is particularly striking that in his anguished prayer in Gethsemane Jesus prays, 'Abba, Father, all things are possible for you. Take this cup from me. Yet not what I want but what you want' (Mark 14.36). God is the Father who loves him, and therefore Jesus can bring him his longing for relief. God is also the Father who has expectations of him and therefore Jesus accepts that ultimately his will is what counts.[8]

3.3.6   The Early Church followed Jesus in teaching that Christians could share in the same relationship to God as Father that Jesus himself possessed (John 1.12-13, Romans 8.14-17, Galatians 4.1-7). It also followed Jesus in teaching that the God who is Father is both a God of outgoing, generous love and also a God who has expectations and demands that are to be obeyed.

3.3.7   Both of these aspects of God as Father are brought out in the opening section of the letter to the Ephesians (Ephesians 1.3-6):

Blessed be the God and Father of our Lord Jesus Christ, who has blessed us in Christ with every spiritual blessing in the heavenly places, just as he chose us in Christ before the foundation of the world to be holy and blameless before him in love. He destined us for adoption as his children through Jesus Christ, according to the good pleasure of his will, to the praise of his glorious grace that he freely bestowed on us in the Beloved.

3.3.8   The first thing that we see in this passage is an emphasis on the grace of God, his outgoing love, which was directed towards us before we were even born, and which has given us in Christ every blessing that heaven can provide.

3.3.9   The second thing we see, however, is that God's grace brings with it a call to holy living in obedience to God.

3.3.10   We were 'chosen', the text says, 'to be holy and blameless before him'. There is an echo here of the language used of the people of Israel in Deuteronomy 7.6 and 14.2, and the point that is being made is that, just as the relationship of Israel with God based on his covenant love for them meant that Israel was called to be a holy people living in obedience to God, so also the relationship of love that the renewed Israel, the Church, has with God as their Father means a call to holy living.

3.3.11   A similar point is made in 1 Peter 1.14-16, which reads:

> Like obedient children, do not be conformed to the desires that you formerly had in ignorance. Instead, as he who called you is holy, be holy yourselves in all your conduct; for it is written, 'You shall be holy, for I am holy'.

3.3.12   Here again there is a reference back to the Old Testament, this time a reference to Leviticus 11.44, and the point being made is that being the children of God the Father means holy living since we are called to reflect his character in the way we live our lives.

3.3.13   Living a life as a human being in relationship to God the Father thus means responding to his love, as Jesus did, by living a life of obedient holiness.

God the Son
3.3.14   From what has just been said, it might appear that our relationship with God as Father is based on a pure *imitation* of Christ. However, this idea would be misleading because it fails to do justice to the kind of language used in Ephesians 1, which stresses that our relationship to God the Father is 'in' and 'through' his Son, Jesus Christ.

3.3.15   According to Ephesians, it is not that God relates to Jesus on the one hand and to us on the other. Rather, there is an identity between Jesus and ourselves to such an extent that, as Richard Hooker puts it: 'Such we are in the sight of God the Father, as is the very Son of God himself'.[9]

3.3.16   Furthermore, Ephesians 1 is just one of a whole series of biblical texts that point us to the fact that Jesus Christ was and is the *vicarious man,* the one in whom we are included, the one in whom we exist before God. Other such texts include John 15.1-11, Romans 5.12-21, 2 Corinthians 5.14-21, Galatians 2.20 and Hebrews 2.10-17.

3.3.17   The overall message of these passages is that our existence is bound up with that of Jesus Christ and has been fundamentally altered by what Jesus Christ has done for us. Our old sinful self has ceased to exist because it has been put to death in Christ and a new self has been raised with Christ beyond sin and death to live with God for ever.

3.3.18   Because Christ is the one in whom our human nature has been recreated in line with God's original intention, we can therefore say with the *St Andrew's Day Statement* on human sexuality:

> There can be no description of human reality, in general or in particular outside the reality of Christ. We must be on guard, therefore, against constructing any other ground for our identities than the redeemed humanity given us in him.[10]

3.3.19   Although the New Testament makes it clear that Christ's action on our behalf, his creation of a new humanity of which we are a part, preceded any response on our behalf it also makes it clear that we have to enter into what Christ has done for us and make it our own. The way we do this is through faith and baptism.

3.3.20   As Protestant theology has rightly emphasized on the basis of texts such as John 3.16, Acts 16.31 and Romans 5.1, faith, in the sense of active trust in the work of God in Christ, is fundamental to a right relationship with God. However, as Catholic theology has rightly emphasized, baptism is also fundamental. In the words of the New Testament scholar Alan Richardson, according to the New Testament:

> What Christ has done for all humanity is appropriated by each individual Christian in his baptism. In his baptism the Christian dies with Christ, is crucified with Christ (Romans 6.6, Colossians 3.3); his death frees him from sin, just as the death of a debtor cancels the

debt (Romans 6.7,18; cf. 1 Peter 4.1). He begins a new life risen with Christ (Romans 6.11-13, 7.4-6, Colossians 3.1).[11]

3.3.21 This does not mean that the New Testament offers us two separate and alternative routes into the new life Christ offers. Rather, faith and baptism belong together since, as Richardson explains:

> 'Justification by faith' must be understood to mean justification by the gracious and saving righteousness of God through baptism and incorporation into Jesus Christ, because 'faith' is not a subjective emotion on our part, but an active decision concerning Christ. This decision expresses itself in the act of obedience and self-denial which is made when we are baptized into his body.[12]

The Christian belief is, therefore, that being properly related to God means accepting the fact that a new way of being human has been created by God the Father through Jesus Christ. It also means entering into it at baptism.

3.3.22 Furthermore, because we have been freed from sin through the death and resurrection of Christ, we are called to live a life that is wholly dedicated to God and in which sin has no place. St Paul emphasizes this point in a key passage in his letter to the Romans, in which he discusses how we should live as those who have been united in baptism with Christ's death and resurrection:

> Therefore, do not let sin exercise dominion in your mortal bodies, to make you obey their passions. No longer present your members to sin as instruments of wickedness, but present yourselves to God as those who have been brought from death to life, and present your members to God as instruments of righteousness. For sin will have no dominion over you, since you are not under law but under grace. (Romans 6.12-14)

3.3.23 As John Calvin puts it in his commentary on these verses:

> Paul now bids us give ourselves wholly to God, so that we may restrain our hearts and minds from straying where the lusts of the flesh may draw us. We are to look to the will of God alone, eager to receive his commands, and prepared to obey his orders.
> Our members, too, are to be dedicated and consecrated to his will, so that all our powers of soul and body may aspire to his glory alone. The reason for this is that, since our former life has been destroyed,

the Lord has not in vain created for us another, to which our actions ought to correspond.[13]

3.3.24   This emphasis on obedience and self-denial was not a Pauline innovation. It was a very clear element in the teaching of Christ himself. We can see this, for example, in the Gospel according to St Matthew. In Matthew 11.28-30 we read as follows:

> Come to me, all you who that are weary and are carrying heavy burdens, and I will give you rest. Take my yoke upon you, and learn from me; for I am gentle and humble in heart, and you will find rest for your souls. For my yoke is easy, and my burden is light.

3.3.25   Here we see a clear combination of grace and obedience. All who are weary and carrying heavy burdens are invited to find rest in Christ, but they can only do so by taking upon themselves the yoke of obedience to his commands.

3.3.26   Furthermore, as Matthew and the other Gospels make clear, this obedience is so radical in character that it involves nothing less than that death of the old self that we embrace at our baptism. In the words of Matthew 16.24-27:

> Then Jesus told his disciples, 'If any want to become my followers, let them deny themselves, and take up their own cross and follow me. For those who want to save their life will lose it, and those who lose their life for my sake will find it. For what will it profit them if they gain the whole world but forfeit their life? Or what will they give in return for their life? For the Son of Man is to come with his angels in the glory of his Father, and then he will repay everyone for what has been done.'

3.3.27   As the *St Andrew's Day Statement* notes, what this means for us today is that:

> 'Adopted as children of God and called to follow in the way of the cross,' we are all summoned to various forms of self-denial. The struggle against disordered desires, or the misdirection of innocent desires, is part of every Christian's life, consciously undertaken in baptism. In any individual case, the form which this struggle takes may be determined by circumstances (wealth or poverty, illness or health, educational success or failure). Often these are not open to choice, but are given to us in a situation in which we

are to live faithfully. We are not promised that the struggle will be quickly and triumphantly resolved, nor even that it will be successful at every point along the way; only that it will be crowned at last by a character formed through patience to be like Christ's.[14]

God the Holy Spirit

3.3.28   The Christian claim that God has recreated us in Christ necessarily raises the issue of the connection between Christ and ourselves. What is it that links Christ and ourselves in such a way that what is true of him is also true of us?

3.3.29   According to the witness of the New Testament the answer to this question is that the link between Christ and ourselves is the third person of the Trinity, God the Holy Spirit. As O'Donovan puts it, 'the Holy Spirit overcomes the problem of the objectivity and externality of God's saving deed in Christ. He makes the objective reality a subjective reality to us.'[15]

3.3.30   We can see this very clearly in Romans chapter 8. In this chapter St Paul uses the terms 'Spirit', 'Spirit of God' and 'Spirit of Christ' interchangeably, and makes clear that the presence of the Spirit within us *is* the presence of Christ within us, so that what is true of him is true of us, and his relationship with God as Father is ours as well.

3.3.31   Thus we read in Romans 8.9-11 that, through the Spirit, we share in the righteousness of Christ and the power of his resurrection:

> Any one who does not have the Spirit of Christ does not belong to him. But if Christ is in you, though the body is dead because of sin, the Spirit is life because of righteousness. If the Spirit of him who raised Jesus from the dead dwells in you, he who raised Christ from the dead will give life to your mortal bodies also through his Spirit that dwells in you.

3.3.32   Thus also we read in Romans 8.14-16 that through the Spirit we are able to call God 'Father' because, like Christ, we too are God's children.

> For all who are led by the Spirit of God are children of God. For you did not receive a spirit of slavery to fall back into fear; but you have received a spirit of adoption. When we cry, 'Abba! Father!' it is that very Spirit bearing witness with our spirit that we are children of God.

3.3.33   However, we also need to note that, sandwiched between these two sets of verses in Romans 8, there are two other verses that make clear that the fact that we have the Spirit dwelling within us brings not only privilege but also responsibility. According to Romans 8.12-13 the responsibility we have is to put to death by the power of the Spirit all that belongs to the 'flesh', which is St Paul's shorthand for the old sinful nature that has been abolished in Christ.

> So then, brothers and sisters, we are debtors, not to the flesh, to live according to the flesh – for if you live according to the flesh, you will die; but if by the Spirit you put to death the deeds of the body, you will live.

3.3.34   St Paul also makes the same point in more detail in Galatians 5.16-24. Here he tells the Galatians that, unlike the Jewish law, the Spirit gives us the power to put to death the patterns of attitude and behaviour that characterize the 'flesh', and to replace them with an alternative way of living:

> Live by the Spirit, I say, and do not gratify the desires of the flesh. For what the flesh desires is opposed to the Spirit, and what the Spirit desires is opposed to the flesh; for these are opposed to each other, to prevent you from doing what you want. But if you are led by the Spirit, you are not subject to the law. Now the works of the flesh are obvious: fornication, impurity, licentiousness, idolatry, sorcery, enmities, strife, jealousy, anger, quarrels, dissensions, factions, envy, drunkenness, carousing and things like these. I am warning you, as I warned you before: those who do such things will not inherit the kingdom of God. By contrast, the fruit of the Spirit is love, joy, peace, patience, kindness, generosity, faithfulness, gentleness, and self-control. There is no law against such things. And those who belong to Christ Jesus have crucified the flesh with its passions and desires.

3.3.35   The radical nature of this Pauline teaching is brought out very clearly by the seventeenth-century Anglican bishop and theologian Jeremy Taylor in the following quotation from a sermon on Romans 8.9-10:

> . . . he that hath the Spirit of God, doth acknowledge God for his Father and his Lord, he despises the world, and hath no violent appetite for secular pleasures, and is dead to the desires of this life, and his hopes are spiritual, and God is his joy, and Christ is his

pattern and his support, and 'godliness' is his 'gain': and this man understands the things of God, and is ready to die for Christ, and fears nothing but to sin against God; and his will is filled with love, and it springs out in obedience to God and in charity to his brother.[16]

3.3.36   Living by the Spirit thus means living in wholehearted obedience to God and this in turn means that, whether viewed in terms of a relationship to God as Father, as Son, or as Holy Spirit, the Christian way of life has a consistent character. It is a way of life that is characterized by obedience to God, manifested in a holy life, marked positively by a new set of attitudes and a new pattern of behaviour and negatively by a willingness to put to death all that is opposed to these.

3.3.37   In order that this teaching may be understood properly, however, a number of points of clarification need to be made.

3.3.38   First, being obedient to God is not simply a matter of the obedience of individuals. Just like the Old Testament, the New Testament teaches that God's people are meant to render a corporate obedience to God and that their life as a community is to be such that this obedience is both enabled and manifested.

3.3.39   Second, putting to death the 'flesh' does not mean rejecting the good things given to us by God in the material creation. There has been a strong tradition of Christian asceticism, influenced by a distinction between the 'material' and the 'spiritual' imported from Greek philosophical thinking, that has seen the enjoyment of the things of this world as incompatible with dedication to God. This way of thinking, however, is itself incompatible with the biblical teaching of the goodness of God's creation, and with the New Testament emphasis that the use of anything that God has made is lawful in itself, providing it is done in obedience to God, and in a way that does not give offence to those around us (1 Corinthians 10.23-30).

3.3.40   Third, a willingness to die to self for the sake of Christ does not imply that we should have a low estimation of our own self-worth or that we should passively submit to the norms of behaviour expected of us by the Church or by wider society. Feminist writers have quite legitimately pointed out, for instance, that women have all too often been the victims of this kind of thinking, being encouraged to think lowly of themselves as women and to accept the norms of a male-dominated Church and a male-dominated society.

3.3.41 What needs to be said strongly in response to this kind of history is that true Christian discipleship needs to be based on a strong sense of the value of our God-given identity as children of God, and, without simply succumbing to any form of currently fashionable 'political correctness', a willingness to challenge those patterns of behaviour in Church and society that fail to reflect this value whether through homophobia, sexism, racism or any other form of intolerance or oppression.

3.3.42 We are able to live a life of self-forgetfulness that expresses itself in active love for God and our fellow human beings precisely because we have confidence in the value that we have for God, and therefore confidence in his care for our well-being. We do not need to spend our time anxiously looking out for ourselves because we know that God is looking out for us as his children (Matthew 6.25-34).

3.3.43 Fourth, and finally, the pattern of discipleship outlined in this section only makes sense in the light of the Christian emphasis on the world to come that we noted at the beginning of the chapter. Living a life in obedience to God will not necessarily mean that we experience the kind of 'happiness' or 'fulfilment' aimed at by contemporary society. Indeed, authentic Christian discipleship will inevitably bring with it pain and suffering. Dying to self is not a painless business.

3.3.44 The Christian message is not that the pain will not happen, but that, as countless Christians have shown, suffering can be used creatively so that we become more transparent to God. This deepening presence of God with us and within us is a foretaste of the eternal life for which we are made:

> ... this slight momentary affliction is preparing us for an eternal weight of glory beyond all measure, because we look not at what can be seen; for what can be seen is temporary, but what cannot be seen is eternal. (2 Corinthians 4.17-18)

3.3.45 It is, of course, the case that this message has been misused in Christian history as a means of justifying oppression. For example, during the eighteenth and nineteenth centuries, white preachers taught

slaves in America and the West Indies that they should accept their
sufferings in this life because they would get their reward in the next.
Repentance for such misuse of this message is vital, but it should not
lead Christians to go to the other extreme and doubt the validity of a
message that is grounded in New Testament teaching.

3.3.46 Furthermore, as the experience of black Christians testifies, the
Christian belief that this life is not all that there is does not simply make
people passive victims of their oppressors. It can also enable them to
live with oppression in ways that give them dignity and hope and also
provides them with the energy eventually to challenge the oppression
itself, as the witness of the Black Churches in North America and
Britain so ably illustrates.

3.4 Christian discipleship and human sexuality

3.4.1 The question that we now have to consider, therefore, is how this
understanding of the nature of Christian discipleship set out above should
shape our understanding of sexuality. What does the new identity that
has been given to us by God in Christ mean in terms of our sexual identity,
and what does the call to radical obedience to God the Father in the
power of the Holy Spirit mean in the context of our sexual activity?

3.4.2 The subsequent chapters of this report will consider some of
the answers that the Christian tradition – including the work of more
recent theologians – has given to the second of these questions, but the
remainder of this chapter will concentrate on the first of them.

3.4.3 As we have already seen, a fundamental part of New Testament
teaching is that in Christ we are new people. Our old sinful selves have
been put to death, and a new self has been raised up to replace them.
This point is made most succinctly by St Paul in 2 Corinthians 5.17: 'if
anyone is in Christ, there is a new creation: everything old has passed
away; see, everything has become new!'

3.4.4 Given that this is the case, the issue inevitably arises as to what
this means for our existing identities. Do they cease to have any
meaning or value? There is biblical material that might appear to imply
that this is the case. Galatians 3.27-28, for example, declares:

> As many of you as were baptized into Christ have clothed yourselves
> with Christ. There is no longer Jew or Greek, there is no longer slave

or free, there is no longer male and female; for all of you are one in Christ Jesus.

3.4.5   At first sight these verses seem to involve a complete abolition of all those things that mark out our identities, our ethnic identity, our place in the social structure, and even that most basic form of our sexual identity, our identity as either male or female, and, indeed, some of the earliest Christians interpreted these verses in this way, attempting to live a radically egalitarian life within a deeply hierarchical society.[17]

3.4.6   However, to interpret Galatians 3.27-28 in this way may be to misrepresent the point that St Paul is intending to make in these verses. The rest of the New Testament suggests that neither St Paul nor any other New Testament writer held that distinctions of race, social status and gender had ceased to exist. Indeed, it is argued strongly that living the Christian life means living responsibly in relation to these distinctions.[18]

3.4.7   How, then, should we understand Galatians 3.28? One helpful interpretation is offered by John Stott in his commentary on Galatians:

> This great statement of verse 28 does not mean that racial, social and sexual distinctions are actually obliterated. Christians are not literally 'colour-blind', so that they do not notice whether a person's skin is black, brown, yellow or white. Nor are they unaware of the cultural and educational background from which people come. Nor do they ignore a person's sex, treating a woman as if she were a man or a man as if he were a woman. When we say that Christ has abolished these distinctions, we mean not that they do not exist, but that they do not matter. They are still there, but they do not create any barriers to fellowship. We recognize each other as equals, brothers and sisters in Christ. By the grace of God we would resist the temptation to despise one another or patronize each other, for we know ourselves to be 'all one person in Christ Jesus' .... .[19]

3.4.8   Not only is it the case that the New Testament does not regard our existence as men and women as having been abolished 'in Christ', but it also points us back to the creation narratives in Genesis 1 and 2 as providing the proper framework for understanding what it means for us to be male and female before God and to relate together as such. We can see this in passages such as Matthew 19.1-9, 1 Corinthians 6.16; 11.7-12, and Ephesians 5.29-32.

3.4.9   Furthermore, these same passages also see the male–female relationship described in the creation narratives as providing the proper context for understanding human sexual relationships, and so it is to these narratives that we shall now turn.

3.4.10   Before we go on to look at these narratives in more detail, however, there are two issues about their interpretation that need to be noted.

3.4.11   First, there is the issue of the relationship between these narratives and the theory of evolution. It is often suggested that we need to rethink the Christian understanding of what it means to be human in the light of evolutionary theory. However, although the theory of evolution may well have implications for various aspects of Christian theology, it is difficult to know why such rethinking is necessary in the specific case of the creation narratives in Genesis.

3.4.12   If we accept, as most commentators now do, that Genesis 1 and 2 are not attempting to provide us with a primitive scientific theory about the emergence of life on earth, but are instead making a theological claim about the creative activity of God, then there is no reason to have to choose between what Genesis has to say about what it means to be human and the account given by evolutionary theory.

3.4.13   Just as Genesis cannot tell us how human life emerged at the biological level, so also evolutionary biology cannot tell us about why God caused it to emerge as it did or how human beings ought to live as a result. These are questions that science is simply not capable of answering. As the geneticist Steve Jones comments in his book *The Language of the Genes*:

> Science cannot answer the question that philosophers – or children – ask; why are we here, what is the point of being alive, how ought we to behave? Genetics has almost nothing to say about what makes us more than just machines driven by biology, about what makes us human. These questions may be interesting, but scientists are no more qualified to comment on them than is anyone else.[20]

What Genesis 1 and 2 provide us with is answers in narrative form to these questions that the natural sciences, evolutionary biology included, simply cannot answer.

3.4.14   Second, there is the issue of the prehistory of the Genesis narratives. There is continuing debate among Old Testament scholars about the development of the creation accounts in Genesis before they reached the form in which we have them today. However, legitimate though such discussion is, what we have to work with theologically is the material in its present canonical form and setting since it is in this form that it is referred to by the New Testament and has been received by the Church.

3.4.15   When we do this the first thing that these texts suggest is that the existence of humankind as male and female is seen as something that is created by God himself and is, therefore, good.

3.4.16   As Mary Hayter notes in her book *The New Eve in Christ*, there have been writers in the history of the Church who have suggested that 'originally humanity was sexless or androgynous and that the fact of the two sexes was a result of the Fall'.[21] In Chapter 1 it was noted, for example, that this was the approach taken by Gregory of Nyssa.

3.4.17   However, it is difficult to see this idea as compatible with the Genesis account. It is clear that, according to the Book of Genesis, human sexual differentiation pre-dated the fall, is an integral part of humanity's creation in the image of God (Genesis 1.27), and is one of the things that comes under the rubric: 'God saw everything that he had made, and indeed, it was very good' (Genesis 1.31).

3.4.18   This then raises the obvious question 'Why did God create humankind as male and female?' One immediately obvious answer to this question would be that the answer lies in biology. It was necessary for human beings to exist as male and female for the purposes of sexual reproduction.

3.4.19   In the first creation narrative in Genesis 1, there is indeed a clear link between human existence as male and female and sexual reproduction in the context of the divine command to exercise dominion over the rest of creation. In the words of the Australian Old Testament scholar Barry Webb:

> In the first account, man is made in the image of God and given the mandate to rule the earth. But this general statement is immediately followed by the more particular statements: 'male and female he

created them ... and said to them, "Be fruitful and multiply, and fill the earth and subdue it." Human beings will be able to rule the earth only if they can reproduce themselves and establish their presence everywhere. In this account, the purpose of the male/female distinction within the human race is reproduction.[22]

3.4.20   As Webb's interpretation here suggests, it can be said that the original purpose for sexual relationships given in Genesis 1 is in order to have children. To this extent we have to agree with the continuing Roman Catholic emphasis on the fact that procreation is a central part of what the sexual act is about, and that, therefore, any form of sexual activity that is by its very nature closed to the possibility of procreation is theologically problematic.[23] However, two things need to be borne in mind.

3.4.21   First, as was noted in Chapter 1 of this report, the Anglican tradition has come to see that, although the procreation of children is an integral part of God's purposes for human sexuality, it may be legitimate for a couple to seek to limit the number of children they have because of their own particular circumstances, the effect of further children upon any existing children they may have, or because of the need to avoid overpopulation. And here we should note that this is an example of the development of tradition being a dynamic process, a dialogue between Scripture and reason, with the biblical teaching being looked at again in the light of reflection upon Christian experience.

3.4.22   Secondly, the account of the origins of sexual relationships given in Genesis 2 makes it clear that there is a perfectly valid reason for the existence of such relationships apart from the begetting of children.

3.4.23   According to this second account the reason why Eve was created alongside Adam is that: 'It is not good that the man should be alone' (Genesis 2.18). To put it simply, the reason that humans exist as male and female is that God wills that human beings should not exist in solitude but in relationship to other human beings.

3.4.24   Even apart from their relationship to other human beings, people are created for relationship with God. As we have seen, the fundamental reason why women and men exist is to be in that filial relationship with God that has been achieved for them by Christ.

3.4.25   However, the God who himself exists in relationship as Father, Son, and Holy Spirit does not will that they should simply exist in this vertical relationship, but that they should reflect their relationship with him in a relationship with other people. That is why the two great commandments that summarize what it means to live rightly before God are the commands to love God and one's neighbour (Mark 12.28-31), and why St John insists that love for God and for our brother (or sister) is inseparable (1 John 4.7-21).

3.4.26   In terms of what was said earlier about what it means to be truly human, this means that God's gift to us in Christ of a relationship with himself is meant to be expressed in relationship to other people. This has been a very strong theme within all branches of Christianity. Even hermits and members of contemplative communities who have followed a solitary vocation, who might seem to provide a counter example, have remained in solidarity with others through prayer. As the Papal encyclical *Familiaris Consortio* puts it:

> God is love and in himself he lives a mystery of personal loving communion. Creating the human race in his own image ... God inscribed in the humanity of man and woman the vocation, and thus the capacity and responsibility, of love and communion.[24]

3.4.27   Christian readings of Genesis 2 have tended to focus on marriage. However, as David Atkinson notes in his commentary on Genesis, our God-given need for relationship is something that can be fulfilled in a number of different ways, and the Christian community needs to be sensitive to this fact.

> Aloneness is not part of God's creation intention. Marriage, as we shall see, is one way in which personal communion with another person may be enjoyed, but as the life of our Lord himself illustrates, it is not the only way. The single life is not without the need or possibility of personal communion. In the Christian Church we have not, however, made it easy for those who are not married, or who are no longer married, or indeed for those whose marriages are more of a struggle than a joy, to find the richness of fellowship for which all of us are made, and which all of us need. One of the problems of those who find themselves unwillingly single is the failure of the church to be a community of friendship. One of the things we need to recover within the Christian community is the beauty and value of friendships both between the sexes and between members of the same sex. Our churches should be communities of friendship – to

stand against all the ways in which our modern patterns of life and thinking push us into individualism and loneliness. We are made for fellowship, and whether in marriage and family, or in a life of celibacy, or community, we need to find ways of dealing with the fact that it is not good to be alone.[25]

3.4.28   Furthermore, as the American ethicist Stanley Grenz explains, relationships of friendship bear their own distinctive theological witness alongside marriage:

> Like marriage, friendship carries theological meaning. In contrast to the marital union, the informal friendship bond is less defined and therefore more open to the inclusion of others. Further, the dynamic of love involved in friendship is generally not contained within exclusive boundaries. For this reason, friendship reflects the open, nonexclusive, expanding aspect of God's love – the divine love that seeks to include within the circle of friendship those yet outside its boundaries.
>
> Marriage reminds us that God demands holiness and hates idolatry and consequently that the community of God must be characterized by faithfulness. The informal friendship bond, especially as formed by single persons, reminds us of a parallel truth: Because God is always seeking the outsider, rather than being limited to a few, God's community is open to 'whosoever will'. As the most explicit example of friendship, relationships among single people are the central exemplar of this theological metaphor.[26]

3.4.29   It can indeed be argued that friendship should be seen as a fundamental model for the Church. The Christian tradition has tended to emphasize the marital model of the Church set out by St Paul in Ephesians 5.21-32. However, in the Bible we also find another picture of the Church, which is the picture of a community of friends. Thus, as *Common Worship* notes,[27] at the Last Supper Jesus shared a meal with his friends, and, in Romans 16, St Paul sends greetings to all his friends in Rome. The Church consists of those who are the friends of Jesus and who are called to reflect this fact in loving relationships of friendship among themselves (John 15.12-17).

3.4.30   One of the most important accounts of friendship in the Christian tradition is the treatise *Spiritual Friendship* by the twelfth-century Cistercian writer Aelred of Rievaulx. Drawing on the work of the Roman orator and philosopher Cicero, Aelred defines friendship as 'that virtue by which spirits are bound by ties of love and sweetness, and out of many are made one'.[28] He then goes on to argue that the origin of friendship lies in the creative activity of God:

> He has willed ... for so his eternal reason has directed, that peace encompasses all his creatures and society unite them; and thus all creatures obtain from him, who is supremely and purely one, some trace of that unity. For that reason he has left no type of beings alone, but out of many has drawn them together by means of a certain society.[29]

3.4.31 In the case of human beings, this principle of unity in multiplicity was established by God's decree in Genesis 2.18, 'It is not good that the man should be alone: I will make him a helper as his partner' and by God's creation of Eve from the substance of Adam to be his perfect companion. As a result of this divine creative activity, declares Aelred, 'nature from the very beginning implanted the desire for friendship and charity in the heart of man, a desire which an inner sense of affection soon increased with a taste of sweetness'.[30]

3.4.32 For Aelred, the desire for friendship is not only something implanted in us by nature at God's behest, but it is also something that finds its origin and goal in Christ:

> And so in friendship are joined honour and charm, truth and joy, sweetness and good-will, affection and action. And all these take their beginning from Christ, advance through Christ, and are perfected in Christ. Therefore, not too steep or unnatural does the ascent appear from Christ, as the inspiration of the love by which we love our friend, to Christ giving himself to us as our Friend for us to love, so that charm may follow upon charm, sweetness upon sweetness and affection upon affection. And thus, friend cleaving to friend in the spirit of Christ, is made with Christ but one heart and one soul, and so mounting aloft through degrees of love to friendship with Christ, he is made one spirit with him in one kiss.[31]

3.4.33 Because friendship has this spiritual significance, Aelred claims that it is a means by which we share the very life of God. In a famous passage that takes the form of a dialogue between himself and his friend Ivo, he writes as follows:

> *Ivo* What does all this add up to? Shall I say of friendship what John, the friend of Jesus, says of charity: 'God is friendship'?

Aelred That would be unusual, to be sure, nor does it have the sanction of the scriptures. But still what is true of charity, I surely do not hesitate to grant to friendship, since 'he that abides in friendship, abides in God, and God in him'.[32]

3.4.34   Although Aelred is now the most well-known monastic exponent of the importance of friendship, his stress on its importance was not unique in his own era. For example, his older contemporary St Anselm also emphasized how important friendship was and described his love for his friends in what to us are strikingly physical terms. For example, in his letter to one of his former pupils, Gilbert Crispin, he writes as follows:

> If I were to describe the passion of our mutual love, I fear I should seem to those who know the truth to exaggerate. So I must subtract some part of the truth. But you know how great is the affection we have experienced – eye to eye, kiss for kiss, embrace for embrace. I experience it all the more now when you, in whom I have so much pleasure, are irretrievably separated from me. He who has abundance does not know what it is to want; he who abounds in delicacies cannot imagine deprivation; likewise, those who enjoy friendship cannot feel the lassitude of the deserted soul. Therefore, since that which has been between us cannot sufficiently be described, and I am speaking to one who knows, I shall say no more, but let us recall our not-forgotten love when we were together eye to eye, exchanging kiss for kiss, embrace for embrace.[33]

3.4.35   The sort of language that is found in this letter has raised the question of whether the hugs and kisses that it mentions are expressions of homosexual love. However, as R. W. Southern explains in his biography of St Anselm, it is unquestionable that this is not what Anselm himself understood them to mean. As Southern notes: 'the only commonly recognized form of homosexuality in the eleventh century was sodomy' and, 'It is clear that Anselm regarded these expressions of love as having nothing in common with sodomy, or with the habits of dress such as long hair and effeminate clothes which were an inducement to sodomy.'[34]

3.4.36   For St Anselm the love between monks was not an expression of illicit homosexual desire, but of the fusion of their souls by the fire of God's love. Similarly, as we have already noted in connection with Aelred, kisses were seen as a symbol of union with God and, in both monastic and secular life, they had a sacramental and symbolic significance that was well understood and, as Southern makes clear, they were not seen as being connected with homosexual practice.[35]

3.4.37   What is significant in the writings of St Anselm on friendship is not that they provide us with evidence of covert homosexuality, but that, like the writings of Aelred, they point us to the importance of loving friendship between human beings within the overarching context of love for God. Those who are united together in Christ ought to have deep relationships of love with each other.

3.4.38   While not necessarily using such startling language as Aelred or Anselm, a number of recent writers have also stressed the spiritual significance of friendship. For example, the contemporary theologian Elaine Storkey writes:

> Deep friendship takes us into a closer encounter with who we are, and shows us a glimpse of who we might be. Even hardened sceptics have talked of friendship bringing them closer to believing in God. For when we are brought face to face with the deep, lasting and faithful love of a friend we experience something which cannot be ultimately explained or understood in any other terms.[36]

3.4.39   Because friendship has the spiritual significance highlighted by Storkey and still more by Aelred and Anselm, it is something that Christians need to celebrate and support. This means that one of the things that the Church needs to consider is how it can give public recognition to the importance of friendship. As a number of writers have pointed out, in the past the Church celebrated the importance of same-sex friendships with rites that gave them an official standing.[37] What needs to be explored is what kind of recognition would be appropriate today, and how we might incorporate into our liturgical life an affirmation and celebration of the value of friendship.

3.4.40   It has also been suggested by a number of recent writers that it may in certain circumstances be right for friendship to be expressed in sexual terms.[38] In order to respond to this proposal it is first of all necessary to look closely at what is meant by the term 'sexual'.

3.4.41   The *New Oxford Dictionary of English* defines the word 'sexual' as an adjective referring to: 'the instincts, physiological processes and activities connected with physical attraction or intimate physical contact between individuals'.[39]

3.4.42 What we are talking about, therefore, is the way in which human beings are physically attracted to each other and have intimate physical contact with each other, intimate physical contact that may or may not include full sexual intercourse. If we start with this definition it is possible to argue that the attraction to others and the desire for intimate physical contact to which it refers are part of a wider human urge to reach out to and bond with other people.

3.4.43 To quote Grenz again:

> Sexuality encompasses our fundamental existence in the world as embodied persons. It includes our way of being in and relating to the world as male or female. Above all, however, sexuality is connected to our incompleteness as embodied creatures, an incompleteness that biological sex symbolizes. Hence, sexuality lies behind the human quest for completeness. This longing for wholeness, which we express through our seemingly innate drive to bond with others, forms an important basis for the interpersonal dimension of existence.[40]

3.4.44 Seen in this light there is certainly a legitimate sexual dimension to all relationships of friendship, since they are about reaching out to transcend our loneliness.

3.4.45 Furthermore, as Grenz goes on to point out, one of the distinctive features of the ministry of Christ himself, recorded in texts such as Matthew 10.37 and 12.50, and Mark 10.29-30 is that he put relationship with himself above the normal human relationships of marriage and family:

> According to Jesus the primary human bond is not marriage and family, important though these are, but the company of disciples. In this manner, human sexuality – understood as the quest to forsake our solitude through relations with others – finds ultimate fulfilment through participation in the community of believers who enjoy fellowship with God through Christ. And our innate incompleteness, related as it is to our fundamental sexuality, points toward the consummation of God's activity in the community of God's eternal kingdom.

En route to that future day, humans enter into a variety of personal relationships. Most of these are informal and somewhat fluid. Some people join together in another type of relationship as well, which in contrast to the first is to be permanent and exclusive. Although both are the outworking of the human drive towards bonding and hence are in this sense 'sexual,' they differ with respect to the type of sexual behaviour proper to each, among other differences.[41]

3.4.46   If we follow Grenz, therefore, what we have to say is that within the community of those who are in Christ there can be a legitimate spectrum of 'sexual' relationships, and the behaviour appropriate to each will depend on the nature of that relationship. Thus, for example, affectionate physical contact might be entirely appropriate within a relationship that was one of friendship rather than marriage.

3.4.47   The biblical injunctions to 'greet one another with a holy kiss' (Romans 16.16, 1 Corinthians 16.20, 2 Corinthians 13.12, 1 Thessalonians 5.26) are not directly related to the question that we are addressing but they do remind us that there can be physical expressions of love by Christians that are manifestations of holiness, and the challenge we face today is to find appropriate forms of these for our own particular culture.

3.4.48   One of the problems in contemporary British culture, and one that has also affected the Church, is that people have come to link affectionate physical contact with sexual intercourse. This means that people are inhibited from showing love in physical ways and, when they do, this it is liable to misinterpretation. One of the things we need to recover both in Church and society is the concept that there can be appropriate physical expressions of love that are not a prelude to, or an expression of, a relationship that involves sexual intercourse. In this connection it has been suggested that what would be helpful would be a new set of 'sexual protocols' that would make clear what forms of behaviour signify and in this context what forms of behaviour are acceptable and what are not.[42]

3.4.49   It is important to distinguish between physical expressions of love in general and sexual intercourse because, if we follow the Genesis narrative, we find that it depicts full sexual intercourse as taking place within a permanent and exclusive bond between two people of the opposite sex.

3.4.50 The Genesis account of the creation of Eve from Adam focuses on two aspects of the relationship between them. The first is their complementarity and the second is their union.

3.4.51 If we take their complementarity first of all, what we find in Genesis 2.18-25 is that the answer God decrees for Adam's solitude is 'a helper fit for him', and that when God finally produces Eve from his rib Adam's reaction is to declare:

> This at last is bone of my bones
> And flesh of my flesh;
> She shall be called Woman,
> Because she was taken out of Man. (RSV) [43]

3.4.52 God's decree that the woman shall be Adam's 'helper' and the fact that she is formed from Adam, together with the fact that Adam is formed first, has led centuries of Christian tradition to see this narrative as pointing to the superiority of Adam over Eve, and hence the superiority of men over women in general. This is also an interpretation of the text that has been subject to critical reflection by many feminist commentators.

3.4.53 However, as Hayter shows in detail, the text itself is not susceptible to this interpretation.[44] Far from emphasizing their *inequality*, it is precisely the *equality* in difference between the man and the woman that Genesis 2 has in view. To quote Atkinson again:

> Whatever the story of the Fall in Genesis 3 implies for the relationship between the sexes, Genesis 1 and 2 make the equality of men and women, as the image of God, unmistakably clear. The removal of a piece of the man in order to create the woman implies that from now on neither is complete without the other. The man needs the woman for his wholeness, and the woman needs the man for hers. Each is equal in relation to the other. Nothing could make clearer the complementarity and equality of the sexes.[45]

Here we may note that a more accurate translation would lead us to speak of woman as the 'counterpart' to man, rather than the 'helpmeet' (a traditional translation). The word 'helpmeet' suggests that women have a secondary and supportive role alongside men whereas 'counterpart' brings out the equality in the context of difference about which Genesis is talking.

3.4.54 It has been objected that this reading of Genesis 2 represents a projection of modern values back into the Genesis narrative. The argument goes that the notion of 'sexual complementarity' is a concept that has its origins in modern democratic society, and that belief in the equality of men and women was highly unlikely in the deeply hierarchical society in which Genesis was written.

3.4.55 This objection serves as a useful warning against imposing our values onto the biblical text. Nevertheless, Hayter's reading seems to be the one that makes the best sense of the text according to the normal principles of biblical interpretation, and it would be foolish to call it into question, either because it accords with the values of modern society, or because of a chronological snobbery that holds that such values could not also have been held by those in the past even in the context of their more hierarchical forms of social organization.

3.4.56 The claim is not that ancient Israelite society was one in which there was social equality between men and women. This was clearly not the case, although there is evidence that Israelite society was comparatively more egalitarian than other Ancient Near Eastern societies.[46] The claim is that the author of Genesis was enabled by God to transcend the limitations of his culture in a way that enabled him to catch a glimpse of God's original intention for the relationship between men and women.

3.4.57 To put it another way, the author of Genesis is not describing how things were in his own society, but how they *ought* to be in spite of the ways in which the relationship between men and women has been distorted by sin (Genesis 3.16). In summary we can say that what Genesis teaches us is that:

- The division of humankind into two sexes was not a biological accident, but something willed by God.

- Both men and women need each other in order to find their fulfilment as human beings.

- The proper relationship between women and men is one of equality in difference.

3.4.58 Having emphasized their complementarity, the text goes on to describe their union:

> Therefore a man leaves his father and his mother and cleaves to his
> wife, and they become one flesh. And the man and his wife were
> both naked, and were not ashamed. (Genesis 2.24-25, RSV)

There has been much debate in recent years about the meaning of this
text. The traditional Christian interpretation of this text is that it
concerns the exclusive attachment of men and women to each other in
a relationship of marriage.

3.4.59 In the words of the Roman Catholic theologian E. Schillebeeckx:

> What cannot be justified from the texts is that Genesis as a whole
> merely refers to the creation of woman and man, and not directly to
> marriage. The intention of the whole text was to restore the social
> fact of marriage to a divine institution.[47]

3.4.60 However, this interpretation has been challenged by a number
of theologians in recent years. For instance, Michael Vasey argues in his
book *Strangers and Friends* that 'it is simplistic to see the story of Adam
and Eve as providing a biblical mandate for the isolated nuclear family
of Western culture'[48] and that 'the confident assertion that Genesis
2.18-25 is simply about monogamous marriage itself reflects the way
that modern society has limited affectionate relationship and the
celebration of gender to domestic life'.[49]

3.4.61 As he sees it, Genesis 2:

> ... does not provide a blueprint for the way in which a particular
> society or culture is to order its public or domestic life. It does not of
> itself preclude the possibility that certain individuals in a society may
> not fit the general pattern and may respond in a different way to the
> mysterious reality of gender.[50]

3.4.62 Vasey is right to claim that Genesis 2 does not provide support
for the 'isolated nuclear family' if this is understood to mean a family
consisting simply of parents and children. Neither Genesis 2, the Bible
as a whole, nor indeed the Christian tradition, suggests that a family
limited to two generations living together is theologically preferable to
a more extended family or household structure. Nevertheless, as we
shall see, there are good reasons for holding that the relationship
between two married parents and their children needs to be at the
centre of family life.

3.4.63   Vasey is also right to protest against the idea that Genesis 2 gives biblical backing solely to monogamous marriage. As we have already accepted, its relevance is wider than that, and the Christian Church needs to give more explicit recognition to that fact.

3.4.64   However, the latter part of his argument is much more problematic.

3.4.65   The reason why the Christian Church has seen Genesis 2 as providing a blueprint for monogamous heterosexual marriage is because this is the human social institution that gives public expression to the ideal of a permanent and exclusive union between one man and one woman, such as Genesis describes.

3.4.66   Vasey's counter-argument is that the Bible itself does not present heterosexual monogamy as an ideal to which human beings should aspire.

3.4.67   Looking first of all at the Old Testament, Vasey suggests:

> What the Old Testament portrays is not a flawed quest for the ideal of the nuclear family but a complex society in which both genders richly participate. The power of Old Testament narrative often comes from the way it engages with the potent images of gender and portrays the passion and wickedness of which human beings are capable. However, its goal is not the domestic bliss of an ideal TV family from the 1950s but a mysterious new creation, which the most powerful gender images are needed to describe (cf. Isaiah 61.10; 66.7-11). When elements of domestic nostalgia do appear – as in the refrain 'every man under his vine and under his fig tree' (1 Kings 4.25; Micah 4.4; Zechariah 3.10) or the domestic happiness of Proverbs 5 – these are quickly revealed as mere resting-places in a story with a different ending.[51]

3.4.68   Moving on to the New Testament, Vasey begins by looking at Jesus' treatment of Genesis 2 in the context of his teaching about divorce:

> The New Testament's treatment of Genesis 1 and 2 follows a similar pattern. Jesus uses the primal vision of Genesis 2 to expose the contempt for women in the Pharisaic approach to divorce (Mark 10.2-12, Matthew 19.3-12; Luke 16.14-18). Wives are not disposable adjuncts to male life; man and woman are created by God to be partners in the one society. The search for convenient legal

justifications for putting a wife aside fails to embrace the duality of gender in God's creation; it does not take seriously either the importance of women or the quality of relationship to which human beings are called.[52]

3.4.69 He then argues that this teaching about divorce does not mean that the New Testament sees monogamous marriage as an ideal:

However, the New Testament does not treat the domestic ideal of marriage as the goal of human aspiration. Jesus' mission is not about the establishing of stable marriages or secure and happy homes. He himself did not marry. It is precisely the passage in which Jesus quotes Genesis 2.24 that commends the renunciation of marriage. His primary thrust is the creation of an affectionate community within which marriage is almost an irrelevance (cf. Mark 3.14-19, Luke 8.1-3; Mark 1.16-18; 29-31; 1 Corinthians 9.5; Romans 16.1-23; 1 Timothy 5.1,2). When the final book of the Bible picks up again the great themes of Genesis 1 and 2 in its vision of the goal of history it has nothing to say about the ideal of marriage, although it harnesses the imagery of gender with great power (Revelation 12; 14.4; 19.7-9; 21.2).[53]

3.4.70 How should we view this argument?

3.4.71 First of all, it has to be acknowledged that the imagery of gender is used in a variety of ways in Scripture and that not all of these refer to marriage.

3.4.72 It is also true that marriage is not seen as the highest state of human existence. As we shall go on to note later in this chapter, the Christian tradition has always accepted that the married state is something that will be transcended by the greater reality of the life to come. Vasey is therefore perfectly correct to state that the Bible does not point us to domestic life as the goal of human history.

3.4.73 However, there are three ways in which Vasey's argument fails to do justice to the biblical material.

3.4.74 First, his description of the Old Testament depiction of human sexuality does not address the issue of the canonical role of Genesis 1–3. As many commentators have noted down the centuries, these chapters provide the basic conceptual framework within which to understand and assess all that follows in the Old Testament.

3.4.75   In terms of human sexuality, this means that the description in Genesis 2 of a permanent exclusive union between one man and one woman ordained by God provides the benchmark by which to assess all the various alternative forms of sexual activity and relationship that the Old Testament describes. In so far as these do not conform to the Genesis 2 pattern, they are to be seen, like all other forms of sin, as the outworking of the fractured relationship between humanity and God described in Genesis 3.

3.4.76   Secondly, it is not clear that Vasey's account of Christ's treatment of Genesis 2 does justice to what Christ is actually recorded as saying. In Vasey's account, Christ's critique of Pharisaic teaching is based on a concern for the importance of women and the quality of human relationships. In the Gospel narratives, however, the focus is not on the consequences of divorce for women or the way it is destructive of human relationships, but on the permanent nature of monogamous marriage as a state of life established by God at creation:

> ... from the beginning of creation, 'God made them male and female.' 'For this reason a man shall leave his father and mother and be joined to his wife, and the two shall become one flesh.' So they are no longer two, but one flesh. Therefore what God has joined together, let no one separate. (Mark 10.6-8)

3.4.77   Thirdly, while marriage is not seen as the highest state of human existence, it is clear that the New Testament affirms monogamous marriage as an institution within which Christians are called to live out their discipleship (1 Corinthians 7.1-40, Ephesians 5.1-32, Colossians 3.18-25, 1 Peter 3.1-7). Indeed, in 1Timothy 4.3 the rejection of marriage as such is highlighted as an example of false teaching, a position that orthodox Christianity has always subsequently maintained, and in 1Timothy 3.1-16, and Titus 1.6, being married to one wife and having a godly family life are seen as criteria for the appointment of Church leaders.

3.4.78   What we do not find in the New Testament is any suggestion that marriage is 'almost an irrelevance' within the new community created by Christ, and the verses that Vasey cites in this connection certainly do not seem to point in this direction.

3.4.79   If we do follow the Christian tradition and see Genesis 2 as being concerned with marriage, we then have to ask what it teaches about marriage. This can be summed up in the two time honoured phrases of 'leaving' and 'cleaving'. The man and the woman leave their existing family relationships to create a new relationship that is marked out by exclusivity and bodily union.

3.4.80   These last two elements go together. It is precisely because the relationship is about permanent exclusive bonding that sexual intercourse is appropriate. As the Roman Catholic ethicist James Haningan argues, the act of sexual intercourse has its full significance as a symbolic or ritual activity: 'Sex, then, finds its proper value as an act which focuses, celebrates, expresses and enhances the meaning of our substantive activities and relationships.'[54]

3.4.81   And as Grenz observes:

> Practised within marriage as a sign of the unconditional covenantal love of husband and wife, sexual intercourse carries several important meanings. It is a beautiful symbol of the exclusive bond between the marriage partners, as through this act wife and husband reaffirm their commitment to each other. Further, it is a beautiful celebration of the mutuality of the relationship, as each partner reaffirms his or her desire to give pleasure to the other. And because of its connection to procreation, the sex act expresses the openness of husband and wife to the new life that may arise from their bond.[55]

3.4.82   Furthermore, precisely as a symbol of the exclusive love of husband and wife for each other, sexual intercourse within marriage underscores the theological significance of marriage. Just as friendship symbolizes the open and inviting aspect of God's love for the world, so marriage signifies the exclusive aspect of God's love for his people in election and covenant, and the exclusivity of their reciprocal love for him:

> In scripture, marriage carries an additional crucial meaning. It provides a metaphor of spiritual truth. The bond uniting husband and wife symbolizes certain aspects of the relationship between God and God's people. The Old Testament prophets found in marriage an appropriate vehicle for telling the story of Yahweh's faithfulness in the face of Israel's idolatry. The New Testament authors drew from this Old Testament imagery (e.g. Romans 9.25, 1 Peter 2.9-10). They spoke of marriage as a picture of the great mystery of salvation – the union of Christ and the church. Marriage illustrates Christ's self-sacrifice for the church as well as the submission to Christ (Ephesians

5.21-31) of a people who anticipate the future coming of the Lord
(Matthew 25.1-13, Revelation 19.7; 21.2; 21.9-10).

In this manner, marriage provides a picture of the exclusive nature
of our relationship to God in Christ. Just as marriage is to be an
exclusive, inviolate and hence holy bond, so also our relationship to
God must be exclusive and holy, for as God's covenant people
we can serve no other gods but the one God (Exodus 20.3).
By extension, the exclusive bond shared by husband and wife reflects
the presence of the divine love present within the triune God, which
in turn overflows from God to creation.[56]

3.4.83   Viewed in this light, marriage is an entirely appropriate symbol
of our identity in Christ. It points us to the mystery of who we truly are
– God's people belonging to God alone.

3.4.84   It is because the act of sexual intercourse carries these
meanings that the Bible[57] and the Christian tradition has seen marriage
as the sole legitimate context within which sexual intercourse should
take place, and has therefore advocated chastity outside marriage and
fidelity within it. Sexual relationships are not meant to be solely for
either procreation or pleasure, but are intended to signify love, fidelity
and commitment, and the God-given context for the exercise of these
virtues is marriage, the relationship given by God to symbolize his
unchanging covenant love.

3.4.85   At the end of Genesis 2 we read in verse 25: 'And the man and
his wife were both naked, and were not ashamed'. In its context this
verse makes the point that there was nothing shameful about the sexual
relationship between Adam and Eve before the Fall. Shame and guilt
come in as a result of the Fall described in the next chapter, along with
the domination of Eve by Adam (Genesis 3.7,16).

To quote Atkinson again:

> The story in Genesis 2 closes by telling us that the man and the
> woman in the Garden were naked and not ashamed. There was
> between them an openness and a unity, not masked by guilt, not
> disordered by lust, not hampered by shame.[58]

3.4.86   As we have already indicated, however, the Genesis account
makes clear that this idyllic state of affairs was not to endure. For those
of us who live after the Fall, the picture of human sexuality given to us

in Genesis 2 is a picture of how human sexuality was intended to be. The reality of human sexuality as we encounter it is very different. In the words of Atkinson:

> The sad truth is, of course, that all our sexuality in its heterosexual and homosexual forms is now disordered. Sexual relationships are sometimes marked more by fear than fellowship or fun; our sexual fantasies get out of hand; sexuality becomes a context for guilt. Increasingly often sexuality can be the vehicle not for love but for human destructiveness and degradation.[59]

3.4.87 Nevertheless, in spite of the disordered state in which we now experience it, the biblical witness is that, in its proper marital context, heterosexual sexual intercourse still retains its character as something created by God and therefore, like everything else that God has made, 'very good' (Genesis 1.31).That is why the Old Testament unashamedly celebrates and commends sexual love between bride and bridegroom and husband and wife in the Song of Songs and Proverbs 5.15-20, and why St Paul directs that husbands and wives should have regular sexual intercourse, in 1 Corinthians 7.2-5.

3.4.88 The disorder caused by the Fall also affects family life. In the past, the Church has succumbed too easily to the temptation to idealize the traditional pattern of family life based on two parents of opposite sex married to each other and their children, and Christian apologists have sometimes suggested that, if this pattern is upheld, all will be well with family life.

3.4.89 This suggestion fails to take seriously enough the fact that the effects of sin are all too common even in traditional nuclear families. The fact that children are living with parents who are married to one another is of itself no guarantee that the family concerned will be a loving and supportive family unit. From Cain and Abel (Genesis 4.1-16) onwards, violence, neglect, abuse and oppression have occurred all too often within traditional family structures. Conversely many non-traditional family units are loving and supportive and enable those within them to flourish.

3.4.90 This having been said, there are two good reasons why the Church should not abandon its support for the traditional pattern of family life and swing to the opposite extreme of simply saying that families come in all sorts of forms and all of these are equally valid.

3.4.91   First, a pattern of family life in which children are the fruit of the love between married parents of the opposite sex is the only one that coheres with the teaching of Genesis 1–2 about human sexuality that we have looked at above. The fact that people flourish in the context of other forms of family life can be seen in Christian terms as evidence of God's grace at work bringing good out of the disorder of a fallen world, and this is certainly something that the Church should affirm and even celebrate. The fact remains, however, that these other forms of family life are at variance with God's plan for human life, and the Church must not be afraid to say so.

3.4.92   Secondly, the Church must also constantly point out that God's plan for human life is not arbitrary, but based on his knowledge of what is best for his creatures. In the case of sexuality and family life, the point that needs to be made in this connection is that, when all due allowance has been made for economic and social factors and for the fact that all forms of human relationship are marred by sin, the evidence still indicates that the traditional pattern of family life is the best environment for the raising of children because it provides them with the greatest degree of security and stability.[60] This is the strongest form of family life and has been experienced as such across a whole range of different societies and historical situations.

3.4.93   In stressing the virtues of heterosexual monogamy, the Christian tradition is therefore not simply concerned with how individuals relate to each other, important though this is. It is also seeking to defend the well-being of society as a whole, and in particular the well-being of children, on the basis of a belief that it is when a man and a woman are committed to each other in a lifelong union that is both symbolized and strengthened by an exclusive sexual relationship that the family unit will be at its strongest and any children they have will have the best chance of growing into responsible, well-adjusted and fulfilled adults who can, in time, make a constructive contribution to the life of the community. As the recent report on cohabitation by a working party from the diocese of Southwark puts it, 'with all its fragility and risk, we are certain that marriage is by far the best framework for a man and a woman to flourish and grow together in love, and for their children to do the same'.[61]

3.4.94   Some contemporary theologians have argued that sexual intercourse is not only a means by which human beings can come to know each other at the deepest level, but that it can also be seen as a means by which we can know God. Adrian Thatcher, for instance, writes in his book *Liberating Sex* that:

> It is through human flesh that God became supremely known, and through the body that God continues to be known. Part of the patriarchal legacy is the assumption that knowing means knowing abstractly, using concepts to move beyond the individual and the particular to universal ideas and truths. Incarnation subverts this procedure. There is a priceless knowing to be had when flesh meets flesh. It is individual and particular. In its intense joy and mutuality it is also the embodied presence of the divine – an experience of bodily holiness which contrasts sharply with the bodiless holiness of too much Christian sanctity.[62]

3.4.95   Thatcher may well be right in his critique of the 'patriarchal legacy'; however, it is hard to find within the biblical witness any support for his idea that there is a continuing 'incarnation' of God in human flesh that allows God to be known through the medium of sexual activity.

3.4.96   As Karl Barth notes, if we are to understand human sexuality aright we must understand it precisely in its limitation as a fundamentally creaturely reality:

> Limitation – this is the first thing which characterises the encounter between man and woman as it is illuminated in the light of the divine command. Its special glory, mystery and significance are not thereby withdrawn. But we see real man, genuine fellow-humanity, man and woman as they truly are. The whole relationship is manifested in its creatureliness. Its glory, mystery and significance are disclosed in its limits. We must not blur these limits if we are truly to live out this relationship or even to perceive it. It certainly does no good, and we help neither ourselves nor others, if in some way we think we must declare that man and wife in union attain to divinity. This is the very thing which they do not do.[63]

3.4.97   In addition, we need to note that sexual relationships are not only limited by their creatureliness, but are also limited eschatologically. They belong to this world rather than that which is to come. We can see this in Luke 20.34-36, where Jesus declares that:

> Those who belong to this age marry and are given in marriage; but those who are considered worthy of a place in that age and in the

resurrection from the dead neither marry nor are given in marriage. Indeed they cannot die anymore, because they are like angels and are children of God, being children of the resurrection.

3.4.98   As *Issues in Human Sexuality* explains, in today's language this means that:

> ... our personhood is indissolubly bound up with our life-story as men or women, and that what that contributes can never be lost when our personal life is fulfilled in eternity. What will no longer be needed, as the passage makes clear, is the physical expression of sexuality, which is required now because of our mortality in order that life may continue. By the same token this will liberate us to grow into the fullest possible relation of love with all, being no longer restricted by the particularity of the flesh.[64]

3.4.99   As was noted at the beginning of this chapter, as Christians we are called to live both in the light of this world and in the light of the world to come. That has always traditionally meant, from a theological point of view, that both marriage and celibacy are possible expressions of discipleship. Marriage is a possible expression of discipleship because it means that we accept that, as long as we are in this world, marriage still has value as a state of life instituted and blessed by God at creation.

3.4.100   Celibacy is also a possible expression of discipleship, as Matthew 19.10-12 and 1 Corinthians 7.1-40 and the examples of Jesus, Paul and numerous Christian ascetics make clear. This form of discipleship has a twofold significance.

3.4.101   First, it is a witness that we belong to the world to come, in which attachments to particular individuals will be transcended in a universal relationship of love to all. Our true fulfilment is to be found in relationships with all of God's people in God's eternal kingdom, and not in the exclusive relationships we enjoy here on earth, valuable though these are.

3.4.102   Secondly, it is a way of life in which some people are called to offer themselves wholly to God in a lifelong commitment. As one Roman Catholic Sister has put it, celibacy is 'a freely chosen response to a personally discerned vocation of charismatically grounded, religiously motivated, sexually abstinent, life-long commitment to Christ which is externally symbolized by remaining unmarried'.

3.4.103 Four further points about celibacy that also needed to be noted are that:

- Celibacy is not the same as singleness. Singleness is a provisional state in which the individual concerned is open to the possibility of marriage. Celibacy, by contrast, is a state of life in which the possibility of marriage has been renounced, often on a permanent basis. Furthermore, whereas singleness may well be a simple matter of circumstance, celibacy is something that is chosen. As *Issues* notes: 'The single state becomes celibacy only when it is freely and deliberately chosen "in order to devote oneself completely to the Lord and his concerns".'[65]

- Celibacy is not about the renunciation of sexuality. As we have noted earlier in this chapter, sexuality is an integral part of being a human being and is therefore not something that can be renounced. What celibacy is about is the sacrificial offering of a person's sexuality to God through a renunciation of the freedom to express that sexuality through sexual intercourse.

- Celibacy has a symbolic or 'sacramental' nature. By being obedient to their particular calling, celibates are a sign of the calling that all Christians have to live in the light of the coming kingdom and to offer themselves wholly to God, even if most are not called to do this in the context of a celibate vocation.

- Celibacy is not about giving things up. It is about the freedom to live for God and for other people, whether this is primarily through prayer in a contemplative vocation or through a life of active service.

3.4.104 If marriage and celibacy are both possible forms of discipleship, ways of expressing our identity in Christ, then how do we choose between them? The answer, to put it simply, is that the choice is not ours but God's.

3.4.105 Both marriage and celibacy may be described as gifts of God in creation. They are both vocations in the strict sense of the term – ways of life to which individuals are called by God. In Christian history the celibate vocation has been given a particular honour in its witness to the coming kingdom of God, from apostolic times onwards. Not least in an age of sexual excess and chaos, such witness remains of abiding value, but it cannot thereby be used to denigrate the honour and importance of marriage. God in his freedom calls men and women to both states of life.

3.4.106 Accepting the vocation that God has given us means acceptance of that 'dying to self' that we saw to be integral to living out the new life in Christ into which we entered at our baptism.

3.4.107 It means dying to self because the fact that our vocation is given to us as a gift by God means that we are invited to accept that vocation, whatever it is, even if it should go against our own wishes and inclinations. That element of unfettered personal choice of lifestyle that we saw to be so important to modern approaches to sexuality and sexual relationships is therefore not appropriate to Christian thinking about these matters. In Christian terms, the appropriate question is not 'what do I want?', but 'what does God want of me?' Or, to put it in other terms, 'what do I most deeply want, given that God is my supreme good; one who desires my well-being infinitely more than I desire it for myself?'

3.4.108 Within this Christian view, then, whatever the vocation to which God calls us, whether this is singleness, marriage or celibacy, it will also involve that putting aside of the narrow, grasping ego, which is a necessary part of being obedient to God in the power of the Spirit.

3.4.109 Whether we are single, married or celibate we are called, as Christians, to discipline the sexual desires and activities considered inappropriate for those who belong to Christ. Texts such as Matthew 5.27-30 and 1 Corinthians 6.9-20 make this point. Inappropriate activities, in the context of Christian discipleship, are therefore to be met with repentance and amendment of life – within the cycle of confession, repentance, forgiveness and amendment of life that characterizes all Christian life. Inappropriate desires are to be honestly faced and placed in God's loving, healing presence.

3.4.110 This is a fact that the Christian tradition, whatever its shortcomings in the area of sexual ethics, has emphasized, and it is a fact that we cannot forget. On the other hand, it is also vitally important that the Church should not swing to the opposite extreme and focus on sexual sins as if they were worse than other forms of sin or were unforgivable.

3.4.111 Appropriate pastoral care will mean neither condoning sinful forms of sexual behaviour nor meeting them simply with condemnation, but realizing that, in this area of life as in all others, growth in holiness comes slowly and will always be incomplete this side of death, and so what people need is help and support as they strive to meet God's standards and obey his commands. As St Augustine rightly emphasized, the Church is not a society of those who are already perfect, but a hospital for sinners in which God gradually and patiently enables us to become the people he wants us to be.

3.4.112 If we are called to be temporarily single or permanently celibate, we also renounce temporarily or permanently the legitimate joys of sexual intercourse and the possibility of enjoying a family life with a spouse and children.

3.4.113 If we are called to marriage, we renounce the freedom that the single life allows, accept the troubles and anxieties that marriage inevitably brings with it (1 Corinthians 7.25-30), and die to our own self-will so that we can submit to what is best for our spouse and any children we may have (Ephesians 5.21-33).

3.4.114 In his book *The Cost of Discipleship*, Dietrich Bonhoeffer writes:

> As we embark upon discipleship we surrender ourselves to Christ in union with his death – we give our lives over to death. Thus it begins; the cross is not the terrible end to an otherwise God-fearing and happy life, but it meets us at the beginning of our communion with Christ. When Christ calls a man, he bids him come and die.[66]

We may take that summons and invitation to apply to our sexuality and sexual relationships as much as to any other area of our lives.

3.5 The traditional approach – a summary

3.5.1 As the twentieth-century Anglican theologian John Macquarrie notes in his *Principles of Christian Theology*, one of the things that characterizes human beings is what he calls their 'open, self-transcending nature',[67] by which he means their innate orientation to relate to that which is other and beyond themselves. From a Christian perspective this drive for self-transcendence has to be understood as a God-given capacity for relationship that reflects the essentially relational nature of God.

3.5.2 In this chapter we have seen that this means that, for human beings to find fulfilment, they need to be in relation to the God who is

Father, Son, and Holy Spirit, and that this is a relationship of faithful response and a setting aside of our desire for immediate self-gratification, which develops over a lifetime and finds its completion not in this world but in the world to come.

3.5.3   We have also seen that this relationship is to be lived out in the community of the Church in which human beings are called to both a 'vertical' relationship with God and also a 'horizontal' relationship with other human beings. This horizontal relationship with other human beings may take a variety of forms that may legitimately be described as 'sexual', and these may well have a 'sexual' dimension in the sense of the dictionary meaning of the term quoted earlier (3.4.41).

3.5.4   However, according to both the mainstream interpretation of the Bible and Christian tradition, the proper context for sexual relations has been and is a permanent and exclusive relationship of love between two people of the opposite sex.

3.5.5   This kind of relationship is only one of the vocations to which we may be called by God, since there also exist vocations to either temporary singleness or permanent celibacy.

3.5.6   Whatever the vocation to which we are called, it will involve self-denial on our part, both the rejection of inappropriate forms of sexual behaviour, to which all Christians are called, and the specific form of self-denial that our particular vocation involves.

3.5.7   This emphasis on the right ordering of our passions in obedience to God may seem unattractive from the perspective of our contemporary secular culture, but from a Christian perspective it is infinitely worthwhile because it is the means by which through the Spirit we are being changed into God's likeness 'from one degree of glory to another' (2 Corinthians 3.18). In this way we see the depth of the divine love for humanity as a whole, the divine creative intention.

3.5.8   That, then, is the Christian sexual ethic as this has been understood down the centuries by the mainstream of the Christian tradition. The question that is now being posed, however, is where gay and lesbian people fit into this picture.

3.6 Some recent rereadings of the Christian tradition

3.6.1   As we noted in Chapter 2, one of the factors we have to bear in mind when we consider the way in which the Bible is interpreted in the Church is that the interpretation of the Bible is a dynamic process in which the biblical material is constantly read in new ways in response to the issues raised in new contexts.

3.6.2   A clear instance of this in our time is the way in which Christian feminist theologians working from within the orthodox Christian tradition have explored the biblical text anew in the light of the questions raised by the feminist movement.

3.6.3   For example, in her essay 'Kenosis and Subversion' the feminist theologian Sarah Coakley reconsiders St Paul's account of Jesus' 'kenosis' or 'self-emptying' in Philippians 2.5-11 in the light of the argument by the post-Christian feminist theologian Daphne Hampson, that the theme of self-abnegation and self-emptying is unhelpful to women because it encourages them to accept subjugation rather than empowering them to challenge oppression.[68]

3.6.4   Having looked at the interpretation of the text both by modern New Testament scholarship and by the Christian tradition, Coakley argues that what the text points us to is 'the possibility of a "strength" made perfect *in* human weakness (2 Corinthians 12.9), of the normative concurrence in Christ of non-bullying divine "power" *with* "self-effaced humanity"'[69] and the idea that 'true divine "empowerment" occurs most unimpededly in the context of a special form of human "vulnerability"'.[70] She then goes on to explore what this vulnerability might mean by looking at the practice of contemplative prayer.

3.6.5   As she sees it, such silent waiting upon God is a way of entering into the pattern of death and resurrection set out in Philippians 2 and:

> By choosing to 'make space' in this way, one 'practices' [sic] the 'presence of God' – the subtle but enabling presence of a God who neither shouts not forces, let alone 'obliterates'. No one can *make* one 'contemplate' (though the grace of God invites it); but it is the simplest thing in the world *not* to 'contemplate', to turn away from that grace. Thus the 'vulnerability' that is its human condition is not about asking for unnecessary and unjust suffering (though increased

self-knowledge can indeed be painful); nor is it (in Hampson's words) a 'self-abnegation'. On the contrary, this special 'self-emptying' is not a negation of self, but the place of the self's transformation and expansion into God.[71]

3.6.6   Coakley agrees with Hampson that it is right for women to seek personal empowerment. However, in her view the sort of vulnerability referred to in Philippians 2 and experienced in contemplative prayer is helpful to women because it challenges traditional gender stereotypes by redefining ideas of power and passivity and has the capacity to be both empowering and transformative.

3.6.7   What we find in this essay by Coakley is a re-expression of the fundamental theme that we have been exploring in this chapter, namely that true human fulfilment is found in relationship with and submission to God. The basic themes that her essay explores, the teaching of St Paul in Philippians 2 and its relationship to the practice of contemplative prayer, are very traditional. However, they are explored in a way that attempts to make connections with feminist concerns and to show how the Christian tradition contains resources that feminists should not ignore.

3.6.8   Just as Christian feminists such as Coakley have begun to reread the Bible and the Christian tradition in new ways in response to feminist concerns, so also an increasing number of theologians have attempted to reread them in the light of concerns raised by gay and lesbian people.

3.6.9   The traditional Christian answer to the question of how gay and lesbian people fit into the picture of human sexuality that has been set out in this chapter, is that they fit into the picture by being called to a life of celibacy. Since they are unable to become married, God's will for them is that they should live a life of sexual abstinence. This will not, of course, prevent them from entering into loving relationships with people of both sexes or preclude appropriate forms of physical intimacy as discussed earlier in this chapter.

3.6.10   Many Christians who feel sexually attracted to members of their own sex would still endorse this approach. There are many other gay and lesbian Christians, however, who do not believe that God is calling them either to celibacy or to permanent singleness. The issue they are raising is whether there are new ways of looking at the Bible and the Christian tradition that would enable us to see full sexual relationships between people of the same sex as being within the will of God.

3.6.11 Some would also suggest that there is an urgent need to develop a positive Christian discipline for same-sex sexual relationships because in same-sex sexual relationships the need to outgrow self-centredness in a genuine concern for the other is equal to that in heterosexual relationships. Some would say that it is even more in evidence. Married couples usually have the support of a wider family and society. They also usually have children to help bind the relationship together. These factors are not usually present or present to the same degree in gay and lesbian relationships. Furthermore, it is often alleged that the gay scene is more naturally promiscuous than the heterosexual one. If this is indeed the case, at least in some contexts, then it could be argued that the need for clear boundaries is even more evident in same-sex relationships than it is in ones of the opposite sex.

3.6.12 This is not merely a gay and lesbian concern, though it touches the lived reality of gay and lesbian lives most deeply. There are church communities and (heterosexual) theologians who seek to support this rethinking of faithful gay and lesbian relationships *within* the Christian tradition on what they see as orthodox theological grounds. Three examples will serve to illustrate this point

3.6.13 The first example is Norman Pittenger's book *Time for Consent*, which was first published in 1967 and was a seminal work in encouraging people to reconsider the traditional Christian rejection of homosexual conduct. The references below are to the second revised edition published in 1970.

3.6.14 In line with the Trinitarian theology we have been exploring in this chapter and drawing on the work of the philosopher A. N. Whitehead, Pittenger argues in his book that the teaching of the Christian faith is that the distinctive thing about human beings is their ability to respond to the love of God at work in creation:

> The 'deep' in man, which is nothing other than the image of God in him, is enabled to say 'Amen' to the deepest in the cosmos, and, more than that, to God himself as 'pure unbounded Love'. The preparation

for this, and the persuasive action within human nature which brings about such conformity of the *within* to the *beyond*, is called in Christian theology the Holy Spirit of God who is one with the divine principle or the 'Father' and one with the divine Self-Expression or the 'Word' or Logos or Eternal Son. With 'them', 'in unity of Godhead', he is to be 'worshipped and adored' by all men. Hence all three *hypostases*, or as we are accustomed to say (and with no great theological accuracy, in view of the specific modern meaning of the word) 'persons', are involved. In this establishment for man, the frustrated and twisted lover, of his capacity to be that for which he is created and which is the true meaning of his life, God is at work. So man is enabled to become a lover, free to love and to receive love, and thus to be fulfilled in love and in loving.[72]

3.6.15   According to Pittenger:

> St Augustine's great words, 'Thou has made us towards thee, O God, and our heart is in disquietude until it finds its rest in thee', stand as the classical statement of this truth about man, who can fulfil his subjective aim only when he is in such a relationship with God that it can be said that 'God dwells in him and he in God'.[73]

and what this in turn means is that human beings can only find their true satisfaction through being in love:

> To say this is to say in other words what is meant when we say that man's only satisfaction, in the last resort, is to be 'in love' – for 'God is love'. Thus in all human striving to love and receive love, in all human sexuality even when it is distorted and twisted and frustrated, there is a working of God. The nasty-minded, the super sophisticated, the over-moralistic, do not see this. Their failure to see it amounts to that condition for which Jesus in the Fourth Gospel, condemned the Pharisees; they are self-blinded. We might put it this way: Love has come into the world, Love is present with us, Love is available to us, and we simply do not wish to recognize its presence, because it somehow offends our delicate sensibility. We wish to be 'more spiritual', shall we say, than God himself. But we are wrong.[74]

3.6.16   If we accept that God is present in all human love and in all human sexuality the question then arises what are we to say about homosexual love and homosexual sexuality? Pittenger acknowledges that the Bible and Christian tradition have seen them as sinful, but he argues that we should be prepared to disagree with their assessment:

> One of the places where I think we must disagree is exactly in the matter of homosexuality. They did not know what we now know; nor can we blame them for not knowing, since they were men of their own time. Furthermore, the dependence which they felt upon Jewish ideas, as well as other aspects of inherited thought, prevented them from seeing some of the implications of the gospel to which they were committed. They cannot be blamed for that, either. Nor am I claiming that we in this day have come to know all the truth. We like them are the creatures of our times and of our circumstances. Yet some things we do know; and it would be false humility to pretend that we do not. One of the things we know is more of what homosexuality is about. Obviously the subject is by no means a matter of complete and precise knowledge; it is in many ways mysterious in respect to its genesis, its developmental aspects, and its physiological-psychological context. On the other hand, we know that the homosexual is like other men. His desires and drives are like theirs, although the sex of the person they can love is different. We know that if the homosexual is to fulfil himself in a sexual way through genital activity it can only be with a member of his own sex. He may try intercourse with a person of the other sex but the result is usually tragedy for both parties. The male homosexual is able to give himself, whole and entire, only to another man, the female homosexual to another woman.[75]

3.6.17   Understanding homosexuality in this way, and in the light of what he has previously said about the presence of God in human love, Pittenger concludes that that there is no problem with loving homosexual sexual activity:

> I cannot see that when two men or women are committed to each other, loyal to each other, hopeful about each other, in such mutuality that each gives and receives, acting with tenderness and with no force or pressure of one on the other, seeking a union which will bring their lives together as fully and completely as possible: I cannot see, if all this is true, why two such persons should be condemned for committing sin when they desire, as almost inevitably they will desire, to act on their love – and that means, of course, to engage in physical acts which for them will both express their love and deepen it.[76]

3.6.18   The second example is Rowan Williams' 1989 Michael Harding memorial address *The Body's Grace*.

3.6.19   In his essay 'Is there a Christian Sexual Ethic?' in his collection of sermons and addresses *Open to Judgement*, Williams argues that human sexuality needs to be understood in the context of the traditional Christian belief that human beings have been given the potential to point towards the reality of God.

> The gospel is about a man who made his entire life a sign that speaks of God and who left to his followers the promise that they too could *be* signs of God and *make* signs of God because of him. Even in this unpromising world, where we are so prone to deceive ourselves, things and persons can come to 'mean', to show, God's meanings – to communicate the creative generosity and compassion which, we learn from revelation, is the most basic reality there is. In more theological language, Jesus is himself the first and greatest *sacrament*, and he creates the possibility of things and persons, acts and places, being in some way sacramental in the light of what he has done.
>
> Now, if my life can communicate the 'meanings' of God, this must mean that my sexuality too can be sacramental: it can speak of mercy, faithfulness, transfiguration and hope. Whatever the temptation, we are not to give up on this aspect of ourselves, as if it couldn't speak of God. For all the danger and complexity, it isn't outside the sacramental potential given us in Christ.[77]

3.6.20 In *The Body's Grace* Williams develops further this 'sacramental' approach to human sexuality.

3.6.21 In this address he argues that at the heart of the Christian faith is the belief that human beings are desired by God:

> The whole story of creation, incarnation and our incorporation into the fellowship of Christ's body tells us that God desires us, as *if we were God*, as if we were that unconditional response to God's giving that God's self makes in the life of the trinity. We are created so that we may be caught up in this; so that we may grow into the wholehearted love of God by learning that God loves us as God loves God.[78]

3.6.22 Building on this point, Williams then argues that the purpose of the Christian community is to help people to understand that they are the objects of God's desire:

> The life of the Christian community has as its rationale – if not invariably its practical reality – the task of teaching us this: so ordering our relations that human beings may see themselves as *desired*, as the occasion of joy.[79]

3.6.23   The link between these theological principles and human sexuality is the fact that, at their best, sexual relationships are occasions of 'grace' in that they are contexts in which two human beings experience each other as the objects of their mutual joy and desire. As Williams sees it, to understand this experience properly we have to see it in a wider theological context:

> ... the body's grace only makes human sense if we have a language of grace in the first place; and that depends on having a language of creation and redemption. To be formed in our humanity by the loving delight of another is an experience whose contours we can identify most clearly and hopefully if we have also learned or are learning about being the object of the causeless loving delight of God, being the object of God's love for God through incorporation into the community of God's Spirit and the taking-on of the identity of God's child.[80]

This means, to put it simply, that the true significance of human sexual relationships is understood when they are seen in 'sacramental' terms as reflecting the delight that God takes in us.

3.6.24   The importance of this for the discussion of same-sex relationships, argues Williams, is that when we see mutual joy and delight rather than the procreation of children as the purpose of sexual relationships, then there is no theological justification for restricting such relationships to heterosexual marriage.

3.6.25   In support of this argument Williams appeals to the way that the Bible talks about sexuality. In the Old Testament he points to the description of God's love for Israel in Hosea 3.1, and the description of Elkanah's love for his barren wife Hannah in 1 Samuel 1.8. In the New Testament he points to what St Paul has to say about sexual relationships in 1 Corinthians 7.4, and the use of marital imagery for Christ and the Church in Ephesians 5.28-29. His conclusion is that, because these texts do not discuss sexuality in terms of procreation, what they show us is that:

> ... if we are looking for a sexual ethic that can be seriously informed by our Bible, there is a good deal to steer us away from assuming that reproductive sex is a norm however important and theologically significant it is.[81]

3.6.26   He then contends that, if the view of sexual relationships that he has described, and to which the Bible gives support, is accepted, then this in turn challenges the rejection of homosexuality:

> If we are afraid of facing the reality of same-sex love because it compels us to think through the processes of bodily desire and delight in their own right, perhaps we ought to be more cautious about appealing to Scripture as legitimating only procreative heterosexuality.
>
> In fact, of course, in a church which accepts the legitimacy of contraception, the absolute condemnation of same-sex relations of intimacy must rely on an abstract fundamentalist deployment of a number of very ambiguous texts, or on a problematic and non-scriptural theory about mutual complementarity, applied narrowly and crudely to physical differentiation without regard to psychological structures. I suspect that a fuller exploration of the sexual metaphors of the Bible will have more to teach us about a theology and ethics of sexual desire than will the flat citation of isolated texts; and I hope that other theologians will find this worth following up more fully than I can do here.[82]

3.6.27   The third example is *Sexuality and the Christian Body* by the American philosophical theologian Eugene Rogers,[83] which is a major attempt to argue the case that a proper Christian understanding of marriage is one that can embrace both homosexual and heterosexual unions alike.

3.6.28   His basic argument, which draws on both *The Body's Grace* and the Orthodox theologian Paul Evdokimov's study *The Sacrament of Love*,[84] is that:

> Marriage in Christianity is best understood as an ascetic practice of and for the community by which God takes sexuality up into God's own triune life, graciously transforming it so as to allow the couple partially to model the love between Christ and the Church.[85]

Drawing on the teaching of St Thomas Aquinas about biblical interpretation, and engaging in critical dialogue with the teaching of Karl Barth about gender and the creation of human beings in the image of God, Rogers contends that this ascetic practice is one that is capable of being undertaken by both straight and lesbian and gay couples and that, therefore, both homosexual and heterosexual unions undertaken with this end in view can legitimately be viewed as Christian forms of marriage.[86]

3.6.29 Rogers further argues that homosexual relationships need the external 'form' or 'rule' that marriage provides:

> Gay and lesbian relationships must exhibit not only the spiritual fruits of faith, hope, and charity, but must also exhibit them in sacramental form. Just as marriage gives form or rule to the sanctifying possibilities of heterosexual sex, so gay and lesbian people need sacramental form, or inspired rules.[87]

3.6.30 Moreover, gay and lesbian marriages ought to be celebrated publicly by the Christian community, because:

> In celebrating, witnessing, guarantying [sic], blessing, delighting in, and feasting the covenanted love of a human couple, a community may, by the Spirit's economic work, be caught up into the Spirit's proper work of doing these things for the love of the Father and the Son, which it eternally celebrates, witnesses, guaranties [sic], blesses, delights in, and feasts in the Trinity's general dance. Thus a married life extensively, and a wedding feast intensively, becomes a mimesis of God, an acting out of God's loving image in Christ.[88]

3.6.31 This is a complex quotation but the basic point that Rogers is making is a simple one. Marriage is a reflection of the loving relationship between God the Father and God the Son within the Trinity and, as the Church celebrates a marriage, the Spirit enables the Christian community to share in this relationship of love.

3.6.32 Like Williams, Rogers sees the fact that gay and lesbian relationships are not open to the possibility of procreation as not being a problem because the possibility of having children is not a necessary part of the good of marriage:

> The marriage covenant itself (human or divine) adds to love time and space for exchanges of mutual gift, with procreation or without. Passages that speak of Israel as God's bride are distinct from those that speak of Israel as God's child, and do not speak of procreation. Jesus and Paul both speak of marriage without mentioning children. That they do so because they expect the imminent end of the world only heightens the point that marriage has an integral, eschatological end in the grace and gratitude of the trinitarian life, apart from childbearing.[89]

3.6.33   In response to the suggestion that homosexuals should adopt a life of sexual abstinence, Rogers refers to the tradition of medieval angeology, that angels are unredeemable once fallen because they have no body that God can assume in order to draw them back to himself. He sees this as making the point that we should not seek for salvation through the rejection of our physical nature and its sexual desires:

> The renunciation of homosexual desires, like the renunciation of heterosexual desires, confuses human beings with – desiccates them into – angels. It gives God nothing by which to redeem them, no hook in the flesh by which to capture them and pull them up.[90]

3.6.34   Like the work of Coakley, the arguments put forward by Pittenger, Williams and Rogers are deeply rooted in traditional Christian thinking about the Trinity and the Incarnation. What they are arguing is that a trinitarian and incarnational theology should lead us to accept and even celebrate same-sex sexual relationships because they have the potential to reflect, and to enable human beings to share in, the eternal love that exists within the life of the Trinity and which has been communicated to us in Christ and through the work of the Spirit.

3.6.35   While, as we have said, it is proper that Christian theologians should seek to reread the biblical text and the Christian tradition in fresh ways in order to respond to the questions that are being asked today, it is proper too that their rereadings should be debated and discussed. It is right to ask critical questions about these rereadings just as it was right for the theologians concerned to ask questions about the biblical material and the way that it has been understood in the Christian tradition.

3.6.36   In the case of Coakley's proposal, for instance, it can be asked whether her understanding of Philippians 2.5-11 as referring to the vulnerability of the human Jesus does more or less justice to the text than the traditional reading, which saw the text as being concerned with the way that the second person of the Trinity humbled himself by assuming human nature at the Incarnation. In addition, it can also be asked how her emphasis on the non-coercive nature of divine power relates to the sovereign Lord of the biblical narrative before whom the peoples tremble (Psalm 99.1).

3.6.37   In the case of the proposals by Pittenger, Williams and Rogers, the question that has to be asked is what we are to make of their arguments for the legitimacy of same-sex sexual relationships in the light of the general biblical picture concerning Christian discipleship and human sexuality that we have looked at in this chapter and the biblical texts that have traditionally been seen as forbidding homosexual activity.

3.6.38   In order to begin to respond to this question the next two chapters will go on to look at how we should understand and respond to what the Bible has to say about homosexuality.

chapter 4
Homosexuality and biblical teaching

Voices from the debate

My partner and I started going to church . . . It was Church of
England with an evangelical feel to it – it was very lively and
always full. At first we went on Sundays, then made ourselves
known to the vicar and curate . . . As we attended church and
became friendlier with the people in it, the curate became aware
that we were a couple. We talked to the curate about being
baptized and he came to the house. When he arrived, we thought
he was going to talk to us about baptism. Instead he said he knew
we were a couple, and that the vicar of the church would not
allow us to receive communion. The curate produced a book
which was basically 'how to become "straight"'. He said he
wanted to meet us for weekly discussions about our sexuality . . .
Our reaction was surprise and hurt . . . Since then we have not
attended church. The memory still hurts very much and we both
feel very angry towards the church. Christians are supposed to be
loving and non-judgemental. We still believe in God and Jesus but
not in the way that the church teaches.

———◀o▶———

We prayed together often that week, and we talked theology. It
became clear that Gary had come not only to say goodbye but to
think hard, before God, about the relation between his
homosexuality and his Christian faith. He was angry at the self-
affirming gay groups, because he regarded his own condition as
more complex and tragic than their apologetic stance could
acknowledge. He also worried that the gay apologists encouraged
homosexual believers to 'draw their identity from their sexuality'
and thus to shift the ground of their identity subtly and
idolatrously away from God. For more than twenty years, Gary
had grappled with his homosexuality, experiencing it as a
compulsion and an affliction. Now, as he faced death, he wanted
to talk it all through from the beginning . . .

In particular, Gary wanted to discuss the biblical passages that deal with homosexual acts. Among Gary's many gifts was his skill as a reader of texts. After leaving Yale and helping to found a community-based Christian theatre group in Toronto, he had eventually completed a master's degree in French literature. Though he was not trained as a biblical exegete, he was a careful and sensitive interpreter. He had read hopefully through the standard bibliography of the burgeoning movement advocating the acceptance of homosexuality in the Church: John J. McNeill, *The Church and the Homosexual*; James B. Nelson, *Embodiment*; Letha Scanzoni and Virginia Ramey Mollenkott, *Is the Homosexual My Neighbor?*; John Boswell, *Christianity, Social Tolerance, and Homosexuality*. In the end, he came away disappointed, believing that these authors, despite their good intentions, had imposed a wilful interpretation on the biblical passages. However much he wanted to believe that the Bible did not condemn homosexuality, he would not violate his own stubborn intellectual integrity by pretending to find their arguments persuasive.[1]

————◄○►————

There have been many times when I've wondered whether I'd have become a Christian at all if I'd been heterosexual. Certainly, my experience of God's grace could not have been the same if I'd been part of the heterosexual mainstream. My return to faith as an adult was entirely the result of another man falling in love with me.

————◄○►————

When I became a Christian, I began to believe it was wrong to be involved sexually in homosexual relationships and struggled to know how to tell my gay friends. We had always been close and supported each other. In fact, if it had not been for my Christian beliefs I would have been happy to continue my homosexual relationships. When I first became a Christian, it was not difficult for me to be celibate. And for this reason I felt that I could be quite open with other Christians about my homosexual past. This was all very new to me. I had previously only been open about my sexuality with other gay men. I was encouraged by what seemed to be a very positive response to my openness from other Christians. A few years later I did struggle with homosexual feelings and temptations, but by this time my faith was meaningful enough to prevent me from abandoning Christianity and becoming involved in homosexual relationships again.[2]

————◄o►————

4.1 Introduction

4.1.1   As we noted in the first chapter of this report, the Christian Church has traditionally seen homosexual behaviour as inappropriate for those who are in Christ. As we also noted, this has been due to a combination of two factors. There has been an acceptance of the positive biblical teaching that sexual intercourse has its sole place within a permanent and exclusive relationship of marriage between two people of the opposite sex. There has also been a belief that the Bible explicitly condemns homosexuality as sinful.

4.1.2   In the last chapter the traditional teaching that sexual intercourse has its proper place within marriage was set out, and the work of some contemporary theologians who have argued that this traditional teaching needs to be reconsidered was also noted.

4.1.3   In this chapter we go on to look at the seven biblical texts that have traditionally been seen as directly addressing the issue of homosexuality, and other texts that are relevant to this issue. We ask what contemporary biblical scholarship tells us about how these texts ought to be read, bearing in mind the principles for the interpretation of biblical texts explored in Chapter 2.

4.1.4   As O'Donovan rightly notes, the theological debate about homosexuality 'cannot rest wholly upon exegesis'.[3] Once we have ascertained what the texts say we still have to ask whether they are binding upon us, and, if they are, how we should apply them today. We therefore also go on to explore the 'in front of the text' issue of how we should respond to these texts today. Drawing on the work of Michael Doe, we note the existence of a continuum of five different responses in the Church, ranging from 'Homosexuality as a whole is rejected by Scripture as sinful' to 'Compatibility with Scripture is not the only consideration' and consider the strengths and weaknesses of each response.

4.2 The Old Testament texts

4.2.1   In Chapter 1, four Old Testament texts were identified as having been seen by the Christian Church as outlawing homosexuality. These texts were Genesis 19.1-14, Leviticus 18.22; 20.13 and

Deuteronomy 23.17-18. We shall look at each of these texts in turn, noting also a number of other texts that are relevant to their interpretation.

Genesis 19.1-14

4.2.2　This text forms part of a cycle of stories about the patriarch Abraham, and is the story of the visit of two angels to Abraham's nephew Lot, who lived in the city of Sodom. Within this text the key verse is verse 5, which states that the men of Sodom, thinking that the angels were ordinary human visitors:

> ... called to Lot, 'Where are the men who came to you tonight? Bring them out to us, that we may know them'. (RSV)

4.2.3　The word translated 'know' in the RSV has generally been seen as a shorthand expression meaning 'have sexual relations with' and the traditional reading of Genesis 19 has been:

> a.　That what the men of Sodom desired was homosexual relations with Lot's visitors.

> b.　That the practice of homosexuality was the reason why Sodom was subsequently destroyed by divine judgement.

4.2.4　In recent years a number of scholars have rejected the traditional interpretation of the text. For example, in his 1955 study *Homosexuality and the Western Christian Tradition* Derrick Sherwin Bailey argues that the word 'know' should be taken in its most straightforward sense as referring to the wish of the men of Sodom to gain more information about the people who were visiting Lot. In his reading of the text the sin of the people of Sodom was lack of hospitality towards strangers.[4]

4.2.5　For another example, Walter Brueggemann contends in his commentary on Genesis that, while it is possible that there is a sexual reference in the narrative, there is also good evidence that the sin of Sodom was not sexual in nature:

> It is possible that the offence of Sodom is understood with specific reference to sexuality. But if such a reading is accepted, the turbulent mood of the narrative suggests gang rape rather than a private act of either 'sodomy' or any specific sexual act.

> However, the Bible gives considerable evidence that the sin of Sodom

was not specifically sexual in nature, but a general disorder of a society organised against God. Thus in Isaiah 1.10, 3.9, the reference is to injustice; in Jeremiah 23.4 to a variety of irresponsible acts which are named, and in Ezekiel 16.49 the sin is pride, excessive food and indifference to the needy.[5]

4.2.6   The majority of commentators, however, while accepting that in the Old Testament Sodom is seen as guilty of a variety of crimes, would nevertheless argue that the specific sin highlighted in Genesis 19 is sexual in nature. The reason for this is that in verse 8 of Genesis 19 the word 'know' is clearly used in a sexual sense with reference to Lot's daughters, and it seems hard to see that it is being used differently in verse 5.[6]

4.2.7   Where the consensus of opinion does agree with Brueggemann is in seeing what is described as an act of homosexual gang rape rather than an example of consensual sexual activity.

4.2.8   It should be noted, however, that the American commentator V. P. Hamilton dissents from this consensus on the grounds that the verb to 'know' employed in Genesis 19 is not a word that is used elsewhere to describe rape, and the way that word is used by Lot in verse 8 indicates that the word is not being used to describe rape in Genesis 19 either. His conclusion is that the narrative in Genesis 19 makes a general reference to homosexual sex rather than a specific reference to homosexual rape.[7]

4.2.9   In summary, we can say that, while there is a spectrum of opinion about the interpretation of Genesis 19.1-14, the scholarly consensus is that the Christian tradition has been correct in saying that sin of Sodom as described in Genesis 19 did involve sexual sin. However, the nature of that sin was gang rape rather than homosexuality *per se*.

4.2.10   As *Issues in Human Sexuality* puts it: '... there is a threatened violation of hospitality consisting in homosexual rape, and ... this is condemned as "wicked"'.[8]

4.2.11   In addition to Genesis 19 there are also three other biblical texts that refer to the sin of Sodom and see a homosexual element in Sodom's wickedness. These texts are Ezekiel 16.49-50, Jude 7 and 2 Peter 2.6-10. Although the interpretation of these texts is also disputed it seems clear that they too see the sin of the people of Sodom as involving an act of sexual immorality of a homosexual nature.[9]

4.2.12 Also related to the story of Sodom in Genesis 19 are two other Old Testament texts, both of which see acts of actual or intended homosexual rape as striking examples of sin. The first of these texts is Genesis 9.20-28, which describes the sin of Ham against Noah, and the second is Judges 19.22-30, which describes the fate that befell a Levite and his concubine at the hands of their fellow Israelites in the city of Gibeah.[10]

4.2.13 If these texts all refer to acts of homosexual rape, it might seem that they have nothing at all to contribute to the modern day debate about the ethics of homosexuality. The current debate is not about whether homosexual rape is acceptable, since everyone agrees that it is not, but about the ethical validity of consenting same-sex relationships.

4.2.14 It is true that the texts we have just looked at say nothing directly about this topic. However, they do serve to remind us that, in the biblical material as a whole, sexual relationships that fall outside the limits that God has laid down are seen as coming under God's judgement. The question that still needs to be addressed is whether homosexual relationships *as such* are seen as coming into this category.

4.2.15 This question brings us to the next two of the classic Old Testament texts relating to homosexuality that we need to consider.

Leviticus 18.22; 20.13

4.2.16 There is a continuing debate about the date and origin of the book of Leviticus, but what is clear is that the function of the book of Leviticus within the Old Testament canon is to bear witness to God's summons to Israel to live as a holy nation.

4.2.17 As the American Old Testament scholar B. S. Childs puts it, according to Leviticus: 'God had separated Israel to himself as a holy people and sanctified them (21.23). Israel was to reflect the nature of God's holiness by separating from all that was unholy.'[11]

4.2.18 The two verses in Leviticus with which we are concerned come in the so-called 'holiness code' in chapters 17–26 of the book of Leviticus.

These chapters contain a comprehensive vision of what the call to holiness means for Israel in every aspect of her national life. In the words of R. E. Clements:

> The holiness which it calls for is no mere private piety, nor even simply a fervent participation in public worship, but a total way of life, involving every aspect of personal, family and social commitment. God's holiness imposes a complete pattern of moral and social behavior upon the people he has chosen so that his holiness makes their responsive holiness an inescapable demand.[12]

4.2.19 Within this call for comprehensive holiness there are a number of verses dealing with various aspects of sexual behaviour, and among these are two verses referring to homosexuality, which read as follows:

> Leviticus 18.22: 'You shall not lie with a male as with a woman; it is an abomination.'

> Leviticus 20.13: 'If a man lies with a male as with a woman, both of them have committed an abomination; they shall be put to death, their blood is upon them.'

4.2.20 These texts have traditionally been seen as a rejection of homosexuality as being incompatible with the holiness required of God's people, and there is general agreement among commentators that this is the meaning of these texts in their original context.

4.2.21 Where there is disagreement is not about *whether* these texts condemn homosexuality but *why* they do so. A number of different suggestions have been made.

- It has been suggested that the use of the word 'abomination' indicates that behind the texts there lies concern about ritual same-sex acts in the context of non-Israelite worship. Seen in this light the real issue is not homosexuality at all but idolatry. Israelites are to avoid homosexual acts because of their connection with idolatry.[13]
- It has been suggested that the condemnation of homosexuality was connected with concern about sexual reproduction. In the words of Jacob Milgrom, commenting on Leviticus 18 as a whole: 'The

common denominator of the entire list of prohibitions, including homosexuality, is procreation within a stable family.'[14] From this perspective, it is the sterility of homosexual acts and the loss of semen that is the problem.

- It has been suggested that homosexual acts are regarded as ritually unclean because they transgress the Israelite understanding of the importance of order in the world. As Philip Budd puts it in his commentary on Leviticus, referring to the prohibitions on both homosexuality and bestiality:

> It seems clear that for Israel a sense of order is profoundly disturbed. It is in the breaking of the boundaries that pollution occurs and there is little doubt that in these cases . . . the boundaries are infringed.[15]

4.2.22 Scholars have identified problems with each of these three suggestions.

4.2.23 The first suggestion overplays the significance of the word 'abomination' and ignores the context of the prohibition of homosexuality. In the words of Barry Webb:

> . . . while 'abomination' is commonly used of cultic offences, especially in Deuteronomy and Ezekiel, it is also used of non-cultic offences, as frequently in Proverbs. And in Leviticus itself it is not used at all outside chapters 18 and 20 – the very passages in question. So there is no established cultic usage in Leviticus to constrain our reading. The matter must be settled contextually, and on that basis the ordinary, non-cultic sense is strongly indicated. The single, blanket prohibition against homosexual intercourse is the counterpart to the whole string of heterosexual taboos which have preceded it, none of which suggests a cultic context (not with your mother, not with your sister, not with your grand-daughter and so on). The fact that no such specifics are given for homosexual relationships makes it clear that it is homosexuality as a whole that is being proscribed. Specification is superfluous. The situation is the same in chapter 20.[16]

4.2.24 The second suggestion rightly notes that Leviticus 18 and 20 are concerned for the stability of family life. However, there is no evidence that the reason for the prohibition of homosexuality in this context is concern for a waste of semen. This is not a point that is made either in this text or anywhere else in the Bible, and it does not explain how the prohibition against homosexuality fits in with the other sexual offences previously mentioned in Leviticus 18 in which loss of sperm would not be an issue.

4.2.25   The third suggestion is difficult because it seems to suggest that the prohibition of homosexuality is simply a matter of ritual purity. This implies that the Old Testament has a separate category of acts that are simply ritually impure rather than morally wrong. *Issues in Human Sexuality* addressed this point: 'the Old Testament does not make distinctions between moral goodness and ritual purity in the way that Christians came to do after the destruction of the Temple and the end of the ancient cult'.[17]

4.2.26   As a number of writers have pointed out, however, where the third suggestion does help us is by pointing out that what is at stake in the prohibition against homosexuality, as also in the other commandments in the Levitical code, is the importance of observing the boundaries that God has laid down.

4.2.27   The commandments regarding human sexuality are intended to prevent the violation of the boundaries between natural and unnatural laid down by God in creation. It is because homosexual acts transgress this boundary that they are an 'abomination'.[18]

4.2.28   However, it also needs to be noted that, in the context of Leviticus 18 and 20, the boundary surrounding human sexual behaviour does not simply prohibit same-sex relationships. As Grenz observes:

> The injunctions of the holiness code regulating sexual behaviour appear to have as their intention the safeguarding and preservation of the marital context in which sexual acts are to occur.'[19]

A similar point is made by Peter Coleman in his discussion of the Old Testament texts relating to homosexuality. He notes that:

> Old Testament morality concerning sexual relationships is in basic principle committed to the defence of family and married life, and everything outside it is seen as a threat and outrage, an abomination not to be permitted in Israel.[20]

4.2.29   From this perspective the sexual injunctions of the holiness code, including the injunctions against homosexuality, are not arbitrary, but reflect the basic perspective set forth in the creation narratives in

Genesis 1–2, that God's appointed place for sexual intercourse is within a relationship of heterosexual marriage. The various sexual prohibitions are the shadow side of this positive divine intention.

Deuteronomy 23.17-18

4.2.30   Just as in the case of the book of Leviticus, there is continuing debate about the date and origin of the book of Deuteronomy. However, as in the case of Leviticus, what is clear is the canonical function of Deuteronomy. Its purpose, highlighted by its form as an address given by Moses to Israel on the eve of their entry into the promised land, is to emphasize how Israel is to live in fidelity to the law given by God to Moses and contained in the Pentateuch.[21]

4.2.31   Chapters 21–25 of Deuteronomy contain miscellaneous laws setting out what fidelity to the Mosaic inheritance will mean in various areas of the life of the people of Israel once they have entered the land of promise. Verses 17-18 of chapter 23 contain laws relating to cultic prostitution and they read as follows:

> There shall be no cult prostitute of the daughters of Israel, neither shall there be a cult prostitute of the sons of Israel. You shall not bring the hire of a harlot, or the wages of a dog, into the house of the Lord your God in payment for any vow; for both of these are an abomination to the Lord your God. (RSV)

4.2.32   In the Authorised Version of the Bible the word that the RSV translates as 'dog' is translated as 'sodomite', and the text has traditionally been seen as condemning male homosexual prostitution.

4.2.33   There has been much scholarly discussion about the precise nature of the male cult prostitute (*qades*) referred to as a 'dog' in v. 18. There are six references to such people in the Old Testament (Deuteronomy 23.17, 1 Kings 14.24; 15.12; 22.46, 2 Kings 23.7, Job 36.14). The precise nature of their activity is never explicitly described, but most scholars, even those of a generally conservative persuasion, while seeing those involved as prostitutes, do not see the text as referring to specifically homosexual prostitution.[22]

4.2.34   However, this consensus still leaves us with an interpretative issue that needs to be solved. If the men involved were prostitutes then they had to be offering either male-female or male-male intercourse, and what needs to be decided is which was being offered.

- The first is something for which we have no evidence in the surrounding culture and which is difficult to imagine in Israel, since it was a society in which female sexual purity was very highly prized.[23]

- The second, however, is a phenomenon that is well documented from the Ancient Near East right down to classical times[24] and, if this is what is being described, it would explain why the texts regard the *qades* with such disapproval. It was not just a case of their being associated with an idolatrous cult, but of their being examples of a form of sexual behaviour that was an 'abomination' to the God of Israel.

4.2.35   Even if we do accept that the phenomenon that is rejected is homosexual prostitution, however, the question still remains about how this is relevant to issues of homosexuality today. The answer may lie in what it tells us about the general Old Testament attitude to homosexuality.

4.2.36   It is now generally accepted that, in the cultural context against which the Old Testament was written, homosexual prostitution was regarded as the most acceptable form of homosexuality, because the person involved had been made homosexual not through their own choice, but through the decision of the goddess whom they represented in the cult. To quote Robert Gagnon in his recent study of the biblical texts relating to homosexuality: 'The Mesopotamian evidence ... makes clear that the *most* acceptable form of same-sex intercourse – not the least acceptable – was precisely same-sex intercourse conducted in a religious context.'[25]

4.2.37   Anyone rejecting homosexual prostitution would, therefore, be rejecting homosexuality *per se*, since, if this most acceptable form of the phenomenon was rejected, all other forms would necessarily be rejected as well, just as in our day someone rejecting consensual same-sex intercourse would be understood as also rejecting all other forms of non-consensual homosexual behaviour.

4.2.38   As Gagnon puts it:

> When the biblical authors rejected homosexual cult prostitutes ... they were in effect rejecting the whole phenomenon of homosexual practice. They were repudiating a form of homosexual intercourse that was the most palatable in their cultural context. If they rejected

that particular form of homosexual practice, how much more all other forms.[26]

4.2.39 The condemnation of cultic homosexual prostitution would thus reinforce the evidence of the texts in Leviticus that the Old Testament regards all forms of same-sex relationship as unacceptable for the people of God.

4.2.40 What, then, can we conclude about what the Old Testament has to say about the issue of homosexuality?

4.2.41 The first thing that can be said is that, in the Old Testament as a whole, proper sexual conduct is seen as a fundamental part of the life of the people of God. Leviticus 18 and 20 and Deuteronomy 23 are just two of many passages in the Old Testament that stress the importance of such conduct.[27] Furthermore, as scholars such as Grenz and Coleman have argued, the basic concern underlying these passages is the defence of marriage and family life, a concern which, we have argued, is built on an understanding of God's intention for human sexuality reflected in Genesis 1–2.

4.2.42 We need to be aware, however, referring back to the hermeneutical principles outlined in Chapter 2, that we cannot simply map back into the Old Testament all our modern notions of what 'marriage' and 'family life' mean. There is obviously a cultural discontinuity between Old Testament family life and family life today.

4.2.43 This raises the issue (that was also outlined in Chapter 2), of how we relate the contingent and culturally particular nature of the laws found in the Old Testament to the universal will of God for the human race. What we learned from O'Donovan was that we have to learn how the universal finds expression through the contingent and particular.

4.2.44 As we have indicated in Chapter 3, the conclusion that the mainstream of the Christian tradition has reached as it has wrestled with this issue is that the universal principle underlying the Old Testament teaching about sexual morality and family life is that which finds its clearest expression in the creation narratives in Genesis 1–2, namely that the foundation of family life and sexual morality is a permanent, exclusive relationship of marriage between two people of the opposite sex.

4.2.45 The reason it has accepted the Old Testament prohibition on homosexuality as permanently binding on the Church is because this prohibition has been seen as the necessary corollary of this positive principle. At the heart of the current debate about homosexuality is the question of whether or not this reasoning is still valid.

4.2.46 The second thing that can be said is that, if we accept that the four Old Testament texts that we have looked at do refer to homosexual activity in its male form, then it is clear that they are unequivocal in their condemnation of it. It is an 'abomination' before God, and its seriousness as an offence is shown by the fact that in Leviticus 20.13 it is punishable by death.

4.2.47 As several scholars have noted, the fact that the Old Testament condemns homosexuality in this unequivocal fashion is one of the things that makes it distinctive among the literature that has come down to us from the ancient Near East. To quote Gordon Wenham:

> The ancient Near East was a world in which the practice of homosexuality was well known. It was an integral part of temple life at least in parts of Mesopotamia, and no blame appears to have attached to its practice outside of worship. Those who regularly played the passive role in intercourse were despised as being effeminate, and certain relationships such as father-son or pederasty were regarded as wrong, but otherwise it was regarded as quite respectable.[28]

4.2.48 As he goes on to explain, this means that:

> Seen in their Old Testament context the originality of the Old Testament laws on homosexuality is very striking. Whereas the rest of the ancient orient saw homosexual acts as quite acceptable provided they were not incestuous or forcible, the Old Testament bans them all even when both parties consented.[29]

4.2.49 What requires explanation is why it is that the Old Testament takes this distinctively severe approach. The claim made by the Old Testament itself, by means of the context of the verses in question in the book of Leviticus, is that it is a reflection of the will of the covenant God of Israel, who willed his people to maintain a distinctive way of life that was different from the nations round about them, and which reflected the pattern for human sexual relations instituted by God at creation.[30] The theological question is whether and to what extent we are prepared to accept this claim as binding upon us. If, as the New Testament claims, the covenant God of Israel is also our God, can we live in an obedient covenant relationship with him while at the same time setting aside the Old Testament teaching about homosexuality? We shall return to this issue at the end of the chapter.

4.2.50   A final issue that needs to be noted is why the Old Testament is silent about lesbian relationships. The honest answer is that we do not know, but what is clear, as we shall see below, is that, when the Early Church was faced with the practice of lesbianism in the Hellenistic world of the first century, it understood the Levitical prohibitions to apply in principle to women as well as men on the grounds that lesbian relationships also violated the framework for human sexuality laid down by God at creation.

4.3 The New Testament texts

4.3.1   In Chapter 1, three New Testament texts were identified as having been seen by the Christian tradition as forbidding homosexuality. As before, we shall look at each of these texts in turn.

Romans 1.24-27

4.3.2   In order to understand these verses properly it is necessary first of all to understand their context in Romans.

4.3.3   Although there has been much debate about St Paul's purpose, or purposes, in writing Romans there now seems to be general agreement that the epistle represents his attempt to give a full account of his understanding of the good news of Jesus Christ and its practical implications.

4.3.4   As J. D. G. Dunn puts it:

> As he stood at one of the most important transition points in his whole ministry he saw both the need and the desirability of such a fully worked out statement – to indicate to others clearly what was the gospel he preached, why as a Jew he preached it, and how it should come to expression in daily life and community.[31]

4.3.5   As Dunn goes on to explain, verses 24-27 of Romans 1 form part of a section of Romans, running from Romans 1.18 to 3.20, which describes why both Jews and Gentiles alike have need of the gospel that

God has called St Paul to preach. In Dunn's words, in this section of Romans, St Paul defines 'the human condition to which the gospel provides an answer'.[32]

4.3.6   In Romans 2.1 – 3.20 St Paul critiques those who hold that they have no need of the gospel because they can be righteous through their observance of the Jewish law, but before beginning this critique he establishes common ground with an imaginary Jewish dialogue partner by describing the unrighteousness of the contemporary Gentile world, in Romans 1.18-32, in order then to turn the tables by arguing that the unrighteousness that he describes is the unrighteousness of Israel as well.

In the words of Charles Cranfield:

> Paul himself reckoned that, by describing – as he certainly was doing in 1.18-32 – the obvious sinfulness of the heathen, he was, as a matter of fact, describing the basic sinfulness of fallen man as such, the inner reality of the life of Israel no less than that of the Gentiles. And the correctness of this view is confirmed by the fact that the 'Wherefore' at the beginning of 2.1, which has proved so baffling to commentators, becomes on this assumption, perfectly intelligible: if 1.18-32 does indeed declare the truth about all men, then it really does follow from it that the man who sets himself up as a judge of his fellows is without excuse. So we understand these verses as the revelation of the gospel's judgment of all men, which lays bare not only the idolatry of ancient and modern paganism but also the idolatry ensconced in Israel, in the Church and in the life of each believer.[33]

4.3.7   He begins in vv. 18-23 with the argument, which is similar to that found in Wisdom 11–15 and would have been accepted by any first-century Jew, that the Gentile world had turned away from the knowledge of God available through nature and had in consequence begun to worship idols:

> For the wrath of God is revealed from heaven against all ungodliness and wickedness of those who by their wickedness suppress the truth. For what can be known about God is plain to them, because God has shown it to them. Ever since the creation of the world his eternal power and divine nature, invisible though they are, have been understood and seen through the things he has made. So they are without excuse; for though they knew God, they did not honour him as God or give thanks to him, but they became futile in their thinking

and their senseless minds were darkened. Claiming to be wise, they became fools; and they exchanged the glory of the immortal God for images resembling a mortal human being or birds or four-footed animals or reptiles.

4.3.8 In verses 24-27 he then goes on to describe how, as a consequence of their rejection of him, God 'gave up' the Gentiles to sexual immorality. That is to say, the form that God's judgement took was to allow human beings the freedom to pursue their own sinful desires, and sexual immorality was the result:

> Therefore God gave them up in the lusts of their hearts to impurity, to the degrading of their bodies among themselves, because they exchanged the truth about God for a lie and worshipped and served the creature rather than the Creator, who is blessed for ever! Amen.

> For this reason God gave them up to degrading passions. Their women exchanged natural intercourse for unnatural, and in the same way also the men, giving up natural intercourse with women, were consumed with passion for one another. Men committed shameless acts with men and received in their own persons the due penalty for their error.

4.3.9 Finally, in verses 28-32, St Paul goes on to describe how God gave the Gentiles up not only to sexual immorality but to all sorts of other forms of vice as well:

> And since they did not see fit to acknowledge God, God gave them up to a debased mind and to things that should not be done. They were filled with every kind of wickedness, evil, covetousness, malice. Full of envy, murder, strife, deceit, craftiness, they are gossips, slanderers, God-haters, insolent, haughty, boastful, inventors of evil, rebellious towards to parents, foolish, faithless, heartless, ruthless. They know God's decree, that those who practise such things deserve to die – yet they not only do them but even applaud those who practise them.

4.3.10 As numerous commentators have noted, what St Paul is doing is giving a vivid, broad-brush description of the consequences of turning away from God. Once the knowledge of the true God has been abandoned the things that he describes are what result.

4.3.11 As part of this catalogue of human wickedness, verses 26-27:

> For this reason God gave them up to degrading passions. Their women exchanged natural intercourse for unnatural, and in the same way also the men, giving up natural intercourse with women, were consumed with passion for one another. Men committed shameless acts with men and received in their own persons the due penalty for their error.

have traditionally been seen to teach clearly that both male and female forms of same-sex sexual activity are shameful and contrary to the natural order established by God. The consensus among commentators is still that this is a correct reading of the text.

4.3.12 There were early Christian commentators who saw the reference to 'unnatural' female sexual activity as meaning that women engaged in unnatural *heterosexual* practices (either through engaging in anal intercourse or through the woman taking the 'superior' position in intercourse). However, it is now generally agreed that the parallelism between the unnatural behaviour of both sexes in these verses taken together with the undoubted reference to male homosexual behaviour means that what St Paul is referring to is in fact lesbianism.

4.3.13 There is also general agreement that St Paul sees homosexuality as a manifestation of that rebellion against God that we have seen to be the theme of Romans 1.

4.3.14 Thus the Methodist New Testament scholar C. K. Barrett writes in his commentary on Romans:

> No feature of pagan society filled the Jew with greater loathing than the toleration, or rather admiration, of homosexual practices. Paul is entirely at one here with his compatriots; but his disgust is more than instinctive. In the obscene pleasures to which he refers is to be seen precisely that perversion of the created order which may be expected when men put the creation in place of the Creator. That idolatry has such consequences is to Paul a plain mark of God's wrath.[34]

4.3.15 Similarly, the Roman Catholic commentator Joseph Fitzmeyer writes in his Anchor Bible Commentary on Romans that what St Paul is teaching is that:

> Homosexual behaviour is the sin of rebellion against God, an outward manifestation of inward and spiritual rebellion. It illustrates

human degradation and provides a vivid image of humanity's rejection of the sovereignty of God the creator.[35]

4.3.16   As a third example, Dunn declares in his *Word* commentary on Romans:

> Paul's attitude to homosexual practice is unambiguous. The third appearance of the word 'changed' . . . seems to imply that the action described (changing the natural use to that which is 'contrary to nature') is of a piece with and direct result of the basic corruption of the glory and truth of God in idolatry, a similar turning from the rule of the creator to that which is simply a perversion of the creature's share in creating. But more striking still is his use of a sequence of words whose import is unmistakable. Homosexuality is seen as a perversion which is 'worthy of no respect'. Homosexual practice is characterized with the emphasis of repetition as 'unnatural' where Paul uses very Greek and particularly Stoic language to broaden the appeal of the more characteristically Jewish rejection of homosexuality, and where he in effect appeals to his own readers' common sense to recognize that homosexual practice is a violation of the natural order (as determined by God).[36]

4.3.17   Dunn goes on to comment that the words in v. 27 'committing shameless acts' are a reference back to Leviticus:

> Paul could not help but be thinking here of Leviticus 18 and 20 which include homosexual acts within the category of illicit sexual relationships as one of the 'abominations' of the surrounding peoples which Israel should avoid on pain of being cut off from the covenant (Leviticus 18.22; 20.13).[37]

4.3.18   In Romans 1 homosexuality *per se* is rejected as an offence against the natural order established by God, and it is a serious offence because it is condemned in Leviticus as an abomination before God that God's people are to avoid.

4.3.19   In his book *The Bible and Homosexual Practice*, to which we have already referred, Gagnon clarifies further Dunn's point that St Paul appeals not only to Leviticus but also to his readers' common sense.

4.3.20   He argues that the reason why St Paul begins his list of Gentile vices with homosexuality is that, in his view, homosexuality is like idolatry in that they are both clear examples of the rejection of that knowledge of God and his will that is provided by nature, and that is, therefore, accessible even to those who do not possess the written law of God contained in the Jewish Scriptures:

> Same-sex eroticism functions as a particularly poignant example of human enslavement to passions and of God's just judgement precisely because it parallels in the horizontal-ethical dimension a denial of God's reality like that of idolatry in the vertical-divine dimension. In other words, idolatry is a deliberate suppression of the truth available to pagans in the world around them, but so too is same-sex intercourse.[38]

4.3.21 We can see that this is what St Paul is saying, he declares, because this is what is meant by the key phrase 'contrary to nature' in v. 26:

> Given the meaning of 'contrary to nature' (para physin) and comparable expressions used by Jewish writers of the period to describe same-sex intercourse, the meaning of the phrase in Paul is clear. Minimally, Paul is referring to the anatomical and procreative complementarity of male and female. Put in more crude terms, Paul in effect argues that even pagans who have no access to the book of Leviticus should know that same-sex eroticism is 'contrary to nature' because the primary sex organs fit male to female, not female to female or male to male. Again, by fittedness I mean not only the glove-like physical fit of the penis and vagina but also clues to complementarity provided by procreative capacity and the capacity for mutual and pleasurable stimulation. These clues make clear that neither the anus, the orifice for excreting waste products, nor the mouth, the orifice for taking in food are complementary orifices for the male member. For Paul it was a simple matter of common sense observation of human anatomy and procreative function that even pagans, oblivious to God's direct revelation in the Bible had no excuse for not knowing.[39]

4.3.22 Gagnon also observes that there are numerous 'inter-textual echoes' that link Romans 1.18-32 back to the creation account in Genesis 1–3. As he notes, the significance of these cross references is that, for St Paul:

> ... both idolatry and same-sex intercourse reject God's verdict that what was made and arranged was 'very good' (1.31). Instead of recognizing their indebtedness to the one God in whose image and

likeness they were made, humans worshipped statues made in their own image and likeness. Instead of exercising dominion over the animal kingdom, they bowed down not only to images of themselves but also to images of animals. Instead of acknowledging that God had made them 'male and female' and had called on them to copulate and procreate, they denied the transparent complementarity of their sexuality and engaged in sex with the same sex, indulging themselves in irresponsible sexual passion on which stable and productive family structures could not be built ... Even though Romans 1.18-32 speaks of events after the fall, for Paul all human rebellions are in one way or another rebellions against God's will for humankind set in motion at creation.[40]

4.3.23   In summary we can say, therefore, that the majority of scholars still hold that in Romans 1.26-27 St Paul rejects all forms of homosexual practice, both gay and lesbian, as sinful. He believes that they represent a rejection of the natural order of things established by God in creation, and, although he uses language taken from contemporary Stoicism, the reason that he believes this is because he is building on the contemporary Jewish belief that, according to the witness of both Scripture and nature, homosexuality is something that is contrary to the will of God.

1 Corinthians 6.9-10
4.3.24   The context of this text is St Paul's concern about the fact that the Corinthians are taking their disputes with each other to court. In v. 7 of chapter 6 he asks the offended party whether it would not be better to suffer wrong rather than bring moral defeat on the whole Church, and in verses 8-10 he then warns the offending party and the Church as a whole against the kind of behaviour that caused the dispute in the first place:

> But you yourselves wrong and defraud, and that even your own brethren. Do you not know that the unrighteous will not inherit the kingdom of God? Do not be deceived; neither the immoral, nor idolators, nor adulterers, nor sexual perverts, nor thieves, nor the greedy, nor drunkards, nor revilers, nor robbers will inherit the kingdom of God. (vv. 8-10, RSV.)

4.3.25   As Gordon Fee notes in his commentary on 1 Corinthians:

> Paul's point in all this is to warn 'the saints', not only the man who has wronged his brother, but the whole community that if they

persist in the same errors as 'the wicked' they are in the same danger of not inheriting the kingdom.[41]

4.3.26 Among those described by St Paul as examples of the unrighteous are those referred to by the RSV as 'sexual perverts'. These have traditionally been seen as practising homosexuals, and understanding the text in this way has led to its being seen as clearly condemning homosexual behaviour as contrary to the law of God and as a bar to inheriting God's kingdom.

4.3.27 In recent years this traditional interpretation of the text has been questioned on the grounds that the Greek words translated as 'sexual perverts', *malakoi* and *arsenokoitai*, are terms that either do not refer specifically to homosexuality at all, or refer to a particular type of homosexual activity, male prostitution involving pederasty. In either case the texts could not be seen as presenting a blanket condemnation of all forms of homosexuality.[42]

4.3.28 Nevertheless, most scholars have continued to maintain that the traditional interpretation is correct.[43] What has been particularly influential in recent discussion of the text has been the recognition that St Paul's language refers back to the holiness code in Leviticus, and that what he is doing is reapplying the Old Testament condemnation of male homosexuality to the situation of the Church in Corinth.

4.3.29 For example, Richard Hays writes as follows in his 1996 study *The Moral Vision of the New Testament*:

> The word *malakoi* is not a technical term meaning 'homosexuals' (no such term existed in either Greek or Hebrew), but it appears often in Hellenistic Greek as pejorative slang to describe the 'passive' partners – often young boys – in homosexual activity. The other word, *arsenokoitai*, is not found in any extant Greek text earlier than 1 Corinthians. Some scholars have suggested that its meaning is uncertain, but Robin Scroggs has shown that the word is a translation of the Hebrew *mishkav zakur* ('lying with a male'), derived directly from Leviticus 18.22 and 20.13 and used in rabbinic texts to refer to homosexual intercourse. The Septuagint (Greek Old Testament) of Leviticus 20.13 reads, 'Whoever lies with a man as with a woman [*meta arsenos koiten gynaikos*], they have both done an abomination' (my translation). This is almost certainly the idiom from which the noun *arsenokoitai* was coined. Thus, Paul's use of the term presupposes and reaffirms the holiness code's condemnation of

homosexual acts. This is not a controversial point in Paul's argument; the letter gives no evidence that anyone at Corinth was arguing for the acceptance of same-sex erotic activity. Paul simply assumes that his readers will share his conviction that those who indulge in homosexual acts are 'wrongdoers' ... along with the other sorts of offenders on his list.[44]

4.3.30   It is, of course, true that homosexuality is only one of the types of sin mentioned in 1 Corinthians 6, and there is no evidence that St Paul saw it as more relatively serious than the other types of sin that he mentions. This is an important point to which we shall return later on in this report.

4.3.31   However, this does not mean that we can ignore the seriousness with which he did regard the issue. We still have to reckon with the fact that St Paul obviously did see homosexual practice as a form of behaviour that would bar someone from the kingdom of God, and also note the point made by Anthony Thiselton in his recent commentary on 1 Corinthians that in this passage St Paul is neither being idiosyncratic nor simply reflecting the cultural prejudices of the surrounding Hellenistic culture. He is instead building on an established Christian catechetical tradition of teaching concerning the nature of the Christian life.[45]

4.3.32   This latter point is significant because, if Thiselton is right, then from the earliest days of the Church there was an agreed understanding of what the Christian life involved and this included a repudiation of homosexual practice. This would in turn explain the point made by Hays concerning St Paul's assumption that his readers will share his convictions.

1 Timothy 1.10
4.3.33   As John Kelly notes in his commentary on 1 Timothy, the setting of this verse is a situation where the Church was being troubled by false teachers who:

> ... read out of the law, i.e. the legal portion of the O.T., fantastic myths and ascetical prescriptions ... which serve to show that they have missed the point both of the O.T. itself and of the gospel.[46]

4.3.34   In response to their teaching, verses 9-10 then explains that the purpose of the Mosaic law is to restrain and correct the wickedness of the ungodly:

... the law is laid down not for the innocent but for the lawless and disobedient, for the godless and sinful, for the unholy and profane, for those who kill their father or mother, for murderers, fornicators, sodomites, slave traders, liars, perjurers, and whatever else is contrary to the sound teaching ...

4.3.35 The word translated 'sodomites' by the NRSV is the word *arsenokoites*, which comes from the same root as the word *arsenokoitai* found in 1 Corinthians 6.9. There has therefore been the same discussion about the meaning of the term in 1 Timothy that we have previously noted in connection with 1 Corinthians.

4.3.36 As in the case of 1 Corinthians 6.9-10 the consensus of scholarly opinion remains that the term in question refers to homosexuality. Thus Luke Johnson comments in his Anchor Bible commentary on the letters to Timothy:

> The translation 'sexual pervert' for 'arsenokoites' is not particularly appealing, but there is no reasonable alternative for a term that means literally 'one who sleeps with' [= has sexual congress with men].[47]

4.3.37 Similarly, I. H. Marshall notes in his ICC commentary on 1 Timothy that *arsenokoites*: 'is a rare word meaning "homosexual"',[48] and Mark Bonnington notes in his Grove booklet *Homosexuality and the Bible*:

> The word *arsenokoitai* appears again in 1 Timothy 1.8-11. Verses 8 and 9 indicate explicitly that the OT law is in view and provides confirmation that Paul and others had Leviticus in view in using the word *arsenokoitai*. Such behaviour is not only contrary to the law but to 'the sound teaching that conforms to the glorious gospel' (1 Timothy 1.10-11).
>
> If we needed a simple modern equivalent for *arsenokoitai* then 'men who sleep with other men' would retain both the generality and the euphemistic quality of the word. Arguments that in using *arsenokoitai* Paul must have had a specific cultural model in mind (like pederasts) are dealt a decisive blow with this simple recognition that Paul's categories were Jewish and biblical. Because Leviticus uses the analogy of sex with a woman, the word can be taken as a rather general one for sexual activity between men and cannot be narrowed down to (say) anal intercourse.[49]

4.3.38   In addition to the argument that the word *arsenokoites* points us back to the holiness code in Leviticus, many exegetes have noted that in 1 Timothy 1.8-10 the text is based on a development of the second half of the Ten Commandments.

4.3.39   For instance, Gordon Fee comments that verses 9-10 contain a two-part catalogue of vices:

> First, there are three pairs of general classifications: lawbreakers and rebels, the ungodly (inwardly irreverent), and sinful (outwardly disobedient), and the unholy and irreligious. Thereafter the catalogue has a remarkable coincidence with the Ten Commandments (the fifth through the ninth), often giving more grotesque expressions of these sins.
>
> Thus these lawless are those who kill their fathers or mothers (fifth commandment); murderers (sixth commandment); the adulterers (lit 'fornicators') and perverts, a word for male coital homosexuality (seventh commandment); slave traders (eighth commandment); and liars and perjurers (ninth commandment). Such coincidences can scarcely be accidental. But what is the reason for such a list here? It is certainly not a hidden reference to the sins of the false teachers, who are guilty of their own kinds of sins, but not these. Most likely the list is a conscious reflection of the Mosaic law as law and expresses the kinds of sins such law was given to prohibit.[50]

4.3.40   What is significant about this observation is that it reinforces the point that the commandments in the Old Testament still provided the basic framework for the New Testament's ethical reflection, and these commandments were seen as prohibiting homosexual behaviour alongside other types of behaviour forbidden by God.

4.3.41   This addresses the current debate about homosexuality directly because it indicates that, if we follow the lead of the New Testament, we are not at liberty simply to disregard the stipulations of the old covenant with regard to same-sex activity: what was forbidden to God's people under the old covenant is still forbidden to God's people under the new covenant.

4.3.42   Thus far we have noted the general consensus that seems to exist among New Testament scholars concerning the interpretation of the texts at which we have just looked.

4.3.43   It needs to be noted, however, that this consensus has been challenged in recent years by a number of scholars who have put forward very different interpretations of this material. Three of the most significant of these challenges have been those mounted by Bernadette Brooten, William Countryman and Robin Scroggs and we shall now look at each of these in turn.

4.3.44   In her book *Love Between Women: Early Christian Responses To Female Homoeroticism*, Brooten sees the fundamental issue underlying what the New Testament has to say about homosexuality as that of gender hierarchy.

4.3.45   Focusing on St Paul's teaching in Romans 1, she argues that his primary concern is not same-sex activity or relations *per se* but rather the ways in which such relations disrupt what St Paul sees as a natural gender hierarchy. She argues that 'Paul's distinction between "natural" and "unnatural intercourse" serves as a window to his vision of gender and sexuality'. Paul adopted his culture's views of women as submissive, and 'lower' than men in the gender hierarchy, and thus he maintained the wider Roman culture's notion that women who engaged in same-sex relations went 'beyond the passive, subordinate sexual role accorded to them by nature'. Such women were described in the wider culture as 'taking on an active role, thereby becoming like men. Brooten therefore argues that 'Paul did not invent the concept of "natural intercourse" but rather adopted it from his culture and gave it a theological foundation.'[51]

4.3.46   As Brooten sees it, therefore, female same-sex activity was 'unnatural' because it meant women taking an active rather than passive sexual role and the male variety was 'unnatural' because, if a man engaged in such activity: 'Even if he does not himself play the passive sexual role, thereby confounding his own nature, he can transgress male nature by causing other men to submit to him.'[52]

4.3.47   In his study of New Testament sexual ethics *Dirt, Greed and Sex*, Countryman also focuses on Romans 1 and argues that St Paul did not regard homosexuality as sinful but simply as 'unclean':

> ... a close reading of Paul's discussion of homosexual acts in Romans 1 does not support the common modern interpretation of the passage. While Paul wrote of such acts as being unclean,

dishonourable, improper and 'over against nature', he did not apply
the language of sin to them at all. Instead, he treated homosexual
behaviour as an integral if unpleasingly dirty aspect of Gentile
culture. It was not in itself sinful, but had been visited upon the
Gentiles as recompense for sins, chiefly the sin of idolatry but also
those of social disruption.[53]

4.3.48   He then goes on to argue further that, according to the
teaching of the New Testament as a whole, such concepts of 'cleanness'
and 'uncleanness' are done away with and replaced with a new emphasis
on 'purity of heart'. From this perspective what matters is not the kind
of sexual relationship but its moral quality.

4.3.49   In his study entitled the *New Testament and Homosexuality*
published in 1988, Scroggs argues that the basis for the New
Testament's rejection of homosexual relationships was the fact that
the prevailing model for such relationships in the Graeco-Roman
world was pederasty, and that the majority of pederastic relationships
were:

> ... both by definition and practice, characterized by lack of mutuality,
> both spiritually and physically. The more one gives attention to the
> call-boy and outright prostitution which 1 Corinthians 6.9-10 and
> 1 Timothy 1.9 attack, the more the practices opposed are those
> abusive of human rights and dignity. Thus what the New Testament
> was against was the image of homosexuality and pederasty and
> primarily here its more sordid and dehumanizing dimensions.[54]

4.3.50   For all three writers the cultural difference between New
Testament times and today means that we cannot apply the New
Testament teaching about homosexuality to today's discussion of the
subject. As Scroggs puts it:

> Biblical judgments against homosexuality are not relevant to today's
> debate. They should no longer be used in denominational discussions
> about homosexuality, and should in no way be a weapon to justify
> refusal of ordination not because the Bible is not authoritative, but
> simply because it does not address the issues involved.[55]

4.3.51   These challenges to the traditional interpretation of the New
Testament texts need to be taken seriously, both in themselves, and as an
indication that we need to engage with the issue, which we have already
mentioned, of the cultural gap between biblical times and today.

4.3.52   However, it also needs to be noted that the arguments put forward by Brooten, Countryman and Scroggs have remained controversial.

- In the case of Brooten, it is argued that she has not established from the New Testament itself that the issue of gender hierarchy was determinative for New Testament sexual ethics and that her reading of 'natural' and 'unnatural' in Romans 1 as meaning 'in accordance with' or 'not in accordance with' gender hierarchy does not do justice to the way in which St Paul uses the word 'nature' elsewhere.[56]

- In the case of Countryman, it is argued that he has not done justice to the way in which the language used by St Paul to describe homosexual activity is used elsewhere in the New Testament to describe sinful behaviour; that he has not done justice to the continuity between verses 23-27 and 28-32 of Romans 1, which suggests that all the activity there described comes under the category of sin; and that he has dismissed too easily St Paul's explicit description of same-sex relations as sinful in 1 Corinthians 6.9-10.[57]

- In the case of Scroggs, it is argued that he has overestimated the importance of pederasty in first-century Graeco-Roman society; that he has underestimated the extent to which St Paul would have been aware of other types of non-exploitative same-sex relationships; that he has failed to note the fact that the New Testament does not use the specific vocabulary that was used to refer to pederasty when it refers to same-sex relations; and that he has also failed to note the significance of the fact that female same-sex relationships (which were not pederastic) are also regarded as sinful.[58]

4.3.53   In summary, we can say that it is still the case that the consensus of scholarly opinion supports the traditional interpretation of these New Testament texts. As Peter Coleman puts it:

> Taken together, St Paul's writings repudiate homosexual behaviour as a vice of the Gentiles in Romans, as a bar to the kingdom in Corinthians, and as an offence to be repudiated by the moral law in 1 Timothy.[59]

4.3.54   Because these texts are the only direct references the New Testament makes to homosexual behaviour, it follows that, as Hays argues:

The only paradigms offered by the New Testament for homosexual behavior are the emphatically negative and stereotypic sketches in the three Pauline texts (Romans 1.18-32, 1 Corinthians 6.9, 1 Timothy 1.10). The New Testament offers no accounts of homosexual Christians, tells no stories of same-sex lovers, ventures no metaphors that place a positive construal on homosexual relations. Occasionally, one encounters speculative claims that Jesus was gay (because of his relationship with the 'beloved disciple'; see John 13.23) or that Martha and Mary were not really sisters but lesbian lovers. Such exegetical curiosities, which have found no acceptance among serious New Testament scholars, can only be judged pathetic attempts at constructing a New Testament warrant for homosexual practice where none exists. If Jesus or his followers had practised or countenanced homosexuality, it would have been profoundly scandalous within first-century Jewish culture. Such a controversy would surely have left traces in the tradition, as did Jesus' practice of having table fellowship with prostitutes and tax collectors. But there are no traces of such controversy. In the paradigmatic mode, the slender evidence offered by the New Testament is entirely disapproving of homosexuality.[60]

4.3.55   Furthermore, as Hays goes on to explain, the New Testament does not just offer three separate negative responses to homosexuality. It also offers an account of reality that explains why these responses are negative.

The mode in which the New Testament speaks explicitly about homosexuality is the mode of *symbolic world* construction. Romans 1 presents, as we have seen, a portrayal of humankind in rebellion against God and consequently plunged into depravity and confusion. In the course of that portrayal, homosexual activities are – explicitly and without qualification – identified as symptomatic of that tragically confused rebellion.[61]

Other New Testament issues

a. The example of Jesus
4.3.56   It is frequently argued that, while the New Testament may contain texts that reject homosexuality, we can obtain a different perspective on the matter from the life and teaching of Jesus. This argument comes in two parts.

4.3.57   First of all, setting aside the extremist argument that Jesus himself might have been gay, or publicly countenanced homosexuality, it is sometimes argued that, because we have no evidence that Jesus said anything about homosexuality, this means that we cannot say that he was opposed to it.

4.3.58   Then, secondly, it is noted that Jesus reached out to those who were seen as morally unacceptable or ritually unclean (Matthew 9.9-13, Mark 5.25-34), that he was prepared to subordinate the Jewish law to human need (Mark 2.23 – 3.6) and that when asked to summarize the law he emphasized the importance of love (Mark 12.28-34). This evidence is taken to show that Jesus took a radical attitude in matters of ethics and was prepared to disregard the written law when this conflicted with the commandment of love. In our context, it is argued a similar attitude would mean setting aside the biblical strictures against homosexuality and obeying the commandment of love by fully affirming our homosexual neighbours.

4.3.59   There are, however, three major problems with this appeal to Jesus.

4.3.60   First, the argument from silence is a weak one. We cannot say that because Jesus did not mention an issue this means that he took a liberal position on the matter. Taking this position to its logical conclusion would mean, for example, also arguing that Jesus was not opposed to bestiality or incest.

4.3.61   There is also some evidence that Jesus did, in fact, make implicit reference to homosexuality, and that what he said affirmed the traditional Jewish standpoint. Thus in Mark 7.21 'fornication' is said to be one of the things that defiles people, and this is a translation of the Greek plural *porneiai*, which was understood to refer to things forbidden by the Levitical law. As Gagnon puts it:

> No first-century Jew could have spoken of *porneiai* (plural) without having in mind the list of forbidden sexual offences in Leviticus 18 and 20 (incest, adultery, same-sex intercourse, bestiality). The statement underscores that sexual behavior does matter. If Jesus made this remark, he undoubtedly would have understood homosexual behavior to be included among the list of offences.[62]

4.3.62   Secondly, although it is at the heart of the Gospel accounts that Jesus welcomed sinners, it is quite clear that he also called them to repentance (Luke 15.3-32), that is, to a new way of life lived in obedience to God. As Rudolf Schnackenburg puts it: 'it was not Jesus' intention to turn men loose in lawlessness and licence. On the contrary he demanded more of the absolute and unlimited obedience to the holy will of God'.[63]

4.3.63 Thirdly, Jesus expressed this call to obedience in terms of a sexual ethic that was more rather than less strict in its interpretation of the Old Testament than that of his contemporaries, and was based on a reaffirmation of the teaching about lifelong, monogamous, heterosexual relationships in Genesis 1 and 2 (Matthew 5.27-32; 19.3-12). It is therefore impossible to conceive that Jesus would have endorsed homosexuality had this been an issue that had arisen during his ministry.

4.3.64 Gagnon's overall conclusion seems a fair summary of the evidence:

> Jesus did not overturn any prohibitions against immoral sexual behavior in Leviticus or anywhere else in the Mosaic law. He did not regard sexual ethics as having diminished importance in relation to other demands of the kingdom. It is highly unlikely that he would have held some sort of secret acceptance of homosexuality in the face of the uniform opposition within the Judaism of his day. Clearly, he did not adopt more liberal positions on other matters of sexual ethics such as divorce or adultery. Instead, he was more demanding than the Torah, not less.[64]

4.3.65 It is true that the Gospels depict the disciples themselves as constantly failing in their obedience to what God required of them. It is also true that Jesus' parable of the Pharisee and the tax-collector (Luke 18.9-14) warns against coming before God with an attitude of self-righteousness. It is therefore entirely correct to say that those who are not attracted to, and do not engage in, same-sex sexual relationships are not entitled to stand in self-righteous judgement over those who are and who do. As in Romans 1–3 so, in the Gospels, it is clear that everyone is a moral failure whose only recourse is to the undeserved mercy of God.

4.3.66 While possibly conceding that the points just made have a certain validity, those who look for a liberalization of the Church's teaching on this issue would remain uneasy with the picture of Jesus so presented. In their view, it does not take seriously enough the point made in 3.3.58 about the implications of Jesus' radical departure from the conventions of his society by not only mixing but eating with those who were regarded as morally beyond the pale. He sought out their company and stayed with them.

4.3.67 For them, Jesus' approach is well captured in a true story about the Baptist preacher Tony Campolo. Arriving in a city for a speaking engagement he was unable to sleep, so he went out and sat in a café. He found it was the one frequented by local prostitutes. Moreover, talking to the girls he discovered it was the birthday of one of them the next day. 'Let's have a party' he said. Next night, after his engagement, he came and gave a birthday party as promised. He neither condoned nor condemned their way of life. He simply included them in a party as a sign of that divine banquet in which Jesus seeks to include them all.

4.3.68 This is not to deny the radical challenge of the rule of God in human affairs that Jesus put before people, or to suggest that he would simply leave people where they were. But, they suggest, if Jesus went into a gay bar, his attitude and approach as we learn it from the Gospels would suggest that he would act much as Tony Campolo did: seeking to include and affirm. The ethical implications would follow, worked out with them.

4.3.69 In turn, those who affirm the Church's traditional position would have their own questions about this alternative portrayal of Jesus. Specifically, they would ask what is meant by the key terms 'include' and 'affirm'.

4.3.70 If 'include' means that Jesus would welcome gay and lesbian people to be part of the kingdom of God, then this is an uncontroversial point that would be generally accepted.

4.3.71 If 'affirm', however, means that Jesus would endorse an active homosexual lifestyle, then this is much more problematic. Those who take a traditional view of the matter would argue that the evidence presented above suggests that 'the radical challenge of the rule of God which Jesus put before people' would mean forsaking such a lifestyle in the same way that the woman caught in adultery was told: 'go, and do not sin again' (John 8.10), and Zacchaeus the tax collector gave half his goods to the poor and made four-fold restitution to those he had defrauded (Luke 19.8).

4.3.72   They would also point out that there is a historical problem with assuming that Jesus would have affirmed those living an active homosexual lifestyle. The Early Church was in a much better position than we will ever be to know what Jesus would have thought about those engaged in such a lifestyle, and the evidence from the Epistles suggests that they believed that he would not have affirmed their homosexual activity. It is difficult to account for the early Church's consistent rejection of such activity on any other basis.[65]

b. The relevance of Acts 15

4.3.73   As well as appealing to the life and teaching of Jesus, those in the current debate who favour a more liberal approach to homosexuality also make appeal to the account in Acts 15. In the words of Jeffrey Siker, they see this text as providing: 'a case for seeing the acceptance of "non-abstaining" homosexual Christians as analogous to how Jewish Christians accepted "non-abstaining Gentile Christians"'.[66]

4.3.74   At the council in Jerusalem recorded in Acts 15, Gentiles who were seen as being sinners because of their non-observance of the Jewish law were accepted into the Church without having to be circumcised or obey the whole of the law of Moses, because evidence was seen of the Holy Spirit at work in their lives (Acts 15.8, see also Acts 11.15-17), and the Church was prepared to set aside parts of the Old Testament to do with ritual purity and food laws in order to make their inclusion possible.

4.3.75   In the same way, it is said, we should be prepared to set aside those parts of the Old and New Testaments that condemn homosexuality and welcome non-abstaining homosexuals into the Church because of the manifest evidence that the Holy Spirit is at work in their lives.[67]

4.3.76   This is an important argument, and raises important questions about the Church's willingness to welcome those it has traditionally rejected, including, of course, those of a homosexual disposition. However, like the previous argument, it also presents serious difficulties.

4.3.77   First, as Andrew Goddard notes:

> Acts 15 is about accepting certain people within the church. This further supposed implication is about accepting certain actions of

those people – patterns of behaviour and relationships. It is simply not possible to leap from one to another.[68]

4.3.78 Secondly, as a matter of fact the Early Church did not see the Old Testament laws relating to homosexuality as not applying to Gentile Christians. Even St Paul, who arguably went beyond the agreement reached in Acts 15 in his willingness to allow Gentiles Christians the freedom not to have to observe fully the Jewish law, remained adamant, as we have seen, that the Levitical laws against homosexuality were still relevant to all Christians.

4.3.79 Indeed, Richard Bauckham has made a persuasive case for arguing that those things from which Gentile Christians are asked to refrain in Acts 15.20 actually include homosexuality, because the logic of the argument in Acts 15.13-21 is that the Gentiles are to be included within the Church on the basis that they are to be seen as the 'alien who resides among them' (Leviticus 17.12) – resident aliens to whom the whole of the Jewish law does not apply. However, those parts of the Old Testament law that are specifically said to apply to such aliens do apply to the Gentiles within the Church. Among these parts are Leviticus 1–18 from which the four prohibitions noted in Acts 15.20 are drawn and which, as we have seen, forbid homosexual activity.[69]

4.3.80 Other scholars, such as Ben Witherington, interpret the prohibitions in Acts 15 differently,[70] but, if Bauckham is right, then Acts 15 is in fact an argument *against* rather than for the acceptance of homosexuality in the Church.

4.3.81 An additional argument for a more liberal attitude to homosexuality put forward on the basis of Acts 15 is that the decision of the Council of Jerusalem that Gentile Christians should observe the Jewish law by refraining from 'what is strangled' and 'blood' came to be abandoned by the Church. This means, it is said, that even the authoritative decree of the first highly authoritative council of the Church reflects a context, an agreed compromise for admitting Gentiles to table fellowship, which is no longer applicable today. The implication of this for the Jewish attitude towards homosexuality is, similarly, that it is no longer binding.

4.3.82 The counter-argument to this point is that, in ceasing to observe the Jewish food laws while continuing to observe the Levitical prohibition on homosexuality, the Church has followed the lead of the New Testament itself in which there are indications that the food laws are not permanently binding (Mark 7.1-23, Acts 10.9-16, Romans 14.1-4, 1 Corinthians 8.1-12) while there are no such indications with regard to homosexuality.

c. The significance of Romans 11.24

4.3.83   In Romans 11.24 St Paul reminds the Gentile Christians in Rome that they have been included into the people of God by an act of unexpected and undeserved divine grace. Using the olive tree as an image for the people of God, he writes that Gentile Christians 'have been cut from what is by nature a wild olive tree and grafted, contrary to nature, into a cultivated olive tree'.

4.3.84   In his important study *Sexuality and the Christian Body*, to which we referred at the end of the last chapter, Eugene Rogers appeals to this verse as pointing towards the acceptance of homosexual partnerships by the Church today. The argument he puts forward is that, although homosexual relations are described as 'contrary to nature' in Romans 1.26-27 this does not close the matter since, according to Romans 11.24, God himself acts 'contrary to nature' in grafting Gentiles into the Church, and God's activity then is paralleled by his inclusion of lesbian and gay couples now.

> It is the wild branches that God grafts according to Romans 11 – the Gentiles with whom Paul associated sexual licence – and on the hearts of whom the Spirit writes a new law – in this case, I will argue the law of marriage. As God grafts Gentiles, the wild branches, onto the domestic covenant of God's household with Israel, structured by the Torah of the Spirit, so God grafts gay and lesbian couples (whom detractors also associate with sexual licence) by a new movement of the Spirit onto the domestic, married covenants of straight women and men.[71]

4.3.85   However, the problem with this reading of Romans is that it overlooks what St Paul and the Early Church as a whole actually argued about the consequences of Gentile inclusion into the people of God.

4.3.86   As Grenz explains:

> The apostles did not urge the new converts to bring their old Gentile ideas and ways into the church. Thus, for example, in the opening

chapter of his letter to the Romans, Paul does not affirm the preferences of Gentiles on the basis of their inclusion into the people of God. Instead the apostle penned a stinging critique of pagan ways. The early church leaders instructed Gentile converts to leave behind their former 'ignorance'. They were to park their pagan religious practices and immoral activities outside the door of the Church.[72]

And among the pagan practices that they were thus to abandon was homosexual sexual activity in both its gay and lesbian forms as Romans 1.24-27, 1 Corinthians 6.9-10, and 1 Timothy 1.10 make clear.

4.3.87   To put it simply, for Gentiles to become part of the people of God meant a call to holiness, and that appears to have meant *inter alia* the abandonment of homosexual practice (as indeed all forms of sexual practice contrary to the heterosexual monogamous norm).

4.4 Responding to the biblical material

4.4.1   Thus far in this chapter we have dealt with what in Chapter 2 we called 'behind the text' and 'in the text' issues. That is to say, we have attempted to explore what the relevant texts meant to their original audience in their original context. What we now have to go on to do is to look at the 'in front of the text' issue of how we should respond to this material today.

4.4.2   In the history of the Church there was, as we have noted, general agreement about how the texts we have looked at were to be applied to the life of the Church. They were to be viewed as providing an authoritative account both of the origins of homosexuality and God's attitude towards it. The proper response to them was seen to be obedience, and, where necessary, repentance and amendment of life.

4.4.3   Today, however, this general agreement has ceased to exist. Instead, as Michael Doe notes in his book *Seeking the Truth in Love*, there is a continuum of responses within the Church.[73]

One: Homosexuality as a whole is rejected by Scripture as sinful[74]

4.4.4   Taking this approach would mean saying that both homosexual orientation (in the sense of a disposition to desire same-sex sexual activity) and its expression in sexual activity are to be regarded as sinful.

4.4.5   The advantage of this approach is that it takes seriously the biblical material that we have looked at in this chapter, and in particular it takes seriously the fact that, according to the New Testament, the desire for homosexual acts as well as their performance is symptomatic of the fact that we live in a fallen world in which sin has disordered God's creation.

4.4.6 The disadvantage of this approach is that if matters are simply left there it becomes very difficult to see how the Bible is being read, as we saw in Chapter 2 that it must be, as a testimony to the grace of God. What seems to be being offered is simply God's 'No' to homosexuals without any corresponding 'Yes'.

4.4.7 Putting the matter in less theoretical terms, this means taking seriously the fact that, even if we accept this position on exegetical and theological grounds, we are still left with the problem of how to provide pastoral support to those who find this particular manifestation of the world's brokenness an extremely heavy burden to bear in their own lives. Anyone who has worked pastorally with homosexual people will be aware of the immense sense of rejection, pain and personal unworthiness that all too many of them feel, and any truly Christian response to homosexuality must find a way of ministering creatively and compassionately to them.

4.4.8 Furthermore, this approach needs to find a way of responding to the fact that there are many homosexual people for whom homosexuality is not an affliction, but a joy, in that they experience both physical intimacy and loving companionship through their relationship with a homosexual partner. A response has to be found to the question 'How can a relationship that brings so much love be a manifestation of sin?', and also to the further question 'What do you have to offer me that will replace the love and support I have as a homosexual, if you are asking me to give these up?'

Two: Scripture may say nothing explicitly about homosexual orientation, but it's very clear that homosexual behaviour can never be acceptable

4.4.9 The advantages of this approach are twofold. First, it takes seriously the evidence that we have looked at in this chapter that, both in the Old Testament and the New, homosexual activity is regarded as sinful. Secondly, by allowing for a distinction between orientation and behaviour, it creates a possible pastoral space for affirming someone who is homosexual as a person while disapproving of their behaviour. To use the old adage, it makes it easier to 'hate the sin, but love the sinner' on the grounds that the disposition itself is neutral, it is what people do or don't do that is the issue.

4.4.10   However, this approach also has two disadvantages. Theologically, it is weak where the first approach was strong, in that it fails to take seriously the fact that the biblical material seems to imply that the very existence of a homosexual disposition is a manifestation of the disorder of a world marred by sin. Seen in this light, a homosexual disposition could not simply be viewed as neutral. Pastorally, it raises the same sort of difficult issues as the previous approach.

Three: Homosexual behaviour is condemned by Scripture, but we have to manage the gap between the biblical world and our own

4.4.11   The point here is the recognition that part of the Bible's humanity, to which we have referred in Chapter 2, lies in the fact that in the first instance it reflects a particular cultural and historical situation. As we noted in both Chapter 2 and in this chapter, the fact that this cultural and historical situation is not the same as ours means that there is a gap between the biblical world and our own that obviously affects the direct applicability of parts of the biblical material.

4.4.12   For example, in Leviticus 19.9-10 and Deuteronomy 22.8 there is legislation about leaving parts of the harvest for the poor and the sojourner, and putting a parapet round a new house that made direct sense in an ancient Near Eastern context but obviously does not apply directly to us in Britain today.

4.4.13   The general point is uncontroversial, and almost all Christians would apply it in their interpretation of Leviticus 20.13 in that, whatever their views on homosexuality, they would not think it proper to impose the death penalty as a punishment for it, believing that this is one of the 'civil precepts' contained in the Old Testament that are no longer applicable today.[75]

4.4.14   However, where this issue does become controversial is when the suggestion is made that the biblical material on homosexuality as a whole is culturally conditioned and therefore no longer applicable. For example, James Nelson writes:

> The specific New Testament judgments against homosexual practice simply are not relevant to today's debate about the validity of caring,

mutual relationships between consenting adults. Nor does the Bible directly address today's question about the appropriateness of homosexuality as a psychosexual orientation.[76]

4.4.15   This suggestion is rooted in the belief that there is a major difference between the sort of homosexual relationships known to St Paul and the homosexual relationships that are encountered by the Church today.

4.4.16   The argument in favour of this belief runs as follows:

4.4.17   In the Roman world of St Paul's time there was a great variety of homosexual behaviour with slaves and prostitutes and between adult men. These forms included some that would be termed 'a marriage' so it was highly likely that he was familiar with a variety of forms of sexual behaviour. To quote Thiselton: 'We must not underestimate Paul's "worldly knowledge".'[77] However, what distinguished these forms of homosexual behaviour is that they were, in our terms, bisexual. Nearly all the examples that we have, at least in literary sources, refer to people who were married or went on to be married.

4.4.18   The same is true of lesbian behaviour, with which again St Paul would have been familiar. The examples of lesbians refer to women who love one another but who were often married to people of the opposite sex.

4.4.19   So, although we can take it that St Paul condemned a wide range of homosexual behaviour, both male and female, the question remains as to how far this is applicable to Christians who want to make an exclusive lifelong partnership with someone of the same sex and who see this as their Christian vocation. St Paul condemns homosexual behaviour, though he would have been aware that people were attracted to, and could love, members of their own sex. But this behaviour went with an equal capacity for heterosexual activity. We are now faced with a situation where a good number of people believe themselves to be irreversibly of a gay or lesbian orientation. Even allowing for the fact that this may be a cultural construct, as bisexuality, to use our term, was the construct for the ancient Roman world, it is difficult to see how we can do other than take people's sense of themselves with the utmost seriousness. St Paul's view needs to be given the greatest possible weight but it cannot be the only consideration.

4.4.20   This argument rightly draws attention to the fact that bisexuality does appear to have been the prevailing cultural model for homosexual behaviour in the Graeco-Roman world of New Testament times. However, three critical points can also be made in response to this argument.

4.4.21   First, it seems to assume that there was no awareness in the ancient world of the idea of homosexuality as an innate or congenital orientation. However, as Grenz notes:

> . . . this assumption is not as self evident as some would have us believe. Certain thinkers in the Greco-Roman world were aware of a type of constitutional homosexuality, even though they did not understand it in the psychosexual categories in vogue today.[78]

He cites Plato *Symposium* 189d–193d, Ptolemy *Tetrabiblos* III.14 and Phaedrus *The Fables of Phaedrus* 4.15 as examples of texts that seek to explain why some people are attracted to members of their own sex rather than to those of the opposite sex. What the existence of such texts means is that not underestimating St Paul's worldly knowledge means accepting the possibility that he may well have been aware that some people had what we today call a 'homosexual orientation'.

4.4.22   Secondly, there is no evidence in St Paul's writings that he condemned homosexual activity because he believed that those involved were capable of heterosexual activity. This issue never arises. Instead, as we have seen, he condemned homosexual activity because he held that it was contrary to God's design in creation as made known through both nature and Scripture. It is therefore unclear that people's belief that they are incapable of sexual attraction to those of the opposite sex would have any effect on St Paul's argument, since it was not based on people's sexual self-perception.

4.4.23   Thirdly, while we should certainly take people's sense of themselves with the 'utmost seriousness' it would mark a radical break with the Anglican theological tradition if it were to be accepted that this should be given priority over the witness of Holy Scripture when making moral decisions. As we argued in Chapter 2 (2.4.2–2.4.11), according to classical Anglican theology, while we have to give due weight to 'reason' (of which people's sense of themselves forms a part), in the last resort it is the witness of Scripture that is normative in revealing God's will to us.

4.4.24   Another, and more radical, attempt to relativize the witness of Scripture is the suggestion by some gay and lesbian readers of the Bible that the reason for the biblical rejection of homosexuality is the cultural bias of a patriarchal society that saw heterosexual males as the norm. This is, for example, the argument put forward by Gary Comstock in his book *Gay Theology without Apology.*[79]

4.4.25   Comstock argues that in Scripture there is deeply ingrained bias towards heterosexual males as the human norm. This, he says, finds expression in such prominent biblical themes as an emphasis on male lineage and genealogy, an emphasis on women as childbearers and the consequent view of barren women as tragic figures, and the use of harlotry as a metaphor for Israel's corporate sin against God. The biblical stress on the wickedness of lesbians and gay men is simply another outworking of this male heterosexual bias: 'Within such a patriarchal framework lesbians and gay men should not be surprised to find passages that malign us.'[80]

4.4.26   Once again, it has to be admitted that there is an element of truth in this argument. There is no doubt, from a sociological point of view, that, as the product of a patriarchal society, the Bible is patriarchal in form. It is clear, for instance, that the Bible assumes a patriarchal ordering of society, and that for the most part the biblical story develops by an exploration of the activities of male characters.

4.4.27   However, this does not mean that the biblical vision for the relationship between men and women is *fundamentally* patriarchal in nature. As we argued in the last chapter, the inequality between men and women that the Bible reflects is seen by the Bible itself as being a result of the Fall, rather than God's original intention for humanity. In so far as the biblical teaching about homosexuality is rooted in the Bible's fundamental vision of an equal and complementary relationship between women and men as God's ideal, it cannot be said to be an expression of a patriarchal ideology.

Four: Homosexual behaviour is not incompatible with Scripture
4.4.28   Within the broad scope indicated by this heading we can identify two distinct approaches.

4.4.29   The first approach is based on the belief that modern research has shown that the biblical texts that were traditionally understood as condemning homosexual behaviour do not in fact refer to the kind of loving same-sex relationships that are under discussion in the Church today.

4.4.30   As Doe notes, this approach is taken, for example, by those:

> … who still take the Bible very seriously, but who see the New Testament passages as referring to pederasty, prostitution or heterosexual depravity (or a combination of all three) and not to the kind of same-sex loving relationships which may or may not have been around then, but are certainly around today.[81]

4.4.31   As in the case of the last approach, it has to be agreed that this approach is based upon an entirely correct premise, which is that it is right to re-examine traditional views of biblical teaching and to see whether they really correspond to what the text is saying. Christians have been doing this throughout the history of the Church, often with results that subsequent generations of Christians have come to see as shedding fresh light on the biblical material.

4.4.32   Thus Luther reread the biblical teaching about the righteousness of God using the tools of humanist scholarship and with the help of St Augustine, and the result was a major theological breakthrough. Then again, in the eighteenth century, a number of Christians re-examined the biblical material relating to slavery and this led to the now universal acceptance that slavery is contrary to the will of God.

4.4.33   More recently, and more controversially, people have reread the biblical teaching to see what light it throws on the place of women in the life of the Church, and many have come to believe that they have gained fresh insights about the roles that women should play in the life of both society and the Church.

4.4.34   However, acceptance of the principle that it is right to re-examine biblical teaching does not mean that the results of every such re-examination are to be accepted. In this chapter it has been noted that the various suggestions for revising the traditional view of the biblical material have not succeeded in changing the consensus of scholarly opinion about the meaning of the key passages in Leviticus and the New Testament. At the moment, the traditional understanding of these passages remains the most convincing one in the minds of most biblical scholars.

4.4.35   Unless this situation changes, it is difficult to see that an appeal to the revisionist reinterpretation of the passages in question provides an adequate basis for a Church that takes the scholarly reading of Scripture seriously to alter either its traditional teaching about homosexuality or its traditional practice, however much it might seem desirable to do so on the basis of the pastoral considerations noted earlier.

4.4.36   The second approach argues that these texts need to be read in the light of Scripture as a whole, and that if we do this we can find resources within Scripture itself for a different approach to the issue of homosexuality. Two examples illustrate this approach.

4.4.37   The first comes from an unpublished paper by Terry Brown, the Bishop of Malaita in Melanesia, entitled *Further Reflections on Homosexuality, Christian Faith and the Church*. In this paper, Brown argues that the proper starting point for an authentically Anglican interpretation of Scripture is the approach taken by the 1958 Lambeth Conference, which declared that:

> ... our Lord Jesus Christ is God's final Word to man, and that in his light all Holy Scripture must be seen and interpreted, the Old Testament in terms of Promise and the New Testament in terms of Fulfilment.[82]

4.4.38   He then goes on to contend that taking seriously the belief that Scripture must be read in the light of Christ provides the basis for a rereading of Scripture that allows for a positive view of homosexuality:

> The traditionalists will reject any interpretation which disregards an anti-homosexuality text in favour of a positive view of homosexuality based on the broader Gospel message of God's unconditional love for humanity. Yet, from my overall reading of the New Testament, I am convinced that (following the 1958 Lambeth resolution) any particular text of Scripture, as a product of the church, must be interpreted 'in [the] light' of Jesus Christ, 'God's final Word' to humanity. It is on this basis that over the centuries the church has slowly changed its teaching on slavery, democracy, the role of women

in church and society, artificial birth control, divorce and many other areas. I continue to believe that homosexuality is another area where this change is taking place and will continue to take place.

I personally resent this theological position being characterized as 'heretical' or even 'liberal' in the pejorative sense. I believe it is the right, indeed, the orthodox way to interpret Scripture on any issue. It is the way Jesus reinterpreted Jewish Scripture. Jesus deeply distrusted literalism with regard to Scripture. To subject a particular text to 'the light of Jesus Christ, God's final Word to humanity', is not a matter of private inspiration or personal preference but the work of the whole church in prayer and study. The 'light of Jesus Christ', working through the Holy Spirit, has the power to reinterpret Scripture, overturning previous interpretations. On the whole issue of homosexuality, then, I cannot accept the entirely negative view of the traditionalists based on a few specific Biblical texts, often taken out of context. I believe that 'the light of Jesus Christ', fully revealed in Scripture, points towards positive Biblical reinterpretation in the area of homosexuality . . .'[83]

4.4.39   While no one would want to question Brown's basic point that a Christian reading of the Bible must be a reading that is centred on the way in which God has revealed himself in Jesus Christ, there are two problems with Brown's proposal that also need to be noted.

4.4.40   First of all, it is not clear precisely what Brown means by the phrase 'the light of Jesus Christ'. This is because the phrase appears to be used in two different ways.

• On the one hand, it is described as if it were something that stands over against Scripture and in the light of which Scripture is to be interpreted. If this is the case, the question that has to be asked is how we can have knowledge of Jesus Christ except through the prophetic and apostolic witness contained in Holy Scripture.

• On the other hand, the light of Jesus Christ is also said to be 'fully revealed in Scripture'. If this is the case, then the problem is how the light of Christ can be used to interpret Scripture when it is through Scripture (including presumably the texts relating to homosexuality) that the light of Christ is made known to us.

4.4.41   In either case, the fundamental problem remains the same. Brown is attempting to counter a traditionalist appeal to Scripture by an appeal to the 'light of Jesus Christ'. However, an appeal to the light of Christ inevitably ends up in practice as an appeal to a particular interpretation of Scripture, because it is only through Scripture that the light of Christ is made known to us.

4.4.42   Secondly, in context Brown appears to be using the 'light of Jesus Christ' as a synonym for 'the broader Gospel message of God's unconditional love for humanity'. As before, no one is going to deny that the message of the gospel is about 'God's unconditional love for humanity', but an appeal to God's unconditional love cannot in itself help us to decide what we should think about the ethics of homosexuality. This is because at the heart of the debate about homosexuality is in fact a debate about how we understand the love of God and what it means to respond to it appropriately.

4.4.43   Those Christians who take a conservative approach to the homosexuality debate argue, for example, that because God loves human beings he has acted in Christ to set them free from sinful patterns of behaviour, including same-sex sexual activity, and that it is for precisely this reason that Christians are summoned to eschew such activity. This understanding of the nature and implications of the love of God is based on a particular reading of the biblical material and, in order to challenge it, Brown would have to show that it misinterprets the biblical texts to which it appeals. Unless he can show that this is the case then it is unclear that his appeal to the love of God takes his argument any further forward.

4.4.44   The second example of material that appeals to other parts of Scripture as a basis for an alternative approach to homosexuality comes from the book *Faith Beyond Resentment: Fragments Catholic and Gay* by the English Roman Catholic theologian James Alison.

4.4.45   In the course of a reflection on the story of Jonah, he argues that the message that we are called to deliver to the Nineveh of our own day is what he calls: 'an emerging understanding of creation that is tied in with the sense of an utterly gratuitous being-held-in-being over against nothing at all'.[84]

4.4.46   His starting point for this fresh understanding of creation is the words of St Paul in 1 Corinthians 1.26-29:

> Consider your own call, brothers and sisters: not many of you were wise by human standards, not many were powerful, not many were

of noble birth. But God chose what is foolish in the world to shame the wise; God chose what is weak in the world to shame the strong; God chose what is low and despised in the world, things that are not, to reduce to nothing things that are, so that no one might boast in the presence of God.

4.4.47   Alison treats St Paul's paradoxes as referring to homosexual people, and on this basis declares:

> We are in fact set free to reimagine creation starting from our position as ones, who, though a thing that is not, have found ourselves held in being by a force of invincible gratuity depending on nothing at all, part of no argument, simply giving life out of nothing. And this, let it be clear, is not only a permission to jump up and play, but it is also an invitation to rescue a portion of the Good News that has fallen prisoner in Babylon.
>
> There are few more important dimensions of the Good News than the access which it gives us to our Creator as our Father, and to the sense of creation as of a given and undeserved participation in an extraordinary and constructive adventure out of nothing, the shape and fulfilment of which becoming and flourishing is as yet very difficult to discern, the rules and natural laws of which are discovered by its participants as they develop. And, wonder of wonders, we who were treated as 'not-part-of-his creation' are beginning to discover ourselves as 'delighted co-workers in my creation' (cf. Isaiah 62.3-5).
>
> Again, what is extraordinary is that this is not a secret gift to us poor downtrodden queers. But rather that God is using his unspeakable creative vitality to make out of what seemed like an excrescence on the face of creation what it really has been all along: a delighted-in, precious and valuable part of his creation which is able to offer to others a quickening of their awareness of what an adventure it is to be a child created from nothing! You have heard it said, 'The stone which the builders rejected has become the head of the corner' (Psalm 118.22). But I say to you, 'Unless we find ourselves sharing in the being rejected, we have no sense of the coming into being of the head of the corner.' And if that sounds blasphemous, then perhaps it is because God who 'was counted among the transgressors' (Mark 15.28) makes a habit of waving blasphemy like a red cape before the horns of the theological wisdom of the world.[85]

4.4.48   The claim that Alison makes here, that gay and lesbian people are a delighted-in, precious and valuable part of God's creation is, hopefully, a claim that no Christian today would wish to question. As people they are as delighted-in, precious and valuable as anyone else. What is problematic is that Alison goes on to argue that, once we accept that gay and lesbian people are the objects of God's creative activity, this means that there is no fixed order of creation in the light of which we are called to live.

4.4.49   When he describes creation as an: 'extraordinary and constructive adventure ... the rules and natural laws of which are discovered by its participants as they develop', what he is pointing us to is the notion that creation is a continuing process in which there are no fixed moral givens. Alison makes this point clear slightly later on in his book when he argues that the experience that homosexual people have of not fitting into the accepted order of creation has led them to see that this order simply does not exist:

> The result is that we have found ourselves forced through into being the advance guard of a serenity about nothing human being simply 'natural', but everything being part of a human social construct, to the extent where we can begin to imagine God quite removed from any justification of the present order, and yet ever palpitating beneath the vertiginous possibilities of the bringing of a divine order into being. This is likely, increasingly, to be immensely important as straight people face the fragility and directionlessness of what seemed natural, except it be received as an invitation to build something for which the rules of the game are being written as we go along. The collapse of the 'natural' is not the collapse of belief in creation, it is part of clearing the human space of violent idolatry and it allows the persistent gentleness of the Creator and his invitation to adventurous participation to become apparent.[86]

4.4.50   It is clear that Alison's argument here is a powerful piece of apologetic for the acceptance of homosexuality. If nothing is natural, then it cannot be said that homosexual activity is wrong because it is contrary to nature. If God is constantly bringing a new divine order into being why should this not be a divine order in which homosexuality is acceptable? However, powerful though this apologetic is, there are serious difficulties with it.

4.4.51   It is obvious that we need to be careful about what we claim to be natural. Alison is quite right to note, for example, that there are institutions such as slavery or a hierarchical ordering of society that were once seen as part of the natural order of things, but which we now see to be human social constructs. However, it is not clear that there is *nothing* natural and God given, but that *everything* is in a state of constant flux with the rules changing as the game proceeds.

4.4.52   The teaching of Scripture as well as the tradition of the Church does seem to suggest that there is a natural order to which human behaviour is meant to correspond. This becomes clear, for example, in Jesus' teaching about marriage and divorce in Mark 10.2-9. As we saw in Chapter 3, the basis of Jesus' argument with the Pharisees is precisely that there is a fixed order in creation, which means that men and women are meant to be joined to each other as one flesh for life. This is not just a human construct, it is something God given. Likewise, in 1 Corinthians 11.2-16, St Paul is concerned that the Corinthians should observe the God-given order of creation in which there is a distinction between the sexes.

4.4.53   This idea of a natural order to which human behaviour is meant to correspond is central to what the Bible has to say about homosexual behaviour. As we have seen in this chapter, the fundamental objection to homosexuality in the biblical writings seems to be precisely that it is contrary to nature, in the sense that it crosses the boundaries for appropriate sexual behaviour established by God at creation.

Five: Compatibility with Scripture is not the only consideration

4.4.54   What this would mean would be acknowledging what the Bible teaches but saying that the Bible alone cannot have the final word on the matter. There are three reasons why this is now argued.

4.4.55   The first reason is a belief that the biblical material simply does not give clear enough guidance to form a proper basis for our evaluation of homosexuality.

4.4.56   This is the position taken by John Habgood, for instance, in his recently published Gifford Lectures *The Concept of Nature*. As part of a wider discussion about the application of the principles of natural law to the issue of human sexuality, he argues that Churches engaged in debate about homosexuality should concentrate on issues arising out of consideration of natural law: 'such as intimacy, fraternity, fidelity, knowledge and sympathy for one another, and spiritual values'[87] rather than basing their discussions on the biblical material. This is because, in his view:

> Among modern biblical scholars, interpretation of the relevant biblical passages has proved to be highly controversial, thus making them unpromising material for an appeal to unequivocal religious tradition.[88]

4.4.57   As we have seen, it is indeed the case that there has been controversy about the meaning of the biblical texts relating to homosexuality. However, it is not clear that this means that we cannot appeal to the Bible for unequivocal teaching about the subject. Before we can say this we have to decide whether the controversy is caused by the fact that the texts really are ambiguous, or whether the meaning of the texts is clear and the controversy is caused by the fact that some people have either misread them, or simply do not wish to accept what they are saying.

4.4.58   The second reason is what is claimed to be the scientific knowledge we now have about the origins and nature of homosexuality. It is argued that we now know that homosexuality is not something that people choose but is an innate condition. This means, it is said, that it must be regarded as natural. As such it is part of the diversity of God's creation and something to affirm and celebrate rather than deplore or condemn.

4.4.59   Thus Bishop John Spong argues that science has shown that homosexuality is a natural phenomenon that is not chosen by the people concerned and that this fact should shape the judgement we make about it:

> When a homosexual orientation is revealed by the development of the science of the brain and its neurochemical processes to be a normal part of the sexual spectrum of human life, a given and not a chosen way of life, then it becomes inhuman to use a person's sexual orientation as the basis for a continuing prejudice. Therefore, the kind of judgment that compromises the worth and well-being of a homosexual person or places limits on the opportunities of that person becomes the activity of ignorance.[89]

4.4.60   This argument may be difficult to sustain for two reasons.

4.4.61 First, the jury is still out on the cause(s) of homosexuality. Spong's argument is based on a belief that science has established a biological basis for homosexuality, but this is by no means universally accepted by those working in the field.

4.4.62 The present state of research into the origins of homosexuality is well summarized by William Byrne and Bruce Parsons:

> Recent studies postulate biological factors as the primary basis for sexual orientation. However, there is no evidence at present to substantiate a biological theory, just as there is no compelling evidence to support any singular psychosocial explanation.[90]

4.4.63 What makes the issue even more complex is the fact that homosexuality is itself a pluriform phenomenon. For the sake of convenience we have talked about 'homosexuality' in the singular, but arguably the evidence provided by scholars such as Greenberg[91] points to the fact that the term properly refers to a whole range of different forms of same-sex relationships.

4.4.64 The problem with talking about 'homosexual orientation' as if this was a fixed phenomenon across all cultures is that a lifelong exclusive attraction to people of the same sex is only one of these different forms of homosexuality. What is just as, if not more, common is people experiencing both heterosexual and homosexual attraction or moving between phases of heterosexual and homosexual attraction depending on their own personal circumstances or the expectations of their particular culture.[92]

4.4.65 In fact, it can be persuasively argued that the category of 'homosexuals' is only useful in so far as it gives us a collective term to describe people who engage in same-sex sexual activity. This makes any 'essentialist' argument that there is a single, fixed cause for homosexuality very difficult to accept, and indeed many homosexuals themselves, particularly lesbians, would want to say that same-sex relationships are something that they choose rather than a response to an inescapable 'orientation'.

4.4.66 Furthermore, even if agreement were reached about what causes homosexuality, this would not in itself determine the ethical status of homosexual activity. This is a point that is well made by Stanton Jones in his essay 'Identity in Christ and Sexuality':

Some argue that acting on homosexual desires cannot be wrong if homosexual orientation develops due to factors beyond the control or choice of the individual. Research on the etiology or causation of the homosexual condition has made some striking advances. The current state of that research might be summarised in three key points – that biological factors may contribute to the development of this proclivity for some people; that there is credible evidence that psychological factors contribute as well; and that simplistic models of causation that focus only on one variable are inadequate. When we examine the research we are forced to think in terms of multiple contributing causal factors. Similar research on other human problems, such as drunkenness and violence, which have clear moral implications has suggested that many different types of factors, including the genetic, can contribute to the development of these patterns. Such research does not answer the moral question – 'should a person who finds himself or herself with such proclivities indulge them?' We each may have received a genetic and/or biological and/or environmental push towards any number of unfortunate proclivities. Understanding those influences may increase our understanding and compassion, and may shape our pastoral response to those conditions, but knowledge of what causes homosexual orientation is irrelevant to the question of whether or not it is right to engage in homosexual behaviour.[93]

4.4.67   The third reason that people feel compatibility with Scripture is not the only consideration is because biblical teaching runs counter to their own moral intuition, and they believe that this moral intuition must be given priority over Scripture. This point is made, for example, by Richard Holloway in his recent book *Godless Morality*:

> ... we no longer treat an injunction from scripture as having moral authority over us simply because it is in scripture. It has to have moral force independent of its scriptural context. We judge scripture by our own best moral standards, not the other way round. We now do this in most areas except the area of sexual behaviour. We must find the honesty and courage to apply this criterion of authenticity to the tangled area of human sexuality.[94]

4.4.68   This approach is certainly one that we need to take seriously since it reflects the approach by many people both outside and inside the Church, and it resonates with the traditional Anglican concern that Scripture should be read in the light of reason, that is to say with reference to the intellectual and moral convictions of contemporary society.

4.4.69   It also has to be remembered that, as we have already acknowledged earlier in this report, it is sometimes the moral convictions of the wider society (partly formed by Christian conscience) that have subsequently proved right, rather than what was put forward at the time as Christian truth. For what is put forward is always a selective truth, seen in a particular light. There are other truths to be uncovered or set in a different context. The interaction between what the Church teaches and the moral convictions of the society in which it is set are too subtle and too varied to allow for a simple countercultural 'no'.

4.4.70   However, by suggesting that our moral intuition is to be the judge of Scripture rather than the other way round, this approach goes against the theological approach outlined in Chapter 2 of this report and traditionally accepted by the Church of England. Taken to its logical conclusion it would mean that the Bible would cease to have a normative function in our ethics and would merely be used to affirm what we already believe on other grounds.

4.4.71   It might seem very tempting for the Church of England to go down this route because it is the route that our contemporary culture finds most congenial. However, if it did so it would be difficult to see how this would be compatible with the affirmations of the authority of the Bible that have been a consistent feature of the Anglican tradition and the Anglican formularies, and it would mean that the Church of England had departed in this respect from the orthodox Christian tradition.

4.5 Conclusion

4.5.1   In this chapter we have reviewed the biblical material that has shaped the approach of the Christian tradition to homosexuality.

In the light of this review it would seem that, while there is room for a legitimate debate about the interpretation of the texts concerned, and while some of the texts (such as Genesis 19, and Deuteronomy 23) address issues that are not directly relevant to the current debate, nevertheless the hermeneutical principles set out in Chapter 2, and the consensus of biblical scholarship, still point us in the direction of the Church's traditional reading of the biblical material.

4.5.2   If we accept the traditional reading of the biblical material, it follows that the conclusion reached by *Issues in Human Sexuality* back in 1991 still remains valid as a summary of the biblical position on human sexuality:

> There is ... in Scripture an evolving convergence on the ideal of lifelong, monogamous, heterosexual union as the setting intended by God for the proper development of men and women as sexual beings. Sexual activity of any kind outside marriage comes to be seen as sinful, and homosexual practice as especially dishonourable. It is also recognised that God may call some to celibacy for particular service in his cause. Only by living within these boundaries are Christians to achieve that holiness which is pleasing to God.[95]

4.5.3   However, even if we accept the 1991 statement as a valid summary of the biblical material, the question of how we should respond to this material still remains.

4.5.4   We have noted five ways of responding to the material, each of which has its own strengths and each of which raises its own problems. In deciding how to react to them there are three key points that we need to bear in mind.

1. It is not possible to hold that these are all equally valid responses to the biblical material. They are incompatible with each other and therefore we have to make a choice between them.

2. We cannot allow either the pastoral issues highlighted under response one or the Church's traditional position on homosexuality to skew our reading of the biblical text or our interpretation of its message. Although it is always very tempting to allow our reading and interpretation of Scripture to be shaped by pastoral concerns or theological tradition, we must seek as objectively as possible to understand what the Bible itself says before considering how this relates to Church tradition or pastoral need.

3. Our final decision on how to read and interpret the biblical material has to be based on the theological principles set out in Chapter 2. We need to apply those principles to the biblical text and then ask which of the responses to the biblical material outlined above seems most valid as a result.

chapter 5

Gender identity, sexual identity and theology

5.1 Introduction

5.1.1   In the previous chapter we looked at the contemporary debate about the interpretation of the biblical texts relating to homosexuality. As we indicated in Chapter 1, however, this debate about the interpretation of biblical texts has to be understood in the wider context of the societal shifts that have caused attitudes towards sexuality and sexual behaviour to change in the modern era. In this chapter we shall explore this wider context in more detail by exploring a number of significant intellectual and political developments within the last few decades, focusing on the rise of the feminist and gay and lesbian movements, and the development of lesbian theology.

5.1.2   We shall look at how the insights from these movements have both challenged and been incorporated into the mainstream of orthodox theology, and how, in some cases, lost traditions have been recovered from the history of Christianity and brought again to light.

5.1.3   We shall also consider both the critical questions that these new ways of thinking raise for traditional Christian theology and also the critical questions that can in turn be asked about these new ways of thinking themselves.

5.2 The quest for rights

5.2.1   In seeking to understand the development of modern rights movements, including feminist, gay and lesbian movements, a number of historians have traced their origins to the Enlightenment discussion about human rights.

5.2.2   In their view, a new understanding of equality and universal rights emerged at the Enlightenment and, in the aftermath of the American and French Revolutions, for example, was put into practice. However, despite the talk of universal rights, not everyone was given rights. Women were excluded and, in America, so, of course, were slaves.

5.2.3   Modern feminism emerged in response to this exclusion of
women from the rights promised at the Enlightenment. For example,
in the 1790s, after the French Revolution (which many saw, at least
initially, as the culmination of Enlightenment ideals), women like
Olympe de Gouges in France, in her *Declaration of the Rights of Woman
and the Female Citizen*, and Mary Wollstonecraft in Britain, in her
Vindication of the Rights of Woman,[1] argued that women should have
equal rights with men.

5.2.4   Modern feminism has often been seen as opposed to
Christianity but, in fact, until recently it was often closely intertwined
with Christianity. Wollstonecraft, for example, argued for equal rights
for men and women on religious grounds, appealing to the eternal
truths of a wise, good and reasonable God, urging men to allow women
to become who God had created them to be.[2]

5.2.5   Feminism remained engaged with Christianity throughout the
nineteenth century and early twentieth century. Feminists such as Sarah
Grimke and her sister Angelina, in America, argued from a Christian
position that women and men are 'both made in the image of God;
dominion was given to both over every other creature, but not over
each other'.[3] Others, such as Elizabeth Cady Stanton, advocated for
women's rights and made a critique of the patriarchal nature of the
biblical texts in her *The Woman's Bible*.[4] Many of these American
feminists also worked with free blacks in the north towards the
abolition of slavery, again on Christian grounds of equality. Similarly,
in Britain, many of those who were in the forefront of the movement
for women's rights – such as Quakers – also worked towards the
abolition of the slave trade and slavery.

5.2.6   The power base for both feminism and the abolition
movements was, therefore, the churches. This was true in both America
and Britain in the nineteenth century. Those Christians who supported
these movements saw the Enlightenment discourse on human rights as
supported by, and in turn supportive of, the biblical teaching that all
human beings are equal before God regardless of their race or sex.

5.2.7   In the second half of the twentieth century a new impetus was
given to movements for human and civil rights in the West. This was a
working out of the Enlightenment legacy, for not everyone yet enjoyed
those universal rights. In the 1950s and 60s, the Civil Rights movement

in the United States emerged and retained its Christian links, largely working from the power base of the Black Churches – as illustrated by the fact that the movement's leader, Martin Luther King, was a Baptist minister.

5.2.8   The Women's Rights movement followed in the wake of the Civil Rights movement. However, by this time, feminism had taken a secular turn, indicated in the groundbreaking feminist work of Simone de Beauvoir, *The Second Sex,* published in the mid twentieth century, which was highly critical of the Church in its treatment of women.[5] There remained, of course, feminists within the Christian tradition, but by now feminism was seen as a largely secular movement and this impression was reinforced by feminism's dovetailing with the 'Sexual Revolution'.

5.2.9   The movement for gay and lesbian equality emerged at this same time, precipitated in America by the police raid of a bar called Stonewall in New York City in 1969 (when homosexual activity was still illegal), when gays and lesbians, perhaps for the first time, seriously fought back. This event is usually regarded as the founding moment of the modern movement for homosexual rights. The theologian Mary Hunt describes its significance as follows:

> When gays first fought back against police at the Stonewall bar on New York's Christopher Street in 1969, they opened up a new era for homosexuals. No longer were same-sex relationships simply the stuff of back rooms and Mafia-run bars. Homosexuals were persons with dignity and (eventually) legal rights equal to all others.[6]

5.2.10   At the Enlightenment there had been no such impulse for homosexual rights – as there had been for slaves and women – and so the gay and lesbian rights movement has developed more recently, and has been largely secular in tone. However, the movements that developed in the 1970s and 80s – often described as gay pride and gay liberation – made the civil rights of gay, lesbian and bisexual peoples a matter of public discourse. More recently, the debates that emerged from those movements have had an impact on public policy in both the USA and Britain. In Britain, for example, we have seen both the lowering of the age of consent for homosexual men in order to make it equal with that for heterosexual men and, conversely, we have also seen legislation prohibiting the promotion of homosexuality in schools under section 28 of the Local Government Act.

5.2.11 Some Christians would argue that the demand by gay, bisexual and lesbian people for full human and civil rights both inside and outside the Church should be supported on theological grounds.

5.2.12 They appeal to the teaching of Genesis 1.26-27, that all human beings are made in the image and likeness of God (regardless of sexual orientation and the *practice* of it), and to Paul's statement in Galatians 3.28, that there is no difference between human beings in Christ. They also contend that Paul's statement must be lived out as a reality in the body of Christ; and that the commandment to love our neighbours as ourselves is the foundation of our relationship with God and central to our life in Christ.

5.2.13 What they are doing is taking the same *theological* arguments made by feminists for the equal rights of women, and by those in the civil rights movement for African-Americans, and applying them to gay, lesbian and bisexual (and indeed transsexual/transgender) people. In this line of argument a Christian anthropology and the biblical notion of justice mesh with the Enlightenment notion of the human person as reasonable and reasoning, equal with his or her neighbour, and entitled to full human and civil rights.

5.2.14 Conversely, as we have seen, there are those in the Christian Churches who argue that a different kind of fidelity to the biblical witness – discussed at length in the last chapter – means that Christians should oppose some of the demands made by those campaigning for gay and lesbian rights. For example, many would object to the recognition of gay and lesbian partnerships by either the Church or the State and would argue that it is right that the Church should bar practising homosexuals from the exercise of ordained ministry. Here, a Christian anthropology finds itself in opposition to the Enlightenment arguments for *universal* rights.

5.2.15 The Christian Churches – while being bound up in the modern impulse for, and at times supporting, full human rights – therefore have a complicated relationship to the modern human rights movement, as witnessed by the Churches' desire to be exempt from some aspects of human rights legislation in recent years in Britain.[7]

5.2.16 The critical challenge that the contemporary discussion of human rights presents to traditional Christian thinking lies in the fact that, for many people both inside and outside the Church, the Church's stand on this issue lacks credibility.

5.2.17   As we saw in Chapter 1, contemporary society has tended to emphasize the freedom of individuals to pursue their search for personal happiness and fulfilment and within this context their freedom to enjoy any kind of consensual sexual activity that they feel appropriate.

5.2.18   The right to pursue personal happiness in this way has come to be widely regarded as an integral part of people's human rights and, therefore, when the Church proclaims a Christian commitment to human rights and yet rejects certain forms of sexual activity, it is seen as being hypocritical and discriminatory.

5.2.19   This challenge needs to be taken seriously, but critical questions can also be asked about it.

5.2.20   First, there is the question of how one balances conflicting claims to the exercise of 'rights'. A classic example of this question is provided by the issue of abortion. On the one hand it can be argued that a woman should have the right to decide whether or not she wishes to have a baby and on the other hand it can be argued that the unborn foetus has a right to life. The appeal to rights does not help because rights can be claimed on both sides of the issue. In a parallel fashion, the right of people to freedom of sexual expression has to be balanced against the right of other people to teach and act according to their particular religious convictions. Once again, rights can be claimed on both sides.

5.2.21   What this means is that the Church is not necessarily being hypocritical or inconsistent when it supports some rights and not others. It is making a choice about which claims concerning rights it supports and which it does not, and this is something that individuals and society as a whole have to do all the time. There is, of course, room for argument about whether the choice the Church has made has been the right one, but that is a different issue.

5.2.22   Secondly, there is the question of how one balances the rights of individuals against the common good. As we noted in Chapter 3, Christians have held that the traditional pattern of family life is that which is most conducive to the flourishing of society as a whole, and the question might therefore be asked as to whether they might not be justified in rejecting patterns of sexual relationship that they see as undermining family life.

5.2.23 Thirdly, there is the question of biblical interpretation. Is it legitimate to appeal to Genesis 1.26 and Galatians 3.28 as supporting the right of gay and lesbian people to freedom of sexual self-expression given the range of other biblical teaching about human sexual activity that we have explored in the last two chapters?

5.3 The human person: gender identity/sexual identity

5.3.1 Questions of identity have been absolutely central to modern understandings of women and men, the family and household, and heterosexuality, homosexuality and bisexuality. The turning point for modern discussions of human identity, or personhood, was the Enlightenment, and some modern scholars have argued that questions about identity have been more bound up with the question of rights than we previously thought.

5.3.2 A number of scholars have suggested in recent years that it was at the Enlightenment that modern notions of sexual difference – of women and men as *distinctly* different from each other – emerged, and that this shift was accompanied by the new idea that our sexuality is a part of our identity, that we *are* homosexual or heterosexual, rather than simply engaging in same-sex or opposite-sex sexual activity, for example.

5.3.3 In the view of these scholars, until the eighteenth century, scientists understood the physical human body in the medical terms of two ancient sources: Galen and Aristotle. They understood there to be one basic model for the human being. The better version of this model was male, the lesser female.

5.3.4 Woman was the imperfect version of man. A woman's sexual organs were understood to be a man's, but internal rather than external; because of a lack of heat in generation, woman's sexual organs remained internal. As a German doctor in the sixteenth century put it, 'Viewing the uterus along with its appendages, it corresponds in every respect to the male member except that the latter is outside and the former inside.' Woman was incomplete because colder and moister, in a system where hot and dry were perfect. Anatomical drawings up until the eighteenth century indicate that this understanding of human nature prevailed in scientific and popular treatises. The historian, Thomas Laqueur, has called this the 'one-sex model'.[8]

5.3.5   According to these scholars, this meant that, before the modern period, people lived with a more fluid understanding of gender. Some medieval historians have argued, for instance, that Christians in the Middle Ages were able to conceive of, and relate to, Christ as both 'female' and 'male' precisely because of the fluidity allowed along the axis of the 'one-sex' model. The historian Caroline Walker Bynum, looking at paintings of the period and analysing the affective spirituality of, for example, the Cistercians in the late Middle Ages, has suggested that the blood shed by Christ was seen as analogous to menstrual blood; the bleeding Christ on the cross was also seen as the nursing mother of humankind; the leakage from the wound in Christ's side was parallel with the breast milk of Mary.[9]

5.3.6   The less attractive side of the 'one-sex' model, from their point of view, is that it reflected and was embedded in a deeply hierarchical society. The order of society, it is argued, was literally patriarchal (patriarchy means 'the rule of the fathers'). In the universe as a whole, God the Father ruled over all. In the state, the king was the head of the nation. In the household – which was not the family, the private entity of the modern period, but rather a social and public institution, a microcosm of the state – the father/husband/master ruled the children, wife and servants.

5.3.7   In the eighteenth century, these scholars say, a shift occurred. Men and women came to be seen as distinctly and biologically different from each other. We might, from a modern viewpoint, assume that at last modern science began to get it right. However, this is only part of the story.

5.3.8   As we noted earlier, the eighteenth century also witnessed the birth of a new discourse about equality and rights. It was only in that context, it is contended, that people began to be interested in looking at the physical and anatomical differences between women and men. For while some women such as Wollstonecraft argued strongly that political and civil rights should be extended to women, few people took this claim seriously. As the historian Londa Schiebinger puts it, 'How were Enlightenment thinkers to justify the inequality of women in the newly envisioned democratic order?'[10]

5.3.9   Historians such as Schiebinger and Laqueur have suggested that one answer to this question was the development of the two-sex model; that is, women and men were now thought to be fundamentally different from each other. On those grounds, women could be, and were, excluded from civil and political rights. As women throughout the nineteenth century pleaded their cause – especially for education and the vote – scientists produced more and more 'evidence' that women were inherently different from men in their anatomy, physiology, temperament and intellect, and this made them unfit to enjoy and exercise such rights. These arguments about women's 'natural' inferiority carried weight because they were brought forward as 'science' but as the historian of science, Cynthia Russet, puts it, 'The situation was one in which a truly modest quantity of reliable data was made to support a formidable body of theory.'[11]

5.3.10   Indeed, supporting the notion that science is very much embedded in culture, Laqueur points to the fact that, although the idea that men and women are different from each other was much propounded in the mid to late eighteenth century, the scientific discoveries that would support it were not made until much later – for example, the significance of ovulation in women was not understood until the nineteenth century.

5.3.11   It is also argued that the idea of women as different from, but complementary to, men also began to prevail at this time or, as Schiebinger puts it, this period saw the 'the triumph of complementarity'.[12] That is, women and men were (and are) perceived as *naturally* having different traits and characteristics from each other.

5.3.12   As we indicated in Chapter 3, it would therefore be argued by many historians that complementarity is such a modern concept that it could not possibly have existed in the mindset of the author of Genesis nor in the societal (hierarchical) structure of the day. To see the 'complementarity' of the sexes in the Genesis creation accounts is merely to map a modern idea back onto an older text.

5.3.13   As was noted at the beginning of this section, it has been further argued by some historians that, if it is indeed the case that people began to think more firmly or clearly in terms of the difference between men and women in the eighteenth century, then this goes some way to explaining why homosexuality and heterosexuality began to emerge as identities at that time. For it is only when that difference becomes more fixed – as opposed to the gender 'fluidity' experienced in the Middle Ages, for example – that attention comes to be focused on that which 'opposes' the difference, namely, same-sex activity and love. Thus the notion of sexual identity began to emerge.

5.3.14   Of course, sodomy was always illegal, between men, between women and men, and even between women as one or two cases (usually unsuccessful in their prosecution) illustrate. But sodomy was simply a sexual *activity*. What emerged from the eighteenth century onwards, it is said, was the new idea that those who engaged in sexual activity with someone of the same sex had a distinct identity, as did someone who engaged in opposite-sex activity, which was, of course, the norm – and legal.[13]

5.3.15   Certainly, in the nineteenth century, many scientists began to explore, explain, analyse and even pathologize the 'homosexual' or 'invert' as a person, male or female, with a distinctly different sexual identity, usually considered abnormal. One historian has explained this change in terms of sexuality going from a verb to a noun.[14]

5.3.16   The theologian and ethicist Linda Woodhead explains it like this.

> Part of a distinctly modern conceptuality, 'sexuality' is understood as an endowment of the individual, a key aspect of individual identity; to say that one is homosexual, heterosexual or bisexual is to say something about who one is quite as much as it is to say something about the other(s) to whom one relates

and she goes on to note that:

> 'Sexuality' is a term that has only recently become current. According to the OED it first appears in 1800 within scientific discourse and in application to lower life forms. It is first applied to a human being in 1879.[15]

5.3.17   For feminists, the shifts in thought that took place at the Enlightenment meant that they were always arguing for equal rights in one of two ways: either by arguing that men and women were (are) equal, with no differences between them; or by taking the argument that women were (are) indeed different from men, and morally superior. Both lines of argument can be seen amongst the suffragists and suffragettes campaigning for the vote in the late nineteenth century and early twentieth century,[16] and in contemporary feminist theory.

5.3.18   Indeed, it can be argued that, to enjoy rights, a person has to have a public identity to which rights can be accorded, and the emergence of the civil rights movement, women's rights movement and gay/lesbian movement in the latter half of the twentieth century all illustrate attempts by different groups to achieve such an identity. However, because of the controversial ways in which both notions of sexual difference and homosexuality came to be defined in the nineteenth century especially – that is, not, on the whole by any women or by gay men and lesbians themselves – debates have raged about the meanings of both gendered identity and sexual identity. These groups have felt the need to (re)claim their identity strongly both in their fight for rights and in order to name themselves.

5.3.19   However, the question of what constitutes female identity or gay identity has been controversial and a matter of much debate amongst feminists and gays and lesbians. Some have even gone so far as to suggest that as a society we are obsessed with such questions of gendered and sexual identity. For example, Luce Irigaray, the French philosopher, has argued that sexual difference is a particular 'fixation' of the modern period. She writes, in almost-theological terms:

> Sexual difference is one of the major philosophical issues, if not the issue, of our age. According to Heidegger, each age has one issue to think through, and one only. Sexual difference is probably the issue in our time which could be our 'salvation' if we thought it through.[17]

What is certain is that it has haunted feminist writing of the last few decades, and continues to be an issue of contention within a much broader context and at a popular level.

5.3.20   Some contemporary feminists propose an 'essentialist' view of women (and men), that is, the idea that women and men have *essential* or *natural* characteristics as women and men; this takes the notion of the difference and complementarity of the sexes and attempts to reclaim it by valorizing the qualities considered 'feminine' – such as nurturing – for feminist purposes. It also often celebrates the 'bodiliness' of women. While there are some high-profile feminists who take this line, most notably Mary Daly in the USA and some of the women known as the 'French feminists' such as Hélène Cixous, this view tends to be in the minority.

5.3.21   The majority of feminist thinkers would point to the ways in which those characteristics designated as 'masculine' or 'feminine' vary over time and place, and therefore cannot be seen as 'natural' or universal. Historians and anthropologists have been particularly important in indicating the ways in which understandings of masculinity and femininity – what we call gender – are cultural and social constructions. As Simone de Beauvoir famously put it, in *The Second Sex*: 'One is not born but rather becomes a woman.'[18]

5.3.22   The work of the American feminist, Judith Butler, especially in her book *Gender Trouble*,[19] has been especially influential in recent years, in suggesting that gender is 'performative' – that is, our understandings of what it means to be a man or a woman need to be reiterated or performed again and again, in order to take effect. She would argue that there is nothing natural in the meanings that we attribute to 'masculinity' or 'femininity'.

5.3.23   This means that there is currently great intellectual uncertainty about what we mean when we speak about what women and men are, and that feminists are engaged in a long-standing debate about sameness vs. difference, reflected at a popular level in numerous newspaper and magazine articles, and popular discussions of science.

5.3.24   One feminist response to this sameness/difference debate is to suggest that sexual difference is but one difference of many, between women, and between men. This leads to the conclusion that, while at present we often construe sexual difference as a key differentiating factor between people, we should instead learn to see it as simply one difference amongst many.

5.3.25   These recent intellectual discussions of gender also throw up a number of questions for the discussion of transsexualism (a topic that we shall look at in more detail in Chapter 7). As we shall see, transsexuals base their arguments for a change of sex on the notion that biological sex and all the attributes that are said to reside in masculinity or femininity, have fixed meanings. Transsexuals rely on a firm notion of sexual difference in their understanding of their own identity as the 'wrong' sex. In that sense, it could be argued that the transsexual is a product of modernity – not only in the scientific technology that enables a 'sex change' but also in the conceptual ideas (absolute sexual difference) behind their very identity as transsexual people.

5.3.26 More recently, the notion of 'transgender' has developed, which covers not only pre- and post-operative transsexuals, but various others: those who choose to live as the opposite sex from that into which they were born (without seeking sex reassignment surgery); the inter-sexed – those with the characteristics of both sexes, usually born with indeterminate genitals; and those who choose to live within both genders or as a 'third gender'. The term transgender suggests a more fluid notion of gender and avoids the thorny question of biology. In the most recent edition of the OED (2002, online), it is defined as 'relating to, or designating, a person whose identity does not conform unambiguously to conventional notions of male or female gender, but combines or moves between these'.

5.3.27 Thus far, we have been using the terms 'sex' and 'gender' rather loosely but, before concluding this section, some more rigorous discussion in the light of our comments so far may be helpful.

5.3.28 It has generally been understood, especially amongst feminist intellectuals, that gender refers to those attributes described as 'feminine' or 'masculine' that change over time and place because they are culturally and socially (some would also say, psychically) constructed. Those attributes do not say much to us about what women and men are essentially, but they tell us something about how women and men have been understood and expected to behave at a certain moment in history, in a certain place and context.

5.3.29 By contrast, sex has generally been taken as a fixed, biological category, as the physical reality of what it means to be a man and woman.

5.3.30 However, the work of historians such as Laqueur, which we have referred to above, makes potentially problematic this otherwise rather useful distinction between gender and sex for, in charting the shift from the one-sex model to the two-sex model, Laqueur points to the ways in which cultural understandings of women and men have in fact had an impact on how men and women were physically described and in influencing how the notion of sexual difference – two sexes –

came to be predominant in the modern era. That is, both gender and sex are influenced by culture. In a way, he is making the simple point that culture does affect science. The problems opened up by this argument are illustrated by the use of language in speaking about transsexuals – for whom the fixed biological category of 'sex' undergirds their very identity – and hence the term 'transgender' has come into being.

5.3.31   As we indicated in the last chapter, a similar debate about nature vs. nurture with regard to homosexuality is also very much alive within the scientific world, and in gay and lesbian communities. Is homosexuality something with which a person is born? Or is homosexuality a matter of cultural influence? And what repercussions would either have, if we could know for sure?

5.3.32   For example, there has been much debate in the last decade about whether there is a 'gay gene'. In 1993, biologist Dean Hamer of the National Cancer Institute in the USA found that, in 40 pairs of gay brothers, 33 had the same set of DNA sequences of the chromosome called Xq28. This was heralded, by those seeking human rights for gays and lesbians, as evidence that homosexuality is something innate to the person. George Rice, an Ontario neurologist, later examined the DNA of 52 pairs of gay brothers and found that their Xq28 sequences were no more similar than what might be expected from sheer chance. This was heralded, by those opposed to giving rights to gay men and lesbians, and by those seeking to 'convert' homosexuals to heterosexuality, as proving that homosexuality is not inborn.

5.3.33   This is a very controversial area, and those two studies were so small that their evidence was, in both cases, inconclusive. Furthermore, learning from the historians of science cited above, we would need to ask: how much does culture play a part in the ways in which scientific research is initiated, carried out and interpreted?

5.3.34   The challenge that the historical research we have just surveyed presents to Christian thinking about human sexuality is twofold:

- First, this research challenges us to reflect on the question of the extent to which Christian thinking in this area has been based on culturally specific understandings of sex and gender that may no longer be universally accepted today.

- Secondly, and more radically, a number of scholars have argued that, once we recognize that the idea of a clear differentiation between the sexes is a cultural construction rather than something that is simply given, this opens up the possibility of thinking about such differences in a new way. It has been suggested, for example, that we should think of a spectrum of sexual identity rather than a clear binary division between male and female and that homosexuality, bisexuality and transsexualism should be accepted as part of this spectrum.

5.3.35 In turn a number of critical responses to the theories about the nature and development of sexual identity that we have just looked at can be made from a Christian perspective.

5.3.36 First, it can be asked how accurate some of the historical reconstruction involved is. For example, is it really the case that it was only in the eighteenth century that people came to see men and women as distinctively and biologically different from each other? Does not the abundant evidence we have that people in the Middle Ages saw men and women as physically, emotionally and even spiritually different in a whole host of ways suggest that Laqueur's 'one-sex' model was, in fact, simply a different way of expressing physical sexual difference on the basis of the prevailing understanding of human anatomy?

5.3.37 Then again, although the use of terms such as 'homosexual' and 'heterosexual' may be modern, we have already suggested in the previous chapter that as far back as classical antiquity people were aware that there were certain individuals who had an innate attraction to members of their own sex and therefore, although the term 'homosexual' may be recent, the idea that lies behind it may be an ancient one.

5.3.38 Secondly, as we suggested in Chapters 1 and 3 above, it is possible to argue that the book of Genesis does in fact teach the complementarity (the 'equality in difference') of men and women and that, on the basis of its teaching, a belief in complementarity has always been a part of orthodox Christian theology, even though this belief has frequently been distorted by a hierarchical view of the male–female relationship.

5.3.39 Thirdly, from a Christian perspective, while it may be both interesting and important to see how people have construed sexual identity in different cultures and in different historical epochs, we need to remind ourselves that the Christian claim is that our identities as human beings are fundamentally determined, not by human social construction, but by the creative and redemptive activity of God. This is a point that we have already made in Chapter 3 with reference to the words of the *St Andrew's Day Statement* on human sexuality:

> There can be no description of human reality, in general or in particular outside the reality of Christ. We must be on guard, therefore, against constructing any other ground for our identities than the redeemed humanity given us in him.[20]

What this claim suggests is that we have to try to assess the various claims that have been made about the nature of men and women as sexual beings and try to see how well they match up to what has been revealed to us about our true identity given to us in Christ. More specifically, this means we still need to wrestle with the biblical material we have looked at in Chapters 3 and 4 and ask what this tells us about the nature of our identity as women and men and how God wishes us to behave on the basis of it.

5.4 The impact of the search for identity on theology

a. Gay theologies

5.4.1   In the last few decades, there has been a proliferation of theologies built on identity, written by peoples previously excluded from the theological discourse. Most obviously, we can point to the rise of Latin American Liberation Theology in the 1970s, beginning with Gustavo Gutierrez's *A Theology of Liberation*,[21] which advocated that theology be done from the standpoint of the poor, and that Christianity should primarily be about solidarity with the poor. We could add to this the rise of Black Theology in the USA in the wake of the Civil Rights movement, and the rise of feminist theology in the USA and Western Europe following the rise of the modern women's movement. Not surprisingly, gay and lesbian theology emerged in these decades too, as a form of liberation theology.

5.4.2   Identity or personhood is at the heart of all these 'liberation theologies' for they are about the liberation of certain marginalized peoples in the name of biblical justice. This poses a considerable challenge to prevailing notions of Christian anthropology. Groups of people that have been traditionally excluded from (formal) Christian theology have come to suggest that the prevalent ideas about their personhood in the Churches and in traditional Christian theology do not match their experiences of who they are or their reading about themselves in the Bible. They have, therefore, sought to add their voices to mainstream theological discourse and to change the Churches' perceptions.

5.4.3　Robert Goss's *Jesus Acted Up: A Gay and Lesbian Manifesto* is an example of a gay liberation theology, self-consciously modelled on the methods and hermeneutics of the earlier Latin American Liberation Theology, and framed within the biblical language of justice. Goss argues that such a theology is about 'solidarity with the risen Christ that challenges crucifixion'. Gay and lesbian Christians 'remember the resistance narrative of Jesus, his struggles, death, and God's liberative practice. In a hermeneutics of solidarity, gay men and lesbians become the bearers of a "dangerous memory", activating and empowering their struggle for the practice of justice.'[22]

5.4.4　Furthermore, Goss goes on to say that this 'theology of liberation is not a private or individual affair'. It is about 'public faith practice'.[23] As such, Goss's theology represents a larger movement in and on the margins of the Churches in the USA, Western Europe and Britain, in which gay and lesbian Christians are seeking a voice, a public identity and justice. This is a reworking of the old feminist slogan that 'the personal is political' and represents a very considerable challenge to the Churches.

5.4.5　Various other strands of gay theology have developed. There have, of course, been many important works that have sought to revise the traditional understanding of the biblical texts that have been seen to condemn homosexuality, notably by scholars such as William Countryman and Michael Vasey, as discussed in Chapter 4. However, as we also noted in that chapter, gay and lesbian biblical scholarship has now moved beyond trying to refute traditional readings of the Bible to the more 'constructive' task of reclaiming homoerotic or same-sex desire within biblical texts, or interpretations of those texts that have actually been a part of the mainstream of the tradition.

5.4.6　Stephen D. Moore, for example, has suggested that, in interpreting the Song of Songs, some patristic writers (such as Origen) and medieval monastic figures (such as Bernard of Clairvaux) shied away from the full-blooded heterosexuality of the text, and tended rather towards the homoerotic. For example, he quotes Bernard:

> Of what use to me the wordy effusions of the prophets? Rather let him Who is the most handsome of the sons of men, let him kiss me with the Kiss of his mouth [Song 1: 1] ... [E]ven the very beauty of the angels Can only leave me wearied. For my Jesus utterly surpasses these in His majesty and splendor. Therefore I ask him what I ask of neither Man nor angel: that he kiss me with the kiss of his mouth.

> For both classical Christian and Jewish commentators, the Song could not be what it seemed, he says. Their subsequent 'queer' allegorical interpretation points, he argues, to 'a lack of homosexual panic in the context in which it was conceived'.[24]

5.4.7 The recovery of 'hidden' traditions, speaking to the existence of same-sex relations in the past within Christianity, has also been important. Most famously the Yale historian John Boswell sparked a great debate in 1994 with the publication of his book *Same-Sex Unions in Pre-Modern Europe*, which we have already referred to in Chapter 1.[25] In this study he argued that a ritual, traditional among Greek Christians, called the *adelphopoiesis* – a rite for the 'making' of 'sisters' or 'brothers' – had functioned in the past as a same-sex union. It seemed to give evidence of 'homosexual marriage' within a part of the tradition of the Christian Church.

5.4.8 In criticism of Boswell's thesis, subsequent examinations of the evidence have pointed to the fact that this rite did not prevent those engaged in it from being married as well, and that the ideals inherent in the rite would not have encompassed sexual intercourse. And yet, further subsequent discussions have suggested that both Boswell and his critics were anachronistic, assessing the evidence of the past too much in terms of our own culture. Such discussions have pointed to the ways in which the 'sexual' is reduced to sexual intercourse in a distinctive way in modern society, which would not have been the case in the premodern era, and to the fact that the sort of voluntary kinship recognized by the rite is missing within modern society or at least not formally or ritualistically recognized today (except within marriage). As Alan Bray puts it in his discussion of Boswell's work and its critics: 'The claim that the relationships blessed by this rite were sexual and akin to marriage *and* the claim that they were not both involve an unsettling degree of anachronism.'

5.4.9   Nevertheless, Bray goes on to argue that, given the fact that there can be no simple passage from the past to the present, the value of recovering history lies rather in: 'its ability to raise radical questions about the terms in which this debate is being conducted'.[26] It raises questions about both ethics and liturgy, and we shall be considering these kinds of questions in this Guide in the discussion of same-sex unions in Chapter 8.

5.4.10   A very different sort of gay theology has been written by the English Roman Catholic theologian James Alison. His work, some of which we have already considered in Chapter 4, has been described as Catholic theology from a gay perspective rather than gay theology *per se*. For what Alison attempts is an entirely different and yet Catholic understanding of the Christian faith in which there are no scapegoats, and in which we have no reason to be resentful.[27]

5.4.11   For faith to be truly transformative, Alison writes, we need to be less rather than more certain of our rightness.

> The beginning of Christian moral life is a stumbling into an awareness of our own complicity in hypocrisy, and a becoming aware of quite how violent that hypocrisy is. Starting from there we can begin to stretch out our hands to our brothers and sisters, neither more nor less hypocritical than ourselves, who are on the way to being expelled ... by an apparently united order, which has an excessive and militant certainty as to the evil of the other. Let us then go and learn what this means: 'I want mercy and not sacrifice'.[28]

5.4.12   This requires a certain vulnerability on the part of all Christians. Alison wishes to create 'something like a space in which a heart might find permission to come close to cracking'[29] for in that space we might begin to understand the loving kindness and audacity of God who invites us just as we are to create fellowship, to open our minds to the new Jerusalem. In that space, we can more easily relax into being loved, more aware of the earth-shaking mercy behind God becoming incarnate and dwelling among us.

5.4.13   What is 'gay' about Alison's theology, we might ask? In some senses, nothing. It is a clear exposition of Catholic doctrine, of the love of God, of how to develop a moral theology and a spiritual practice that lead to fullness of life rather than narrowness and bitterness. But it is written from the perspective of a gay Roman Catholic priest, who has not had an easy experience in the Church and could so easily have lapsed into such bitterness, and yet whose faith enables him to be completely free. And so he writes that God's mercy may especially be witnessed by gay and lesbian people at this time precisely because 'they' could lapse into resentment at the Church – like many others who are scapegoated and marginalized. Instead, their experience may have created 'something like a space in which a heart might find permission to come close to cracking' and there the crucified Christ and thus life in God is to be found.

5.4.14   While gay male theology and lesbian theology have tended to be written from different standpoints, as we shall see in a moment, more recently the notion of 'queer theology' has sometimes seen dialogue and agreement between gay and lesbian theologians. For example, Robert Goss writes:

> The new coalition between lesbians, feminist women, and gay men form an ongoing learning process, a dialogue that achieves relative understandings and effects social change. In this dialogue, lesbians and gay men have adopted the common term *queer* to describe themselves and their sexuality. *Queer* is a term of political dissidence and sexual difference. It is part of the movement to reclaim derogatory words from oppressive culture.[30]

This brings us to the development of lesbian theology, but first we need to think about female sexuality in the Christian tradition generally.

b. Female sexuality

5.4.15   It is not within the remit of this report to give a full survey of the impact of feminism on Christian theology: this would make several reports – indeed heavy tomes – in itself. It is, however, appropriate to consider the ways in which feminists have pointed to the near-total absence of any proper discussion of female sexuality (heterosexual, bisexual or lesbian) in the Christian tradition, and look specifically at the development of lesbian theology.

5.4.16   Where would one go in the Christian tradition to find a positive portrayal of female sexuality? The absence of women from the more formal field of theology has meant that women's identity and sexuality have largely been viewed through male eyes and, therefore, defined by men.

5.4.17   Those women who have been able to speak and write theologically have often done so precisely because they have been freed from the ties of family and household. We have the writings and sayings from the early Christian desert mothers because their wisdom was sought; and their wisdom was sought because, in pursuing the ascetic life, they were seen to have transcended their own gender and their sexuality for a greater good. And, indeed, their removal from the primary arena of sexual activity – marriage – eventually brought many elite women to positions of authority in monasteries in the early Middle Ages and a subsequent exercising of power that would never have been possible for them as married women. In order to exercise power, the absence of sexuality was required for a woman.

5.4.18   We have the writings of medieval and early modern mystics such as Catherine of Siena and Teresa of Avila. These are often highly erotic but, while an exploration of the erotic in their relationship to God is important, it is all too easy and probably mistaken to interpret their writings in a flat-footed way by sexualizing their language from a modern perspective – though scholars have done it. Jacques Lacan, the influential French psychoanalyst could, for example, only understand Teresa's ecstasies in terms of sexuality, ignoring the significant and intricate stages of prayer required to reach such heights.[31]

5.4.19   We have the arguments for the good of marriage in the writings of the sixteenth-century Protestant Reformation, but these come from Luther and other male reformers and, it is argued, their largely hierarchical view of marriage gives no room for a distinctively female view of the matter. To put it simply, while we have Luther's views on marriage and sexuality, what we do not have is what his wife Katherine thought about these matters.

5.4.20   The idealization of woman, which happened in the Victorian era, much promoted by middle-class evangelical faith, understood women as inherently different from men: weaker in many ways, but the guardian of family morals and 'naturally' more spiritual than men. Women were therefore thought to be lacking in sexual desire; sexual activity for women was to be endured for the sake of motherhood rather than enjoyed.

5.4.21   It is to what they see as this absence of any real discussion of female sexuality, especially by women themselves, in the Christian tradition, then, that feminists have pointed. Those who have highlighted this most especially, perhaps, are lesbian feminists whose agenda has been much wider than simply demanding the right to have sexual relations with other women.

5.4.22   It is important to discuss lesbianism separately from male homosexuality because, as Bishop Michael Doe notes in his recent book on sexuality and the Church, in comparison with male homosexuality:

> Lesbianism has had different origins and aims, and amongst these have been a desire to find expressions of sexuality which redefine its nature and purpose, seeking alternatives to a patriarchal understanding of the world.[32]

5.4.23   Doe is making two important points about lesbianism here. The first is that the origins of modern lesbian identity are not the same as those of the male movement for gay liberation, although there is a connection between the two. The second is that among the aims of the lesbian feminist movement has been a desire for a complete rethinking about the nature of human sexuality in order to create a new way of looking at the matter that is no longer dominated by the needs and concerns of men.

5.4.24   Like male homosexual activity, lesbian activity is a phenomenon that has been known throughout human history. It is, for example, something that can be well documented from the Greco-Roman world, and, as we have noted, it was something that was both known and rejected by St Paul.[33]

5.4.25   However, like its male counterpart, the modern Lesbian movement is something that has developed very recently. As Mary Hunt explains, it is a movement that has three roots – the sexual revolution of the 1960s, the rise of the women's movement, and the rise of the movement for homosexual equality.

5.4.26   Hunt is very critical of the 'so-called sexual revolution', arguing that it was a social movement that was still dominated by men and that: 'For women it meant the need for more birth control, more abortions, and ultimately less freedom to really choose'.[34] However, she notes that it did at least mean that issues concerning human sexuality could now be talked about:

> ... if anything positive did come out of this rather virulent period
> it was the fact that people began to talk more freely about sexuality.
> This was no small matter when we reflect that even to the present
> day, discussion of sexuality is still taboo in some circles, including
> most of theology.[35]

5.4.27   Hunt argues that a far more significant influence on the
development of lesbianism was the rise of the women's movement with
its emphasis on the way in which human sexual relations reflect male
('patriarchal') oppression of women:

> In consciousness raising groups women not only mentioned
> sexuality but took it as a major focus, seeing it as the mirror which
> reflected all of women's treatment in the society. The woman who
> was oppressed in bed, who was raped or beaten, whose husband or
> lover did not use birth control, the woman who was called frigid,
> the postmenopausal woman, all these are various facets of the same
> woman, namely the oppressed woman in patriarchy.[36]

5.4.28   As Hunt explains, the significance of this critique of patriarchal
oppression for the development of lesbianism lies in the fact that, from
the early 1970s onwards, specifically lesbian feminists began to argue
that there was a link between male oppression of women in general and
the belief that heterosexuality is and should be the norm for human
sexual behaviour.

5.4.29   Only when heterosexuality was no longer the norm could
women be free to make their own choices about the kind of
relationships *they* wanted:

> The point is not that every woman act in a particular way, but
> that every woman be freed from the constraints that patriarchal
> heterosexism places upon her. Then and only then can women make
> real choices about relationships with particular people, not excluding
> a whole class of people (women) from the beginning. This same
> dynamic of instant exclusion of whole classes of people is operative
> in racism, in classism, in discrimination toward the differently able,
> those from Third World countries, etc. It is this dynamic that lesbian
> feminists seek to change in its many manifestations.[37]

5.4.30   This meant that it soon became clear that it was not enough
for lesbian feminists simply to form part of the wider homosexual
community:

Feminists quickly became aware that being part of the gay community was important but no panacea. *Gay* had become another false generic like *man*, referring to both male and female homosexuals. This symbolised the values of the movement as well, which were focussed on making male homosexual expression valid, and little else. Feminists could not stop our analysis with the sexual, but always understood our sexuality within the complex constellation of racism, sexism, classism etc. The 'natural alliance' between lesbians and gay men was not so natural after all. This is not to say that there are not some obvious and important links, but it is to say that very different emphases have been made from the two perspectives.[38]

5.4.31 One very important difference in emphasis noted by Hunt is that, for lesbian feminists, sexual liberation is not the key issue:

Gay males, for example, have emphasized their sexual lives as the locus of their liberation. But since *gay* is not a generic word we can conclude that the lesbian emphasis is quite different and not to be homogenized. Lesbian feminists have not defined ourselves according to sexuality, although that has been important. Rather, we have defined ourselves according to certain relational commitments to other women, or what I am calling female friendship. The nature of our relationship with regard to the specifically sexual aspect is quite simply no one else's business. That is not to say that lesbian feminists are in the closet about our sexuality, nor that we advocate continuing the hidden relational lives of our foresisters with the women they loved. Far from it. Rather, the goal from a lesbian feminist perspective is that persons eventually be allowed to love whom they will without current heterosexist gender constraints.[39]

5.4.32 The fact that the lesbian movement's agenda is about the development of meaningful relationships with whomsoever a women chooses to relate, rather than simply about the development of homosexual relationships, reflects the fact that many lesbians would see their homosexuality as a matter of choice rather than necessity. Theologian Rosemary Radford Ruether writes:

Lesbians are more likely to say that their homosexuality is an expression of their general capacity to be sexual, and that this reflects their general capacity to love, to be attracted to and affectionate toward other people, female or male. These women see their lesbianism less as a fixed biological necessity than as a social choice. They would say that they have chosen to love women because, in a patriarchal society, lesbian relations are less violent and coercive and more conducive to loving mutuality than are relations with males. Since patriarchal society sets up heterosexual marriage as a relationship of domination and subordination, fully moral – that is, loving and mutual relations – are possible only between women. Lesbianism is an expression of this social morality.[40]

The French writer Monique Wittig makes the point very starkly in her essay 'One is not born a woman' in which she argues that the very concept of 'woman' is a social construct that serves to keep a large part of the human race in permanent servitude. For her, the importance of lesbianism is precisely that it enables people to avoid being 'women' in the ways that society has dictated:

> Lesbian is the only concept I know of which is beyond the categories of sex (woman and man), because the designated subject (lesbian) is not a woman, either economically, or politically, or ideologically. For what makes a woman is a specific social relation to a man, a relation that we have previously called servitude, a relation which implies personal and physical obligation as well as economic obligation ('forced residence', domestic corvée, conjugal duties, unlimited production of children, etc.), a relation which lesbians escape by refusing to become or stay heterosexual. We are escapees from our class in the same way as the American slaves were when escaping slavery and becoming free.

> For us this is an absolute necessity; our survival demands that we contribute all our strength to the destruction of the class of women within which men appropriate women. This can be accomplished only by the destruction of heterosexuality as a social system which is based on the oppression of women by men and which produces the doctrine of the difference between the sexes to justify this oppression.[41]

c. Some key issues in lesbian feminist theology

5.4.33   Lesbian feminist theology is a rapidly developing theological movement, and one that is very varied in its expression. However, a survey of the relevant literature shows that there are a number of key issues that are important to this movement as a whole. We shall look at some examples of these key issues.

The critique of heterosexuality as 'natural'

5.4.34   As we have seen, within the Christian tradition it has been believed on the basis of the teaching of Genesis 1–2 that heterosexual

sexual relationships are natural because they are the form of sexual relationship instituted by God at creation.

5.4.35   Lesbian theology has responded to this belief by making the suggestion that heterosexuality is not natural, or God given, but is, in fact, simply a social construct designed to control human sexuality for what is perceived to be the benefit of society as a whole. Genesis 1–2 can be understood in that context, as an explanation, in its own setting, of how things were or ought to be.

5.4.36   Rosemary Radford Ruether points instead to the important insights made in modern thought about the nature of sexuality. She suggests that:

> … we return to the Freudian insight that we are 'originally' bisexual and polymorphously sexual. Instead of seeing this as an infantile 'perversity' we should see it as a clue to the nature and potential of human sexuality. Human sexuality is not narrowly programmed towards genital sexuality, heterosexuality, or reproduction. Indeed what makes human sexuality 'human' is its tendency to transcend the limits of biological reproduction and to be oriented toward human relationality. This more generalized capacity for sexual attraction is both exciting and frightening. It is the body's basic experience of vital, pleasurable feelings, awakened in sensual contact with other humans. This is frightening since it also suggests vulnerability, loss of control, giving oneself up to others.[42]

5.4.37   According to Ruether, human societies have responded to the ambivalent nature of human sexuality:

> … with various social strategies that channel its use. Sexuality is channeled socially toward heterosexuality and toward committed family relationships in order to assure not only reproduction, but also the stable relationship of the generations in child raising, mutual care, and the support of the aged. Western cultures particularly have channeled sexual feeling away from general body experience to a functional, genital sexuality. We develop into adults by deadening most of our bodies, and most of our relationships, sexually.[43]

5.4.38   What this means, in a paraphrasing of de Beauvoir, is that: 'We are not born heterosexual. We are taught to become heterosexual'.[44]

Furthermore, our channelling towards heterosexuality also reflects the values of a male-dominated society:

> Heterosexuality represents not only a channelling of polymorphous bisexuality toward heterosexual marriage for the purpose of procreation and child raising, but also a socialization that has taken place historically under conditions of patriarchy – that is, under systems of male, ruling-class (and race) domination. We are conditioned to respond sexually to persons not only of the right gender, but also of the right race and class – this is, people who are 'marriageable' according to racial and ethnic endogamy – and hierarchy.[45]

5.4.39 In Ruether's view, this channelling of human sexuality along approved lines has been tremendously damaging, not only to those for whom the conditioning has not worked and who have become homosexuals, but to everybody, because it has meant that everyone has had to repress aspects of their sexuality in order to fit in with the expectations that society has placed upon them.

5.4.40 In theological terms, for a lesbian woman, denying one's God-given sexuality – in the pressure to conform to 'approved' heterosexuality – might be seen as sinful. Theologian Melanie May has argued this, saying that when she 'passes' as heterosexual, then that is a sin of omission, and in that silence:

> I omit myself from being the fullness of the image of God as God created me to be. I thereby put God's glory at risk as well as my own being, for ... God's glory is dimmed whenever and wherever women and men created in God's image are violated and diminished.[46]

5.4.41 As Ruether sees it, what we have to do is to acknowledge the truth about the development of human sexuality in the past so that we can then develop a new and better sexual ethic in the future:

> As we recognize the pluriformity of our sexual potential and experience, and the way we have been shaped in our identities by conformity to or reaction against the dominant social conditioning, we can begin to explore a new sexual and social ethic of moral development toward mutual, loving, and committed relationships. Such moral development does not entail a denial of our capacity for many-sided asexual feeling, but it does entail choosing, out of a multiplicity of possibilities, certain particular people with whom we

open ourselves to deeper relationships and vulnerability, with whom we choose to journey into the bonding of committed love and friendship. In the context of such a committed relationship we can then appropriate our sexuality not as something biologically necessitated, or as socially coerced, but as a freely chosen way of expressing our authentic humanness, in relation to the special others with whom we wish to share our lives.[47]

Marriage as a problematic ideal

5.4.42　Linked to the lesbian feminist critique of the idea that heterosexuality should be viewed as the human sexual norm is a critique of the idea that marriage should be seen as the ideal model for a human sexual relationship. The grounds for this critique, which have already been suggested in an earlier quotation from Ruether, are that marriage developed within a patriarchal society as an institution designed to ensure male economic and social control over women. As a result, it cannot provide a suitable basis for a relationship based on mutual love.

5.4.43　Elizabeth Stuart, for example, notes that the *Alternative Service Book* (ASB) marriage service stresses the relational character of marriage as the context for the development of mutual love between husband and wife, but asks whether marriage can provide the right framework for this sort of development:

> Part of the problem is that we have burdened marriage with too much. We have taken an institution which began as an economic contract, a union of two sets of assets in a male-dominated society, in which love's place was not defined, and in the space of but a few hundred years we have redefined it so that now we see it, in our culture at least, as a lifelong commitment of love where the people involved, motivated by romantic love, are supposed to fulfil the other's emotional needs in a relationship based upon equality. A feminist would want to ask: can an institution conceived on the premise of unequal power relations ever fulfil the purposes of marriage outlined in the ASB? The evidence is not convincingly positive and that is why many lesbian and gay people ask whether they should be looking to marriage as a model for structuring and understanding their relationships.[48]

The importance of friendship

5.4.44　Consequently, one concept that has become increasingly important for lesbian and feminist theologians as a way of talking about both our human relationships and our relationship with God is 'friendship'. While this has long been important in female culture, this has been reflected more recently in the theological work of Mary Hunt, Elizabeth Stuart, and Elisabeth Moltmann-Wendel.

5.4.45 Reflecting on the importance of friendship in the experience of women, lesbian and other feminist theologians have argued that the characteristics that can be found in friendships between women provide a model for the sort of relationships that need to be seen in the Church and in society as a whole.

5.4.46 Mary Hunt writes, for example:

> I have suggested that women's friendships are mutual, community seeking, honest about sexuality, nonexclusive, flexible and other-directed. These qualities, it seems to me, have tremendous potential not simply for relationships among women, though that potential has yet to be explored, but for the whole church. It is these characteristics which will transform our culture and create the preconditions for the possibility of the reign of God. I am not arguing that all women's friendships participate in these qualities as yet. That is wishful thinking. Rather, by naming them I hope to make it so, or at least bring to consciousness what might be possible in women's lives so that our contribution to the whole church can be forthcoming.[49]

5.4.47 Hunt also argues that a theology based on the concept of friendship provides a promising framework within which to develop a theology of sexuality. This is because:

> ... it acknowledges that it is not sexuality per se but friendship that determines what the quality of life can be. In patriarchy it is certainly the sexuality dimension that makes the difference. But after patriarchy it is the entire relationship that makes the difference.[50]

5.4.48 The point that Hunt is making here is that, while traditional theological approaches to sexuality tended to view the sexual act in isolation and to judge a relationship in terms of its sexual component, an alternative and better approach is to explore how the sexual dimension enhances or fails to enhance the quality of the friendship between the people involved. It is friendship that really matters, sex is a secondary issue.[51]

5.4.49   Reflecting on women's experience of friendship, and on biblical texts such as 2 Chronicles 20.7 and John 15.12-17, which use the concept of friendship as a way of describing a relationship with God and the kind of community Jesus sought to establish, a number of lesbian and/or feminist theologians have explored the idea that friendship provides us with another useful model for speaking meaningfully about God.

5.4.50   Hunt, for example, argues that the characteristics of 'mutuality' and 'the urge towards community' that are to be found in female friendships are also useful ways of understanding God.

5.4.51   Mutuality, she says:

> ... is suggested by process theologians who are concerned with how God is affected by humankind, and obviously vice versa. Mutuality is that quality of the otherness of God which is really God's oneness with us. To characterize otherness as mutuality is to say that God can not only be understood in human terms, but that the very understanding is affected by our belief in God. In short, mutuality means that our relationship with God, like all friendships, is freely chosen on both sides (unlike family or government images like Father and Lord, in which the relationships are not necessarily intentional or gratuitous). More needs to be explored, of course, but it is clear that God as friend opens up a new paradigm for our understanding.[52]

5.4.52   In similar fashion, the urge towards community enables us to make sense of another essential aspect of a Christian understanding of God, namely, the way in which God cooperates with human beings in order to achieve God's saving purposes:

> The idea of the reign of God, the omega point, the gathering of all that is into a harmonious community, these are all Christian ways of talking about the God-human co-operation which will result in salvation. Jesus is the force in Christianity, the friend whose relationship with us is manifested in our being part of the Christian community. This membership is evidenced in the work of love and justice. This is not the pietistic 'what a friend we have in Jesus'. Rather it is the experience of being part of a historical group of friends. Jesus' friendships, especially the example of his particular friendship with the beloved disciple (John 13.23; 21.17, etc.) as well as his immediate community of men and women are a model for contemporary Christian life. Again, much remains to be explored,

but we can conclude that the missionary urge which springs from Christianity is in fact to go and make friends of all nations.[53]

5.4.53 Stuart also sees the concept of friendship as a useful way of understanding what we mean by God. In *Just Good Friends* she builds on Hunt's work to present her own picture of God as a sometimes unreliable friend:

> The metaphor of God as friend(s)[54] has roots in the Hebrew and Christian scriptures. We have already observed the reference to those with whom God made covenants as 'friends' in the Hebrew scriptures. Hochma (*Wisdom*) is portrayed as a friendly presence, immanent in the creation she loves, summoning us to justice whilst inviting us to share a meal with her. This image is taken up in the figure of Jesus who in God's name establishes a community of friends and invites all to join it. In his own body Jesus bears the tragedy of friendship failed, passion transmuted into destruction. Mary Hunt believes that it is important that we should not be afraid to take our experience of the frailty of friendship into our experience of God, and I think she is right. At a workshop I attended on our images of God, a collective sharp intake of breath greeted my revelation that I often experience God as an unreliable friend. Yet many of us have the experience of crying to God 'why have you forsaken me?' Christianity, unlike Judaism, has always had problems in dealing with the absence of God and voicing the pain and betrayal felt in this experience. Sometimes when we need God most she is on the cross with us rather than in a position of strength to help us, or just achingly absent. It is right and proper, if we are seeking to exist in honest and mutual friendship with the divine, that we should call her to judgement as she calls us.[55]

5.4.54 As Stuart sees it, a major advantage in seeing God as friend is the ability of the term friend to:

> ... contain within it multilayers of other images; parent, lover, wisdom, sister/brother can, and indeed should, also be friends. In worship it is one of the very few images of God that is truly inclusive.[56]

5.4.55 Stuart also argues that it is the God who is friend whom we experience in the context of our friendship with other people:

> We often experience friendship as an experience of what some would call 'grace'. We are surprised by a blossoming love which we neither

expected nor consciously sought. In this experience of the graciousness of friendship we touch the sacramental presence of God, of Sophia craftily weaving a web between us and then stretching the ends of the twine to bind us to others. Many no longer find anthropomorphic images of God helpful and we should remind ourselves of the biblical location of God in the betweenness of persons as the passionate power that binds them together. We must never forget, 'it is, and *it is not*'. What we can detect in the shadows on the faces of those around us is that there is something of friendship in God, not idealized sentimental friendship but real messy friendship of which we are an integral part and which we incarnate in our relationships. We become sacraments of God's wanton passionate love when we endeavour to relate in friendship. In relationships of radical vulnerability we experience and incarnate something of what it could be like in the reign of God.[57]

Lesbians in the Church

5.4.56   Much of the theology discussed in these last sections is potentially wide-reaching in its methods and insights, and some of the possible consequences of this will be discussed at the end of this chapter. However, it should not be forgotten that for all those lesbians who leave the Church or hold rather lightly to the Christian tradition, there are many who choose to stay despite not always feeling welcomed or, worse, despite feeling or being persecuted. The lesbian women who experience the dilemmas of being both lesbian and Christian most sharply are those women who are also called to be priests.

5.4.57   For any lesbian or gay person, the paradoxes inherent in finding they are both homosexual and Christian can be deeply painful.[58] This is particularly the case for those who find themselves not only Christian and homosexual, but with a vocation to the priesthood in a Church that officially declares that practising homosexuals should not be ordained. Should they answer the call and keep quiet about their sexuality or live openly as lesbians with an insistent call to priesthood that remains unanswered? Many lesbian priests feel that they already suffer discrimination in the Church because they are women. Such discrimination and feelings of 'not belonging' are compounded by their sexuality.

5.4.58   There is not much written about this for it is to 'speak the unspeakable'. One helpful article is that by Dorothy Austin, an Episcopal priest, a psychotherapist and university professor, and a lesbian. Austin writes:

> How do I speak the unspeakable? . . . When I speak on gay and
> lesbian issues in an ecclesiastical or church-related context, in the
> theological school classroom, I often find myself – in spite of myself
> – lurking somewhere in the cloistered closet. Like some creature in
> Narnia, having made my way through the ecclesiastical vestments, to
> the back of the wardrobe, I find it's quite possible, seductive even, to
> disappear, cloaked and passing – out of the sight of my own gaze.[59]

The dilemma of the lesbian priest is expressed by Austin thus:

> Just look at the scope of my dilemma: If my whole life is a secret and
> its secrecy a source of unremitting shame; if what lies at the heart of
> who I am is a story I cannot utter aloud because I might lose my job,
> lose the respect of my colleagues, lose my orders as a Christian
> priest, lose my family, lose my mental stability, maybe even lose my
> life for telling the truth, then let me lose this life. Let it die and be
> buried without 'me,' that 'I' might rise to a more livable life.[60]

5.4.59 It might fairly be said that this, too, is the dilemma of the gay
male priest. This would, in many ways, be true. Certainly, Michael Doe,
in his work on the Church and homosexuality, sees these parallels.
His three stories in the Epilogue to his book, *Seeking the Truth in Love*,
of two gay male priests and one lesbian priest, speak to the equal
feelings of oppression amongst gay and lesbian clergy, though it is
his story of the lesbian priest that ends his book, with that priest
committing suicide, unable to face the dilemma of her position in the
Church. It was for her that Doe wrote the book.[61]

5.4.60 The acute personal dilemmas faced by lesbian Christians in
general, and by lesbian priests in particular, mean that the Church's task
is not only to respond to the feminist theological work discussed earlier
in this chapter, on the patriarchal nature of the Church itself and of
marriage, but also to think how to support people wrestling with these
dilemmas. The lesbian writer Melanie May suggests that it is only when
a gay or lesbian person is free to live out their sexuality that they can
fully incarnate God's glory. One question we might ask is: how should
we respond to this suggestion in the light of the material we have
looked at in Chapters 2 to 4?

5.5 Gender, sexuality and the household within the mainstream of theology

5.5.1 Some of the ideas discussed in this chapter are now beginning
to have a considerable impact on the mainstream of theology. We have

already looked at a number of examples of this phenomenon at the end of Chapter 3 but, in this section, we will examine two more aspects of this: fresh analyses by mainstream theologians in the Christian tradition on the subject of gender and sexuality, and discussions of the nature of the Christian household.

a. Revisiting the tradition

5.5.2   As gaps in the Christian tradition about certain aspects of gender and sexuality have been highlighted, or dominant Christian views on these matters challenged, some theologians have begun to look at the tradition with fresh eyes. In recent years, for example, several prominent theologians, including Rowan Williams and Sarah Coakley, have looked at ideas about gender and sexuality in the patristic writers. As an example of this we will take a brief look at some contemporary rereadings of St Gregory of Nyssa, the influential fourth-century Cappadocian Father, about whom much has been written in this regard.

5.5.3   Verna Harrison has argued that Gregory of Nyssa's understanding of unity in Christ is a state 'in which the distinction between male and female no longer exists'.[62] This is a form of gender transcendence that, for Gregory, 'is a surpassing of the limitations and divisions that can hinder each man or woman from acquiring a fullness of human life and goodness'.[63] Harrison focused especially on the ways in which this occurred through asceticism – indeed the notion of transcending one's gender through the disciplining of the body was a common notion in the asceticism of the fourth century – and the Eucharist.

5.5.4   Some theologians have explicitly related this insight about gender to current theological and ecclesiological issues. Rowan Williams, for instance, has argued that Gregory's writing has: 'considerable import for politics, sexual politics' particularly in relation to the ordination of women.[64]

5.5.5   Sarah Coakley has made the connection between Gregory and recent feminist theory, which was discussed in this report at 5.3.20–5.3.25, which challenges the idea that there are essential characteristics to women and men and proposes that gender is a construct. Indeed, Coakley makes an explicit connection between the work of the influential feminist theorist Judith Butler and Gregory, suggesting that Gregory denaturalizes sex and gender in the just the way that Butler does. For him, the understandings of gender that exist in unredeemed humanity are overthrown in the eschatological community of the redeemed.[65]

5.5.6   What these scholars are arguing is that Gregory understands any differences between man and woman as transient, and abolishes the gender hierarchies that were the norm of his day. Most notably he does this in his life of his sister, the famous ascetic Macrina, who is seen as transcending her gender through her piety and thereby witnessing to a transformation for which we all might hope. She is an example of divinely restored humanity in which there is, as Rowan Williams puts it, 'a fundamental spiritual equality between male and female'.[66]

5.5.7   This sort of interpretation of the Fathers is an example of work being done within the mainstream of the Christian tradition that nevertheless tells a different story about both gender and sexuality from that which has generally prevailed.

5.5.8   A somewhat similar argument about the transcending of sex and gender within the Christian community is put forward by Elizabeth Stuart in her most recent work, *Gay and Lesbian Theologies: Repetitions with Critical Difference*.[67] In this work she argues very clearly that both gender and sexual orientation are culturally constructed rather than fixed. She argues that an earlier generation of liberal gay and lesbian theology has been unable to deliver what it promised for it was built on the premise that homosexuality is/has a fixed identity; in taking an 'essentialist' position that theology identified too closely with the modern secular construction of homosexuality.

5.5.9   She writes:

> The gay self is not an incontestable truth. If the social constructionists are right and it was a creation of modernity then it is the creation of heterosexual culture and needs to be not just reclaimed as liberals attempt to do, but scrutinised more closely, as does the accompanying assumption that sexuality tells the profoundest 'truth' about a person.[68]

5.5.10   Indeed, Stuart to some degree repudiates her own earlier work, and that of some of the lesbian theologians discussed earlier in this chapter, such as Mary Hunt, for the ways in which they relied too much on the experience of the individual for their starting point. She suggests that: 'there is a danger that theologies based in experience end up ... advocating a thinly disguised form of essentialism'.[69] In a footnote about Hunt's work and her own, on friendship, she writes (referring to herself in the third person):

> In constructing a theology of friendship both Hunt and Stuart make huge claims about the nature of women's and gay experience which are impossible to substantiate. In arguing that lesbian and gay people tend to define their primary relationships in terms of friendship Stuart has to ignore or down play the experiences of those who do not.[70]

Again, she criticizes such theologies for going outside the tradition for their foundations and for their understanding of identity.

5.5.11 Stuart proposes, instead, that Christianity itself must be the source for gay and lesbian (or queer) theology because it is 'queer' in a way that we have been unwilling to admit – precisely because the Christian tradition refuses to accept the stability of gender and sexual desire. She draws here on the work not only of feminist theorists like Judith Butler, but also of theologians such as Sarah Coakley and Rowan Williams on Gregory of Nyssa. She recognizes the eschatological significance of that work and suggests:

> In the end gay is not good, straight is not good, no one is good but God alone and redemption does not come through gender or sexuality, rather these are taken up into the process of redemption. The Church as the community of the redeemed must play out gender and sexuality in such a way as to reveal their lack of eschatological significance. In the end as my body lies in its casket before the altar my hope will not lie in my sexual orientation, or my gender but my baptism, and my family and friends rightly absorbed into the wider ecclesial community at that moment will be reminded that this is their only hope as well.[71]

5.5.12 For Stuart, it is baptism that is the focal point of our identity as Christians – as, for example, it is for the authors of the *St Andrew's Day Statement*, discussed in Chapter 2 – because: 'the baptised manifest a new type of creaturehood/humanity'.[72] It is by baptism and not by biology that one enters the Church, and baptism reveals the inadequacy of all other forms of identity. Thus, from the same theological starting point for Christian identity as the authors of the *St Andrew's Day*

Statement but with a different interpretation of the scriptural and the Christian tradition's understanding of gender and sexuality, Stuart argues:

> Heterosexuality and homosexuality and maleness and femaleness are not of absolute importance, they are not determinative in God's eyes and in so far as any of us have further behaved as if they are we are guilty of the grave sin of idolatry and if we have further behaved as if they are grounds upon which to exclude people from the glorious liberty of the children of God we are guilty of profanity and a fundamental denial of our own baptismal identity which rests in being bound together with others not of our choosing by an act of sheer grace.[73]

In this, she echoes the emphasis on the gift of freedom through grace, through baptism, which is to be found in the work of 'gay' theologians such as Eugene Rogers and James Alison, and other theologians such as Rowan Williams.

b. The Christian household

5.5.13   A number of theologians and ethicists have turned their attention to the resources of the Christian tradition in order to think about what constitutes a holy household. They have asked how, in our age – in the light of all the shifts in sexual behaviour and changing patterns of marriage and family outlined in Chapter 1, and the related intellectual developments outlined in this chapter – the Church might hold to ideals of holiness in the forms of living together that it sanctions, while at the same time meeting the new challenges inherent in changing social and sexual patterns.

5.5.14   The moral theologian, Thomas Breidenthal, has addressed this question directly in his book *Christian Households: The Sanctification of Nearness*, which he describes as 'a theology of the Christian household'. He writes: 'To ask why Christians value life together is to ask what a Christian household is and what kind of householding Christian faith inspires.' He defines a household in the following way:

> ... two or more people sharing the daily round of life to a significant degree and over a significant period of time, whether the sharing is freely chosen or not. This intentionally loose definition covers a broad range of living arrangements, from the partnership of two people who share shelter, sleep, sex, food, childrearing, financial

resources and so forth, to communities on the monastic model, to people who live alone but whose daily life is a rich weave of shared meals, hospitality, deep attachments, and daily care for others, or whose solitude is heavy with the remembered presence of the dead. What all households have in common is a very high degree of familiarity – knowing and being known just not without public faces on, but more the way God knows us – in our sleeping and our rising, in our going out and our coming in, as Psalm 121 puts it. Whenever we use the word 'family' we are highlighting this aspect of life together.[74]

5.5.15   Breidenthal points to the apparent ambivalence within the Christian tradition – and seemingly of Jesus himself – about life together. But he goes on to provide a biblical understanding of connection and 'nearness' over and against a secular individualism that 'is the self's bid to replace God', based on the command to love our neighbours for that compels us to assent to nearness. He writes, 'And because our fellowship with one another is itself God's will for us – indeed, it is for companionship in the praise of God that we truly yearn – Christians not only reject the myth of radical individualism, but embrace our connection with one another both as truth and as good news.'[75]

5.5.16   The household is the best way, argues Breidenthal, of sanctifying this nearness. It is the place where we learn genuine neighbouring for a wider circle (hospitality and care for the stranger, for example) in balance with the sanctification of familiarity within the household. Indeed, the Christian household is both a training ground and a preview of the social life of heaven.[76]

5.5.17   This means that each of us 'must take responsibility for the care we pledge to one another when we choose to live together in Christ's name'. For, Breidenthal argues, 'Where genuine care is exercised in the context of familiarity, there the Christian household may be found.' He gives a definition of this form of care:

> Care is the working out of the embrace of nearness, through familiarity with a limited number of people, in the name of nearness with all, under the condition of sin.[77]

5.5.18   For Breidenthal, then, the presence of such care is a litmus test: it provides a criterion by which we can measure the holiness of a household. On these grounds, he extends the notion of the Christian or holy household beyond Christian marriage and monastic life, to any household in which that care is found, in which love of God and love of neighbour are hallmarks, including those of same-sex couples.

5.5.19 Breidenthal concludes:

> Householding is a way of sanctification. It can heal us of our inattention to one another, and teach us how to enjoy our nearness to one another in Christ. If this twofold purpose is served, it hardly matters what form the householding takes. There is no healing in any form of householding that does not take our sinfulness and our need for discipline seriously, and there is no joy in any householding that does not ally itself with the claim of every neighbour and with all who place their hope in a universal reign of peace. Christian marriage and monasticism are justified by this discipline and this hope; apart from this justification neither marriage nor monasticism has any claim upon us. If other ways of construing the Christian household can demonstrate a similar discipline and a similar hope, they too should be taken seriously and honoured. This is the basis on which I have endorsed the blessing of same-sex unions.[78]

5.5.20 Breidenthal's support of same-sex unions is not based on equality or rights – as with some of the writers we have looked at earlier in this chapter – but rather is based on a different set of ethical and theological grounds. He looks at the marks of the holy household within Scripture and the Christian tradition and argues that, wherever such marks of holiness appear within a household, then we must honour that household.

5.5.21 This is not an easy path, however. Breidenthal stands rigorously within the Christian tradition in making his case.

> But the gate is narrow. Redeemed familiarity is arduous, not cheap. *Capital* for the Christian, holy familiarity begins with Jesus and works itself out from there, sometimes with fear and trembling, sometimes in joy and confidence. Promiscuous relations do not make for schooling in familiarity. This is the tension at the heart of the Christian (and I suppose of any truly religious) householding: we must distance ourselves from some in order to learn what it means to be a neighbour to all ... Christian householding is preparing us for holy familiarity with everyone by providing an opportunity for concrete familiarity with just a few people; the church, as a sign of

my bond with all followers of Jesus, is a constant reminder that in heaven my experience of familiarity is going to transcend household ties. Thus the church challenges all her households not to make Idols of themselves, but to remember their ultimate loyalty to Jesus and to all for whom he died.[79]

5.5.22   The question of same-sex unions will be discussed in a later chapter, but the argument of Breidenthal's book is set out here as an example of rethinking the issue from a distinctly theological starting point and within the mainstream of Christian thinking about the nature of the household.

5.6 Critical questions raised by the new theological thinking

5.6.1   The kind of new theological thinking that we have been considering in the latter part of this chapter is becoming increasingly important within the Church, and it raises a number of important questions that more traditional forms of Christian theology need to take seriously:

- Does the teaching of early Fathers like Gregory of Nyssa not point the way to a more flexible understanding of human sexuality?

- Does the use of homoerotic imagery and the existence of rituals such as the *adelphopoiesis* indicate that there was in the Early and Medieval Church an acceptance of same-sex sexuality that was subsequently lost?

- Do gay Christians who have remained in the Church in the face of rejection and marginalization have something to teach us about becoming open to divine grace?

- Have the Church and its theology been complicit in the construction of a social system that oppresses women? If so, have they ceased to act in this way?

- Has the Church's teaching on marriage taken seriously enough the emphasis on mutual submission and mutual love set out in Ephesians 5.21-33, or has it allowed marriage to become an institution in which men are allowed to dominate women?

- Have distinctive female perspectives on human sexuality been ignored because of the fact that theology has until very recently largely been produced by men?

- Would it not be less oppressive to embrace a pluriform model of sexuality in which all women and men were to explore their own particular sexuality in a way that best suited them?

- Is the concept of friendship not a better way of conceiving of both human relationships and the nature of God than the models that have traditionally been used in the history of the Church?

- Does the new identity given to us in baptism not transcend our normal categories of sexual differentiation?

- Might the concept of the Christian household provide us with a model that enables us to honour both heterosexual and same-sex relationships that demonstrate the marks of holiness?

5.6.2　On the other hand, there are also important questions that can be addressed in return to this new theological thinking and that need to be taken equally seriously:

- Does the appeal to the writings of Gregory of Nyssa take sufficient note of the fact that his teaching on the eschatological abolition of sexual differentiation was based on beliefs about the originally androgynous nature of humanity and the spiritual nature of the resurrection body that have generally been seen as incompatible with the teaching of Scripture and of the Church?

- As before, is the historical scholarship accurate? As we noted in Chapter 1 and also in this chapter with reference to the work of Bray, Boswell's argument for the existence of same-sex unions in the Early and Medieval Church has been subject to severe criticism from other historians and has not been widely accepted. In addition it can be asked whether the argument that the interpretation of the Song of Songs by writers such as St Bernard of Clairvaux was homoerotic has taken into account the argument by Southern that we looked at in Chapter 3 that, while early medieval writers regularly used language that might appear to us to be homoerotic, it had a spiritual rather than a sexual meaning.

- Is it legitimate to contrast baptismal identity with sexual identity? Does not the evidence of the New Testament point to the belief that our new identity given to us at baptism does not abolish the sexual difference established by God at creation? As the recently published paper *True Union in the Body?* puts it:

The apostolic teaching clearly was not so eschatological that it believed our identity as male and female was stripped away through our baptism into Christ. Indeed, it may be a false belief, similar to this that led to some of the errors in Corinth which Paul (especially in 1 Corinthians 5–7) seeks to rectify. It is clear that the apostles continued to address and counsel believers as men and women, husbands and wives, fathers and mothers: and ... nuptial imagery remains of great importance in New Testament Christology, ecclesiology and eschatology.[80]

- In the light of the biblical material that we have explored in Chapters 3 and 4, is it possible to accept Breidenthal's suggestion that same-sex unions should be honoured providing they can demonstrate a similar discipline and similar hope to other types of Christian household? Does his argument not leave out of consideration the question of whether same-sex sexual relationships are intrinsically incompatible with a life of Christian obedience?

- Does the fact that gay and lesbian people often find their experience of the Church a very painful one, and the fact that they may indeed experience God's grace in a very powerful fashion, constitute a legitimate argument in favour of the acceptance of same-sex sexual activity, or does it simply mean that the Church needs to offer gay and lesbian people more effective pastoral care and needs to have a greater appreciation of the gifts that they have to offer? We shall explore this issue in detail in Chapter 8.

- Even if, over the centuries, marriage has been linked with the social and economic control over women by men does this mean that the fundamental Christian understanding of marriage as a lifelong mutual commitment of love between two people freely entered into is oppressive by nature?

- Is there any empirical evidence to support the Freudian claim that human beings are naturally bisexual? Does the available evidence not in fact suggest that the vast majority of human beings are naturally heterosexual?

- Is friendship not different from marriage both in its nature and in its theological significance, and does this not mean that friendship cannot simply replace marriage as the model for the relationship between men and women?

- Although the use of the term 'friend' alongside other metaphors for God may help to illuminate certain aspects of the biblical witness, is there not the danger that a focus on friendship as a controlling metaphor for God will lead to a sidelining of other biblical images that stress the sovereignty and authority of God over human beings?

5.6.3   The fundamental issue underlying all the questions that we have just listed is the same one that has already arisen in our consideration of homosexuality in the previous chapter, namely, how one assesses the validity of fresh developments in theology. Like the revisionist theologians we looked at in the last chapter, many of the writers whose work we have considered in their chapter are not seeking to reject the Christian tradition, but to develop it in new ways that resonate with their experience and that of other women and other lesbian and gay people. They also seek to explore and bring to light parts of the Christian tradition that have been forgotten, suppressed or lost.

5.6.4   Seeking to develop the Christian tradition in new ways is a legitimate exercise, and one in which the Church has always been engaged, but it carries with it the inevitable danger of developing the tradition in a direction that no longer remains faithful to the divine self-revelation on which Christian theology is based. Gnosticism and Arianism were rejected by the Church as false developments, for example, because in their different ways they made it impossible to confess with full seriousness the apostolic testimony that 'in Christ God was reconciling the world to himself' (2 Corinthians 5.19).

5.6.5   What needs to be discussed is whether the kind of theology at which we have been looking is a legitimate development. In their desire to rethink Christian theology in the light of gay and feminist concerns have the writers concerned remained faithful to what God has made known to us – and continues to make known to us through the Holy Spirit – about who God is, how God relates to us, and how, in response, we are called to relate to each other?

5.6.6   Finally, we need to remember that important and significant theological work – which goes on to become central to the Church's beliefs and practices – often emerges initially on the margins. This is entirely in keeping with the witness of the Gospels. For example, in Matthew 15, it is an outsider, the Canaanite woman – a Gentile, a woman, on the margins of Jesus' Jewish world – who raises the issue of Jesus' mission beyond the House of Israel to the Gentiles, anticipating the universal mission of the Church set out in Matthew 28, and the teaching in Acts and the Epistles of St Paul that the Christian community is a community where barriers of ethnicity, gender, social status and prevailing prejudices have no place.

5.6.7 If Christian people take to heart the full critique of traditional Christianity as set out in this chapter, many will experience it as a direct threat to their identity as Christians. It will be perceived as undermining the very foundations of their faith. The temptation, therefore, will also be either to reject instantly or ignore such radically challenging perspectives. They are relatively new and most of us have not even begun to understand, let alone assess, them. This is not, of course, to imply in any way that everything that has been put forth as a criticism of traditional Christianity is correct. As the nineteenth-century Anglican theologian F. D. Maurice used to say, people are more usually right in what they affirm than in what they deny. But we can only work our way through to a genuine discernment of what is legitimate and what is illegitimate development of Christian truth by sympathetic, honest and patient dialogue.

5.7 Concluding questions

5.7.1 The material in this chapter has been designed to show the range of recent thinking on gender and sexuality within, on the margins of, and outside the Christian tradition. It has also shown what may be the historical roots of modern assumptions about sex, gender and sexual identity, and has laid out the complicated relationship between the Churches and modern thinking about personhood, identity and rights.

5.7.2 The questions raised by this material are really about the nature of the Christian tradition, and the relationship between gospel and culture. To what extent is the Christian tradition always dynamic? How much are Christian beliefs and practices necessarily shaped by culture? What is the significance of forgotten traditions and stories, or new readings of orthodox texts? And should we restore or bring them to the centre of the Church? How do we enable the marginalized in the churches to speak theologically and how much are they the prophetic voices in our midst? And finally, how important are questions of gendered and sexual identity? – and have we exaggerated their importance in the modern era?

chapter 6

Bisexuality

6.1 Introduction
6.1.1   As was noted in Chapter 1, homosexuality is not the only issue that is currently raising questions about the Church's traditional understanding of human sexuality. This is also true of bisexuality.

6.1.2   The purpose of this chapter is to look at the theological issues raised by bisexuality. The phenomenon of bisexuality will be described, an account will be given of the current theological debate about this phenomenon, and the critical questions arising from this debate will then be noted.

6.2 What is bisexuality?
6.2.1   The most straightforward definition of bisexuality is that given by Elizabeth Stuart and Adrian Thatcher in their book *People of Passion*. They note that, like the term 'homosexuality', the term 'bisexuality' is a nineteenth-century term and that it is used to describe 'those men and women who feel sexual attraction to those of both sexes'.[1]

6.2.2   Thatcher gives a more detailed explanation of the nature of bisexuality in his book *Liberating Sex*, drawing on the testimonies of bisexual people recorded in the volume *Bisexual Lives*.[2]

> Bisexual people experience erotic attraction towards members of both sexes. They are likely to be more hidden even than gays and lesbians, and to be misunderstood by both groups as failing fully to 'come out' or as attempting to have the best of both worlds. The over-used and over-tidy classifications of 'heterosexual' and 'homosexual' leave little room for further orientations, yet according to the orientation scale ... everyone from points 1–5 has at least incidental sexual experience with people of both sexes while only those on point 3 are classified as primarily bisexual.[3] Classification almost breaks down at this point. A bisexual person might be one equally attracted to women or to men, yet if the balance is slightly altered he or she might be classified 'basically heterosexual' or 'basically homosexual'. Such a person may in any case be unable or unwilling to engage in such precise self-definitions. It is suggested

that, according to one reading of orientation, 'There are enormous numbers of bisexuals in the world – probably over one third of the population – but most do not call themselves bisexual yet.' The very existence of bisexual people 'in significant numbers', let us say, provides further support for the assumption that there is a basic bisexuality in all of us which biological and social influences help to channel towards our eventual sexual orientation.[4]

6.2.3   This quotation from Thatcher helpfully points us to a number of significant issues that are raised by the phenomenon of bisexuality.

6.2.4   The first of these is the vulnerability of people with what are perceived as 'unusual' sexual desires. As Thatcher notes, openly bisexual people are a minority within a minority who are likely to attract criticism from heterosexuals for failing to conform to a heterosexual norm and from homosexuals for failing to have the courage to 'come out' and declare themselves as lesbian or gay.

6.2.5   The second is the difficulty that attends the attempt to provide clear and precise definitions of people's sexual orientation given that, as we noted in Chapters 1 and 4,[5] people experience different phases of sexual attraction and activity.

6.2.6   For example, if someone has homosexual sexual experience at school or university and then goes on to marry and to have solely heterosexual experiences thereafter, how should their sexuality be defined?

- Are they someone who is heterosexual but has had a few homosexual experiences?

- Are they someone who is homosexual but has denied the fact because of social pressure?

- Are they bisexual but unable or unwilling to admit to the fact?

Alternatively, should we give up the attempt to define people in terms of a fixed sexual orientation and simply note the fact that people have a range of sexual attraction and experiences, which may take different forms at different points in their lives?

6.2.7   The third issue, which is related to the second, is the question of the prevalence of bisexuality. Thatcher notes the claim made by some bisexuals that over a third of the population are, in fact, bisexual, and the further claim that this points to a basic bisexual orientation in everyone. The problem with deciding this issue relates to the question of definition outlined in the previous point.

6.2.8   If people are asked about how they define themselves sexually the figures for bisexuality turn out to be remarkably low. For example, the extensive research undertaken by E. O. Laumann and others in the United States and published in 1994 found that 0.8 per cent of men and 0.5 per cent of women identified themselves as bisexual.[6]

6.2.9   It could be argued, however, that this low self-identification merely reflects social prejudice against the concept of bisexuality and a much higher figure would be obtained if it included everybody on points 1 to 5 of the Kinsey scale. It is on this basis that the figure of over a third of the population's being bisexual could be obtained.

6.2.10   This conclusion could itself be criticized, however. Kinsey's figures for same-sex sexual experience have been widely criticized as overinflated[7] and, even if they were accepted, the difficulty noted above about how to classify someone with both heterosexual and homosexual attraction and/or experience would still remain.

6.2.11   It is even more problematic to follow Sigmund Freud and to argue that all human beings are basically bisexual and become either heterosexual or homosexual as a result of biological and social factors. This is a hypothesis that, in the nature of the case, would be difficult to prove and it does not seem to have attracted widespread support.

6.2.12   The reason it is important to note these issues is that they feed into the theological discussion of bisexuality, and it is to this discussion that we shall now turn.

6.3 Bisexuality – the theological debate

6.3.1   As Thatcher rightly notes; 'Bisexual people are almost always overlooked in discussions of sexuality',[8] and what is true generally is also true in regard to the theological discussion of sexuality.

6.3.2   In most of the theological discussion of sexuality, bisexuality is totally ignored. For example, the Evangelical Alliance report *Faith, Hope and Homosexuality* has no mention of bisexuality and the same is true of the URC's *Human Sexuality Report* and the Roman Catholic

Catechism of the Catholic Church. A reading of these documents and most of the studies of Christian attitudes to sexuality by individual authors would lead to the conclusion that human sexuality exclusively occurs in heterosexual or homosexual forms.

6.3.3　A theological debate about bisexuality is now beginning, however, and as we shall see, it is a debate that raises the same basic issues about human sexuality as are raised by the discussion about homosexuality.

6.3.4　A good way into the debate is by looking at the brief statement about bisexuality contained in *Issues in Human Sexuality* and the reaction to it by Thatcher and Stuart.

6.3.5　Paragraph 5.8 of *Issues* reads as follows:

> We recognise that there are those whose sexual orientation is ambiguous, and who can find themselves attracted to partners of either sex. Nevertheless it is clear that bisexual activity must always be wrong for this reason, if for no other, that it inevitably involves being unfaithful. The Church's guidance to bisexual Christians is that if they are capable of heterophile relationships and of satisfaction within them, they should follow the way of holiness in either celibacy or abstinence or heterosexual marriage. In the situation of the bisexual it can also be that counselling will help the person concerned to discover the truth of their personality and to achieve a degree of inner healing.[9]

6.3.6　There are three points made in this paragraph:

- Bisexuality is an ambiguous condition and those who are bisexual may need counselling to discover who they really are and to obtain inner healing.

- Bisexual activity is always wrong, principally because it inevitably involves infidelity.

- The right course for bisexual Christians is either celibacy or heterosexual marriage.

6.3.7　Thatcher challenges all three points in *Liberating Sex,* calling into question the whole framework within which the *Issues* paragraph is operating.

6.3.8   First of all he challenges the idea that bisexuality is an ambiguous condition by suggesting that the very idea of people having fixed homosexual and heterosexual dispositions is itself questionable: 'Bisexual orientation is ambiguous only in relation to fixed alternatives. Might it be that these are ambiguous rather than bisexual people?'[10]

6.3.9   Secondly, he challenges the notion that bisexuals need inner healing by pointing out that: 'The reference to healing makes sense only if one is sick,'[11] and this is precisely the issue under dispute.

6.3.10   Thirdly, he challenges the idea of offering bisexual people the choice of either celibacy or marriage by arguing that celibacy cannot be compulsory and that, if a bisexual person gets married, this may lead to complications at some later date:

> The stark choice between celibacy or heterosexual marriage places it within a framework that knows nothing of bisexuality and cannot cope with it. Even homosexuals were allowed the right of conscience. Bisexuals have only compulsory celibacy to choose from. But, as we have observed, celibacy is a gift not a requirement, and heterosexual marriage, while it is an option, may lead to serious complications later.[12]

6.3.11   Finally, he challenges the notion that bisexuality necessarily involves infidelity by suggesting that we need to listen to the testimonies of bisexual people and ask what kind of fidelity might be appropriate for bisexual people, given their specific sexual desires or needs:

> Whatever heterosexual filter is placed over the lens that scrutinizes bisexual people, they will continue to report, honestly, that attraction to both sexes is powerful and integral to their lives. Much attention needs to be given to them which is not based solely on past solutions involving procreation and abstinence. The bishops are right to identify fidelity as a central issue. Is a bisexual person someone who is attracted to people of either sex or someone who needs sexual contact with people of both sexes? Do we know? Can we know? A 'need' can be confused with a 'want' yet the two are very different. Is there a married person alive who has never at some time wanted someone sexually other than his or her spouse? Is there a case for bisexuals behaving differently?
>
> Perhaps marriage is unsuitable for bisexual people? It is difficult to see how marriage can withstand the strain of one partner also in a

homosexual relationship outside the marriage, but such marriages exist, inside and outside the Church, and some of them appear strong, fortresses of acceptance and love.[13]

6.3.12   What Thatcher is calling for is a paradigm shift in our thinking about bisexuality so that we no longer try to fit bisexuality into a simplistic view of the world, in which people are basically either heterosexual or homosexual, but take bisexuals seriously on the basis of what they have to say about their own experience, and construct an ethic for bisexual conduct that makes sense in the light of this experience.

6.3.13   The challenge that such a paradigm shift poses for traditional Christian sexual ethics is well expressed by Stuart and Thatcher in *People of Passion*. They note that:

> ... bisexuals undermine the whole sexual system, the neat classification of people into homosexual and heterosexual, the pathologizing of homosexuality as a heterosexual disorder and so on. Bisexuality represents desire unfettered, and perhaps that is why those who experience it are so studiously unacknowledged in church documents, and on the odd occasion where they are acknowledged they are pathetically misrepresented as sexually indiscriminate and promiscuous.[14]

6.3.14   The point they are making is that the reason that the Church has been unwilling to take bisexuality seriously is that, once we view bisexuality as an ethically valid option, then this means accepting that sexual desire and its gratification in sexual intercourse are things that are good in themselves regardless of the number or sex of the people involved. It means rejecting any attempt to classify people as 'heterosexual' or 'homosexual', and instead adopting a pluralist, 'postmodern', approach that lets people explore and define their own sexual identity in any way they see fit.

6.3.15   This point is expressed in terms of personal experience by Sue George in her book *Women and Bisexuality*:

> I love having no limits on who I can get close to, and having several people who are 'special'. I love the richness of my experience and life. It can be a way of expressing a sexuality which sees the person rather than the gender; it can be a way of having relationships that do not

rely on stereotypes; it can be a way of relating more closely to people of both sexes; it can encompass many types of sexuality and many different people. Ideally, bisexuality is a way of forming relationships without putting boundaries on them because of gender.[15]

6.4 Critical questions raised by the theological debate about bisexuality

6.4.1   The statement about bisexuality in *Issues in Human Sexuality* and the response to it by Stuart and Thatcher, together with the witness of Sue George about her own bisexual experience, raise a number of questions that will need to be considered in the course of future discussions of bisexuality.

6.4.2   The first question is the methodological one about the correct starting point for Christian reflection on sexual activity, which has already been noted in the course of this report. Should we start from the picture of human sexuality that we believe to be the one contained in the biblical witness and then evaluate the various forms of human sexual activity and inclination on this basis, or should we begin with the experience of human beings, in this case bisexual human beings, and then seek to interpret and evaluate the biblical material in the light of this experience?

6.4.3   Obviously we cannot make an absolute distinction here since, in practice, there is a constant interplay between experience and biblical interpretation. Nevertheless, if the argument of the previous chapters has been valid, it would be difficult to see how it would be consonant with the Anglican theological tradition to give the last word to personal experience. The Bible has to provide the framework within which to interpret our experience rather than the other way around.

6.4.4   The second question is the status of research into human sexual orientation in the development of Christian sexual ethics. As we have noted, sexual orientation is something that is very hard to define, and some of the claims that have been made for the prevalence of bisexuality seem exaggerated. However, the question of what relevance it would have for Christian sexual ethics if it could be established that a large proportion of the population were in fact bisexual is one that still needs to be faced. Would it make it difficult or impossible to present heterosexuality as the norm for human sexuality?

6.4.5   The third question is whether the discussion of bisexuality can be separated from a discussion of Romans 1.26-27.

6.4.6   It is sometimes assumed that bisexuality is a modern phenomenon about which the Bible is silent. However, as we have already noted (4.4.16–4.4.19), while the term is modern – and the mentality that suggests that bisexuality is an 'identity' is modern – the phenomenon or activity that it describes is definitely not. This is a point that is made very clearly by Mark Smith in his article referred to in Chapter 4. He argues that, far from being unknown, bisexuality was in fact the dominant sexual 'model' in the Hellenistic world of the first century:

> What may we conclude from this survey of ancient homosexual practices? The picture that emerges is characterized by great diversity. If we could take the time to include evidence for heterosexual activity, it would become clear that if there was any one sexual 'model' in Ancient Greece and Rome, it can best be described as bisexual ... Our modern use of the English language has served to distort the issue. We tend to speak of homosexuals or heterosexuals, gay or straight. The Greeks and Romans had no such language at their disposal. From their point of view humans are simply sexual, and they have expressed that sexuality in many different ways, with their own sex or the opposite or, perhaps more commonly, if pederastic practices tell us anything, with both at different times, maybe even at the same time ... My primary conclusion is that the bisexual 'model' that characterized the Greco-Roman world admitted of a plethora of sexual practices and attitudes, as different as human desires and the potential for human creativity, from multi-party orgies to platonic love, from pure heterosexuality to true bisexuality to committed adult homosexual marriage.[16]

6.4.7   As Smith goes on to argue, it seems 'highly probable' that, as a well-informed and well-travelled Roman citizen, St Paul 'knew that bisexuality was the standard "model" for sexual behaviour among his contemporaries'.[17] If this is indeed the case then it seems clear that his general condemnation of same-sex sexual relationships in Romans 1.26-27 would have included bisexual behaviour. Given this, the question arises as to whether we can still regard bisexuality as ethically valid if we accept the world view sketched out by St Paul in Romans 1 as ethically normative.

6.4.8   The fourth question is whether the overall biblical picture of God's intention for human sexuality allows room for any alternatives to a heterosexual monogamous norm other than abstinence or celibacy. This is an issue that has already been raised by the previous discussion of homosexuality, but it is raised even more acutely if recognition of bisexuality means moving to a position in which all forms of sexual activity are to be accepted if they meet the needs and desires of the people concerned.

6.4.9   The fifth question is the question of the meaning of marital fidelity. Traditional Christian teaching, based on the prohibition of adultery in the seventh commandment, has been that faithfulness within marriage necessarily entails the exclusion of all sexual relations outside marriage. Indeed, such fidelity has been seen as one of the defining characteristics of marriage. The question that Thatcher raises, however, is whether this traditional teaching meets the particular needs of bisexual people. What if someone who is bisexual is someone who needs a sexual relationship with people of both sexes in order to find personal fulfilment? Is this ruled out if they are married, because of the seventh commandment, or do we need to rethink what fidelity means in their particular case?

chapter 7
Transsexualism

Voices from the debate

Gender identity is assumed by many to be 'natural'; that is,
someone can feel 'like a man', or 'like a woman'. When I first
started giving talks about gender, this was the one question that
would keep coming up. 'Do you feel like a woman now?' 'Did
you ever feel like a man?' 'How did you know what a woman
would feel like?'

―――――◄○►―――――

I've no idea what 'a woman' feels like. I never did feel like a girl
or a woman; rather, it was my unshakeable conviction that I was
not a boy or a man. It was the absence of feeling, rather than its
presence, that convinced me to change my gender.[1]

―――――◄○►―――――

The four decades of living a secret life were over. As I progressed
along in counselling and emotional restoration, I came to see that
I had believed so many lies about myself. God hadn't made a
'mistake' in creating me with a male body. It was he that had
formed my body from the beginning. He had a destiny for me.
'My frame was not hidden from you when I was made in the
secret place. When I was woven together . . . your eyes saw my
unformed body.' (Psalm 139.15-16, NIV). God had planned for
me to become a man before I had even been created![2]

―――――◄○►―――――

My experience has shown me that to seek to change the mind
orientation of the transsexual is not only useless, but also wrong
and against the will of God. Let me explain. For over 30 years
I agonized before God in prayer over my condition. My cultural
religious conditioning had taught me that such thoughts, and the
desires which followed, were evil, and I sought God for healing in
earnest desperation. Although after severe self-abasement before
the Lord I seemed to have a short period of release, this never
lasted long, and certainly I was not granted healing by God in this
way. I turned to the only way I believe healing is possible, which

is by seeking the way of changing my bodily form to the gender
I knew to be my real gender. I have found healing now through
full gender reassignment.[3]

————◀○▶————

The process of healing my gender confusion began almost as soon
as I entered the kingdom, in October 1993, but it was more than
two years before I came to understand that the Lord was leading
me to reclaim my manhood. During 1995, I had become
increasingly uncomfortable with my artificial, self-made identity
of Patricia, and the necessary deception of maintaining its facade.
By then I had begun to share the truth of my past, initially with
my pastor and his wife, and gradually with others in the church.
This was a frightening time, as I could never be entirely sure of
people's reactions. Of course, my fears were never realized: the path
I was taking was ordained of God. He had prepared the way, and
the hearts of (almost) all the people with whom I shared my past.

The crunch came in December, when, during a Sunday service,
I clearly felt the Lord telling me that the time had come to
abandon my alter ego and begin to live my life as the man that
God had intended me to be.

————◀○▶————

7.1 Introduction

7.1.1   The purpose of this chapter is to look at the theological issues
raised by transsexualism. The format of this chapter will be the same as
in Chapter 6.

7.2 The nature of transsexualism

7.2.1   'Transsexuality', a term popularized by the American
psychiatrist Harry Benjamin in the late 1940s and early 1950s, is the
word that has been commonly used to refer to an extreme form of the
condition known as 'gender identity disorder' or 'gender dysphoria'.
More recently, the term 'transgender' has emerged – which suggests a
more fluid understanding of gender, that is, what we mean by the
constructed terms 'masculinity' and 'femininity'. We, however, have
chosen to use the word 'transsexualism' because this seems to have
taken over from transsexuality as the preferred way to refer to this
condition.

7.2.2   Transsexualism is an extreme form of gender identity disorder in that, as the Home Office's *Report of the Interdepartmental Working Group on Transsexual People* puts it, those who are transsexual:

> ... live with a conviction that their physical anatomy is incompatible with their true gender role. They have an overwhelming desire to live and function in the opposite sex.[4]

7.2.3 More detail about the nature of transsexualism is provided in the recently published Evangelical Alliance report on the subject. It explains that:

> Transsexuality may often be marked by a strong rejection of the individual's physical sexual characteristics and, again at its most extreme, may be absolute, overwhelming and apparently unalterable. A transsexual man, for example, may feel an attraction towards other men, but unlike a homosexual will prefer to relate to them as female. Transsexuals seek to live in their preferred gender role and may undergo surgery to conform their body to that of the opposite sex. They remain well aware of their actual anatomical sex, and for the 'condition' of transsexuality to be present no doubt will exist concerning the actual biological sex of the individual. Transsexuality is seen by psychologists as the end stage of gender identity disorder. Some have described it in terms of a state in which the mind can no longer accept the body. Accordingly, a definition frequently encountered is that of 'feeling like a man trapped in a woman's body' or vice versa.[5]

7.2.4 Two key points to note from the Evangelical Alliance report are:

a. The fact that, in the case of transsexuals, there is no doubt about their biological sex.[6] In terms of their genetic, physical and hormonal characteristics they unambiguously belong to the sex to which they believe they do not belong. To quote Rodney Holder:

> With transsexualism the standard biological tests for sex are unequivocal, i.e. the sex chromosomes, gonads (testes and ovaries) and genitalia of transsexuals are uniformly all male or female. This is in contrast to hermaphroditism, which is a congenital disorder in which both male and female gonads are present and the external genitalia are not clearly male or female. Hermaphroditism is generally treated in early childhood by surgery and hormone therapy, whereby the patient is assigned an unambiguous phenotype of either male or female.[7]

b. Because the biological sex of transsexuals is unambiguous, medical intervention takes the form of 'sex reassignment surgery' in which, as far as possible, the physical characteristics of the individual concerned are altered to those of the opposite sex. The treatment involved is described by Holder:

> Treatment is often by sex reassignment surgery (SRS) but this should follow a protracted period of psychological consultation, and a period living in the psychologically perceived sexual role, while undergoing hormone treatment. The latter will produce secondary sexual characteristics, e.g. facial hair and deepening of the voice in the case of a female-to-male transsexual. Surgery comprises mastectomy and hysterectomy for female-to-male and removal of penis and testicles in male-to-female. Reconstruction of genitalia of the reassigned sex is successful in the case of male-to-female but so far it has proved impossible to construct a functional penis in the female-to-male case – a fact which might well impinge on an ethical judgment as to the validity of marriage following the operation in this case. In either case certain features of the original biological sex remain, not just the genetic inheritance of the sex chromosomes, but bodily features such as bone structure.[8]

7.2.5   It also needs to be noted that SRS is not the only form of treatment. Holder quotes the researches of L. M. Lothstein and S. B. Levine, who cite a 70 per cent incidence of successful adjustment to the person's bodily sex in response to psychotherapy without surgery in a sample of fifty patients.[9]

The history of transsexualism
7.2.6   The first known example of SRS occurred in 1930 when Danish artist Einar Wegener became Lily Elbe but, according to the researches of A. Bolin cited by Victoria Kolakowski in her article 'Towards a Christian Ethical Response to Transsexual Persons', medical research into the condition really began in the early 1950s.[10]

7.2.7   The question of whether transsexuals have always existed is one to which there is no agreed answer.

7.2.8   Transvestites, those who dress as members of the opposite sex, have been known throughout history but, since people are often transvestite without being transsexual, this does not tell us anything about the history of transsexualism.

7.2.9   However, Mark Dainton and Keith Tiller argue in their booklet *Ministry to the Gender Confused* that gender confusion and the desire to change sex has in fact existed from ancient times.

> Though only recently gaining significant media attention and public knowledge, gender confusion is almost certainly not a new problem, all ancient mythologies include examples of people wishing to change sex. There are a number of historical examples of gender confusion, the earliest probably being that described by the Jewish philosopher Philo in around 20 BC, of men wishing to be women. The Roman emperor Nero, full of remorse after murdering his wife, apparently arranged for a male slave who resembled her to be transformed into a female, though no record survives as to how this was achieved. Indian society has a long history of male eunuchs who live as women, who are very highly regarded and often thought of as possessing supernatural powers.
>
> An often quoted case is that of the Chevalier d'Eon who supposedly rivalled Madame de Pompadour for the favours of Louis XV. With no possibility of surgery d'Eon's deception was soon discovered, but the king was fascinated by his story and made him a diplomat, after which he lived in retirement as a woman. There are many other historical examples of gender confusion both from men who wish to be women and women who wish to be men.[11]

7.2.10   While accepting that transsexualism as we know it is a twentieth-century phenomenon, Kolakowski also suggests that transsexuals did exist before the twentieth century but were either undetected or assumed to be homosexual.[12]

7.2.11   On the other hand, writers such as B. L. Hausman have argued that transsexualism was created by the medical profession during the last century by its labelling of a diverse set of gender disorders as transsexualism and by its offering surgery as a treatment.[13]

The causes of transsexualism

7.2.12   The differences between Kolakowski and Hausman on the history of transsexualism reflect the fact that there are different understandings of the causes of this phenomenon. These can be classified as the physiological, psychological and the social explanations.

7.2.13   The *physiological* explanation holds that there are certain physiological differences between transsexuals and the rest of the population. There have been various suggestions as to what these differences might be. As the Evangelical Alliance report notes:

> Some have suggested that it is due either to an abnormal gene, altered levels of hormones in the body, or because some part of the body (often the brain) is more like the opposite sex in the way that it works.[14]

7.2.14 The *psychological* explanation holds that in terms of physiology transsexuals are like everyone else but for some reason they have come to see themselves as trapped in a body of the wrong sex. In the words of the Evangelical Alliance report:

> Others have suggested that these physical causes are not important, and rather than transsexual people being born with their sexual identity pre-set, influences in the person's environment, such as an abusive father or an emotionally cold mother, are more likely causes which give rise to feelings of rejection of the body and a life of denial with regard to one's biological sex.[15]

7.2.15 The *social* explanation holds that the cause of transsexualism is to be found neither in physiology nor in psychology but in the way in which society has developed. As has already been noted, there are those who would argue that medical developments have been crucial in leading to the development of a self-conscious transsexual identity. Alternatively, others would argue that transsexualism is the response to the way in which male and female gender roles have developed in Western society. Fraser Watts, for example, notes the argument that:

> ... the current way in which we currently distinguish between male and female in our society is over-rigid and that this in turn gives rise to the concept of transsexualism. It is possible that drawing a less sharp boundary between male and female would allow people to operate much more easily in an in-between area and that transsexualism as we know it would become unnecessary.[16]

7.2.16 Because physiological and psychological factors are not susceptible to change in the same way as social factors, those who favour a physiological or psychological explanation for transsexualism are more likely to be open to its being a phenomenon that has occurred throughout history than are those who favour a theory of social causation.

7.2.17   One last point that needs to be noted on this subject is that these explanations are not necessarily seen as mutually exclusive. For instance, the American writer John Money declares:

> Causality with respect to genetic identity disorder is subdivisible into genetic, prenatal hormonal, postnatal social and postpubertal hormonal determinants . . . .There is no one cause of a gender role. It develops under the influence of multiple factors, sequentially over time, from prenatal life onwards. Nature alone is not responsible, nor is nurture alone. They work together, hand in glove.[17]

7.2.18   What all sides in the causation debate are agreed about is that transsexualism is not a matter of voluntary choice by the individual concerned. No one chooses to be transsexual. They are either born or develop that way for reasons beyond their control. This does not necessarily mean, however, that a transsexual person cannot come to accept his or her biological sex, a point to which we shall return later in this chapter.

The growth of the debate about transsexualism

7.2.19   As Dainton and Tiller explain, transsexualism first came to public attention in the early 1950s at much the same time that it became the subject of serious medical research.

> The first transsexual case to excite real media attention was that of American GI George Jorgensen who became Christine Jorgensen following gender reassignment by Dr Christian Hamburger in Casablanca in 1952. Jorgensen's story was widely published in both America and Europe and in its aftermath many transsexuals who had probably resigned themselves to forever remaining in their original gender began to seek similar treatment.
>
> Since the publicity surrounding Christine Jorgensen many other transsexuals have come to public attention, sometimes by producing their autobiographies or selling their stories to the press, or often through uninvited exposure. In Britain the case of the transsexual phenomenon came to prominence in 1970 when the transsexual model April Ashley fought a case for her marriage to a man to be legally recognised, ironically to allow for a divorce. Ashley lost with the legal precedent set that gender is irrevocably fixed by chromosomes at birth.[18]

7.2.20   Since the Ashley case, transsexuals in Britain, alongside transsexuals in other countries, have waged an increasingly high-profile

campaign for a reversal of the Ashley judgment, and for legal
recognition of their right to live as members of their preferred sex,
including the right to marry as a member of that sex and to have their
birth certificates amended. As a result of this campaign the issue of
transsexualism is now firmly on the political agenda and has also
become a subject for discussion and debate within the Church.

In the words of the Evangelical Alliance report:

> ... during the past few years the issue of transsexuality has become
> increasingly high profile, not only in the media, but also in the
> political arena and in the courts, where recently employment
> legislation has been widened to take account of people who are
> transsexuals. In response to interest group pressure, further
> government legislation is anticipated soon to address the subject,
> including, for example, questions of identity and marriage. Groups
> of Christian transsexual people have also emerged to argue a case
> for acceptance of their particular lifestyle on Biblical and other
> grounds. In Christian circles, notably in churches, Bible colleges,
> Christian organisations and national conferences, the question of
> transsexuality has begun to surface with increasing frequency,
> involving complex and perplexing practical and theological
> consequences.[19]

7.3 The Christian debate about transsexualism

7.3.1   The amount of literature generated by the Christian debate
about transsexualism has so far been quite small, but what literature
there is reveals a clear pattern to the Christian debate on this subject.

7.3.2   The first thing that emerges is that, unlike in the case of
homosexuality and bisexuality, there is general acceptance that there are
no biblical texts that can be seen as addressing transsexualism as such.

7.3.3   The statement in Deuteronomy 23.1: 'No one whose testicles
are crushed or whose penis is cut off shall be admitted to the assembly
of the Lord' might be seen as a prima facie rejection of those who have
undergone male-to-female SRS, and by extension SRS itself. However,
it is generally accepted that this verse is cancelled out in the Old
Testament by the removal of the ban on eunuchs in Isaiah 56.4-5, and in
the New Testament by the acceptance of the genitally mutilated by Jesus
himself in Matthew 19.12, and by the account of the conversion of the
Ethiopian eunuch in Acts 8.26-39.[20]

7.3.4   Similarly, the statement in Deuteronomy 22.5: 'A woman shall not wear a man's apparel, nor shall a man put on a woman's garment; for whoever does such things is abhorrent to the Lord your God' might seem to rule out cross-dressing by either transvestites or transsexuals. However, there is general acceptance that this text is primarily addressing the need for the people of Israel to avoid copying Canaanite religious practices, although it may also reaffirm the need to reflect the principle that the distinction between male and female established at creation should be upheld.

7.3.5   As the Evangelical Alliance report puts it:

> ... whilst some Christians see reference in Deuteronomy 22.5 to a clear divine condemnation of transsexuality, most commentators suggest that this passage of Scripture contains minimal relevance to the debate at all, or indeed to twentieth century society. It is likely that, in keeping with God's covenantal concern to preserve the holiness of his character reflected within the covenant community of Israel, and to avoid anything which threatened Israel's existence and harmony, the cross-dressing prohibition was introduced to prevent involvement on the part of Israelites in contemporary Canaanite religious rituals of the day, which involved swapping of sex roles and cross-dressing. Whatever the significance of this particular verse of Scripture it is probably doing a disservice to reasonable hermeneutics to apply it directly to transsexuals. Nevertheless, the strength of the Hebrew word translated as 'abomination' or 'detests' indicates that in the sight of God such practices were fundamentally incompatible with identity with God's people, and therefore it remains likely that what this passage of Scripture is intended to signify is a reaffirmation of divine intent, in that the sanctity of the distinctiveness between the two created sexes is to be maintained.[21]

7.3.6   What the Christian debate concerning transsexualism has in fact been about has been the question of how to honour the principle expressed in Genesis 1.26-27 that God has created humanity as male and female, and that human beings are called upon to live in the light of that fact.

7.3.7   Those Christian writers on this subject who have been unwilling to accept the transsexual claim that they have a body of the wrong biological sex and the wish to have SRS to rectify the situation have based their objections on the ground that the biological sex of the transsexual is their true self. As they see it, for transsexuals to seek to change this is to reject the way that God has chosen to make them.

7.3.8   This is the argument that is put forward, for example, by Oliver O'Donovan in his 1982 Grove Booklet *Transsexualism and Christian Marriage*, described by Watts as: 'far and away the best piece of Christian writing about transsexualism'.[22]

7.3.9   O'Donovan's starting point for his consideration of transsexualism is his Christian conviction that humankind was created by God to be sexually 'dimorphic'. That is to say, according to God's creative intention, there is a clear difference between male and female human beings. Furthermore, the difference between males and females is at root a biological one. In his words:

> One can express the Christian perspective like this: the either-or of biological maleness and femaleness to which the human race is bound is not a meaningless or oppressive condition of nature; it is the good gift of God because it gives rise to possibilities of relationship within which the polarities of masculine and feminine, more subtly nuanced than the biological differentiation, can play a decisive part. Through masculinity and femininity we claim the significance of maleness and femaleness for relationship, and give it, through relationship, an interpretation which can express our individuality as persons. But this enjoyment of masculinity and femininity in relationship always evokes biological maleness and femaleness, and only as that biological opposition is taken up into a structure of life which fully exploits its capacity for enabling relationship, can masculinity and femininity be more widely enjoyed without fear of degeneration and exploitation.[23]

7.3.10   On the basis that it is one's biology that determines one's sex, and this is something God given, O'Donovan rejects the idea that someone can rightly claim to have a real sex that is different from the sex of their body:

> If I claim to have a 'real sex' which may be at war with the sex of my body and is at least in a rather uncertain relationship to it, I am shrinking from the glad acceptance of myself as a physical as well as a spiritual being, and seeking self-knowledge in a kind of Gnostic withdrawal from material creation.[24]

7.3.11   He also rejects the idea that someone's sex is constituted both by a unity of their biological sex and their psychological orientation. In particular he is opposed to the idea that he finds in the work of John Money that sexual differentiation is brought about by a process of both biological and psychological development stretching from conception to puberty. In the case of transsexuals the outcome of this process is ambiguous because their physical sex is at variance with their psychological sex because of hormonal factors, and it is therefore acceptable to remove this ambiguity by assigning them a unified sex through SRS.

7.3.12 According to O'Donovan this way of understanding transsexualism involves an unacceptable determinism. As he sees it, Money's argument that the psychological and biological development of human beings should be regarded as a unity means: 'The abolition of distinct spheres of biological and psychological sexuality' and this in turn means:

> ... our forgetting, or ignoring, all that we have learned through philosophy or science of the difference between causality in behaviour and causality in bio-mechanical systems. The sexual psychologists who have striven to free the concepts of masculinity and femininity from the strictness of biological dimorphic alternatives, have every reason to dislike what Money is saying. No philosophy of mind which desired to rise above the crudest materialism could be happy with it. And Christian thought, too, for all its concern with psychosomatic unity, does not intend that unity to be understood as the ascription of all sexual behaviour and relationship to a total neurological and chemical determinism. The price paid for a unified conceptual field at this point is extraordinarily high.[25]

7.3.13 As O'Donovan sees it, however, this is the price we have to pay if we want to accept Money's theory:

> But can the thesis that transsexualism is a form of intersex manage without such a unified conceptual field? Would the hormonal hypothesis, perhaps, if it were demonstrable, entitle us simply to class transsexualism as a physical condition without embarking on these more radical philosophical adventures? I think not; for the most that is claimed even for the hormonal hypothesis is that physical conditions can produce a predisposition to transsexualism, to which later psychological influences may or may not give effect. The character of transsexualism as a distinctly psychological disorder

is not called into question. Only such a categorical abolition of the distinct categories of psychological and biological could entitle us to question it.[26]

7.3.14   O'Donovan further rejects the notion that: 'the surgeon's art, by equipping the transsexual with functioning genitalia, can qualify him as a member of his assumed sex'.[27] For O'Donovan, this notion ignores the distinction between that which is God given and that which is an artificial human creation.

> To know one's body as self is to know the difference between that givenness from which one's freedom begins and all the artefacts which are the product of one's freedom. Artificial organs which are moulded onto or into one's body do not cease to be not-self and become self. They are properly called 'artificial' because their reality is not congruent with the reality of the body itself. Of course this does not as such prohibit their use. It is important, certainly, to the meaning of sexual intercourse that the organs with which we engage in it are ourselves; but if our organs are incapable of performing their duty and need artificial assistance, I know nothing that can be said against it in this case any more than against the use of crutches in walking. The point is simply that such assistance never becomes anything more than a substitute to make good the body's deficiency. Whatever the surgeon may be able to do, and whatever he may learn to do, he cannot make self out of not-self. He cannot turn an artefact into a human being's body. The transsexual can never say with justice: 'These organs are my bodily being, and their sex is my sex.'[28]

7.3.15   To put it simply, for O'Donovan human beings are either male or female because of their God-given biology and nothing a surgeon can do can alter this fact. SRS can never make a man a woman or vice versa.

7.3.16   The Evangelical Alliance report takes a similar line to that put forward by O'Donovan. It too argues that our sexual identity is determined by our biology and is to be regarded as something God given rather than something that we can choose for ourselves.

> The doctrine of *creation* with the story of Adam and Eve and the insistence that 'male and female he created them' points to the fact that our sexual identity is part of the 'givenness' of how we have been made. It is not therefore something we can select for ourselves

on the basis simply of how we feel. A Christian understanding of morality firmly resists treating human beings as somehow completely in charge of their own destiny and so justified in excluding the Creator and his purposes from the equation.

This text also underlines the basic and clear distinction between men and women (rather than, as some allege, a 'spectrum' with maleness and femaleness at each end and an ambiguous blend in the middle). This at least suggests that the individual who claims ontologically to be 'a woman trapped in a man's body' (or vice versa) is fundamentally mistaken given the Biblical assertion of the priority of the physical. Whether someone should have the freedom to undergo gender reassignment surgery on other grounds is, of course, a different question. The point is that a Christian understanding of what it is to be human cannot easily take at face value an individual's claim that their 'true sex' may be different from their birth sex as indicated by their chromosomes, gonads and external genitalia. Sex is so fundamental to human existence that it cannot be dissected out and viewed in isolation. And whilst it is true that the appearance of sexually-differentiated gonads and external genitalia is part of a process of development, this is not the case at the sex chromosomal level since these are, in the vast majority of cases, clearly either XX or XY from the outset.[29]

7.3.17   Because of the belief that sex is God given, the report concludes that it is not appropriate in normal circumstances for Christians to support either a transsexual lifestyle or SRS, and advocates that non-surgical responses to transsexuality should be explored and supported instead.

We affirm God's love and concern for all humanity, including transsexual people, but believe that human beings are created by God as either male or female, and that authentic change from a person's given sex is not possible. We further affirm that an ongoing transsexual lifestyle and gender reassignment is incompatible with God's will as revealed in Scripture and in Creation. We would oppose recourse to gender reassignment surgery as a normal valid option for people suffering from gender dysphoria on a Biblical basis, noting in addition that no long term research exists which validates the effectiveness of surgery in effecting gender change. Rather, we believe that acceptance of the Gospel of Jesus Christ offers real opportunities for holistic change in the context of non-surgical solutions. We appeal to the medical and psychiatric professions to prioritise research for the purposes of holistic treatment into the root psychological, social, spiritual and physical causes of 'transsexuality' rather than develop purely technical cosmetic options which remain essentially irreversible and require lifetime recourse to hormone therapy. We appeal to society as a whole to use Christian community values of love and care as a basis for thought and action.[30]

7.3.18 The report's advocacy of an holistic non-surgical approach to transsexualism is based on the conviction that, with appropriate support, transsexual persons can learn to accept and live according to their biological sex. This is the position taken by some Christians working with transsexuals such as Parakaleo Ministry,[31] but others working in the field would deny that such change is possible.

7.3.19 The report does note, however, the possibility that there may be occasions where support for someone choosing SRS can be seen as the only valid pastoral response to an emergency situation.

> The church may find that one of the most difficult situations arises where a transsexual person in contact with the church, despite every well intentioned effort to advise them otherwise, comes to the conclusion that the only alternatives open to them are gender reassignment surgery or suicide. Whilst not wishing to condone a course of action believed to be inherently opposed to God's revealed will, the lesser of two evils in such a case may necessarily and unavoidably be seen to be authentic practical support of the transsexual person throughout the operative phase as the only realistic compassionate option.[32]

7.3.20 The Roman Catholic ethicist Luke Gormally puts forward a similar argument to that put forward by O'Donovan and the Evangelical Alliance, although in his case there is a particularly Catholic emphasis on the effect of SRS on the ability to procreate children.

7.3.21 In a letter that he says reflects the consensus of 'sound Catholic moralists' he argues that a person's biological make-up is what determines their sexual identity:

> It is important to recognise that one's given biological sexual capacity (most importantly, gonads: testes, capable of producing sperm in men; ovaries, capable of producing ova, in women) is the normal basis of sexual identity in the human person. Factors in psychological development may lead people to a sense of self which is at odds with their actual sexual nature. But the truth about their

sexuality is manifested in their physical make-up and not primarily at the level of consciousness, which may be false.

7.3.22   He also argues that SRS is not acceptable because, in pursuit of a person's 'fantasy' about their true sexual identity, their overall 'personal good' is sacrificed in the destruction of their ability to have children:

> The human person is a unity of the biological, the psychological and the spiritual, and what we rightly mean by the 'personal good' of a human being involves all the fundamental or basic human goods that are at issue in these dimensions of our lives. And so, for example, it is in virtue of the generative capacity given with our bodily sexual make-up that we are capable of realising the basic human good of the transmission of life in marriage. Sacrifice of the choice to realise that good, as in voluntary celibacy, for the sake of another good ('for the sake of the Kingdom'), continues to honour the begetting of children as an integral part of the human good; it remains a realisable good, and recognised as a good, that one foregoes. Sacrifice of the capacity to realise that good, as in the voluntary destruction of generative capacity, in order to sustain a fantasy of sexual identity, treats the begetting of children as no part of the integral human good, the scope of which one has redefined on the basis of one's fantasy. Bodily integrity may not be sacrificed for 'personal good' so understood. Bodily mutilation is acceptable only when and as necessary to preserve health or life.

7.3.23   As Gormally sees it, because transsexualism is a psychological problem in which someone is alienated from their unambiguous sexual identity, the appropriate treatment is psychotherapy:

> Most studies suggest that such alienation is due to 'psychological causes' of one kind or another influencing the course of emotional and cognitive development. If that is so, then it would appear that something like psychotherapy is the appropriate approach to overcoming the alienation.

7.3.24   Those who take a more positive view of the transsexual claim and SRS as an appropriate response to transsexualism than either O'Donovan, the Evangelical Alliance, or Gormally do so on the basis that sexual differentiation cannot be seen simply as a biological given to be determined by an examination of the chromosomes, the gonads and the genitalia.

7.3.25   Holder, for example, accepts that: 'Human beings are indeed male or female and we relate to each other as sexual beings.'[33] However he then argues against O'Donovan that:

> The medical evidence seems to indicate that gender identity is not fixed irrevocably with the triad of chromosomes, gonads and genitalia. Brain differentiation occurs later, and psychosexual identity may be disrupted by physical and social pressures either side of birth. Psychologically perceived sexual identity, when in conflict with the biological triad, is highly resistant to change, though there is some evidence that psychotherapy works in some instances . . . . But SRS to change the bodily determinants to match those of the psyche is both indicated and successful in many cases.[34]

7.3.26   As Holder sees the matter, because human sexual identity is a function of both the body and the mind, transsexuals have an ambiguous sexuality and giving them a unified sexual identity through SRS is no different in principle from giving a unified physical identity to children born with ambiguous physical characteristics.

> I do not believe that we have to agree with O'Donovan that the surgeon has given the transsexual his sex, thereby rendering human sexuality an artefact. No, sexuality is given. In the case of the transsexual hormonal and/or psychosocial pressures have resulted in gender identity deviating from its normal path. Surgery, which has merely brought the two into line, admittedly by giving the primacy to the psychological perception over the physical evidence, is in principle no different from that in the case of hermaphroditism, where the assignment is arguably made on a more arbitrary basis.[35]

7.3.27   Kolakowski takes a similar line to Holder. She argues that we should accept the suggestion that there is some kind of biological component in the development of transsexualism.

> Although no clear consensus exists regarding its cause, experts agree that the condition is developmental in origin and uncorrectable by psychotherapy in most cases. The presently preferred belief that the condition is psychological is beginning to yield to recent studies showing a far greater biological component than previously thought.[36]

7.3.28   For Kolakowski the belief that transsexualism is a developmental condition with a strong biological component leads to the view that transsexual people have a mixed sexuality. She sees this as analogous to the mixed sexuality of the eunuchs mentioned by Christ in Matthew 19.12 and of the Ethiopian eunuch in Acts 8, and argues that the acceptance shown to them in the face of prevailing cultural prejudice provides a precedent for acceptance of both transsexuals and SRS by the Church today.

> ... this argument supports a more compassionate view of transsexuals and thereby of sex reassignment surgery. Since the transsexual, like the eunuch, is of mixed sexuality, and no condemnation is made of eunuchs, there is far greater reason to support surgical intervention where it compassionately meets a need in the transsexual person. This is especially true if research concludes that there is a strong biological component making surgery a more fitting response.[37]

7.3.29   Watts takes a slightly different position from either Holder or Kolakowski. He challenges the premise assumed by O'Donovan that the sex of the human body is something God given. Arguing that an evolutionary understanding of the world means accepting the idea that God has 'allowed considerable freedom about how evolution has proceeded',[38] he suggests that this freedom may extend to improving our bodies, and therefore: 'I do not see that a Christian need regard every aspect of material nature, even the sex of their bodies, as God-given and therefore sacrosanct.'[39]

7.3.30   As he sees it:

> ... O'Donovan needs to explain much more clearly why people should regard their bodies as a given. Christians would not, I think, regard people's personalities as a given that they should not attempt to improve. We do not accept personality problems in this way as something that simply limits our freedom, and about which we should not attempt to do anything. And if personalities are not regarded in this way, why should bodies be? Also, it is not clear that all aspects of our physical nature are a given that must simply be accepted. Most Christians would raise no objection to operations that corrected minor physical deformities. So why is transgendering different? O'Donovan might reply in terms of the ethical importance of a distinction between remedying deficits and attempting positive improvements. (Such a distinction is often made in ethical discussion about genetic engineering.) However, for O'Donovan's position to carry conviction he would have to go much further than he does in

spelling out where the boundary comes between what should and should not be accepted as a given by Christians, and why gender comes into the category of what should be accepted.[40]

7.3.31   Watts' view is that:

> ... rather than saying we must respect and work with nature as we find it, I would want to say that we should approach the modification of nature in a way that is constrained and guided by what we discern to be the creative purposes of God, and to carry these purposes forward as best we are able. On this view, the transsexual modification of physical sex should be approached in terms of whether or not it is seen as consistent with God's creative purposes.[41]

7.3.32   Watts does not explore the issue as to whether it should be seen as consistent with God's purposes in this way. He merely notes the possibility that transsexuals could be regarded as a third indeterminate sex, and notes that there are examples of 'transgendering' in Christian history. He does not make clear, however, what weight such considerations should have in determining the ethical validity of SRS today other than saying that the historical examples 'should at least be pondered before the Church condemns transgendering as sinful'.[42]

7.3.33   A fourth approach is that put forward in an unpublished paper by Peter Forster. He argues that the existence of gender dysphoria is a consequence of the fact that we live in a fallen world and that it is right for us to take action to correct the consequences of its fallenness:

> The fundamental theological point is a recognition that we live in a dynamic, imperfect, evolving world, which produces all sorts of phenomena which to varying degrees are ambiguous, dubious, distorted, mistaken, etc. ... These are set amid the essential beauty and goodness of creation, as life is set in the midst of death. Transsexualism appears to represent a dissonance, or fault-line, between certain features of the physical body and the self-perception of gender. How can we be certain that it is the perception which always needs to be corrected? In Christian theology, the fallenness of the world includes its physical being, as Genesis 3 makes clear. Modern cosmology reveals a physical universe on the way either to heat death or to catastrophe. In such a universe, each of our lives is subject to multiple fault-lines. If so, are we not permitted, within the limits of what is possible and desirable, to seek to correct gender-

related faults? All human action in this respect will be provisional, risky and subject to the recreative judgement of God, but that is no reason to refuse to countenance it. Such a refusal would be an example of the tendency in Christian ethical thinking to evade contact with the empirical realities of life in its present, provisional, fallen form.

7.3.34 Two particular issues that arise with transsexuality are the question of marriage, and the modification of birth certificates.

Marriage

7.3.35 There are two specific problems connected with the question of marriage.

7.3.36 The first problem is that of the person who marries and then undergoes SRS. What is the status of their marriage? The only person who comments on this is Holder who suggests that there are two ways of looking at the matter.

- The first is to argue that a marriage entered into by someone with transsexual feelings is one that requires annulment (rather than divorce) on the grounds that such a person was not capable of entering into a valid marriage in the first place.

- The second is to see the matter in terms of a disability which gradually emerged and which made sexual intimacy impossible and inappropriate (as in the case of a married man who lost his genitalia in an accident). In this case the disability would not of itself constitute grounds for divorce or annulment.[43]

7.3.37 Holder goes on to argue that a pre-operative transsexual who knew themselves to be transsexual ought to refrain from marriage. However, if they did marry and subsequently had SRS they ought to remain celibate in their new identity should their marriage not survive:

> Even if it were agreed that the first marriage were in principle null, on the grounds that for a valid marriage psychologically perceived gender identity and biological sex should be aligned, the vocation of a Christian transsexual, out of duty to his children and former spouse, would be to remain single.[44]

7.3.38 The second problem is that of someone who undergoes SRS and then wishes to marry as a member of their newly assigned sex.

7.3.39   There is a division of opinion on this problem, a division that reflects different attitudes to the whole question of transsexuality.

7.3.40   Under rulings given in the cases of April Ashley in 1970 and Elizabeth Bellinger in 2001[45] such a marriage is not legal in this country. However, in the case of Christine Goodwin, the European Court of Human Rights declared that the fact that transsexual people could not marry under British law was a breach of Article 12 of the European Convention on Human Rights[46] and so the law may well have to change. However, O'Donovan and the Evangelical Alliance report would still be opposed to the Church's recognizing such a marriage on the grounds that the transsexual is still a member of his or her original biological sex and, therefore, what is taking place is not a marriage between a man and a woman.

7.3.41   In the words of the Evangelical Alliance report:

> ... however apparently loving and mutually supportive a transsexual relationship may be, and however much society may be justified in wishing to offer such relationships the same freedoms and privileges that married couples enjoy, efforts to elevate them to the status of Christian marriage should be resisted on the grounds stated earlier.

> Such a relationship cannot be regarded as truly being contracted between a man and a woman but between two partners of the same sex, one of whom has adopted a gender identity which is at variance with their biological sex.[47]

7.3.42   Two further objections to the marriage of transsexual people have been noted by the Roman Catholic ethicist George Woodall in an unpublished paper entitled *Trans-sexual Persons and Catholic Moral Theology.*

7.3.43   His first objection is based on the fact that in Catholic moral theology the possibility of procreation is a necessary part of marriage. In the case of a post-operative transsexual this possibility will have been ruled out as a result of SRS and for Woodall, this means that it has to be asked: '... whether what is at stake is a form of simulation of marriage'.[48]

7.3.44   He would see this as a different issue from the marriage of someone who was sterile through no choice of their own, because in that case the person concerned would not have deliberately ruled out the possibility of procreation.

7.3.45   His second objection is rooted in his acceptance of a psychological basis for transsexualism.

7.3.46   Referring to the work of three American writers on transsexualism he declares that: 'both Coleman and Ashley and O'Rourke argue persuasively that trans-sexual persons have their problems of core gender identity rooted above all in psychological factors of a serious and enduring nature'.[49] As he sees it, the implication of the existence of these psychological factors is that someone who is transsexual 'is not adequately integrated to the minimum degree necessary to be capable of living out a married life'.[50]

7.3.47   He notes that Roman Catholic teaching as set out in documents such as *Gaudium et Spes* and *Humanae vitae* is that marriage requires:

> . . . a sufficient degree of self-possession to be capable of the self-gift and of the reception of the other on an enduring basis. Without such a minimal capacity, a person could not fulfil the obligations of marriage even if these had been grasped.[51]

7.3.48   As a result:

> A trans-sexual person would almost certainly be considered as being incapable of marriage in the terms of the Catholic Church's Canon Law.[52]

7.3.49   Holder and Kolakowski, by contrast, accept the idea of marriage for post-operative transsexuals. Both are aware of the problems raised by the fact that any such marriage will necessarily be barren, and that the limitations of SRS mean that full physical consummation of the marriage may not be possible. However, they argue that this would not make a Christian marriage impossible.

7.3.50   As Holder puts it:

> Despite these difficulties, it can be argued that the intention of a post-operative transsexual in marrying, i.e. to enter a heterosexual union which will be consummated, is good. The operation was carried out to remedy a severe dysfunction; the legacy of imperfect

genitalia constitutes a side effect of a procedure carried out to achieve personal integration and to enable pursuit of the vocation of marriage. The transsexual is doing the best he possibly can in adverse circumstances to achieve these goods, God's will for him in creation, of personal wholeness and union with a member of the opposite sex.[53]

7.3.51 Kolakowski, though not Holder, also argues that the growing recognition of same-sex unions is relevant to the issue: 'the compelling arguments of gay and lesbian people for recognition of same-sex unions also favours granting church recognition to the marriages of transsexuals'.[54]

7.3.52 The precise relevance of same sex unions to the marriage of transsexuals is not explained by Kolakowski, but presumably the point is that these are other examples of union in which neither procreation nor full consummation is possible.

Birth certificates

7.3.53 The issue of birth certificates is concerned with the question of whether they should be altered to reflect the newly assigned sex following SRS. This is something that is pressed for by groups campaigning for transsexuals, on the grounds that it reflects who they really have been all along, and would prevent distress caused by the revelation of their previous identity. As in the case of marriage, the altering of the birth certificates of transsexuals is not currently permitted under British law, but this situation has again been challenged by the Goodwin judgement, which declared that this was in breach of the right to private life enshrined in Article 8 of the European Convention on Human Rights.[55]

7.3.54 Both the Evangelical Alliance and O'Donovan comment on this issue and they are against the proposal to allow birth certificates to be altered.

7.3.55 The Evangelical Alliance report argues that amending birth certificates would be to support officially an illusion and would encourage moves towards transsexual marriage:

> Notwithstanding the arguments in favour, we nevertheless believe the case for transsexual people to be allowed to amend their birth certificates, except in rare cases of genuine mistake, to be

fundamentally flawed, open to abuse, and tending to undermine accepted realities by condoning illusion and denial. In particular, we believe it would lead to unacceptable legitimisation of currently illegitimate 'marriage' relationships and remove protection against deception.[56]

7.3.56   O'Donovan does not comment so explicitly on the issue but he cites the amendment of Canadian birth certificates as an example of the kind of 'public fiction' necessarily entailed by any public recognition of the preferred sex of post-operative transsexuals.[57]

7.3.57   By contrast to the Evangelical Alliance and O'Donovan, Forster sees no objection to altering a birth certificate:

> There is no reason why an amended birth certificate, detailing the change of gender identity, should not be issued, subject to appropriate scrutiny in individual cases, and medical certification. From that point, legally, the new gender should apply.

7.3.58   It should be noted, however, that Forster's position falls short of the desire of some transsexual people that what they would regard as their 'true' identity should be recognized to have existed from the time that they were born. As they would see it, their identity has not changed, rather their bodies have been brought more closely into line with who they really have been all along.

7.4 Critical questions raised by the debate about transsexualism

7.4.1   A number of questions arise out of the Christian discussion of transsexualism to date. These questions can be divided into seven categories.

a. A question about what it means to be a person

7.4.2   One way of approaching the debate about transsexualism would be to suggest that the primary thing to note is the obvious: that transsexuals are people and that, therefore, when we consider such issues as the pastoral care they may require, and their fitness to hold office in the Church, what we must look at is their needs and gifting rather than the question of their sexual identity.

7.4.3   This suggestion has merit in so far as it reminds us that transsexuals are not to be viewed simply in terms of the issues surrounding their sexual identity. However, in so far as it suggests that someone's personhood can be divorced from their sexual identity, it does raise the basic question of what it means to be a person.

7.4.4   As we noted at the beginning of Chapter 3, the Christian understanding of what it means to be is rooted in the teaching in Genesis 1.26-27 that human beings are made in the image of God. As we also noted, being made in the image of God means being made for relationship with God. In Atkinson's words, to be made in the image of God is to have the vocation to relate to him as 'his counterpart, his representative and his glory on the earth'.[58]

7.4.5   Furthermore, as the creation narratives in Genesis 1 and 2 make clear, the basic form in which human beings are created by God to relate to him in this way is as male and female: 'So God created humankind in his image, in the image of God he created them; male and female he created them' (Genesis 1.27).[59] This means that, from a Christian perspective, it is impossible to conceive of a person as a kind of abstract soul without an embodied sexual existence. That may be true of angels but it is not true of human beings. To be a human person is to exist bodily as either male or female and to relate to God and other people as such.

7.4.6   This further means that, from a Christian point of view, it has not traditionally been possible to separate the question 'who are you?' from the question 'what sex are you?' The two necessarily go together. And, indeed, it has to be said that transsexual people themselves are concerned to keep the two questions together because their whole struggle is precisely with the question of their sexual identity and how this is or is not expressed by their bodies.

b. Questions about divine order

7.4.7   As in the case of the debates about homosexuality and bisexuality, the fundamental questions surrounding transsexuality are questions about the ordering of human sexuality by God, and how this relates to the self-perceptions and desires of particular individuals.

- What constitutes the sex given to us by God? Is this determined by our biology, our psychological self-perception or a mixture of the two?

- Should we regard the sex given to us by God as sacrosanct or are we free to rectify or improve it if this can be seen to be in line with God's overall creative purposes?
- If it were to be established that either genetic or hormonal influences are the cause of transsexualism, should this affect our estimate of the sex of a transsexual person, or should these influences be viewed as pathological and therefore irrelevant to their true sexual identity?
- If we say that gender dysphoria is a consequence of the fallenness of creation, should we see that fallenness as being manifested in a person having the 'wrong' body for their true sexual identity, or in their belief that they have the wrong body?

c. Questions about the Bible

7.4.8   Although the discussion about transsexualism has not been focused on the interpretation of biblical texts, nonetheless, questions about biblical interpretation have arisen:

- Does Genesis 1–2 point to a basic dimorphic distinction between the sexes instituted by God at creation? If so, how do we relate the teaching of Genesis to the questions about sexual differentiation raised by modern medicine and contemporary explorations of the nature of gender?
- Does the prohibition of cross-dressing in Deuteronomy 22.5 have anything to contribute to a Christian view of transsexualism?
- Does the acceptance of eunuchs in Matthew 19 and Acts 8 say anything about the attitude Christians should take to transsexualism today?

d. Questions about medical intervention

7.4.9   In the light of the questions that have just been noted, a further question that needs to be addressed is the question about the proper limits of medical activity. The specific question in this connection is when does the use of medical techniques become an illegitimate attempt to transcend the proper limitations of our humanity?

7.4.10   The ethicist Robert Song addresses this question in his book *Human Genetics: Fabricating the Future*. He begins by contrasting the understandings of the status of our human bodies in the ancient heresy known as 'Gnosticism' and in orthodox Christianity:

The issue at dispute between gnosticism and orthodox Christianity with regard to the body was, and remains, something like this: is one's true self to be found in separation from or identification with one's body? Gnosticism gave the former answer. It held the dualist view that the spirit was to be separated from the body. Ethically, this might have the consequences that the body be treated with licentious abandon, since the condition of the body made no difference to one's moral purity (the 'antinomian' alternative); or that it be rigorously controlled in order to demonstrate one's moral worth (the 'legalist' alternative). Either way, the body was separate from one's true self. It was something that could be objectified or treated instrumentally. Within this view the idea becomes intelligible of the body as something which can be made indefinitely malleable to suit the self's ends, which can serve as raw material to be improved. The body is open to being seen as inherently faulty, needing human intervention to perfect it. Within the orthodox Christian view, by contrast, the physical body is something which is inseparable from the self. For Christians the process is more nearly that of learning identification with one's body rather than separation from it. Human bodiliness is something to be inhabited as the creation of a good God. Finitude is not to be regarded as an obstacle to true fulfilment or as something which is to be opposed or feared, nor is it the imposition of limits which it is the task of human endeavour to transcend.[60]

7.4.11 He then goes on to argue that the Christian approach to this issue has implications for the ethics of medical activity:

It does not follow, however, that Christians are committed to a certain kind of passivity because of their acceptance of human physical createdness. On the contrary, they are called to participation in God's action of restoring and redeeming the created world, and one of the central features of this is the practice of medicine . . . . There is, in other words, a proper role for therapeutic intervention against disease and bodily disorder, as a sign of the Kingdom which is the restoration and fulfilment of creation. But, if this is so, somehow a distinction needs to be made between those activities which are genuinely therapeutic, and those which, in a more gnostic spirit, amount to efforts to transcend the created order. Despite the difficulties we have already seen, and although the distinction still needs to be properly located, some kind of distinction between therapy and enhancement is at the heart of Christian claims about the nature of human beings and the meaning of salvation.[61]

7.4.12 As he sees it:

> One way of getting at the question is to ask about suffering. What kinds of suffering may we properly oppose, and what kinds should we properly learn to accept. What kinds of suffering are the appropriate role realm of medicine, and what kinds of suffering would it be wrong for medicine to try to banish? [62]

7.4.13 Although Song's argument is directed in the first instance to the debate about the development of medical technologies that utilize our increased knowledge of human genetics, what he has to say also addresses the issue of medical intervention as a response to gender dysphoria. No one questions that those who suffer from gender dysphoria do genuinely suffer. The ethical question raised by Song, however, is whether the attempt to address their suffering through SRS is an appropriate use of medicine. In Song's terms, is it a form of therapy that can be seen as a sign of the coming of the kingdom because it restores order to what is disordered in line with the healings recorded in the Gospels? Or is it an illegitimate attempt to use medicine to transcend the proper limits of our creatureliness by attempting to escape the body given by God?

7.4.14 In addition, we also have to give attention to the issue raised by Gormally about the destructive nature of SRS, in the sense that it destroys the capacity of the post-operative transsexual to have children. Is it morally right to destroy someone's God-given reproductive capacity in the course of SRS in order to treat gender dysphoria? Does the good that might be achieved outweigh the destructive nature of the activity involved?

7.4.15 What the issues raised by Song and Gormally mean is that the question of whether we should treat gender dysphoria with psychotherapy, SRS or a combination of the two is not simply a technical question about what is the most effective form of treatment. It is also an ethical question about the proper limits of medical treatment.

e. Questions about marriage and birth certificates

7.4.16 As well as the question we have just noted about the nature of gender dysphoria and its most appropriate treatment, there are also questions about the desire of transsexual people to marry and to have what they see as their true identity recorded on their birth certificate.

- Should the marriage of a pre-operative transsexual be regarded as a valid Christian marriage?

- Should a married person who undergoes SRS divorce on the grounds that they are now of the same sex as their spouse and should they remain celibate for the sake of their former spouse and any children they may have?

- Should the marriage of a post-operative transsexual be regarded as a marriage between two people of different sexes or two people of the same sex?

- If a marriage involving a post-operative transsexual cannot produce children and may not be able to be fully consummated can it still be a valid Christian marriage? If not, what does this say about the marriages of non-transsexual people where the same circumstances apply?

- Is it fair to regard the alteration of a transsexual's birth certificate as a 'public fiction'. Even if so regarded, could it still be justified as an act of compassion?

f. Questions about transsexuals in the life of the Church

7.4.17   As well as the questions already noted there are four specific questions about the place of transsexual people in the life of the Church.

- What is the best way to give pastoral support for pre- and post-operative transsexual people?

- What challenges do transsexual people pose for the church that is seeking to support them?

- Is it appropriate for transsexual people to engage in ordained ministry?

g. A question about discipleship

7.4.18   The fundamental question that pulls together all these questions is a question about discipleship. What does it mean for a transsexual person to live in obedience to Christ?

7.4.19   Does such obedience mean learning to accept and live with their given biological identity because this is the identity that God has given them, or does it mean seeking a new post-operative identity on the grounds that it is this that will enable them to express more fully the person God intends them to be?

7.4.20   As this chapter has shown, the issues surrounding transsexualism are very complex and controversial. However, this is no excuse for retreating into a gut reaction that simply says that transsexualism is unnatural and therefore wrong, or a simplistic approach that says that any course of action that enables people to feel more comfortable with their own identity must be the right one.

7.4.21   There are serious theological issues at stake here to do with the nature of sexual identity as created by God and as affected by a fallen world, and it is these theological issues that must be allowed to shape any responsible Christian approach to this subject.

7.4.22   At the heart of the matter is the question of the Christian understanding of what constitutes our God-given identity as human beings. It has traditionally been held that one of the implications of the Christian belief in the resurrection of the body is that it shows that our bodies are integral to who we are before God. We are not simply people who inhabit bodies, rather our bodies are part of who we are. If this is the case, what are the theological grounds for saying that, in the case of people with gender dysphoria, their 'true' identity is different from that of the body with which they were born? Can we go down this road without moving to a new form of gnostic dualism in which the body is seen as separate from the self?

chapter 8

Homosexuals, bisexuals and transsexuals in the life of the Church

Voices from the debate

As a gay man, I cherish the priests and congregations who will not look askance at my life and my partner. I rejoice that the Church of England retains a breadth and lack of authoritarianism and so, tacitly, permits such acceptance. Yet I mourn the fact of so many lesbians and gay men who, through bitter experience or understandable assumption, spurn organized religion. They have come to believe the cruel untruth that Christianity will not welcome their lives and their loves. I see in their eyes a mix of puzzlement and incredulity that a gay man will even set foot in a church.

———◀○▶———

Homosexuality comes in a very attractive package; books, videos, magazines, clubs, support groups and affirmative action are all freely available. Despite the presence of discrimination, it is comparatively easy to declare oneself gay and to live the lifestyle. We are less hung up about one another's sexuality than we think. Yet if something is attractive, if it is easy, does that also mean that it is right? As the dissatisfaction grew, I began to ask myself the hard questions: could I really cope with the possibility of a celibate, single lifestyle, when the alternative seemed so easy, so attractive and so available? Could I honestly have a relationship with God that was real, yet also give myself to someone of the same sex?

I wrote earlier about dissatisfaction in the depth of my being. I believed then and I believe now that to practise the sexuality that seemed to invade my mind would be wrong. I cannot name an exact date and time but the first decision I made was to acknowledge that the practice was wrong in God's eyes and however hard and despite the longing, obedience to him would come first.[1]

———◄○►———

What is it like, being a priest and having my primary human relationship with another woman? It's living an impossibility, it's listening to people on the radio or in conversation talking about 'them' and knowing it's me. It's living with a 'white noise' of anxiety and fear that is a tinnitus I can't shake. This fear is debilitating and echoes around the institution I move in. I can see it in the eyes of others too; the fear of being 'found' or the fear of being 'wrong' or the fear of having to make a relationship with someone they don't understand. It's listening to brothers and sisters to whom I am bound by my baptism, or ordination say that I can't be. And wondering if they are right. And knowing that they can't be right – as I live and breathe the delight and love I have found in the world. My home is with this woman; she is the 'right human face' that I thought I might never find. She is a gift to me and I thank and curse God by turns for giving me the contradictory (in our day) gifts of vocation to priesthood and vocation to relationship. It's wanting to take up my cross and follow Christ but refusing to be told my 'cross' is celibacy, by married men. It's knowing that my relationship is a resting place not a battle ground. It's wanting to say 'we' but being careful to say 'I'. It's accepting the institutional demand to lie well.

It is laughter, acceptance, support and friendship. It is knowing that I am a better priest and I walk the Way more closely because she travels with me.

It is living a paradox. I'm not the end product of an argument. I can't be. But I am. And that's where I live.

———◄○►———

I now experience sexual attraction in heterosexual, not homosexual, ways. For a while certain mental habits stayed with me, but that is all that they were – mental habits freed of their force – and as I write they have virtually disappeared. I forget for long periods that I have ever been 'gay', and when I do it seems like a bad dream. What gives me the greatest joy is the sense of being in right ordering, in being a woman as was intended in the creation of the world, not as marred by sin. This makes it much easier for me to take the full part in Christian life and service which I desire. I now see homosexuality primarily as a regrettable psychological handicap, open to God's healing. I have no easy way of accounting for the fact that I have been given what many others who struggle with their orientation long for and do not experience. In the end healing is a mystery, and we must trust in the rightness of God's way for each individual.[2]

———◀○▶———

... the transsexual condition as a human disorder which destroys the quality of normal life is not the creative will of God. In fact I have come to understand that, not only is it God's will that I should be female, but that the only way, and the way approved by God, is that I should have been healed by full gender reassignment. Far from sinning against God's creative purpose, I was fulfilling it by the means God has now provided in medical science.

In view of this conclusion, to discriminate against a transsexual who has received gender reassignment in any way so that that person is prevented from serving God in their calling is the serious sin, and it is not the sufferer from Gender Identity Disorder who has sought healing by gender reassignment that has sinned.[3]

———◀○▶———

At the time of writing, Jane and I have been married for fifteen months, with all the ups and downs that befall most marriages in their first year! We have both begun Christian training through an excellent locally run course, and I have just been selected to be a cell group leader in our church. I continue to work as a nurse, having gained promotion about eighteen months ago, and am also studying for a nursing degree. What of my spiritual life? I had hoped that marriage might finally kill stone dead all those old desires, but it didn't, at least not overnight. They resurfaced a few months into our marriage and I have had occasional periods of temptation since. However, I have not fallen into despair as before, recognizing the strategy of the enemy.

Rather, I have learned to turn to the Lord when the tempter strikes. Unless the Lord brings about a complete physical healing in me, which I don't discount and often pray for, I recognize that my foray into the world of transsexuality has left me with physical and mental scars that I may carry to the grave. My hope is that the Lord may enable me to use them to give hope to others and perhaps prevent them from falling into the same mess.[4]

————◄◦►————

8.1 Introduction

8.1.1   It should be noted at the outset of this chapter that those at the sharp edge of this debate are the gay, lesbian, bisexual and transgendered people in the Church. They live the painful reality of the paradoxes of their position, and can be subjected to homophobia – violence, and unkindness and exclusion based on prejudice.[5] This is especially true for gay, lesbian, bisexual and transgendered priests who struggle to reconcile their sexual identity and their vocation, while all the time continuing to serve the Church faithfully as their vocation demands. Any consideration of this whole issue has to take this reality into account, and make it a central pastoral concern.

8.2 The teaching of *Issues in Human Sexuality*

8.2.1   The 1991 report *Issues in Human Sexuality*, to which reference has already been made in Chapter 1, concludes that homosexuality cannot be regarded as an equally valid expression of God's intention for human sexuality as heterosexuality. It declares that:

> . . . homophile orientation and its expression in sexual activity do not constitute a parallel and alternative form of human sexuality as complete within the terms of the created order as the heterosexual. The convergence of Scripture, Tradition and reasoned reflection on experience, even including the newly sympathetic and perceptive thinking of our own day, make it impossible for the Church to come with integrity to any other conclusion. Heterosexuality and homosexuality are not equally congruous with the observed order of creation or with the insights of revelation as the Church engages with these in the light of her pastoral ministry.[6]

8.2.2   The report is also very clear, however, that this does not mean that those who are homosexual are of less value as people than those who are heterosexual or that God loves them any less. It lays down as a 'second fundamental principle' that:

> . . . homosexual people are in every way as valuable to and as valued by God as heterosexual people. God loves us all alike, and has for

each of us a range of possibilities within his design for the universe. This includes those who, for whatever reason, find themselves with a homophile orientation which, so far as anyone at present can tell, cannot in their case be changed, and within which therefore they have the responsibility of living human life creatively and well. Every human being has a unique potential for Christlikeness, and an individual contribution to make through that likeness to the final consummation of all things.[7]

8.2.3   Having laid down these two principles the report then goes on to explore how these principles should find expression within the life of the Church.

8.2.4   It begins by noting that some Christian homosexuals feel called 'to witness to God's general will for human sexuality by a life of abstinence'.[8] This, it says, 'is a path of great faithfulness, travelled often under the weight of a very heavy cross. It is deserving of all praise and of the support of Church members through prayer, understanding and active friendship.'[9]

8.2.5   It also notes, however, that there are others:

> ... who are conscientiously convinced that this way of abstinence is not the best for them, and that they have more hope of growing in love for God and neighbour with the help of a loving and faithful homophile partnership, in intention lifelong, where mutual self-giving includes the physical expression of their attachment.[10]

8.2.6   The report suggests that in thinking how to respond to such people we need to bear in mind that, alongside its belief in a God-given moral order, the Christian ethical tradition has also emphasized 'respect for free conscientious judgement when the individual has seriously weighed the issues involved'.[11] Application of this tradition of respect for the conscientious judgement of the individual means, the report says, that the Church must not reject those who believe that homosexual sexual activity is appropriate for them:

> While unable ... to commend the way of life just described as in itself as faithful a reflection of God's purposes in creation as the heterophile, we do not reject those who sincerely believe that it is God's call to them. We stand alongside them in the fellowship of the Church, all alike dependent upon the undeserved grace of God. All those who seek to live their lives in Christ owe one another

friendship and understanding. It is therefore important that in every congregation such homophiles should find fellow-Christians who will sensitively and naturally provide this for them. Indeed, if this is not done, any professions on the part of the Church that it is committed to openness and learning about the homophile situation can be no more than empty words.[12]

8.2.7   It also maintains however, that what it says about the need for the Church to accept those in sexually active homosexual relationships has to be qualified in four ways.

- It does not mean an acceptance of bisexuality since, as has been noted in a previous chapter, the report sees bisexual sexual activity as inevitably involving infidelity.

- It does not mean an acceptance of the argument put forward by some homosexual activists that short-term or casual sexual partnerships are acceptable in the case of homosexuals. This argument, the report declares, 'is simply a pretentious disguise for the evil of promiscuity'.[13]

- It does not mean an acceptance of paedophilia whether this be homosexual or hetereosexual in nature:

  > Paedophilia breaches the limits of what is healthy in the child-adult relationship, and in Christian terms is a sin not only against chastity but also against charity and justice.[14]

- Finally, it does not mean that it is acceptable for members of the clergy to enter into sexually active homosexual relationships:

  > We have, therefore, to say that in our considered judgement the clergy cannot claim the liberty to enter into sexually active homophile relationships. Because of the distinctive nature of their calling, status and consecration, to allow such a claim on their part would be seen as placing that way of life in all respects on a par with heterosexual marriage as a reflection of God's purpose in creation. The Church cannot accept such a parity and remain faithful to the insights which God has given it through Scripture, tradition and reasoned reflection on experience.[15]

8.2.8   Summing up the 'essential points' of its argument, the report declares:

> The Church in its pastoral mission ought to help and encourage all its members, as they pursue their pilgrimage from the starting points

given in their own personalities and circumstances, and as they grow by grace within their own particular potential. It is, therefore, only right that there should be an open and welcoming place in the Christian community both for those homophiles who follow the way of abstinence, giving themselves to friendship for many rather than to intimacy with one, and also for those who are conscientiously convinced that a faithful, sexually active relationship with one other person, aimed at helping both partners to grow in discipleship is the way of life God wills for them. But the Church exists also to live out in the world the truth it has been given about the nature of God's creation, the way of redemption through the Cross, and the ultimate hope of newness and fullness of life. We have judged that we ourselves and all clergy, as consecrated public and representative figures, entrusted with the message and means of grace, have a responsibility on behalf of the whole body of Christ to show the primacy of truth by striving to embody it in our own lives. But we also wish to stress the Church's care for and value of all her clergy alike, and that where the Church's teaching results for any ordained person in a burden grievous to be borne we, the bishops, as pastors to the pastors, will always be ready to share in any way we can in the bearing of that burden.[16]

8.3 Challenges to this teaching

8.3.1 The teaching of *Issues in Human Sexuality* that has just been outlined does not have legally binding authority in the Church of England since it has never been put forward by General Synod, although General Synod commended it for study by the Church. In addition, *Issues* itself claims that it is an educational document intended to encourage further reflection rather than 'the last word on the subject'.[17]

However, because it reflects the current collective position of the House of Bishops, and because the Church of England is an episcopally led Church in which bishops have a particular responsibility for guiding the Church in matters of faith and morals, it should be accepted by those in the Church as possessing considerable theological and pastoral authority.

8.3.2 On the other hand, the Church of England is also a Church in which episcopal teaching is open for discussion and debate, and as part of this discussion and debate the teaching of *Issues in Human Sexuality* has been criticized from two different directions.

8.3.3 There are those who argue that this teaching is not sufficiently clear-cut in its rejection of homosexuality, and that it is wrong to make a distinction between the standards of behaviour expected of the clergy and the laity.

8.3.4   For example, in an article entitled 'Divine Order and Sexual Conduct', Simon Vibert responds to the endorsement of the teaching of *Issues* in the 1995 *St Andrew's Day Statement* by arguing that 'the Anglican Church must be more radical' in its rejection of homosexuality, and that 'The Bishops' Statement on Human Sexuality has been interpreted by many as being a double standard and endorsing a two-tier ethic.'[18]

8.3.5   Vibert argues that:

> It is a mistake to assume that the pastoral epistles espouse two standards of ethics, one for clergy and the other for lay people. Surely what Paul is calling for is a greater exemplification of the one standard amongst those who are going to lead the flock, not a lower standard for the *laos*?

> One of the reasons why the 'Bishop' is called to higher standards is in order that he may model the Christian life. But the other reason is in order that bishops may exercise pastoral discipline. Surely nowhere in the New Testament are they called to 'respect the integrity' of those who dissent in such a way that does not call sinners to repentance and a chaste lifestyle along the lines of 1 Corinthians 6. The frustration for many evangelicals is that 'respecting the integrity' has come to mean an almost total lack of Church discipline.[19]

8.3.6   He also questions the assumption that pastoral sensitivity and clear teaching are mutually exclusive:

> Surely the pastorally sensitive will want to speak out about the damaging effect of endorsing unbiblical same-sex sexual relationships? Surely, the Church must take up the prophetic challenge and call people to recognise the damage which is done by ignoring biblical principles? To fail to do this is far from compassionate, it is weak and dishonouring to God.[20]

8.3.7   In contrast, there are also those who feel that the teaching of *Issues in Human Sexuality* is still too condemnatory in its attitude to homosexual relationships among both the laity and the clergy.

8.3.8   On the general issue of its rejection of an equality between homosexual and heterosexual sexual activity this criticism is based on the conviction that the report as a whole has not taken sufficiently seriously the arguments for a rethinking of the Christian understanding of sexual relationships.[21]

8.3.9   On the specific issue of its rejection of the acceptability of same-sex sexual relationships among the clergy two arguments are put forward.

8.3.10   First, objection is taken to the contention in *Issues in Human Sexuality* that the clergy are called to exemplify the Church's ideal in terms of human sexuality, and that clergy in homosexual relationships cannot do this.

8.3.11   Jeffrey John, for instance, writes:

> Of course for the majority of people heterosexual marriage is the ideal – and there are faithful married clergy to exemplify it. For those who are called to celibacy, faithful celibacy is the ideal, and there are faithful celibate clergy to exemplify that also. I have argued that for homosexuals who are not called to celibacy a faithful covenanted partnership is ideal (and in the case of lay people the bishops, at least in certain paragraphs, seem to accept it) – and there are in fact many clergy partnerships to exemplify it too.[22]

8.3.12   Developing this point he declares that:

> The current situation is the more depressing because same-sex couples need more than almost any other category of people to be 'offered' an ideal by the Church – a positive theological framework within which to conduct a holy life – and to have it exemplified for them. It is the experience of many clergy in a same-sex relationship who have allowed this to be known that they generally draw a large pastoral clientele of other gay Christians who cannot find the kind of positive Christian counselling they need anywhere else. In this situation the example and role-model of the priest really is an indispensable source of hope, and a rock on which others can build. But of course it is intolerably hard for clergy to fill this need if they receive no support from the Church.[23]

8.3.13   Secondly, it is argued that a strict policy against same-sex relationships among the clergy is both unenforceable, and also fails to acknowledge the reality that there is a significant number of dedicated homosexual clergy in the Church of England who require support rather than rejection.

8.3.14 Both these points are made by Michael Vasey in his book *Strangers and Friends*:

> The policy may be defensible; it is less clear that it is workable. An obvious difficulty is enforcement. The problem here includes the usual difficulties of definition and evidence. In the case of incumbents with the freehold it would also involve extended public trials in which the scandalous and immoral nature of such relationships would have to be established. More deeply, the policy fails to come to terms with the fact that a significant minority of the clergy of the Church of England are gay. They include many of the church's finest clergy, and it is precisely their homosexuality that has drawn them to Christ and gives them the insight and sensitivity that the Church of England values in their ministry. Often they are willing to undertake tasks from which other clergy shrink. Given the evidence that the Church of England now has of the stress that its policy causes to such clergy, it is hard to see how it can continue to justify not allowing them to address their own spiritual, emotional and relational needs in ways that seem appropriate to them. The policy does not sit easily with the hope that the clergy will minister out of a personal experience of the grace of Christ and model mature and responsible personal relationships.[24]

8.4 Possible responses to these challenges

8.4.1 How might the Church of England respond to these challenges to the policy on homosexual relationships contained in *Issues in Human Sexuality*?

There are five possible responses that it might make.

- It might cease to have any policy at all and simply declare that homosexual relationships are a matter for the individuals concerned, and it is not for the Church as a corporate body to make any pronouncement about them.
- It might seek to impose a stricter pastoral discipline on homosexual clergy and laity.
- It might take a more inclusive approach and declare that homosexual relationships can be of equal validity to heterosexual ones. This approach might then lead to the Church's accepting the ordination of

practising homosexuals, and the introduction of services of blessing
or even marriage for gay and lesbian couples who desire this.
The introduction of gay and lesbian marriages would, of course,
require a change in civil as well as ecclesiastical law.

- It might decide that, while homosexual relationships fall short of
God's ideal and should not be seen as an alternative to marriage, a
committed homosexual relationship might nevertheless be the best
choice for some gay and lesbian people, and that it would be right to
offer some sort of official Church recognition to it in terms of a
service of prayer or blessing.

- It might decide to maintain the present policy.

What are the pros and cons of these possible responses?

Not having any policy at all

8.4.2   This is the policy with least to recommend it. The only possible
reason for introducing it would be the hope that controversy about the
subject might cease if it was accepted that the Church as a body took no
stance on the matter and that it was up to each individual to make up
his or her own mind.

8.4.3   It does not seem likely, however, that such a move would put
an end to controversy. Those who support the Church's traditional
approach would still campaign in support of their convictions and
would seek to have them endorsed by the Church once again.
Conversely, those on the other side of the debate would continue to
campaign in support of their convictions, and would in all probability
argue that, in the face of continuing homophobia both inside and
outside the Church, it was the Church's responsibility to take a firm
stand in support of homosexual relationships.

8.4.4   Furthermore, even if such an approach could be justified on
pragmatic grounds, it would still not be an approach that any Christian
Church could adopt with a clear conscience.

8.4.5   This is because it would represent an abdication of the
responsibility of the Church as a corporate body to bear witness to
God's standards for human conduct. It is the Church as a whole, and
not simply the individuals within it, that is called to bear witness to
God by being a holy nation that lives according to God's ways

(Exodus 19.5-6, Leviticus 19.2, 1 Peter 2.9). It would also represent an abdication of the duty laid upon the leaders of the Church, as ministers of the word, to give clear instruction to the faithful concerning what God requires of them.

Taking a stricter approach

8.4.6   This could be seen as a more consistent implementation of the theological principles that are set out in *Issues in Human Sexuality*, which may appear to be a reason to commend it.

8.4.7   If it really is the case that, as *Issues* maintains, there is 'an evolving convergence on the ideal of lifelong, monogamous, heterosexual union as the setting intended by God for the proper development of men and women as sexual beings' with the result that, 'Sexual activity of any kind outside marriage comes to be seen as sinful, and homosexual practice as especially dishonourable,' and if it really is the case that, 'Heterosexuality and homosexuality are not equally congruous with the observed order of creation', then it could be argued that it is incumbent on the Church to proclaim this fact clearly and unequivocally, and to take disciplinary action against those who refuse to accept the Church's teaching or to live accordingly. It is true that it is important to recognize the right of each individual to act according to his or her conscience, but the recognition that, in a fallen world the conscience of the individual may be ill informed or misled, means that it is proper for the Church to act as it always has done and to take action against those whose beliefs are at variance with Christian truth as this is understood by the Church as a whole.

8.4.8   The argument would be that it is not enough simply to 'stand alongside' those in sexually active homosexual relationships as *Issues* suggests. What is needed is a positive attempt to help them break free from such relationships either by changing their orientation so that they are able to live as heterosexuals or by learning to embrace chastity as God's call to them in their particular situation. Pastoral discipline would have a place in this process along the lines set out by St Paul in 1 Corinthians 5.1-5, as a means of bringing people to realize the gravity of their behaviour and their need for amendment of life. Furthermore, saying that clergy ought to live lives that conform to the Church's teaching and then failing to discipline those who do not leads to the inevitable conclusion that the Church is not really serious about its teaching and gives tacit acceptance to homosexual activity.

8.4.9   There are, however, three arguments against this approach.

8.4.10   The first argument is that such a policy would lead to increased conflict with groups campaigning for homosexual equality both inside and outside the Church, and would also alienate the Church further from a society in which homosexuality is becoming ever more accepted, particularly in the media and among young people.

8.4.11   This argument has some weight but it cannot be a decisive argument given that it may sometimes be the Church's duty to endure conflict and unpopularity in order to bear witness to the truth. According to St Luke's version of the Sermon on the Mount, it is precisely when all people speak well of Christians that they ought to be worried, because this is the mark of a false prophet (Luke 6.26).

8.4.12   A second and more important argument is that a stricter policy would be difficult to enforce across the Church as a whole, and would lead the Church into a series of scandals. There is a perception that there are certain dioceses in the Church that take a clear line on this issue and others that are more tolerant and even supportive of homosexuality, and this means that it would be difficult to convince people that any disciplinary policy was being implemented uniformly and therefore equitably.

8.4.13   It might be that there would be dioceses where active homosexuals were disciplined and others where they were not, and this discrepancy, alongside the problems that Vasey has identified about bringing disciplinary action against the clergy, would mean that the whole disciplinary policy would be likely to fall into disrepute.

8.4.14   In the meantime, the press would be bound to cover the story, in all probability in a sensational fashion, representing it as a 'witch hunt' and, as a result, the Church's image would come into disrepute and its ability to bear witness to the gospel would be compromised.

8.4.15   This could be argued to be a situation where a theologically ideal approach would do more damage to the Church than a less ideal but more pragmatic and realistic approach that recognized that because the Church is *in via* – on the way to perfection but not having yet achieved it – it has to make compromises and learn to live with messy and ambiguous situations. In the General Synod debate in 1987 active homosexual relationships were not condoned, but nevertheless the idea of disciplining the clergy on this issue was specifically rejected.

8.4.16   The third and most important argument, however, is that a stricter policy would actually mean that the Church would fail to give gay and lesbian people adequate support and pastoral care. The dilemmas and painful paradoxes faced by lesbian and gay clergy have already been discussed briefly in Chapter 5. This sort of policy would make life extremely difficult – more difficult than it already is – for gay and lesbian priests throughout the whole Church.

8.4.17   There is a growing consensus, even among those who take a generally conservative line in matters of sexual ethics, that a simple policy of condemnation and discipline is inappropriate for three reasons.

a.   It does not do justice to the fact that the Church as a whole is a community of sinners and, as such, cannot exclude other sinners who are sincerely seeking to follow Christ, however much it may disapprove of aspects of their behaviour.

This is a point that is very well made within a Presbyterian context by the United Presbyterian Church in the United States of America in its 1978 report *The Church and Homosexuality*:

> As persons repent and believe, they become members of Christ's body. The church is not a citadel of the morally perfect; it is a hospital for sinners. It is the fellowship where contrite, needy people rest their hope for salvation on Christ and his righteousness. Here in community they seek and receive forgiveness and new life. The church must become the nurturing community so that all whose lives come short of the glory of God are converted, reoriented, and built up into Christian community. It may be only in the context of loving community, appreciation, pastoral care, forgiveness and nurture that homosexual persons can come to a clear understanding of God's pattern for their sexual expression.
>
> There is room in the church for all who give honest affirmation to the vows required for membership in the church. Homosexual persons who sincerely affirm 'Jesus Christ is my Lord and Savior' and 'I intend to be his disciple, to obey his word, and to show his love' should not be excluded from membership.[25]

It is also important to note in this regard that there has long been a danger of the Church's becoming too obsessive about sexual sins. There is a need to avoid the hypocrisy of singling out homosexuality as a particular bar to participation in the life of the Church while conveniently overlooking forms of sin to which others in the Church may be subject.

For example, we noted in Chapter 4 that homosexuality was only one out of a number of serious forms of sin highlighted by St Paul in 1 Corinthians 6.9-10 as barriers to inclusion in the kingdom of God. Likewise, we need to remember that what St Paul says about homosexuality in Romans 1.26-27 has to be balanced by what he has to say about other forms of sinful activity in Romans 1.28-32, and by his condemnation of the morally self-righteous in Romans 2.1-29.

b. It may fail to allow room for appropriate pastoral discrimination between different kinds of homosexual behaviour, and for variations in what may be asked of someone at different stages in their Christian journey. This is an important consideration because, as David Atkinson writes:

> We need ... to recover a sense of the pilgrimage of Christian faith. This may enable us to live with the view that certain patterns of behaviour, though not in themselves God's will, are a least detrimental option – or a morally best choice at a particular stage in a person's pilgrimage – in a flawed situation. We need to avoid regarding all homosexual behaviour as morally equivalent. Promiscuity is one thing, a committed sexual relationship is another. Both are different from uncertain sexual explorations at a particular stage in a person's journey of faith and self-discovery, in their journey towards wholeness.[26]

Pastoral flexibility is clearly vital, and the question is whether a more hard line approach would allow or encourage this.

c. Even those advocating this approach will need to acknowledge that it does not give sufficient importance to the fact that what will most help homosexual people to embrace a traditional approach to sexual ethics is the witness of a loving and supportive community that gives them the sort of acceptance that they may not have received from other parts of society or even, in the past, from the Church itself.

Atkinson gives another important warning to the Church on this point:

The existence of Gay churches stands as a rebuke to the lack of love and friendship in many of the mainline churches towards homosexual people. As we noted earlier, we are only at liberty to encourage homosexual people to see their orientation as most likely a calling towards celibacy, and encourage them to spread their relationships with their brothers and sisters in Christ, if support for the former and opportunities for the latter are available in genuine love. Where such support and such opportunities are not available, the homosexual person has then to choose an optimum morality within a difficult situation. It ill behoves an unloving heterosexual community to stand in judgement on a homosexual person in such circumstances for choosing a loving sexual partnership within which to express, as well as he may, something of the love of Christ – however objectively wrong such a liaison may be considered to be.[27]

8.4.18   While the proponents of a stricter approach have a point in drawing attention to the need for the Church to give a clear explanation of why it cannot accept that homosexual relationships fall short of God's intention for human sexuality, and while the use of ecclesiastical discipline should never be ruled out as a last resort, the major flaw with this approach is its failure to see the need to stress the grace rather than the law of God when seeking to help people to live in accordance with God's will. It represents a harsh policy, not in keeping with a gospel of love.

8.4.19   Once again Atkinson explains the point helpfully:

Sadly, the first word the homosexual person usually seems to hear from the Christian church is one of moral rebuke. The picture of God reflected in such a response is of a Creator of moral boundaries and the Judge of sinful aberrations. And of course at many stages in our Christian pilgrimage we all need to make responsible choices for our lives in the light of the Creator's will and his judgement, to ask his forgiveness for our sins, and seek his grace for a change in our lifestyle. But what many of us need to hear first and foremost – especially those of us struggling with emotional needs, with relational starvation, with sexual guilt or sexual temptation, or simply with confusion concerning our identity or role, is that God is loving, caring, understanding and accepting. To begin with 'sin' may be to add guilt to guilt, isolation to isolation, and rejection to rejection. To begin with 'love' may be to provide a context of personal relationship within the safety of which change can be contemplated, forgiveness can be received, and growth towards wholeness in Christ can be furthered. It is often only when we have learned what love means through the experience of sharing in the love of a supportive community that we are able to set out the changes of lifestyle which the demands of love require.[28]

Taking a more inclusive approach

8.4.20   There are two things that the arguments for a more inclusive approach have to commend them.

8.4.21   First, they attempt to take seriously the questions about the traditional Christian approach to homosexuality raised both by the revisionist approach to the relevant biblical material and by the natural and social sciences. These questions, which we have outlined in the previous chapters of this report, are ones that all Christians certainly do need to take seriously. For example, there is a need to ask seriously whether the biblical texts that have been seen as condemning homosexuality are relevant to our assessment of loving same-sex relationships today, and whether what we know about the origins of same-sex attraction mean that it has to be viewed as a natural part of God's creation rather than as some form of abnormality.

8.4.22   Secondly, they attempt to take seriously the need to ensure that the Church is a truly inclusive community in which people can feel welcomed and supported whatever their sexual orientation, and in which gay and lesbian people can find role models to help them to express their sexuality in relationships that are pleasing to God. It would enable gay and lesbian priests, especially, to be able to get on with their vocational work without living in fear. As before, these are issues that all Christians need to take very seriously indeed.

8.4.23   However, this having been said, the proposal that the Church should take a more inclusive line also involves a number of difficulties.

8.4.24   The first and major difficulty is that, while the advocates of this approach are right to note the questions that have been raised about the Church's traditional teaching, taking a more inclusive line would conflict with the fact that the majority of scholarly and Christian opinion still sees the traditional teaching as basically valid.

8.4.25   The line on sexual morality taken in *Issues in Human Sexuality* still reflects the consensus of biblical scholarship and the prevailing mind of the Church of England, and it would be both wrong and impossible for the Church to move officially to a more liberal position as long as this remains the case.

8.4.26 It would, for example, be difficult for the Church of England formally to recognize homosexual partnerships as a form of Christian marriage or to abandon a requirement that the clergy should refrain from sexually active homosexual relationships while still upholding its traditional teaching about the nature of marriage and its role as the proper locus for human sexual activity.

8.4.27 The Church could not both teach, as it always has done on the basis of Genesis 2.18-24, that marriage as ordained by God is a permanent union between one man and one woman, and at the same time agree that gay and lesbian relationships could rightly be described as marriage.

8.4.28 Equally, the Church could not call upon its clergy to act as teachers and exemplars of the Christian way of life, and yet say that they are free to live in ways that are contrary to that way of life as this is understood by the Church. As Michael Banner notes:

> This is not a matter of the religious being subject to counsels of perfection which do not apply to the laity, for the Bishops do not say that it is right for the laity to have homosexual relationships and wrong for the clergy, but only that where the clergy have such relationships they, unlike the laity, create a scandal which consists in the fact that one whose authority is derived from the authority of the Church challenges that very authority.[29]

8.4.29 It is, of course, primarily the responsibility of the clergy concerned to respect their ordination vows by being obedient to the Church's teaching and, as *Issues* notes, it would be wrong for the Church to 'carry out intrusive interrogations in order to make sure that they are behaving themselves'.[30] Nevertheless, it is right that the Church should set out what it expects from its clergy in terms of their personal behaviour as it always has done from biblical times,[31] and that this expectation should reflect the Church's moral standpoint.

8.4.30 It is also important to note that, from New Testament times onwards, it has been expected that the personal sexual behaviour of the clergy will model biblical teaching about sexual morality. This is what is meant when it is stated in 1 Timothy 3.2 that: 'a bishop must be above reproach, the husband of one wife' (RSV) and in Titus 1.6 that an elder should be 'blameless, the husband of one wife' (RSV). As the American commentator Thomas Oden notes, what these passages tell us is that:

> An overseer of the flock is expected to be sexually accountable and responsible within the framework of covenant marriage – husband of one wife. This places the overseer clearly within the frame of the fundamental New Testament teaching of marriage and sexual fidelity: 'Let marriage be held in honor among all, and let the marriage bed be undefiled' (Hebrews 13.4). There was in the surrounding Greco-Roman culture a general indisposition towards marital fidelity, particularly in a port city like Ephesus. There is abundant evidence that marriage was at this time being undermined by frequent divorce, widespread adultery and homosexuality on the one hand, and by an extreme reactionary asceticism on the other. In a few spare words Paul made it clear that the leadership of the Christian community had a firm commitment to the family, to healthy sexuality, and covenant fidelity within marriage. Pastors must understand how important sexual fidelity is, for they will inevitably be serving as a model of fidelity for the flock.[32]

8.4.31   In line with this teaching, the question in the ordinal in the *Book of Common Prayer*:

> Will you be diligent to frame and fashion your own selves, and your families, according to the doctrine of Christ, and to make both yourselves and them, as much as in you lieth, wholesome examples and patterns to the flock of Christ?

has always been understood to mean that the clergy ought to be exemplary in their sexual conduct and that it was scandalous if they were not.

8.4.32   This does not mean that clergy are not at liberty to question and challenge the Church's understanding of what proper sexual conduct involves, but it does mean that, while this understanding remains unchanged, the clergy have a general obligation to live according to it, and the Church has the right to expect them to do so, and in cases where their behaviour causes grave scandal to take appropriate disciplinary action against them. This would be as true for heterosexual clergy as for homosexual clergy.

8.4.33 There is, of course, the argument that openly gay and lesbian clergy in active homosexual relationships are required in order to provide 'role models' for other gay and lesbian Christians. The question here is what kind of 'role model' is required.

8.4.34 What the clergy are expected to model is the Christian way of life. At present the Church of England continues to affirm the traditional Christian teaching of sexual relationships within marriage and abstinence outside it and therefore this is what the clergy are called upon to model. If the Church were to present openly practising homosexual clergy as role models this would contradict its own teaching. Furthermore, those who believe that social factors play an important part in leading people towards homosexual practice would fear that young people, in the age of uncertainty and insecurity, would be open to a misreading of their sexual desires and seek mistakenly to own a homosexual identity blessed and modelled by the Church.

8.4.35 As has been noted above, one possible option would be for the Church to maintain its present teaching concerning marriage, but nevertheless to be willing to offer services of prayer for gay and lesbian couples either publicly or semi-publicly in a similar way to the way it now offers a service of prayer and dedication after civil marriage.

8.4.36 There are three main arguments in favour of this proposal.

8.4.37 First, in contrast to the previous option, this proposal would mean that the Church still upheld its commitment to the traditional biblical teaching that the ideal framework for human sexual relationships is heterosexual marriage, and that homosexual relationships cannot be seen as an equally valid alternative.

8.4.38 Secondly, however, it would offer space for the recognition that, because we live in a fallen world, not all human beings have the capacity to enter into heterosexual relationships, and that it is not reasonable to expect that those who cannot enter into heterosexual relationships should embrace celibacy. The reason that this is not reasonable is because celibacy is a gift from God (1 Corinthians 7.7), and some people with a sexual attraction to those of their own sex may not have received this gift.

8.4.39 In their situation, the argument goes, the principle set out by

St Paul in 1 Corinthians 7.9: 'But if they are not practising self-control, they should marry. For it is better to marry than be aflame with passion' should be applied by analogy to people who are homosexual. This would mean that, if they have not received the gift of celibacy, then they should enter into long-term, committed, homosexual relationships instead.

8.4.40 This is, for example, the approach taken by the German theologian and ethicist Helmut Thielicke in his book *The Ethics of Sex*. He argues that homosexuals cannot change their sexual predisposition and therefore the question that has to be addressed is:

> ... how the homosexual in his actual situation can achieve the optimal ethical potential of sexual self-realisation. To deny this would in any case mean a degree of harshness and rigor which one would never think of demanding of a 'normal' person. Celibacy cannot be used as a counter argument, because celibacy is based upon a special calling and, moreover, is an act of free will.[33]

8.4.41 Similarly, the 1998 report on homosexuality and the Church, *Living With Tensions*, produced for the Evangelical Church in Germany, states that on the basis of 1 Corinthians 7:

> ... the advice to be given to those who have not received the charisma of sexual abstinence must be to form a single-sex life partnership which is in line with the commandment of love and thus based on ethical responsibility.[34]

8.4.42 Thirdly, by being prepared to offer some form of prayer for homosexual couples in this situation, the Church would be showing that it was prepared to give support to those who were seeking to live in this ethically responsible fashion in the face of pressure both from a frequently hostile heterosexual culture, and from a culture of promiscuity that exists within parts of the (male) gay community in particular. It is suggested that such an approach would be in line with the refusal of *Issues in Human Sexuality* not to un-church those who have made a conscientious decision to enter into same-sex relationships, and its argument that the right of lay people to make such a decision should be respected.

8.4.43 It is sometimes argued that there is an analogy to be drawn with the increasing willingness of the Church to accept the remarriage of those who have been divorced that we have noted in Chapter 1. Here too, it is argued, the Church has learned to temper its commitment to the ideal of lifelong marriage with the realization that it needs to give pastoral support to those whose first marriages have failed and who now wish to make a fresh start. If the Church is willing to do this in the case of those who have fallen short of God's intention through divorce, why should it not offer the same pastoral compassion to those who are homosexual?

8.4.44   This proposal is in some ways an attractive option, but serious questions still remain.

a.   Would it prove a tenable mediating position? Is it not more likely to attract criticism both from those who believe that the Church has no business praying for such relationships, and from those who would object strongly to the suggestion that homosexual relationships should be viewed as in any way inferior to heterosexual marriage?

b.   Is there any grounding either in Scripture or the tradition of the Church for saying that a long-term homosexual relationship is ethically responsible even though it falls short of God's ideal? As we have seen, Scripture and tradition are unanimous in saying that, because homosexual acts are an 'abomination' before God, they are quite simply to be avoided in exactly the same way as one simply avoids other sexual sins such as fornication or adultery. There is no suggestion that abstinence from homosexual relationships is a special gift that is only granted to some people, and to suggest that St Paul's teaching in 1 Corinthians 7 points in this direction is to distort the apostle's teaching and to use his words to support a position that he himself would have condemned.

c.   Even if what is prayed for is, as the EKD document suggests,[35] not the relationship as such but the individuals involved, the question would still remain about what form such a blessing should take. If the Church's teaching remains that same-sex relationships are not in accordance with God's will, consistency would require that a service of prayer and dedication for people in such relationships should include a prayer that God would lead them to a better way of life, and this would be unlikely to be acceptable to the people concerned.

8.4.45   It can also be argued that the analogy with the remarriage of divorcees is not persuasive because it fails to recognize that both the

Bible and the Christian tradition allow for the possibility of divorce and even remarriage,[36] whereas they give no such support to same-sex relationships.

8.4.46 In response to these objections a number of further points have been made by those in favour of offering services of prayer to those in same-sex relationships.

- Opposition from both sides might suggest that this position is the correct one. Moreover, as has been argued earlier, opposition by itself cannot be taken as the overriding consideration. It could also be argued that the blessing of same-sex relationships has been advocated not on the basis that it is a mediating position, but on the basis that it reflects the Church's calling to try to hold together the Christian ideal and what is pastorally required in a less than ideal world.

- People who have lived together faithfully for 30 years or more in a mutually supportive same-sex relationship sometimes show the fruits of the spirit that are sadly lacking in some heterosexual marriages, and it would be grotesque either to describe such loving long-term relationships as 'an abomination' or to refuse to celebrate them before God.

- Many people would want a service of dedication and blessing that was rooted in a sense of thanksgiving to God for the relationship as a gift from him and as a prayer that he would continue to deepen and bless it.

8.4.47 In support of the analogy with the Church's pastoral response to divorce, they would argue that many scholars, perhaps the majority, would argue that the teaching of Jesus on marriage sets out an absolute standard that should not be broken but to which the Church soon had to make exceptions, as we see in Matthew's version of the teaching of Jesus. In other words, there is, within the New Testament, evidence of a developing tradition as the Church had to grapple with the realities of marriage breakdown. In the light of Jesus' teaching on marriage, there should only be divorce and remarriage on an exceptional basis. It should be possible, and rightly so, because we live in a frail, fallen world. Pastoral necessity requires it. Pastoral care also requires the blessing of committed same sex-relationships.

8.4.48 Given the existence of these different approaches to the matter, how do we decide between them? At the heart of the matter is the basic issue of what blessing same-sex couples would involve.

8.4.49 If it were simply a matter of giving pastoral support to the individuals concerned there could be no objection. As we have insisted earlier on in this chapter, homosexual people require all the pastoral support the Church can give them.

8.4.50 There would also be little problem if what was taking place was simply the celebration of a relationship of love and friendship. We have argued earlier in this report that the Church needs to provide appropriate ways of celebrating such relationships.

8.4.51 The nub of the problem lies in the fact that the Church would be understood by all concerned to be also giving recognition to a sexually active same-sex relationship.

8.4.52 This becomes clear if one looks at the various unofficial liturgies for the blessing of same-sex relationships that have already been produced.

8.4.53 For example, the liturgy produced by St Luke's Charlton contains the prayer:

> Almighty God, source of all being, we thank you for your love, which creates and sustains us. We thank you for the physical and emotional expression of that love; and for the blessings of companionship and friendship. We pray that we may use your gifts so that we can ever grow into a deeper understanding of love and your purpose for us, through Jesus Christ, our Lord. Amen.[37]

In the context it is clear that what God is being given thanks for is not just 'companionship and friendship' but the sexual side of the relationship as well.

8.4.54 The same is true of the 'Act of Confirmation and Commitment' written by Jan Berry for the blessing of a lesbian relationship, which declares:

> We have come here today to create a space –
> A space where love can be celebrated
> A space where passion can be honoured
> A space where commitment can be affirmed

and in which the couple say to each other in turn

> N. I have chosen you as my partner.
> I love you and I delight in you.
> I promise to share my life with you
> in tenderness and passion
> holding to you in good times and bad,
> in anger and forgiveness
> in pain and in hope.
> Forgive me when I fail;
> support me when I am weak.
> Please go on trusting me,
> as I grow in love and trust you.[38]

It is clear from these two extracts that it is not only the sexual side of the relationship that is being celebrated and affirmed, but it is also clear that this side of the relationship *is* being celebrated and affirmed.

8.4.55   The fundamental question is whether this kind of celebration and affirmation of same-sex sexuality would be 'legitimate' in the light of the theological issues explored in Chapters 3 and 4 of this report.

8.4.56   In his unpublished paper to which we have already made reference in Chapters 3 and 4, Terry Brown argues that 'homosexuality is to be seen as a more pastoral than doctrinal issue'.[39] If this argument is accepted then the issue raised by the blessing of same-sex relationships is the simple one of whether or not it would be helpful for the people concerned.

8.4.57   However, it is questionable whether it is possible to separate out pastoral and doctrinal issues in the way that Brown suggests. Christian pastoral care has to have as its basis a Christian understanding of what makes for human flourishing and this in turn has to be based on a Christian understanding of humanity informed by the doctrines of creation and redemption. Therefore, the theological issues in Chapters 3 and 4 do need to be borne in mind.

8.4.58   It also has to be borne in mind that liturgy has a declarative and educational function within the Church. That is to say, in its liturgy the Church declares what it believes about God and how we should respond to God, and in so doing it aims to inform and shape the understanding of the faithful about these matters. It is because this is the case that the Church of England is very careful about the production of new liturgical material and it is why it has clear rules about what liturgies may be used.

8.4.59 This being the case, if the Church were to move to the authorization of liturgies celebrating same-sex relationships, it would be more than simply a compassionate response to a perceived pastoral need, it would be a de facto declaration by the Church of England that it accepts the legitimacy of such relationships and is happy for them to become an accepted part of the life of the Church. As J. I. Packer has argued in the context of the debate about same-sex blessings in the Canadian context:

> To bless same-sex unions liturgically is to ask God to bless them and to enrich those who join in them, as is done in marriage ceremonies. This assumes that the relationship, of which the physical bond is an integral part, is intrinsically good and thus, if I may coin a word, blessable, as procreative sexual intercourse within heterosexual marriage is.[40]

8.4.60 This would mark a departure from the position taken in *Issues in Human Sexuality*, since to quote Banner again, in *Issues* there is no suggestion that the choice of a same-sex relationship is morally justifiable: 'but only that those who have taken a morally wrong decision ought not for that reason to be "rejected"'.[41]

It would constitute a considerable shift in the Church of England's position if it were to move from saying that people in homosexual relationships were not for that reason to be rejected by the Church, to saying that the Church should give its official approval to the liturgical celebration of such relationships.

8.4.61 Another point that needs to be noted is that if one looks at the kind of liturgies for the blessing of same-sex unions to which we have already referred, they can, or might be, interpreted as same-sex marriage services. They may not be called marriage services but there are of course parallels in terms of content with other marriage services. They are indeed celebrating a relationship between two people in the way that a marriage service does.[42]

8.4.62 The significance of this is that by giving its permission for such services the Church of England would effectively be supporting marriage-like unions between gay and lesbian couples. There are those who are of course campaigning for the acceptance of such services and are explicit about this point. Jeffrey John, for example, declares that:

> An officially endorsed liturgy of blessing, as well as affirming God's love for the couple themselves, would help immeasurably towards creating in society the same acceptance and support for gay partnerships that any marriage needs to flourish.[43]

8.4.63　In a social context where there is growing pressure for official recognition by the State for same-sex 'civil-partnerships', with many of the social rights and privileges of marriage, any move by the Church of England in the same direction could only serve further to undermine its traditional argument that the State should continue to give a distinctive place to heterosexual marriage as one of the key building blocks for British society.

8.4.64　One alternative that has been suggested to services of prayer for gay and lesbian couples officially endorsed by the Church of England is allowing individual members of the clergy to offer such services in circumstances where this would be appropriate.

8.4.65　*Issues in Human Sexuality* accepts, and indeed encourages, sensitive pastoral care for gay and lesbian people. All those who exercise licensed ministry need training and support in forming appropriate systems for such pastoral ministry. This can be part of a pattern of strengthening the ministry of the Church to the variety of contexts in which people live and form key relationships.

Much of this is uncontroversial:

- the practice of confidential pastoral counselling;
- the ministry of Absolution;
- praying with people as they seek God's wisdom for the choices confronting them.

8.4.66　There are, however, occasions when ministers are asked to exercise more public and potentially controversial ministries, and these may include offering prayers in church with and for same-sex couples and the blessing of these relationships in circumstances in which gay and lesbian people who are Christians seek the support of the Church in rooting their relationships inside their Christian vocation.

8.4.67 Parish priests considering how to respond to such requests will need help in considering how they can uphold the teaching of the Church as they seek to offer pastoral care in these situations. If the Church is not to drift into action that, in the absence of careful consideration, might compromise the canonical responsibilities of those who hold the bishop's licence, guidance is needed. Bishops will need to reflect on what sort of guidance should be offered and priests should always seek the bishop's comments and direction before proceeding to act.

8.4.68 The argument in favour of this approach is that it would give individual parish priests the flexibility to take appropriate action in particular circumstances without committing the Church as a whole. It would also work towards a more genuinely loving and inclusive Church.

8.4.69 Those who have problems with this approach would, however, question whether this argument is valid. As they see the matter, if the Church as a whole agrees that it is right for individual priests to take this line of action and if bishops give their assent to it then this still means that the Church of England is giving support to the offering of prayers for relationships that the Bible describes as sinful. In their view, the proper course of action for a bishop asked for advice about the matter would be for him to tell the priest involved to support the individuals involved but to avoid doing anything that might suggest that their relationship had some particular standing in the eyes of the Church.

8.4.70 They also fear that what might start off as a practice that happens only in very exceptional circumstances would soon come to be seen as a normal part of the Church's ministry in the same way that the marriage of divorced people in Church has moved from being a rare event to a relatively frequent occurrence.

8.4.71 Another difficulty with the idea that the Church of England should adopt a more liberal policy towards homosexual relationships is the effect that this would have on those homosexual Christians who accept the Church's traditional teaching and struggle, often at great personal cost, to live lives that are in conformity with it. They would inevitably feel that their convictions and struggles had not been taken seriously by the Church. Their opinions are often overlooked in the discussion of this issue, but they do need to be taken into account.

8.4.72 Martin Hallett, who is himself in this position, made this point forcefully in his Grove booklet *Sexual Identity and Freedom in Discipleship*:

> The Christians just mentioned with a homosexual orientation, who do not agree with the more liberal theological approach to it, are usually silent. Sometimes they may be in leadership and vulnerable to the effects of exposure. There are ordained ministers in the Church of England who say to me that they will consider resigning if the Church of England supports the practice of homosexuality. Even though aware of homosexual feelings themselves, they will feel betrayed if the Church establishment changes its position. The debate in the Church of England seems to involve gays and lesbians seeking the acceptance of homosexual relationships and those who are sympathetic to them, versus campaigners against the acceptance of homosexual relationships for whom it is not a personal issue. I sometimes wonder if the Church is aware that this is not an accurate picture of the real situation. Those who are silent in this debate, but nonetheless homosexually orientated and seeking celibacy, may be less of a minority than is often assumed.[44]

8.4.73 The reference in this quotation to clergy considering resignation brings us to the fourth major difficulty with the Church's moving towards a more inclusive position, which is the effect it would have on the unity of the Church.

8.4.74 There can be no question that, for many Christians, particularly, although not exclusively, on the conservative evangelical wing of the Church, the Church's attitude to homosexuality is a fundamental theological issue. This is for two reasons.

a. They see it as a test of the Church's willingness to be faithful to the will of God as this has been revealed to us in the Bible. This is because for them it is crystal clear that the teaching of the Bible as a whole makes it impossible to see same-sex sexual relationships as anything other than a sinful deviation from God's intention for human sexuality. Any attempt to compromise this principle would be for them a rejection of the authority of God in favour of modern secular standards of behaviour. As John Stott puts it:

... ultimately it is a crisis of faith: whom shall we believe? God or the world? Shall we submit to the lordship of Jesus, or succumb to the pressures of prevailing culture?[45]

b.   Even more importantly, they see it as a matter that involves salvation. This is because they take seriously St Paul's teaching in 1 Corinthians 6.9-10 that sexual immorality in its homosexual form is one of the types of behaviour that will prevent people from entering the kingdom of God. From this perspective the Church must never encourage homosexual conduct because to do so would lead people down the path to damnation.

8.4.75   For these two reasons those who hold this position will oppose any change in the Church of England's position extremely strongly. If we ask why they feel that the Church cannot simply live with differences of opinion and practice on this matter as it does on numerous other matters, the answer is because they see the matter in the terms just described. This is a matter on which for them the teaching of Scripture is crystal clear and which involves salvation and therefore there is simply no room for compromise. As Packer puts it in the article to which we referred earlier, a decision to move away from the Church's traditional teaching, like the one taken by the diocese of New Westminster, would be one that:

> ... falsifies the gospel of Christ, abandons the authority of Scripture, jeopardizes the salvation of fellow human beings, and betrays the church in its God-appointed role as the bastion and bulwark of divine truth.[46]

8.4.76   A question that has been raised is whether those taking this position are *newly* emphasizing the issue of homosexual activity. It has been argued that their emphasis on the importance of homosexuality is something new and that it has emerged as a by-product of the growth of conservative evangelicalism that we discussed in Chapter 1. On the other hand, those who take this position (whether or not they are evangelical) would maintain that they are simply upholding the Church's traditional teaching and that they have only responded to the challenges to this teaching made by others.

8.4.77   The certainty of conflict would not in itself be a decisive argument against making such a move if there were overwhelming arguments in its favour, but, as this report has indicated, the consensus of opinion seems to be that such arguments have not yet been produced, and in this situation the likely effect of any change on the unity of the Church does carry weight.

8.4.78   The fifth difficulty with the Church of England's taking a more inclusive position is the effect this would have on the Church of England's relationship with the other Churches of the Anglican Communion, and with Churches of other traditions, particularly the Roman Catholic and Orthodox Churches and those Churches that are part of the Evangelical Alliance. As we shall see in the next chapter, relations with many of these Churches would be seriously impaired by the introduction of a more liberal policy. As with the previous difficulty, this is not a decisive argument, but it is certainly something that needs to be taken into account.

8.4.79   In response to these difficulties, those favouring a more liberal approach would again raise points of their own.

8.4.80   They would argue that:

- The personal decision of someone like Martin Hallett should not be something that is imposed on other Christians who take a different view of the matter.

- For them also, the Church's attitude to homosexuality is a fundamental theological issue to do with the Church's willingness to be the inclusive, compassionate and just community willed by God.

- The unity of the Church cannot be the final consideration. Every change in the Church's position that we now endorse caused dissension when it was first mooted. Furthermore, the true unity of the Church needs to be a unity that includes a diversity of both opinion and practice.

8.4.81   As with the issue of the blessing of same-sex couples, the question arises as to how we should evaluate these differing positions. As before, we have to go back to the fundamental theological issues at stake of which there are two:

- What path of discipleship in the sphere of sexual conduct is required of an individual in order for them to live the life of holiness that Scripture describes?

• What approach to the issue of sexual conduct is required of the Church if it is to be faithful to Christ and to have that unity in obedience to his word which is his will for his people?

8.4.82 To put it simply, the question that has to be asked is whether, in the light of the material we looked at in Chapters 3 and 4, moving towards a more inclusive position would enable the Church of England as a whole and those individuals within it to be more faithful to Christ?

We will return to this point in the final chapter.

Maintaining the present policy

8.4.83 As we have seen, the present policy has been criticized both for being too permissive and for being too restrictive.

However, it does have three big advantages:

• It reflects what seems to be the consensus of scholarly and Christian opinion on the matter in question.

• It allows room for sensitive and discriminating care of homosexual people, and provides a space in which the Church can continue to grapple with the issue while seeking to remain faithful to its traditions

• It enables the Church of England to maintain its internal unity and its relationships with its Anglican and ecumenical partner Churches.

8.4.84 Nevertheless, it is not enough simply to maintain the present position. A number of other initiatives also seem to be required.

• There needs to be more education about the issues under debate. The discussion of homosexuality is not something that is going to go away and, if this is to be a responsible discussion, then both clergy and laity need to be made aware of the issues that are being discussed so that they can make up their own minds before God and make an informed contribution to the development of the Church's mind.

• There needs to be an encouragement of informed discussion concerning the status of the debate about human sexuality. People need to be encouraged to explore why homosexuality is such a divisive issue in the Church today, and whether there is in fact an unhealthy obsession with sexual sin that prevents people focusing on other forms of sin that are also important and in which we are, in the West, implicated, and which perhaps more urgently require attention – such as commercial greed, poverty and inequalities of wealth. Furthermore, yet others would point to the fact that 'heterosexual sin' is often bypassed: the focus on homosexual activity is one way in which discussion about and correction of heterosexual sin is avoided.

• There needs to be more education about the specific pastoral needs of gay and lesbian people and how these might be addressed within the framework of the Church of England's current position. The sort of welcoming and supportive community advocated by David Atkinson will not happen by accident. It needs to be developed and for this to happen both clergy and laity need education in how to go about this.[47]

• There needs to be continuing work by the Church to combat homophobia and homophobic violence both within the Church and within society as whole.[48] This can be a difficult area given the way in which the label 'homophobia' is sometimes used as a political slogan to attack any opposition to homosexual equality on issues such as the age of consent, but nonetheless all Christians must necessarily oppose discrimination and violence against homosexuals as people and join with all others of good will in preventing this happening.

8.5 Bisexuality

8.5.1   In Chapter 6 of this report it was noted that the treatment of bisexuality in *Issues in Human Sexuality* has come in for severe criticism. It is not clear, however, how a different approach to bisexuality could be taken within the overall understanding of human sexuality that *Issues* advocates.

8.5.2   As was also noted in Chapter 6, there are those who argue that the sexual needs of bisexual people do not fit into the framework of traditional Christian sexual morality and that this shows that the framework itself is in need of revision.

8.5.3   Those taking this line seem to be suggesting that bisexual people should be encouraged to explore whatever types of sexual relationships best suit their particular needs, providing the quality of those relationships is such that it mirrors the love of God.

8.5.4   If this position were to be accepted then clearly the correct approach for the Church would be to provide support for bisexual people as they engage in this kind of exploration.

8.5.5   If, however, it is felt to be right to maintain the traditional Christian framework in which the God-given context for sexual relationships is heterosexual marriage, then the basic points in what *Issues* says about bisexuality do seem to remain sound.

- If bisexual sexual activity involves simultaneous sexual relations with people of both sexes then, from the standpoint of traditional Christian ethics, this would either imply promiscuity or infidelity or both. If there are multiple partners of both sexes this must mean promiscuity, and if there is an existing permanent sexual relationship and sexual activity takes place outside it then this would involve infidelity.
- If God's overall intention for human sexual activity is that it should take place in the context of marriage with someone of the opposite sex, then clearly the Church needs to encourage bisexual people who are capable of entering into such a relationship to do so, and to discourage them from entering into a homosexual one.
- If the proper Christian alternative to marriage is abstinence, then it is clearly right for the Church to advocate this for bisexuals just as much as anyone else.
- There does not seem to be any place within the traditional Christian framework for the idea that bisexual relationships should be accepted as part of a process of sexual development in which people come to be able to make a lasting commitment to a partner of one or other gender. This may indeed be what happens to a majority of bisexual people – and may be the experience of a significant minority of younger people today whether they call themselves bisexual or not – but this fact would not in itself make a process of sexual experimentation ethically acceptable.
- Finally, it may well be the case that counselling can help bisexuals to come to terms with their sexual identity and to make responsible Christian decisions in the light of it.

8.5.6   Overall, what this means is that, from the standpoint of traditional Christian ethics, bisexual people do not come into a separate ethical category of their own. The issues that are outlined above are issues that bisexuals face in common with everyone else.

8.5.7   It also needs to be stressed that, as in the case of homosexuality, sexual desires are not in themselves the issue. For example, a married bisexual person who is attracted to a member of their own sex is no better or worse than a married heterosexual person who is attracted to a member of the opposite sex who is not their spouse. The issue is not whether such desires exist, but what the person concerned does about them.

8.5.8   The fact that the issues faced by bisexual people are not unique also means that the issues relating to their pastoral care and their suitability for ordination are not unique.

- Just like everyone else, what bisexual people require is a welcoming and supportive community within which they can find the security to explore issues relating to marriage, celibacy, and the resistance of sexual temptation.

- Just like everyone else, it may be right for bisexual people to be ordained if they have a genuine calling from God, and if they are able and willing to exemplify in their personal lives the Church's teaching about God's intention for human sexuality. Clearly, if a bisexual person's sexuality causes them severe psychological or emotional problems or they are unwilling or unable to live out the Church's teaching about sexuality, then they would be unsuitable for ordination. However, exactly the same would be true of an exclusively heterosexual person with similar problems.

8.6 Transsexualism

8.6.1   When considering the question of the transsexual in the life of the Church, the two key things to be noted are firstly, that transsexuals are to be welcomed and offered pastoral support by the Christian community, just as anyone else, and that, secondly, the presence of transsexual people does raise some specific pastoral issues that the community will need to think how to face.

8.6.2   Both these points are well made in the Evangelical Alliance report *Transsexuality* which, though specifically addressing an evangelical context, also says things that are relevant to Anglican churches in general:

> It has to be acknowledged that there are no easy answers to the potential dilemmas posed by the presence of transsexual people in

the church context, and any solutions will necessarily involve careful planning and lengthy timescales to permit attitudes and sensitivities on both sides to be accommodated. The fundamental pastoral challenge may be seen as the need genuinely to welcome transsexual people into a caring and compassionate Christian community in which all stand in need of the love, mercy and grace of God, and which recognises that the transsexual person is as 'human' as anybody else. In practice it should nevertheless be understood that the presence of transsexual people within the body of Christ may unfortunately provoke human reactions of hostility, together with a wide range of concerns which may especially include any perceived impact on the younger members of a church community where attempts at explanation may be well nigh impossible, let alone offensive and unadvisable. In seeking to welcome transsexual people into a Christian community, it also needs to be remembered that whereas the process of sanctification can appear to many people long and arduous, for the transsexual individual who typically has experienced extreme anguish and pain throughout a lifetime, the resolution of inner conflict may appear particularly laborious. The need for patience, long term commitment, and the active seeking of God for wisdom by all those who are concerned cannot be over-emphasised.[49]

8.6.3   In terms of specific pastoral issues, the approach that is taken will inevitably be shaped by the debate about how to evaluate the phenomenon of transsexualism, which we looked at in the last chapter.

8.6.4   As we saw in the previous chapter, the fundamental debate is whether someone's God-given sexual identity is determined by their physical nature regardless of their psychological self-perception or whether this identity lies both in their biology and in their self-perception. How people respond to this debate necessarily has important implications in the areas of treatment, marriage and ordination.

8.6.5   In the area of treatment, those taking the first approach will tend to feel that the preferred approach to meeting the needs of the transsexual will be an approach, possibly involving both psychological and spiritual help, which will enable the person concerned to come to terms with their biological identity. Sexual reassignment surgery may, however, be accepted as a last resort in cases of extreme psychological distress.

8.6.6   Those taking the second approach will tend to be much more open to the use of surgery to help people develop a sexual identity that expresses who they feel they truly are, while acknowledging that this is a difficult course of treatment, which has no guarantee of a successful outcome.

8.6.7   In the area of marriage, those taking the first position will have concerns about post-operative transsexuals marrying in their new identity, since this will mean that they are really marrying someone of the same sex as themselves. This will not be a problem for those who take the second position, though, as we saw in the last chapter, questions could still be raised about the status of any marriage entered into by a transsexual in their previous sexual identity. Furthermore, it would have to be asked of any transsexual wishing to be married whether they were sufficiently secure in their identity to give the marriage a reasonable chance of success – though this is, of course, not an issue unique to transsexuals.

8.6.8   It also needs to be noted, as we have already said, that such a marriage would not be legal under current British law, although this position may well change as a result of the Goodwin judgement.

8.6.9   In the area of ordination, those taking the first position will probably have problems with transsexuals being ordained or serving as ministers. There are two reasons why this view is taken.

8.6.10   The first reason is the belief that they cannot present a proper role model for other Christians. The Evangelical Alliance report, for example, declares that:

> Whilst we are reluctant to impose hard and fast rules, nevertheless it would in principle be clear that, on the basis of biblical passages such as 1 Timothy 3.1-13 and Titus 1.6-9, excellent and unquestioned role models are foundational requirements for Christian leadership. As transsexual people are role models so fundamentally distinct from accepted examples, we consider their appointment to leadership or counselling positions within the church to be unwise on Biblical as well as other grounds.[50]

8.6.11   In Church of England terms, the argument would be that transsexuals could not fulfil the requirement in Canon C 4 to be 'a wholesome example and pattern to the flock of Christ'. The reason for taking this line would be the conviction that their repudiation of their God-given sexual identity means that they would be unable to bear witness to the Church's belief that sexual differentiation is something given by God at creation that Christians are called to accept and exemplify in their patterns of behaviour.

8.6.12   This is the argument put forward, for example, by the evangelical pressure group Reform in relation to a recent case in the diocese of Bristol in which a male to female transsexual was permitted to remain in parish ministry. Their press release stated:

> The Bible clearly differentiates between the sexes. Whilst our sex does not affect our status in Christ, God has made us the way we individually are, so that we can give glory to Him by the way we cope with our strengths and weaknesses. Giving in to our desires when they are contrary to what the Bible shows us about God's will, should never be affirmed by anyone in Church leadership, nor should it be allowed to be a model of leadership.[51]

8.6.13   The second reason is the belief that transsexual people are not sufficiently stable psychologically to fulfil a ministerial vocation. This is a point made by George Woodall in his unpublished essay referred to in the previous chapter. He writes that:

> The deep-rooted psychological problems of trans-sexual persons, their profound difficulties in inserting themselves into stable relationships, the question of fantasising and pursuing illusory hopes and solutions are all bound to call into question the judgment of the trans-sexual person who might seek priestly ordination. The issue of that person's capacity to undertake a life-long ministry in the priesthood is as much a problem here as it would be, were he contemplating marriage.[52]

8.6.14   Those taking the second position will probably not have objections in principle to transsexuals being ordained.

8.6.15   They would hold that transsexual people could serve as 'wholesome examples to the flock' because they would hold either that the Church's belief in absolute sexual differentiation needs to be modified, or that in the case of transsexual people their true God-given sexual identity was not simply determined by their biology. In either case, the argument that a transsexual person would be a counter-witness to what the Church believed about human sexuality would cease to apply.

8.6.16   They would also question Woodall's depiction of transsexuals as people with deep-rooted psychological problems and argue that there are examples of well-adjusted transsexuals who would be able to fulfil a ministerial vocation perfectly adequately, and might even argue that they could act as 'role models' for other transsexuals. However, even for those taking this position, specific problems regarding the ministry of transsexuals may still remain.

8.6.17   Fraser Watts, for instance, writes:

> One of the key issues that the Church may face is that of a priest who has transgendered. The quality of adjustment such a transsexual priest was able to make in their new gender would clearly be relevant to whether it would be appropriate for them to function as a priest. Given the unpredictability of the adjustment of transsexuals, there may be wisdom in suggesting that a transsexual has a period out of ministry (or at least out of full-time ministry) until it becomes clear that the problems of re-adjustment are not going to eclipse, or detract from, other aspects of ministry. Another key matter is the acceptability of a transsexual priest to a congregation which is clearly separate from whether it was permissible in principle for a transsexual to have an ordained ministry.
>
> My own view is that there is no objection in principle, but that it might be difficult to find a parish where being a transsexual incumbent would not be divisive and a distraction from the broader work of the Church. Some might argue that the Church had a duty to find such a parish, but I am not sure about that. It seems to me that a priest who decided to [sic] would be knowingly embarking on a course of action which would make their ministry unacceptable to many people, and that the institutional Church could not shield them from the consequence of their action. There might, of course, be special forms of ministry, where potential problems would be minimised.[53]

8.6.18   Watts' comments apply directly to someone who is already ordained, but the issue of the emotional and psychological stability of the person concerned would also apply in the case of the transsexual seeking ordination.

8.6.19   In the recent case in the diocese of Bristol referred to above, the priest who underwent SRS received strong support from their parish. In a parallel case in another diocese, however, difficulties occurred and it was felt inappropriate for the priest concerned to continue to minister.

chapter 9

Handling some current controversies over sexual morality

In this chapter we shall be looking at how the Church of England should seek to handle the currently controversial issues of homosexuality, bisexuality and transsexualism. These are obviously not the only issues that currently face the Church of England in the area of sexual morality. The question of cohabitation, which is addressed in the Southwark diocesan report to which we referred in Chapter 3, would be another such issue, for example.

However, since the issues of homosexuality, bisexuality and transsexualism are the ones on which we have concentrated in this report, it is the handling of these issues that will be the focus of this chapter.

9.1 The official approach of the Church of England
9.1.1   Although there is a range of views on homosexuality within the Church of England there are two official statements.

9.1.2   The General Synod motion, which was noted at 1.3.17–18 above, remains on the record as the last synodical expression of the mind of the Church as a whole.

9.1.3   *Issues in Human Sexuality,* which came out four years after the Synod debate, is a different kind of statement, which is more pastoral in tone and, unlike the Synod statement, does not include a call to repentance. However, its overall stance on sexual morality is the same, as is its insistence that holiness of life is particularly required of Christian leaders. *Issues in Human Sexuality* does not claim to be the last word on the subject and in 1997 it was commended by Synod for discussion and response by the Church. Nevertheless, it does express the theological position and pastoral practice of the House of Bishops. As such, it has considerable authority within the Church.

9.2 Diversity within the Church of England
9.2.1   As was suggested in the last chapter, it seems likely that the approach taken by General Synod and by the House of Bishops still

reflects the consensus of opinion within the Church of England. However, as has already been explained in this report, this overall consensus, and the consistency of the Church's official teaching, conceals the fact that within the Church of England there is a diversity of approaches to the issue of homosexuality. This diversity is both theoretical and practical.

9.2.2   In terms of *theoretical* diversity it is clear that the Church of England is divided along the lines that we have explored elsewhere in this report between those who hold that homosexual relationships are contrary to the revealed will of God, those who feel that they should be accepted as part of the range of human sexual expression that God has created, and those who feel that, while they do not conform to God's ideal, they may in certain circumstances be the best option ethically for those with a sexual attraction to those of the same sex as themselves.

9.2.3   The range of the debate within the Church of England is indicated by the statements about human sexuality produced by the conservative evangelical Anglican pressure group *Reform* on the one hand and by the *Lesbian and Gay Christian Movement* (LGCM) on the other. Although the LGCM is not an Anglican organization, it does express the views of those who are pressing for a change in the Church of England's traditional position.

9.2.4   These two groups are only two among a number of groups who have produced such statements. Others that could be mentioned are the *True Freedom Trust* on the conservative side of the debate and *Changing Attitudes* on the liberal side. The reason for using statements by *Reform* and LGCM is that, as we have noted, these statements give a clear indication of the difference of opinion that exists within the Church.

9.2.5   Section (d) of the *Reform* 'covenant' states that *Reform* holds to:

> The rightness of sexual intercourse in heterosexual marriage, and the wrongness of such activity both outside it and in all its homosexual forms.

And the commentary on these words declares:

> In the face of enormous confusion today the biblical pattern for sexual activity must be spelt out. Both fornication (sex before

marriage) and adultery (sex outside marriage) are condemned as sinful heterosexual behaviour in the Bible. Homosexual behaviour (which can appear in a variety of ways) is also condemned as sinful. This part of the covenant is not singling out sexual behaviour as the worst form of sinfulness, it is rather that this is the area where the Bible's authority and teaching is so often denied today. And of course when we find our behaviour is condemned as sinful by the Bible, in whatever area, we are encouraged to seek forgiveness through the gospel of Jesus Christ and to lead a new life in him.[1]

9.2.6 By contrast the statement on 'Homosexuality and the Church' on the web site of the LGCM notes that:

> Most Christians have believed and most churches have taught that you cannot be a Christian and express your love for another person of the same sex in a sexual relationship. They believe that God has condemned this through the Bible.[2]

The statement goes on to question this belief.

9.2.7 First of all, it gives a brief overview of the biblical material. Developing the kind of revisionist approach to the biblical evidence that we looked at in Chapter 4, it argues that there is nothing in the biblical material that condemns loving and compassionate homosexual relationships.

9.2.8 It then goes on to argue that attitudes in the Church have progressed over the centuries and the time has now come for a reconsideration of homosexuality:

> In many respects the Church was limited by the social outlook of the times and places where the Gospel was preached. Attitudes have always changed, however slowly. Only in the last century was slavery abolished, but Paul accepted it without question. And it is only in recent times that the churches have started to examine the position of women in their own organizations and in society in general. The time is now right to have a critical look at homosexuality in a Christian context.[3]

9.2.9 It concludes by declaring that the LGCM is seeking to implement the values of the gospel:

> The Lesbian & Gay Christian Movement is not selling out on Christian truth. It is working for the very love and freedom that

Christ brings to his people through his life, death and resurrection. Our Movement is working for love, for peace, for justice, and for the promotion of the Christian faith. God's work is always a struggle. Let us try to be at the heart of it.[4]

9.2.10 In terms of *practical* diversity it is clear, on the one hand, that there are clergy and laity in the Church of England who will:

● Seek to dissuade gay and lesbian people from forming same-sex sexual relationships;

● Seek to persuade gay and lesbian people either to marry, seek to change their sexual orientation or live celibate lives;

● Be unwilling to accept the ministry of practising homosexual clergy and who will seek to prevent the ordination and appointment of such clergy;

● Dissociate themselves from those in the Church of England who take a different view of the matter;

● Campaign for some continued legal restriction on homosexual activity.

9.2.11 It is also clear, on the other hand, that there are clergy and laity in the Church of England who will:

● Encourage gay and lesbian people to form same-sex relationships if this is what they feel is right for them;

● Welcome and encourage the ministry of openly homosexual clergy;

● Give an unofficial blessing to those gay and lesbian couples who desire it;

● Campaign for an end to legal restrictions on homosexual activity.

9.3 Diversity within the Anglican Communion
9.3.1   The diversity that exists in the Church of England on this matter is part of a wider diversity within the Anglican Communion.

9.3.2   The Anglican Communion also has a recently established position on the matter of homosexuality. We should not forget, however, that this position or 'line' was reached after a fierce and painful debate that has had many repercussions throughout the Anglican Communion and opinion on it remains divided.

9.3.3   This position of the Anglican Communion is contained in resolution 1.10 of the 1998 Lambeth Conference, which was referred to in the first chapter of this report.[5] It will be argued by many that this resolution, with its rejection of homosexual practice as 'incompatible with Scripture' expresses the opinion of a large number of Anglicans around the world, particularly, though not exclusively, in the two-thirds world, a state of affairs reflected in the fact that a large number of the bishops at Lambeth '98 voted for resolution 1.10.

9.3.4   Those who accept the authority of Lambeth 1.10 hold that, because this resolution reflects the clear teaching of the Bible and the mind of the Communion as a whole, it ought to be accepted by all Anglicans. They therefore react with both dismay and anger when it appears to be ignored in some provinces of the Communion, most notably the Episcopal Church of the United States of America (ECUSA).

9.3.5   This reaction has found expression in a number of ways, including the irregular consecrations in Singapore and Denver of bishops to serve what are often called 'traditionalist' parishes within ECUSA, and the recent proposal contained in the report *To Mend the Net*[6] that the Anglican Primates' Meeting should have the power to initiate action against those provinces or dioceses that act in a way that exceeds the limits of acceptable Anglican diversity. It is quite clear from what is said in *To Mend the Net* that its authors have ECUSA and its stance on homosexuality principally in mind.

The issues raised by the irregular consecrations and by the proposals in *To Mend the Net* have been taken seriously by the Primates of the Anglican Communion and are the subject of continuing reflection, debate and concern.

9.3.6   Those who support the Lambeth resolution are, of course, opposed both to encouragement being given to homosexuals to enter into same-sex relationships and to the ordination or appointment of practising gay or lesbian clergy.

9.3.7   On the other hand, there are other Anglicans who feel that they cannot accept the teaching of Lambeth 1.10. Those who take this approach are particularly influential in ECUSA and the Anglican Church of Canada, but they exist in other parts of the Communion as well.

9.3.8   There are two reasons why they are unable to accept the teaching of the Lambeth resolution. First, and most simply, they hold that the view of homosexuality taken by the Lambeth Conference is theologically wrong. This is the view taken, for instance, in the response of the Diocese of California to Lambeth 1.10, which has already been referred to in Chapter 4. This concludes by declaring that:

> Scripture tells us that we are beings in a creation that is ongoing, to whom more is revealed by God over time. It is a creation in which all the law and the prophets are summed up in the commandment to love God and our neighbors as ourselves. In such a creation, it is inadequate to conclude, as does the 1998 Lambeth conference, that homosexual practice is incompatible with Scripture because same gender sex is condemned in Leviticus. In such a creation there is every reason to revise our thinking in order to make an equal place in the church for gays and lesbians.[7]

9.3.9   Secondly, they argue that Lambeth '98 should not mark the end of the debate on homosexuality within the Communion because the Lambeth Conference did not listen adequately to the views of gay and lesbian people, and take their pain, dismay and anger sufficiently into account.

This is, for example, the view put forward in *A Pastoral Statement to Lesbian and Gay Anglicans from Some Member Bishops of the Lambeth Conference*, published in August 1998. This declares:

> Within the limitations of the Conference, it has not been possible to hear adequately your voices, and we apologize for any sense of rejection that has occurred because of this reality. This letter is a sign of our commitment to listen to you and reflect with you theologically and spiritually on your lives and ministries. It is our deep concern that you do not feel abandoned by your Church and that you know of our continued respect and support.
>
> We pledge that we will continue to reflect, pray, and work for your full inclusion in the life of the Church. It is obvious that Communion-wide we are in great disagreement over what full inclusion would mean. We ourselves have varied views and admit, as the report of the Human Sexuality Sub-section of the Conference says, that there is much we do not yet understand. But we believe it is an imperative of the Gospel and our faith that we seek such understanding.

> We call on the entire Communion to continue (and in many
> places, begin) prayerful, respectful conversation on the issue of
> homosexuality. We must not stop where this Conference has left off.
> You, our sisters and brothers in Christ, deserve a more thorough
> hearing than you received over the past three weeks. We will work
> to make that so.[8]

9.3.10   Particularly in ECUSA and in the Anglican Church of Canada,
there have been those who have been prepared to take practical action
to support gay and lesbian Anglicans living in same-sex relationships.
For example, in February 2000, the Very Revd Robert Taylor, an openly
gay priest, was appointed Dean of St Mark's Cathedral in Seattle, and
even though the ECUSA General Convention has declined to approve
official services of blessing for gay and lesbian unions, such services do
exist in some American dioceses. Such services were recently proposed
in two Canadian dioceses as well, and in June 2002 the synod of one
of these dioceses, the diocese of New Westminster, agreed that they
should be permitted to take place.

9.3.11   The diversity within the Anglican Communion has been
further highlighted by the recent report of the International Anglican
Conversations on Human Sexuality convened by the Archbishop of
Canterbury following the 1998 Lambeth Conference in order to 'help
move the whole Communion forward from the Lambeth resolution'.

9.3.12   These conversations between bishops from around the
Anglican Communion did result in a number of points of agreement.
For example, it was agreed that:

- The Scriptures are foundational for all aspects of our work.

- The questions at issue centre on homosexual behaviour, not on
  homosexual people. We are called to love homosexual people as
  we are called to love any other people.

- Homosexuality is a much more varied phenomenon than the
  singular noun suggests; there are no 'assured results' available to
  us from medical and other research into origins, causations, etc.
  Even if there were, Christians would not be relieved of the
  responsibility of making theological and ethical judgments.

9.3.13   However, the conversations also 'revealed and clarified' a
number of points of disagreement:

- We were not able to reach a common mind regarding a single pattern of holy living for homosexual people.

- We have different perceptions of the relationship of the authority of Scripture to that of Reason and Tradition and contemporary experience.

- We approach and interpret Scriptural passages in different ways.[9]

9.3.14   An attempt to enable as many Anglican bishops as possible to make a *common* statement in response to Lambeth was initiated in 1999 by Bishop Steven Charleston, the President of Episcopal Divinity School in Cambridge, Massachusetts, one of the eleven Episcopal seminaries in the USA. He drew up the Cambridge Accord – an invitation to every bishop in the Anglican Communion to make a shared statement on behalf of homosexual people throughout the world.

9.3.15   Because the Cambridge Accord focuses on condemning the violence perpetuated against homosexuals globally, it seeks to focus on an issue that all Anglican bishops might feel able to support. As the letter introducing the Accord states:

> Recently the global persecution of homosexuals has reached alarming proportions. For example, in the United States, hate crimes against gay and lesbian persons has risen with deadly consequences; in Africa, particularly in Uganda, Kenya and Zimbabwe, national leaders at the highest levels of government have made public statements vilifying homosexuals with a claim to justification through the Christian faith. The Cambridge Accord seeks to respond to this kind of pogrom against homosexuals by clarifying the Anglican position through a shared statement of the bishops of the Church.

9.3.16   The Accord notes that, because the Anglican Church's debates about homosexuality have been in the limelight (especially during the Lambeth Conference), 'the responsibility for us to calm the passions of hate have become even more acute' and 'to stand united in our Anglican tradition of peace and the protection of human rights with dignity'. Bishop Charleston continues in his letter to his brother and sister bishops:

> After Lambeth I am also acutely aware of the uniquely Anglican need to make such a public statement. The African nations that are currently in the spotlight are all strong areas for our Communion.

Their bishops need our support in resisting this kind of misuse of the Christian faith.

9.3.17   The strength of the Accord in the whole Anglican Communion is that it recognizes that 'bishops have divergent views on the "biblical, theological and moral" issues surrounding homosexuality' but invites them to stand in unity on three essential points, the key points of the Accord:

a.   that no homosexual person should ever be deprived of liberty, property or civil rights because of his or her sexual orientation;

b.   that all acts of violence, oppression and degradation against homosexual persons are wrong and cannot be sanctioned by an appeal to the Christian faith;

c.   that every human being is created equal in the eyes of God and therefore deserves to be treated with dignity and respect.

9.3.18   By 2000, Anglican bishops from the USA, Canada, Puerto Rico, England, Scotland, Wales, Honduras, Cyprus and the Gulf, South Africa, Melanesia, New Zealand, and Australia, had signed the Cambridge Accord. This included 22 bishops from England, Wales and Scotland, including the new Archbishop of Canterbury, Rowan Williams.[10]

9.3.19   Most recently, the paper *True Union in the Body?* commissioned by the Archbishop of the West Indies, Drexel Gomez, suggests that there should be a moratorium on Anglican dioceses and provinces taking actions in the area of homosexual conduct that would depart from the Church's traditional teaching:

> ... given both the lack of agreed procedures at the Communion level and the need for a period of stability under a new Archbishop of Canterbury, it would be preferable if within the Communion as a whole a moratorium could be placed on actions in this area which seek to alter the traditional public teaching and practice of the Christian Church. That traditional teaching must be upheld, even if at the same time some room is allowed for the protection of private conscience and the use of pastoral discretion which does not create public scandal.

> This commitment to the Lambeth 1998 decision and a moratorium on actions opposed to it should remain in force at least until there

are agreed procedures by which the Communion can respond to innovation in this area. These procedures would likely require a future Lambeth Conference (or some similarly representative body) to conclude that such actions are 'not against God's Word', thereby giving permission to provinces to proceed as they believe right in their own setting. If instead unilateral action is taken in this area before the Communion as a whole gives its consent, then almost inevitably this will rupture the overall unity of the Anglican Communion. This will have serious consequences, because this unity is 'essential to the overall effectiveness of the Church's mission to bring the gospel of Christ for all people' (Lambeth 1998, III.2). Is it right to threaten that mission? [11]

9.4 **Diversity in the Church worldwide**

9.4.1   The diversity that exists within the Church of England and the Anglican Communion also exists within the whole Church of Christ worldwide.

9.4.2   In this country, for instance, although the Roman Catholic Church takes a clear line opposing homosexual relationships and the same is true of the Evangelical Alliance, the Methodist Church and the United Reformed Church remain somewhat divided on the issue.

9.4.3   Thus the 1993 Methodist Conference passed two different motions on sexuality that reflect the Methodist Church's divided mind. The first declared:

> This conference reaffirms the traditional teaching of the Church on human sexuality: namely chastity for all outside marriage and fidelity within it. The conference directs that this affirmation is made clear to all candidates for ministry, office and membership.

The second declared:

> Conference recognises, affirms and celebrates the participation and ministry of lesbians and gay men in the Church. Conference calls on the Methodist people to begin a pilgrimage of faith to combat repression and discrimination, to work for justice and human rights and to give dignity and worth to people whatever their sexuality. [12]

9.4.4   Although it is not immediately apparent from the quotations themselves, the second resolution was supported by those advocating a more liberal attitude to homosexuality as a counterbalance to what they saw as the excessive conservatism of the first resolution.

9.4.5   The URC has been and remains one of the most welcoming and affirming of the British Churches to gay and lesbian people; nevertheless, in the aftermath of a general Assembly debate on the issue, resolution 14 of the URC General Assembly 2000 decided:

> ... that there is a lack of agreement relating to issues of human sexuality, and that any further resolution attempting to declare the mind of the church on this subject would be unlikely to find sufficient support at this time.[13]

Although there is currently a seven-year moratorium on official discussion of the issue, it is clear that, at the national level of the URC General Assembly, homosexuality remains a subject of continuing discussion and debate, while individual churches maintain – as is proper in a Church with a strong congregationalist tradition – individual autonomy and decision-making on the matter of gay and lesbian clergy, and other matters pertaining to the broad question of homosexuality.

9.4.6   Looking around the globe a similar picture of diversity emerges. The Orthodox and Roman Catholic Churches, officially at least,[14] maintain the traditional rejection of homosexual activity, and the same is true of conservative Protestant bodies such as the Southern Baptist Convention in the United States. By contrast, the United Churches in the United States and Canada agreed in 1985 and 1988 respectively to permit sexually active same-sex partnerships within their membership and to ordain sexually active lesbians and gay men.[15]

9.4.7   In between these two positions there are many Churches that take a much less clear-cut line. For example, the Evangelical Lutheran Church of America is divided on the issue, with its 1993 report merely rehearsing the arguments on both sides and issuing a prayer that the Holy Spirit would guide the Church on the matter.[16] For another example, although the Evangelical Church in Germany, the EKD, contains Christians who take a conservative view of the matter, nevertheless, as we have seen, the EKD report on homosexuality and the Church, published in 1998, argued that a lifelong single-sex relationship was the best option for homosexuals who had not received the gift of celibacy, and recommended the blessing of people in such relationships.

The report is also open to the possibility of practising homosexuals' being ordained in circumstances 'where the homosexual way of living is expressed in an ethically responsible way',[17] although it holds that there would need to be ecumenical consensus with sister Churches before such a step was taken.

9.4.8   Among the Nordic and Baltic Lutheran Churches with which the Church of England is in communion as a result of the Porvoo agreement there is also diversity.

9.4.9   The Lutheran Churches in the Baltic republics (Estonia and Lithuania) do not, as yet, have the issue on their agenda. This reflects the fact that these are conservative Lutheran Churches in what are still quite traditional societies.

9.4.10   The situation is different with the Lutheran Churches in Finland, Iceland, Norway, and Sweden. These are, generally speaking, more liberal Churches, in societies where there has been widespread public acceptance of homosexual relationships for quite a long period of time. This means that there is pressure building up within them for the blessing of same-sex relationships and the ordination of practising homosexuals.

9.4.11   However, this having been said, none of these Churches has officially gone down this road, and there some opposition remains to the idea that they should do so. The case of the Evangelical Lutheran Church in Finland illustrates the point.

9.4.12   Since last year it has been possible in Finland for people of the same sex to register as a legally recognized partnership. This is not legally equivalent to marriage but, except for the right to adopt a child or to accept the family name of the other party, the rights conveyed to the people involved are virtually the same.

9.4.13   After the first homosexual couples had publicly celebrated their registration in March 2002, two motions were proposed in the Synod of the Finnish Lutheran Church

- The first requested material for a liturgical blessing for such a couple.

- The second requested that a paragraph be inserted in the Finnish Church Order (their equivalent of the Canons) preventing anyone who had registered a same-sex partnership holding ministerial office in the church.

9.4.14 After a long discussion, the Synod did not make a decision on either motion, but instead remitted the issue to a church commission, which is still in the initial stages of its work. A decision on the matter is not expected in the near future.

9.5 Diversity over bisexuality and transsexualism

9.5.1 As explained earlier in this report, the discussion of bisexuality and transsexualism is more recent and less developed than the debate about homosexuality. As a result it is a debate that has a much lower profile in the Church, and is consequently the cause of much less division. However, it seems likely that the efforts of those campaigning for the needs of bisexual and transsexual people, the increasing numbers of those seeking sex reassignment surgery, and the variety of responses to this, mean that the profile of these issues will continue to be raised.

9.5.2 Given the range of opinions on these issues, which this report has noted, it is probable that they too will be the cause of increasing diversity in the years to come. As we have explained, there is already discussion within the Church of England on the propriety or otherwise of ordaining transsexuals, sparked off by the case of a transsexual priest in the diocese of Bristol.

9.6 Handling diversity over sexual morality

Things we cannot do
9.6.1 Given the existence of this diversity, the question that arises is how the Church of England should respond to it in a theologically responsible fashion that draws both on theological first principles and its long experience of living with differences of belief and practice. We suggest, first of all, that there are four things that the Church cannot do.

a. We cannot ignore the fact that this diversity exists
9.6.2 Whatever views we hold on the matters under debate, we cannot bury our heads in the sand and pretend that the view we think correct is the only possible one. There are two reasons why we cannot do this:

- We should always work on the assumption that views that differ from our own have something to teach us. None of us knows everything or is infallible in the interpretation of what we do know, and therefore we must always be open to correction. However, this correction cannot take place if we only take note of ideas that support our existing opinions. At the heart of this assumption is a continued need for genuine dialogue.

- We cannot help others to see what is wrong with opinions we view as erroneous if we have not come to grips with them ourselves. Unless we engage seriously with opinions that we think are wrong we will never be able to mount a convincing case to show that our own approach is to be preferred.

b. We cannot say that ethical differences simply do not matter because there is no objective scale of moral values against which to compare them

9.6.3   This is a position that has been advocated by many supporters of the currently fashionable philosophical approach known as 'postmodernism', which we have already encountered when looking at principles of biblical interpretation in Chapter 2.

9.6.4   The American writer Kenneth Gergen sums up the postmodern approach to ethics in this way: 'For the post modern there is no transcendent reality, rationality, or value system with which to rule between competitors.'[18]

9.6.5   Postmodern philosophy and thought therefore tends to challenge claims to universal validity for human systems of thought and culture. These are seen to be social constructs, not absolutes that make a universal claim upon us. In Christian theology and biblical study there has been a parallel development of emphasis on the diversity of modes of Christian thought and an insistence that there is no one overarching systematic theme with which to approach the resources both of the Bible and the Christian tradition.

9.6.6   The strength of the postmodern approach is that it acknowledges the variety and changeability of human thought, culture and experience. In so far as it does this it is an approach that Christian theology has to take seriously.[19]

9.6.7   However, postmodernism is more than a salutary protest against overinflated claims to absolute intellectual objectivity. It is, in effect, if not in intention, an alternative world view, an all-embracing account of how things really are. As J. R. Middleton and Brian J. Walsh put it in their book *Truth is Stranger than it Used to Be*:

> Do postmodernists consider their own worldview as simply one option among many? Not at all. Postmodernity, as the master discourse which guides our understanding that all stories are mere human constructs, does not appear on the table. It *is* the table on which all the other dishes are served. Postmodernity thus functions as the larger interpretive frame that relativizes all other worldviews as simply local stories with no legitimate claims to reality or universality.[20]

9.6.8   Understood as a world view, postmodernism has a number of serious limitations.

- It is self refuting. Ethically, postmodernists reject moral absolutes because they believe that belief in them always leads to the oppression of those who fail to conform to the prevailing moral norm and, philosophically, they reject moral absolutes because they hold that 'truth' is merely a human social construct that gives one no purchase on how things really are. However, if the postmodernists are right, there can be nothing wrong with oppressing people and, therefore, nothing ethically wrong with the use of the concept of moral absolutes and, if they are right, we can never know that it is true that 'truth' is a human social construct, since this idea of a social construct would itself be simply a social construct.

- If taken seriously it would mean that we could not say that any action whatsoever was right or wrong, and most people, including most postmodernists, would find this an impossible approach to take in practice. Most people, for example, would argue that the Holocaust was morally wrong, not simply that they happen to disapprove of it. Any philosophical system has to give an adequate explanation for the stubborn human conviction that there is such a thing as right and wrong, and postmodernism simply fails to do this.

- It confuses the context of a moral belief with the question of its truthfulness. As we have said, it is certainly true that all moral truth claims arise in the context of particular cultures. However, as Nicholas Rescher points out, this is irrelevant to the question of their correctness:

The fact that the affirmation of a fact must proceed from within a historico-cultural setting does not mean that the correctness and appropriateness of what is said will be restricted to such a setting. The fact that we make assertions within time does not prevent us from asserting timeless truths.[21]

- Most importantly, postmodernism fails to do justice to the fact that God has established an objective moral order through his creative and recreative activity in Jesus Christ. It is on the basis of this moral order that we recognize in God the source and standard of all that is beautiful, good and true and, as we saw in Chapter 3, it is only by living in conformity to this moral order that human beings can find the fullness of life for which God created them.

9.6.9   For all these four reasons, and particularly for the last one, we must go on saying that ethical differences, including differences about sexual ethics, really do matter because they are not just arbitrary differences of opinion or cultural convention, but differences rooted in better or worse understandings of how things really are. The existence of a moral order established by God means that some ways of behaving are better or worse than others because of their conformity or lack of conformity with what this moral order requires.

c. We cannot claim that differences of approach to sexual ethics are only superficial

9.6.10   In the face of differences of conviction that threaten to disrupt the unity of the Church, it is very tempting to suggest that really, deep down, everyone is saying the same thing. In the case of the current differences concerning human sexuality we cannot make this suggestion because it simply is not true.

9.6.11   It is true that, within the current diversity about sexual ethics in the Christian Church, there is a large degree of common ground:

- All would agree that, although in a fallen world all sexual activity is to a certain degree affected by sin, there is nothing intrinsically evil about sexual activity as such, and that both marriage and celibacy are equally valid forms of Christian discipleship.

- All would also agree that sexual relationships must be marked by the virtues of love, fidelity, and respect for the integrity of one's sexual partner. They would therefore say that casual, exploitative and violent forms of sexual conduct are wrong, and would therefore condemn promiscuity, adultery, paedophilia and rape.

9.6.12   However, beyond this, agreement ceases and significant disagreements emerge. As has been noted in the course of this report:

- There is real disagreement between those who believe that homosexual relationships can have ethical validity and those who would argue that they are sinful in all circumstances.
- There is real disagreement between those who believe that it is appropriate to give a blessing to long-term same sex-relationships and those who would argue that such a blessing is theologically inappropriate.
- There is real disagreement between those who would hold that practising homosexuals are as fit for ordination as anyone else, and those who would argue that their way of life is sinful and makes their ordination inappropriate.
- There is real disagreement between those who believe that the normal requirements of heterosexual monogamy are applicable to bisexuals and those who would argue that, in the case of bisexuals, such requirements may not be appropriate.
- There is real disagreement between those who believe that a person's God-given sexual identity is determined by their physical nature and those who would argue that their self-perception about their identity is equally or more important.

9.6.13   These are real and important differences that, when translated from theory to practice, make a significant difference both to how people should behave and how the Church should react to their behaviour.

9.6.14   If, for instance, it really is the case that homosexual sexual intercourse is sinful in all circumstances then it would clearly be wrong for those giving pastoral care to homosexual people to give them any encouragement to engage in such behaviour. Instead, as the 1987 General Synod motion suggests, such behaviour would have to be met by compassion, a call to repentance, and an assurance of God's forgiveness.

9.6.15   If, however, it is the case that such activity is permissible for those who have a homosexual orientation and have not received the gift of celibacy, then clearly those giving them pastoral care would need to encourage them to develop an intimate, exclusive, loving relationship, and might feel it appropriate to affirm a long-term homosexual relationship by means of a service of blessing.

9.6.16   Likewise, if it really is the case that a person's sexual identity is determined by their physical nature, then it would be right to encourage people to seek to come to terms with that identity rather than to undertake sex reassignment surgery, and it would be difficult to accept that they could marry in their preferred identity, since this identity would not truly exist. Conversely, if the key thing is someone's self-perception and their ability to live comfortably with their bodily appearance, then it might be right to encourage them to undergo SRS, and to accept their desire to marry in their post-operative identity.

9.6.17   The differences here are clearly far more than superficial, particularly to those involved in such situations in real life. For questions of sexual identity and practice constitute areas of extreme vulnerability for many people.

d. We cannot say that the differences do not matter because matters of sexual conduct are not really all that important
9.6.18   We cannot say this because the Christian faith clearly teaches that 'each of us will be accountable to God'[22] and, whatever view of sexual ethics is taken, failure to take the correct approach clearly cannot be regarded with indifference.

9.6.19   For those who take a traditional line, those who engage in sexual practices that deviate from the married norm are guilty of fornication, adultery and sexual perversion, and those who practise such things run the risk of forfeiting heaven.[23] For those who take a revisionist line, those who oppress others by condemning their sexual practices and denying them the possibility of sexual fulfilment are guilty of a major failure of love towards them, and whoever fails in love does not know God and does not abide in him.[24] What we are dealing with here touches deep things and therefore cannot be a matter of no consequence.

Things we have to do
9.6.20   Given, therefore, that we cannot simply ignore the fact that there is a diversity of Christian approaches to sexual ethics, and that we

cannot say that these differences do not matter or are merely superficial, how should we handle them?

9.6.21 There are four things we have to do.

a. We have to ask whether these are matters that fall within the scope of legitimate diversity

9.6.22 Recent ecumenical theology has strongly affirmed the importance of diversity in the life of the Church. The *Porvoo Common Statement,* for example, declares that:

> Visible unity, however, should not be confused with uniformity. 'Unity in Christ does not exist despite and in opposition to diversity, but is given with and in diversity.' Because this diversity corresponds with the many gifts of the Holy Spirit to the Church, it is a concept of fundamental ecclesial importance, with relevance to all aspects of the life of the Church, and is not a mere concession to theological pluralism.[25]

Likewise the 1999 ARCIC statement *The Gift of Authority* argues that:

> In the rich diversity of human life, encounter with the living Tradition produces a variety of expressions of the Gospel. Where diverse expressions are faithful to the Word revealed in Jesus Christ and transmitted by the apostolic community, the churches in which they are found are truly in communion. Indeed, this diversity of traditions is the practical manifestation of catholicity and confirms rather than contradicts the vigour of Tradition. As God has created diversity among humans, so the Church's fidelity and identity require not uniformity of expression and formulation at all levels in all situations, but rather catholic diversity within the unity of communion. This richness of tradition is a vital resource for a reconciled humanity. 'Human beings were created by God in his love with such diversity in order that they might participate in that love by sharing with one another both what they have and what they are, thus enriching each other in their mutual communion (*Church as Communion* 35).[26]

9.6.23 Furthermore, the principle of accepting and respecting diversity has come to be used, particularly within the Anglican Communion, as a way of enabling Churches to live together in spite of differences of belief and practice over such issues as the ordination of women to the priesthood and the episcopate. Thus, for example, the Eames Commission invoked the principle of diversity as a way of enabling Anglicans who disagreed over the propriety of the ordination of women to the priesthood and the episcopate to remain together as part of one communion.

9.6.24   However, the principle of the acceptance of diversity cannot be lazily invoked as a way of avoiding conflict by tolerating all forms of belief and practice. This is because there are limits to diversity. One cannot simply say that all forms of diversity are legitimate. As *The Gift of Authority* argues, diversity has to be controlled by fidelity to the divine self-revelation given to us in Jesus Christ and witnessed to by Scripture.

9.6.25   For example, it would not be legitimate to deny the existence of God,[27] or that Jesus Christ came in the flesh,[28] or that he died for our sins in accordance with the Scriptures.[29] All these are beliefs that are central to the Christian faith, the denial of which would take one outside the sphere of orthodox Christianity altogether. It is because agreement on such matters is vital that the recent ecumenical agreements that the Church of England has entered into, such as the Meissen agreement with the EKD or the Porvoo agreement with Scandinavian and Baltic Lutheran Churches, or the Fetter Lane agreement with Moravians, have all contained statements of agreement on such matters. They are there because agreement on such things matters if we are to be a united people before God.

9.6.26   Moreover, these agreements also highlight the fact that, for the Church of England, as for the Anglican Communion as a whole, the areas of legitimate diversity not only exclude disagreement on the fundamentals of the faith as set out in the Bible and the Catholic Creeds but also exclude disagreement on the need to celebrate the two dominical sacraments of baptism and the Eucharist or the necessity of the historic episcopate. The 'Lambeth Quadrilateral', which sets out the basic Anglican understanding of what a united Christian Church would look like, insists that there would have to be agreement on all these areas for such a united Church to exist. Where agreement on these matters has not proved possible, as in the case of the refusal by the EKD to accept the need for the historic episcopate, the journey towards unity has run into difficulties.

9.6.27   The question that is now being raised in some quarters is whether these non-negotiables ought to be extended to include agreement on sexual morality. For example, the Montreal declaration of Anglican essentials produced by 'traditionalist' Anglicans in Canada in 1994 listed as one of these essentials an affirmation concerning standards of sexual conduct:

> God designed human sexuality not only for procreation but also for the joyful expression of love, honour and fidelity between wife and husband. These are the only sexual relations that biblical theology deems good and holy.
>
> Adultery, fornication, and homosexual union are intimacies contrary to God's design. The church must seek to minister healing and wholeness to those who are sexually scarred, or who struggle with ongoing sexual temptations, as most people do. Homophobia and all forms of sexual hypocrisy and abuse are evils against which Christians must ever be on their guard. The church may not lower God's standards of sexual morality for any of its members, but must honour God by upholding these standards tenaciously in face of society's departures from them.[30]

9.6.28 Regardless of whether one agrees with what this statement says about Christian sexual conduct, its inclusion in a list of Anglican essentials does raise the question as to whether fundamental ethical issues ought not to be seen as an area where there has to be agreement both within and between Churches and on which an acceptance of diversity is not appropriate.

9.6.29 The classic argument against this position is that what ought to be regarded as essential is that which makes the Church the Church and that, on everything else, diversity may be tolerated. Thus, it has been argued, there has to be agreement about the basics of the faith, about the sacraments, and about the ministry of word and sacrament, since without these the Church could not exist, but it is possible for the Church to continue to exist while embracing a variety of approaches to ethics. Therefore, agreement about ethical matters is not required for a united Church.

9.6.30 However, this argument ignores the point that we have already made, that ethics, including sexual ethics, also matter if the Church is to live up to its calling. The will of God for his people is that they should be holy as he is holy,[31] and this means walking in obedience to his commandments, 'walking in the way of the Lord' as the Old Testament puts it. This means that it is vital that God's people should know what he requires of his people, obey it, and teach others to do likewise. To this end there needs to be agreement concerning Christian ethics. Furthermore, as we have seen, in the case of the disagreement about sexual ethics the disagreement is about matters that go to the heart of people's relationship with God, and which cannot therefore be treated as subjects on which we can simply learn to live with diversity.

9.6.31 Therefore we have to say with Michael Doe:

> ... we cannot as Christians just give way to a 'you believe this, I believe that' approach to being together, or moving apart, in the Church. Nor even can we be content with the rather cheap model of 'reconciled diversity,' meaning benign tolerance, which many Christians find an easier option to the costlier pursuit of real, 'visible', unity. We need to continue to struggle together for the truth, to find the right and godly balance between the call to solidarity and the recognition of difference. Nowhere is this more important – especially in the Anglican Communion – than in the area of sexuality.[32]

b. We have to ask how a common mind can be achieved on sexual ethics if it is not enough simply to tolerate diversity

9.6.32 As we have argued in Chapters 2 and 3, we cannot simply choose any approach we like for determining the correct approach to sexual morality, because God himself has laid down the approach we must take through his self-revelation in Jesus Christ.

9.6.33 This was the truth acknowledged in a different context by the *Barmen Declaration* of 1934 in its famous statement that:

> Jesus Christ, as he is testified to us in the Holy Scripture, is the one Word of God, whom we are to hear, whom we are to trust and obey in life and in death. We repudiate the false teaching that the church can and must recognize yet other happenings and powers, images and truths as divine revelation alongside this one Word of God, as a source of her preaching.[33]

9.6.34 The findings of rational reflection upon the natural and social sciences, changes in behaviour and attitudes, and the personal experiences of individuals, what in classical Anglican terminology we may collectively call 'reason', all have their own importance, and provide the context that the Church's teaching and preaching need to address. They are among the vehicles that the Holy Spirit uses to push us to think again about the content of God's self-revelation; but it is that self-revelation, and nothing else, that has to be the basis and control of all of the Church's thinking.

9.6.35   To put it simply, what this means is that what we as Christians have to do is to seek together to understand what the biblical witness to Jesus Christ has to say concerning the current diversity of sexual attitudes and practice and how we should behave accordingly.

9.6.36   This means, that first of all, as we have already emphasized, we will need to listen carefully to each other. It is all too easy to assume that our understanding of the biblical witness is the right one and to disregard or even demonize those who think differently. As we argued in Chapter 2, we have to be constantly aware of the provisionality of our reading of the Bible, and this means we have to cultivate what has been called 'holy listening'. That is to say, we have to spend time and effort in seriously and prayerfully seeking to understand what those with whom we are in conversation are really saying, as opposed to what we think they might be saying, making the charitable assumption that they too are seeking to discern the will of God, and being open to the possibility that they have in fact heard God speaking through his word and by his Spirit, and that we therefore need to take heed of what they have to say.

9.6.37   Secondly, we will need to listen carefully but critically to the tradition of the Church. As Karl Barth puts it:

> ... in order to serve the community of to-day, theology itself must be rooted in the community of yesterday. Its testimony to the Word and the profession of its faith must originate, like the community itself, from the community of past times, from which that of to-day arose. Theology must originate also from the older and the more recent *tradition* which determines the present form of its witness. The foundation of its inquiry and instruction is given to theology beforehand, along with the task which it has to fulfil. Theology does not labour somewhere high above the foundation of tradition, as though Church history began to-day. Nevertheless, the special task of theology is a *critical* one, in spite of its relative character. The fire of the quest for truth has to ignite the proclamation of the community, testing and rethinking it in the light of its enduring foundation, object, and content.[34]

9.6.38   It is particularly important that the voices of tradition are listened to in the area of human sexuality, because the fact that current attitudes have diverged so much from what has been the accepted Christian norm can lead to a strong temptation to think that what the Christian tradition has to say can have no relevance to our situation. In fact, it is in times like this that we need to pay special attention to the tradition, and to allow its voice to raise critical questions about current attitudes. If we do not do this, we allow the present to operate a tyranny over our thinking when, in fact, the present is just as likely to be wrong as the past.

9.6.39   However, this having been said, two further points need to be borne in mind:

- We need to recognize the diversity within tradition, and recognize the voices and views that may have been silenced or forgotten, as we suggested in Chapter 5.

- As we noted in Chapter 2, we cannot absolutize the importance of tradition. The past was no more infallible than the present, and the questions that were asked in the past may not be those that we need to ask today. Tradition is an invaluable resource, but it must not become a straitjacket completely constricting our current thinking. What matters, as Barth says, is a critical conversation with the past that is honest about the negative aspects of Church history and previous Christian thought, but which is also open to learning from them.

9.6.40   The last thing to say about this process of listening is that it is never ending. While we should not live in a situation of perpetual doubt or suspension of belief, we always have to be open to hearing God more clearly and more deeply than we have done before and amending our thinking and our acting accordingly. As has already been said, none of us is infallible and, until we see God face to face and know as we are known (1 Corinthians 13.12), we have to go on growing in our knowledge of God and what he requires of us.

c. We have to be honest about the implications of disagreement over sexual ethics both for our own internal unity, and for our ecumenical relationships

9.6.41   Although our unity as Christians is based on our common membership of the one body of Christ and, as such, is something that is invisible, this unity that we share through our relationship with him is one to which we are called to give visible expression. Our ability to do this is, however, compromised by our inability, either internally or ecumenically, to achieve agreement over our different approaches to sexual ethics.

9.6.42   As we have previously noted, it has long been recognized in the ecumenical field that there have to be limits to diversity. This is because visible unity that is not based on agreement in truth is simply not worth having. We can only have that degree of visible unity that is justified by the degree of our agreement as to the will of God for his people.

9.6.43   Furthermore, as the Roman Catholics and the Orthodox have frequently reminded the ecumenical movement, the issue of what we believe in the field of sexual ethics cannot be left out of the picture. We have to be honest about the implications for Christian unity of our disagreements in this area as well.

9.6.44   There is no point in trying to create or sustain an artificial unity that simply papers over areas of important difference. This is dishonouring to God, because it means that we do not take issues of truth with a proper degree of seriousness. It is also counterproductive in terms of the Church's mission because those outside the Church will not see the Church as providing an example of how to live with difference. They will instead receive the message that the Church is not worth listening to because it is as confused as the rest of the world.

9.6.45   If we find that we do disagree with others and our visible unity with them is thus impaired, this does not mean that we cannot recognize them as Christians. As has been argued above, our understanding of Christian ethics, and how we behave in this area, does have important implications for the issue of whether we are living faithfully before God. However, what makes us Christians is our common relationship with Christ, which is rooted in repentance, faith, baptism and the gift of the Holy Spirit, and not the correctness of our beliefs about matters of sexual conduct or the impeccability of our own behaviour.

9.6.46   It therefore makes perfect sense to recognize someone as a Christian who we think is at fault in these areas, and to this extent there is a proper place for Christian inclusivity. What does not make sense, however, is to overlook their beliefs or their conduct or to think that these do not matter.

9.6.47   It is always difficult to walk the narrow path that avoids the sin of judging others when we ourselves are guilty, but also avoids condoning what we believe to be contrary to the will of God. However, this is the hard path that we have to take if we are to obey the biblical injunction to speak the truth in love so that the whole body of Christ may grow in him.[35]

d. We have to be willing to act in accordance with our beliefs

9.6.48   This is true for us as individuals, but it is also true for the Church of England as an institution. If we believe that we have discerned the will of God, then we have a duty to act accordingly as a Church so that there is a corporate as well as an individual obedience to God's will. It is this kind of corporate obedience that we see depicted by St Luke in Acts 2.41-47, a passage that has long been taken as a model for how God wants his people to be.

9.6.49   If we ask how this kind of corporate obedience can be brought about, the two key factors that we need to bear in mind are the proclamation of the gospel and the provision of appropriate forms of pastoral care.

9.6.50   If those in the Church of England are to be faithful to the will of God, then the Church needs to proclaim the gospel in word and sacrament, and to explain in general terms through preaching and catechesis what it understands the implications of the gospel to mean for people's behaviour, their sexual behaviour included.

9.6.51   Those with pastoral responsibility will also need to help people to apply the gospel to their own individual lives through the provision of pastoral care. What such pastoral care should involve is a controversial matter.

9.6.52   There are two points to do with pastoral care upon which everyone would agree.

9.6.53   First, it always needs to be remembered that issues to do with human sexuality are issues that involve real people with real feelings that can be hurt. In Scripture as a whole, and particularly in the ministry of Christ, we see that God addresses and ministers to people as individuals, and those engaged in pastoral care need to take this as their model.

9.6.54 Pastoral care should not be given to anyone, be they heterosexual, homosexual, bisexual or transsexual, as if their sexuality was all that needed to be known about them. Just like heterosexual people, each homosexual, bisexual, and transsexual person is a unique individual, with a unique life story, and, consequently, unique pastoral needs. Anyone who is called to ministry must constantly bear this in mind and be prepared to invest the time and effort necessary to get to know all people properly, whatever their sexual orientation, in order to offer appropriate pastoral help that is relevant to their particular situation. Furthermore, such pastoral care should never be patronizing.

9.6.55 Secondly, as we have already indicated in this report, homosexual, bisexual and transsexual people must be treated with compassion and as equal Christians. It is likely that they will have encountered misunderstanding or hostility from members of the Christian Church in the past and, if the Christian gospel is to be meaningful to them, it will need to be incarnated in terms of Christ's love. If this is in the context of pastoral care, then that must offer them understanding, support, and unconditional love as they seek to meet the challenges to Christian discipleship that their particular form of sexuality raises.

9.6.56 There is, however, a third point to do with pastoral care on which opinion is divided.

9.6.57 On the one hand, there are those who would say that the kind of compassionate pastoral care just advocated and the respect for the conscience of the individual advocated in *Issues in Human Sexuality* preclude the possibility of challenging homosexual, bisexual or transsexual people about matters to do with their sexuality or making the way that they exercise their sexuality a matter for pastoral discipline.

9.6.58 On the other hand, there are those who would say that what is truly compassionate is helping people to walk in obedience to the will of God and that challenging people about their sexuality and making the way that they exercise it a matter for pastoral discipline can be a way of helping people to do this. How, it is asked, can anyone turn from a wrong path unless someone makes clear to them the fact that they are on a wrong path, and how can the holiness of the Church be maintained if sinful behaviour continues unchecked?[36]

9.6.59   The disagreement between the supporters of these two options is not simply a disagreement between homosexual, bisexual and transsexual people on the one hand and heterosexual people on the other. It is a disagreement that divides homosexual, bisexual and transsexual people themselves. For example, in terms of the debate about the pastoral care of homosexual people, organizations such as the *Lesbian and Gay Christian Movement* and *Changing Attitude* would support the first position whereas *True Freedom Trust* would be sympathetic to the second.

e. We must beware of ignoring the work of the Spirit
9.6.60   Those advocating that the Church of England should have a more inclusive attitude to gay, lesbian, bisexual, and transsexual people might well contend, however, that the argument in the previous paragraphs is based on the erroneous assumption that it is such people who are the problem: a problem to be addressed more or less strictly, more or less tolerantly, but a problem. They would suggest that the problem is not homosexual, bisexual, or transsexual people, but rather the Churches' corporate failure to recognize the Spirit of God at work in our times.

9.6.61   As we noted in Chapter 4, they would note that Acts records how some of the most venerable Christians in the early Church failed to recognize the Spirit at work among the Gentiles, and the implications of this for their understanding of the Christian faith. They would also draw attention to the way in which white Christians have failed to see the Spirit of God at work in their black sisters and brothers or in the implications of this for the ordering of both the Church and wider society. As they see it, there is an analogy between these past failures and the failure of the Church today to recognize the Spirit at work in homosexual, bisexual and transsexual people.

9.6.62   Those who take a more conservative approach would note, however, that there is also a danger of confusing the Spirit of God with the prevailing attitudes of contemporary culture. They would not deny that the Church has failed to recognize the work of the Spirit in the past. However, they would argue that we cannot see behaviour that is contrary to the teaching of the Bible as being inspired by the Spirit, since this would mean that the Spirit who inspired the Scriptures was now contradicting himself. As they would see the matter, unless and until it can be shown that the Scriptures teach otherwise, the Church must maintain its traditional stance, because only by so doing can the Church remain obedient to the Spirit of God speaking through God's word.

9.7 Summary and conclusion

9.7.1   In this report we have done three things

- We have looked at the background and nature of the current debate about some aspects of human sexuality, and noted the diversity that exists on this issue in society, in the Church of England, and in the Church as a whole.

- We have looked at the theology of human sexuality as a whole and considered the specific issues raised by homosexuality, bisexuality and transsexuality. We have also noted the particular challenges and questions raised for traditional Christian theology by feminist, gay and lesbian theologians working from within the Christian tradition, and the issue of whether female sexuality has been adequately handled within the tradition.

- Finally, we have considered the place of homosexuals, bisexuals and transsexuals in the life of the Church, and we have explored how the Church of England should respond with integrity to the current diversity of thinking about this matter.

9.7.2   As the discussion in this report has developed, it has become clear that at the heart of the debate about human sexuality is the question of what it means to respond appropriately to the grace of God.

9.7.3   In *The Cost of Discipleship* Bonhoeffer makes a famous distinction between cheap and costly grace.

Cheap grace, he says, means grace taught as an abstract theological principle and therefore:

> ... grace without discipleship, grace without the cross, grace without Jesus Christ living and incarnate.

Costly grace, by contrast:

> ... is the treasure hidden in the field; for the sake of it a man will gladly go and sell all that he has. It is the pearl of great price to buy which the merchant will sell all his goods. It is the kingly rule of Christ, for whose sake a man will pluck out the eye which causes him to stumble, it is the call of Jesus Christ at which the disciple leaves his nets and follows him.[37]

9.7.4   As we saw in Chapter 3, the Christian calling is to follow the path of costly grace, for it is to this path that we are summoned by our baptism into Christ's death and resurrection. This is true whether we define ourselves as heterosexual, homosexual, bisexual or transsexual.

9.7.5   We can all agree on the sheer graciousness of that grace. Christ says to each one of us, you are cherished, welcomed, included. Where there is continuing disagreement concerns what is entailed on our part by the cost of that grace.

9.7.6   We can all agree that the very fact of God's grace means that the Church is summoned to be a welcoming community in which all who seek to follow Christ in the path of discipleship may find unconditional love and support. Where there is continuing disagreement is what shape this love and support should take in the case of homosexual, bisexual and transsexual people. Does it mean respecting and endorsing whatever decisions they may make regarding sexual activity or sexual identity – and if so, what should our attitude be to the Church's traditional understanding of biblical teaching? Or does it mean asking them to reconsider such decisions and then supporting them through all the pain that such reconsideration will involve?

9.7.7   It is our hope that, as each reader comes to the end of this guide, she or he will be able to reflect about which issues in human sexuality need to be thought about again, and how to engage in the continued journey of dialogue and learning with others.

At this stage in the debate, our corporate discipline as a Church is to continue our journey together in dialogue, mutually supporting each other in continued listening, sensitive engagement of the issues, and discernment. As Rowan Williams has written:

God is not to be known unless we grasp the depth of our freedom and our unfreedom, unless we give up fictions about our purity or our innocence and become committed to searching out those we exclude and suppress, creating with them the promised community of mutual gift.[38]

9.7.8   In engaging in sensitive discussion with others, we thus commit ourselves to demonstrating the love of God to one another, and we remember that that love is the love of the Creator God who made each one of us in his image and likeness. Respect for a fellow human being is always grounded in that central piece of Christian theology.

9.7.9   Our prayer is that, as we continue to reflect with the Anglican Communion and our ecumenical partners on the biblical witness to the grace of God, we may be led into a truer and deeper understanding of what responding appropriately to that grace means in terms of our individual and corporate discipleship, and what it means for the formation of church communities that express and demonstrate the mysterious and extraordinary depths of God's love for each one of us.

Appendix: The Oxford diocesan study days on *Issues in Human Sexuality*

This is a paper produced by Jo Saunders from Oxford diocese reporting on the study days on the topic of issues in human sexuality. It is included as an example of how a study of this matter might be undertaken at a diocesan level.

Growth through listening

A diocesan process for understanding issues in human sexuality

When in 1997, the Bishop of Oxford asked me to head up an educational process within the Diocese of Oxford on issues in human sexuality, the task seemed immense. A study guide had been produced in 1992 and 100 copies sold, but a survey had shown that only a small percentage of these had actually been used.

In 1997 a facilitating group was formed comprising gay and straight people, men and women, academics, clergy and lay, and from all strands of 'churchmanship'. Firstly we updated the study guide and promoted it within the diocese. We gathered information from other dioceses as to resources and methods of presenting issues to church groups and synods. This showed a great variety in approach and method, each suited to its own diocesan culture, and so we decided that we must devise a method best suited to the Diocese of Oxford.

Over the following year we visited three chapters and three parishes, using the study guide as a basis for discussion and as a 'taster' for people to use locally. One course was run through a Christian Training Scheme and this proved very worth while because it was ecumenical and the Anglican 'angst' was diluted.

After Lambeth

With the Lambeth resolution in 1998 the agenda changed. Two deaneries received motions from PCCs about endorsement of the

Lambeth Resolution and 'traditional' teaching, and possible movement up through the synodical structures. The group decided that we must take on board the challenge to listen to each other embedded in the Lambeth resolution. All that followed has been with that in mind.

The Bishop of Oxford did a 'teach-in' at diocesan synod in March 1999, which gave a broad overview on homosexuality – causality, gay history, philosophical ethics, the Bible and hermeneutics, and covered issues such as permanent relationships, cultural and worldwide contexts and homophobia.

At about the same time the group facilitated presentations at the two deanery synods mentioned, and one speaker covered the historical process in the churches and scripture and a gay person gave a personal testimony on their faith and sexuality. In both cases the motion did not go forward to diocesan synod, either voted out, or the synod deciding not to vote. With invitations to two more synods to discuss scriptural issues and a few visits to parishes, we realized that we needed something more proactive if we were to reach over 600 parishes and 29 deaneries.

We decided that we needed to enable clergy to discuss the issue of same-sex relationships in a 'safe' unthreatening way, before they could feel comfortable enough to introduce it in the parishes. Bishop Richard and the senior staff agreed to invite their clergy to study days, which the bishops would chair. A programme was decided.

Preparing to listen
Once the bishops had set dates for summer/autumn 2000, venues had to be found for nine days each catering for 75 clergy. This proved to be one of the more time-consuming tasks of the process as we had to fit into venues on specific dates and needed accommodation without toddlers' groups, Mothers' Union meetings and all the other community activities which large church centres cater for. Once date and venue were decided, each area bishop and the diocesan bishop personally invited every incumbent, curate, NSM and OLM to one of the days – three in each archdeaconry.

Speakers were recruited through the Lesbian Gay Christian Movement, Changing Attitude, the Courage Trust and True Freedom Trust. I was heartened by the ready response from these organizations and from the people they suggested I might approach to speak.

The facilitating group planned the Scripture session and between them undertook to lead it. (Despite the resource in Oxford of eminent theologians, the dates we had were either in exam time or at the beginning of the academic year.)

The day was to start with an overview from Bishop Richard and he recorded his input on to a CD. On the days when he was not present, participants listened to his talk on the CD with the script for them to follow. This proved a very welcome method of preparing participants for the rest of the day.

Clergy responded in surprising numbers to the invitation – in all nearly 400 clergy attended either their local day or switched to another day which was more convenient. The process was financed through Continuing Ministerial Education and with hall hire, speakers' fees and expenses, the cost of each day averaged out at £165. Added to this must be the cost of the hours of work put in by myself and my secretary to prepare papers, organize resources and daily teams.

At each day a small library was on display plus leaflets and literature to be taken away. Once speakers, group leaders and the chairman had been briefed, we were ready to go!

The programme
Each day started with prayers and then listening to Bishop Richard, either in person or on the CD, and his paper entitled 'Same Sex Relationships – the unresolved questions'. After coffee we listened to two speakers; one from an openly gay perspective, often in a stable partnership; one from the perspective of a gay friendship without sexual practice, or celibacy. This was followed by small group work on case studies relating to pastoral issues. After lunch there would be an introduction to the scriptural issues and materials to be used. After an hour or so in groups there was a plenary reflection on issues raised by the Bible study. The day ended with prayer.

Three days were run in the summer, and evaluated with the senior staff team in July. It was agreed that the process worked and, beyond tweaking timings here and there, the programme should remain unchanged. In preparing for the autumn, we decided to include sector ministers, and new invitations were sent to them and to those parish clergy who had not yet replied.

The content of the day

a. Same-sex relationships

One important feature of the day was the set of ground rules offered before the first session and posted at group locations. These included – confidentiality, respect for others and their differences, only disclosing what is comfortable to disclose, allowing others to speak, and not making assumptions about each other. This with the prayers and Bishop Richard's measured exposition of the issues created a calm, 'safe' atmosphere for the day.

The personal testimonies of the speakers were, by all measures, the most important, compelling and effective part of the day. I am very indebted to all who spoke. We heard from women and men, young and older, one person who had just celebrated 50 years' partnership, some who were experiencing partnership after years of loneliness. We also heard from those who have struggled with their sexuality and chosen not to enter into same-sex relationships, some choosing marriage. All spoke with great openness and honesty both of their personal lives and their faith journeys and their experiences of the Church within that. The questions were always slow to start but overrunning time once the participants recognized that honest questions received honest answers.

The case studies raised some pastoral issues around recognition of gay/lesbian partners in a congregation, who discloses and to whom, and about leadership roles for lay homosexual people. The whole issue of vocation to celibacy was aired and of the pressures to adopt a lifestyle which may not be a true vocation. In the case of marriage despite being homosexual, issues were raised about pastoral care for wives and children, and the purpose of marriage if entered into solely for companionship.

b. Scripture

The whole afternoon was devoted to the study of texts. These were in three sections: 1. Romans 1.18-32 and Acts 15.1-22a. 2. Genesis 1.26-30 and Genesis 2.18-24 and the Prefaces to the Marriage Ceremony in the *Book of Common Prayer* and the *Alternative Service Book*. 3. Contemporary texts from Stanley Grenz – *Welcoming but not Affirming*, *Permanent, Faithful, Stable* by Jeffrey John and *Strangers and Friends* by Michael Vasey.

Each group looked at one set of texts and all three were brought together in the reflection. As there were sometimes seven or eight groups, this took good management!

We therefore looked at a seminal passage when considering homosexuality, with discussions on idolatry, the context of the Early Church and Greco/Roman practice. In Acts we tried to determine whether the inclusion of the Gentiles in the Early Church had any messages for today.

The Genesis passages generated long, heated discussions about what sex is really for, procreation or companionship, and some groups never moved on to the Marriage Prefaces. The general consensus was that, though thinking has moved on over the centuries, and procreation is now not the first purpose of marriage, same-sex partnerships are different and not 'marriage' as such.

The contemporary texts proved difficult for those who expected only to look at Scripture itself. Three perspectives on same-sex relationships, traditional prohibition, marriage model and friendship model, were compared and contrasted. This generally led to a discussion around true friendship, its invisibility in our modern society and the need to reaffirm friendships between people of both the same and opposite gender.

Conclusion

The aim of this process was to listen, actively, to the thoughts, opinions and feelings of others. There was no aim to change people's minds and I do not think the process did that. It did enable clergy to listen to test their thoughts to others and to understand that, from whatever end of the spectrum comes, others hold different views with great sincerity. The complexity of this whole issue was highlighted. Hearing the 'voices' of those who have had a personal struggle with their faith because of their sexuality was a humbling, moving experience for many.

In discussion very opposing views were expressed. At no time was there any public conflict, name-calling or animosity, which we had witnessed at some deanery synod meetings. The Diocese of Oxford has pursued this process and we now wait to see its effects. We recommend it to other dioceses and churches. Any details of papers produced can be obtained from the BSR at Oxford, telephone 01865208214, and the CD may be purchased from Oxford Diocesan Publications Limited, Diocesan Church House, North Hinksey, Oxford OX2 ONB. Cheques for £4.50 should be made payable to 'ODPUBS Ltd'.

Jo Saunders

Notes

foreword
1 'A Final Report from the International Anglican Conversations on Human Sexuality', *Anglican World*, Trinity 2002, Issue no. 6, pp. 17, 18.

chapter 1
1 O. Guinness, *The Gravedigger File*, Hodder & Stoughton, 1987, p. 100.

2 As Richard Bauckham notes, this is part of a wider emphasis on individual human autonomy in much modern thought: 'Much of the modern age, with its distinctive aspirations and achievements, has been inspired by a vision of human beings as the sovereign subjects of history, capable of transcending all limits and mastering all the conditions of their life. Freedom is conceived as radical independence. Nothing is received, all is to be freely chosen. Freedom is the freedom to make of oneself what one chooses.' (R. Bauckham, *God and the Crisis of Freedom*, Westminster John Knox Press, 2002, p. 32.)

3 A. McLaren, *Twentieth-Century Sexuality: A History*, Blackwell, 1999.

4 It has been argued, for instance, that the increase in human longevity has put an increased strain upon marriage because it has meant that, while in the past people could expect to be married for an average of about 15 years, married couples today need to survive all the changes in a relationship that could last 60 years or more.

5 D. Greenberg, *The Construction of Homosexuality*, Chicago University Press, 1988, p. 462.

6 Mark D. Jordan, *The Ethics of Sex*, Blackwell, 2002, p. 132 (see Chapter 6 of this book for Jordan's survey of these changes and their impact in the churches).

7 C. S. Lewis, *Mere Christianity*, Fontana, 1955, p. 86.

8 D. S. Bailey, *The Man-Woman Relation in Christian Thought*, Longmans, 1959.

9 It is true that St Gregory of Nyssa held that the division of humanity into male and female was a secondary action by God that followed on after his creation of humanity in his image and was intended to provide for the propagation of the race after the Fall (*On the Making of Man* XVI–XVII in The Nicene and Post Nicene Fathers 2nd series, vol. V, T&T Clark/Eerdmans, 1994, pp. 405–7) and that a number of writers, such as the twentieth-century Orthodox theologian Nikolai Berdyaev, have been sympathetic to his ideas. However, these are the exceptions that prove the rule. The overwhelming consensus of the Christian tradition has been that the division of humanity into two sexes was an original and integral part of God's creative plan.

10 J. Calvin, *Commentary Upon the Book of Genesis*, Banner of Truth, 1975, p. 128.

11 St Augustine, *On the Good of Marriage* in The Nicene and Post-Nicene Fathers 1st series, vol. III, T&T Clark/Eerdmans, 1998, pp. 397–413.

12 For St Augustine's teaching on this point see *The City of God* Bk XIV, Chapters 17–24.

13 St Thomas Aquinas, *Summa Theologiae*, Part III Supplement Q.49a, Burns, Oates & Washbourne, 1932.

14 L. S. Cahill, *Sex, Gender and Christian Ethics*, Cambridge University Press, 1996, p. 193.

15 *Catechism of the Catholic Church*, Geoffrey Chapman, 1994, p. 506. It should be noted of course that official Roman Catholic teaching holds that such acts of pleasure should be open to the possibility of procreation.

16 The distinction between abstinence and celibacy needs to be noted here. Abstinence means refraining from sexual relationships in a context in which they would be inappropriate, while celibacy means the renunciation of all sexual relationships for the sake of the kingdom of God.

17 The *Catechism of the Catholic Church*, for instance, declares that the 'religious state' in which an individual embraces the 'evangelical counsels' of poverty, chastity and obedience is:

... one way of experiencing a 'more intimate' consecration, rooted in baptism and dedicated totally to God. In the consecrated life, Christ's faithful, moved by the Holy Spirit, propose to follow Christ more nearly, to give themselves to God who is loved above all, and, pursuing the perfection of charity in the service of the Kingdom, to signify and proclaim in the Church the glory of the world to come. *(Catechism of the Catholic Church* p. 212.)

18 Tertullian, *To his Wife*, Chapter III, The Ante-Nicene Fathers, vol. IV, T&T Clark/Eerdmans, 1994, p. 45.
19 See E. Schillebeeckx, *Marriage, Secular Reality and Saving Mystery*, vol. II, Sheed and Ward, 1965, pp. 108–46.
20 John Chrysostom, *On Virginity, Against Remarriage* (trans. Sally Rieger Shore), 10:1, vol. 9 in Studies in Women and Religion, E. Mellen Press, 1983.
21 See J. Boswell, *Christianity, Social Tolerance and Homosexuality*, Chicago University Press, 1980 and *Same Sex Unions in Pre-Modern Europe*, Villard Books, 1994.
22 See, e.g. M. M. Sheehan, 'Christianity and Homosexuality' in *Journal of Ecclesiastical History*, vol. 33, no. 3, July 1982, pp. 438–46.
23 *Catechism of the Catholic Church*, pp. 504–5.
24 *The Official Report of the Lambeth Conference 1998*, Morehouse Publishing, 1999, p. 93.
25 *Issues in Human Sexuality*, Church House Publishing, 1991, p. 18.
26 *Issues in Human Sexuality*, p. 22.
27 *Marriage*, Church House Publishing, 1999, p. 8.
28 *Marriage*, p. 14.
29 *Common Worship Pastoral Services*, Church House Publishing, 2000.
30 See G. Bray, 'The Strange Afterlife of the Reformatio Legum Ecclesiasticarum' in N. Doe, M. Hill and R. Ombres (eds), *English Canon Law*, University of Wales, 1998, pp. 37–47.
31 O. Chadwick, *Michael Ramsey: A Life*, SCM Press, 1998, p. 150.
32 *Putting Asunder*, SPCK, 1966.
33 Chadwick, *Michael Ramsey*, p. 151.
34 Chadwick, *Michael Ramsey*, p. 153.
35 *Marriage, Divorce and the Church*, SPCK, 1971; *Marriage and the Church's Task*, CIO, 1978; *Marriage – and the Standing Committee's Task*, CIO, 1983; *An Honourable Estate*, Church House Publishing, 1988; *Marriage in Church after Divorce*, Church House Publishing, 2000.
36 The latest estimates are that one in seven Church of England weddings now comes into this category.
37 *Marriage in Church after Divorce*.
38 R. Coleman (ed.), *Resolutions of the Lambeth Conferences*, Anglican Book Centre, 1992, p. 35.
39 Coleman, *Resolutions of the Lambeth Conferences*, p. 72.
40 Coleman, *Resolutions of the Lambeth Conferences*, p. 72.
41 Coleman, *Resolutions of the Lambeth Conferences*, p. 147.
42 Coleman, *Resolutions of the Lambeth Conferences*, p. 160.
43 Chadwick, *Michael Ramsey*, p. 154.
44 *Abortion – An Ethical Discussion*, CIO, 1965.
45 *General Synod Report of Proceedings July 1983*, CIO, 1983, p. 815.
46 *General Synod Report 1983*, p. 815.
47 D. S. Bailey, 'The problem of sexual inversion', *Theology*, vol. LV, February 1952, pp. 47–52.
48 *The Problem of Homosexuality – An Interim Report*, CIO, 1954, p. 13.
49 Chadwick, *Michael Ramsey*, p. 149.
50 There has recently been disagreement within the Church of England about whether the age of consent for homosexuals should be lowered to 16 or remain at 18 but no one has suggested that there should be a return to the situation prior to 1967.
51 These were the unpublished report of a Board of Social Responsibility Working Party produced in 1970,

the 1979 BSR report *Homosexual Relationships – a Contribution to Discussion*, CIO, 1979, and the unpublished 1989 'Osborne' report, which was commissioned by the BSR for the House of Bishops.

52 Text in P. Coleman, *Christian Attitudes to Homosexuality*, SPCK, 1980, p. 269.

53 *General Synod Report of Proceedings*, vol. 18, no. 3, Church House Publishing, 1987, pp. 955–6.

54 *Issues in Human Sexuality*, p. 40.

55 *Issues in Human Sexuality*, p. 41.

56 *Issues in Human Sexuality*, p. 42.

57 *General Synod Report of Proceedings*, vol. 28, no. 1, Church House Publishing, 1997, p. 340.

58 This criticism is stated most forcefully in J. Barr, *Fundamentalism*, SCM Press, 1977.

59 For the sophistication of contemporary evangelical approaches to Scripture see for example C. Bartholomew, C. Greene and K. Moller (eds), *After Pentecost: Language and Biblical Interpretation,* Paternoster/Zondervan, 2001.

60 See for example J. Stott, *Issues Facing Christians Today*, Marshalls, 1984.

61 Coleman, *Christian Attitudes*, p. 182.

62 Coleman, *Christian Attitudes*, p. 226.

63 Coleman, *Christian Attitudes*, p. 226.

64 *The Official Report of the Lambeth Conference*, p. 94.

65 *The Official Report of the Lambeth Conference*, p. 94.

66 *The Official Report of the Lambeth Conference*, p. 381.

67 *The Official Report of the Lambeth Conference*, p. 381.

68 *The Official Report of the Lambeth Conference*, p. 381.

69 *The Official Report of the Lambeth Conference*, p. 381.

70 E. Stuart and A. Thatcher, *People of Passion*, Mowbray, 1997.

71 Stuart and Thatcher, *People of Passion*, p. 190.

72 See for example The Evangelical Alliance, *Transsexuality*, Paternoster Press, 2001; D. Horton, *Changing Channels? A Christian Response to the Transvestite and Transsexual*, Grove Books, 1994; R. Holder, 'The Ethics of Transsexualism', *Crucible*, April–June 1998, pp. 89–99 and July–September 1998, pp. 125–36; and V. Kolakowski, 'Towards a Christian Ethical Response to Transsexual Persons', *Theology and Sexuality*, no. 6, March 1997, pp. 10–23; O. M. T. O'Donovan, *Transsexualism and Christian Marriage*, Grove Books, 1982.

73 Putting the challenge in this way presents a slightly misleading picture of the Church simply responding to changes in the wider culture by either accepting or rejecting them. The reality is that the Church, and in particular individual Christians, has often played a key role in bringing about such changes, as was noted earlier in relation to both contraception and the possibility of civil divorce.

74 O. M. T. O'Donovan, 'Homosexuality in the Church: Can there be a fruitful theological debate?' in T. Bradshaw (ed.), *The Way Forward?*, Hodder & Stoughton, 1997, p. 24.

chapter 2

1 Text in J. H. Leith (ed.), *Creeds of the Churches* (revised edition), Blackwell, 1973, p. 232.

2 *The Official Report of the Lambeth Conference 1998*, Morehouse Publishing, p. 32.

3 *The Porvoo Common Statement*, Council for Christian Unity, 1993, p. 18.

4 Dogmatic Constitution on Divine Revelation *Dei Verbum* 21.

5 See A. C. Thiselton, *New Horizons in Hermeneutics*, HarperCollins, 1992, pp. 178–85. It could indeed be argued that a central concern of the leading Protestant Reformers was that the Bible should be properly interpreted using the new interpretative tools provided by Renaissance humanism.

6 See, for example, A. C. Thiselton, 'Hermeneutics' in S. B. Ferguson and D. F. Wright (eds), *New Dictionary of Theology*, IVP, 1988, pp. 293–7.

7 W. Brueggemann, *Theology of the Old Testament*, Fortress Press, 1997, pp. 61–2.

8 T. Hart, 'Tradition, Authority, and a Christian Approach to the Bible as Scripture' in J. B. Green and

Notes

M. Turner (eds), *Between Two Horizons*, Eerdmans, 2000, pp. 194–5.

9 Hart in Green and Turner, p. 195.

10 Hart in Green and Turner, p. 196.

11 Hart in Green and Turner, p. 196. A similar point is made by Thiselton, who declares in his essay '"Behind" and "In Front Of" the Text' that:

> Meaning is not *grossly* indeterminate and unbounded. Nevertheless, hermeneutical agenda are not simply replicated from era to era. New questions and thought-forms arise in relation to which new paradigms exhibit both continuity and discontinuity as traditions of interpretations expand. (Bartholomew, Greene and Moller (eds), *After Pentecost: Language and Biblical Interpretation*, Paternoster/Zondervan, 2001, p. 105.)

12 Hart in Green and Turner, p. 196.

13 St Augustine, *Certain Sermons or Homilies*, 1.1, quoted in G. B. Bentley, *The Resurrection of the Bible*, Dacre Press, 1940, p. 123.

14 S. Fowl, *Engaging Scripture*, Blackwell, 1998, p. 91.

15 A. C. Thiselton, 'Authority and Hermeneutics' in P. E. Satterthwaite and D. F. Wrights (eds), *A Pathway into The Holy Scripture*, Eerdmans, 1994, pp. 136–7.

16 Thiselton in Satterthwaite and Wright, p. 137.

17 M. Turner, 'Historical Criticism and Theological Hermeneutics of the New Testament' in Green and Turner, *Between Two Horizons*, pp. 44–70.

18 O. M. T. O'Donovan, *On the Thirty Nine Articles*, Paternoster Press, 1993, pp. 56–7.

19 R. Sanderson, *Lectures on Conscience and Human Law*, 1647, IV.5 in Bentley, *The Resurrection*, p. 66.

20 D. Brown, *Choices: Ethics and the Christian*, Blackwell, 1983, p. 35.

21 Sanderson, *Lectures*, IV.19 in Bentley, *The Resurrection*, p. 68.

22 O'Donovan, *On the Thirty Nine Articles*, pp. 89–90.

23 *The Official Report of the Lambeth Conference* 1998, Morehouse Publishing, p. 32.

24 Thomas Cranmer, from his 1547 homily 'A Fruitful Exhortation to the Reading and Knowledge of Holy Scripture', text in J. H. Leith (ed.) *Creeds of the Churches* (revised edition), Blackwells, 1973, p. 232.

25 ARCIC, *The Gift of Authority*, Catholic Truth Society, 1999, p. 17.

26 *The Official Report of the Lambeth Conference* 1998, p. 32.

27 *The Virginia Report*, p. 245.

28 For a more detailed discussion of the place of tradition in the interpretation of Scripture see R. Bauckham, 'Authority and Tradition' in R. Bauckham, *God and the Crisis of Freedom*, Westminster John Knox Press, 2002, pp. 91–115.

29 O'Donovan, *On the Thirty Nine Articles*, p. 200.

30 *Issues in Human Sexuality*, Church House Publishing, 1991, p. 5.

31 K. Barth, *The Humanity of God*, Fontana, 1967, p. 69.

32 O'Donovan, *On the Thirty Nine Articles*, pp. 63–4.

33 D. Atkinson, *Pastoral Ethics in Practice*, Monarch, 1989, p. 19.

34 Atkinson, *Pastoral Ethics in Practice*, pp. 19–20.

35 O. M. T. O'Donovan, *Resurrection and Moral Order*, IVP, 1984, pp. 25–6.

36 O'Donovan, *Resurrection and Moral Order*, p. 26.

37 S. C. Barton, 'Is the Bible Good News for Human Sexuality? Reflections on Method in Biblical Interpretation', *Theology and Sexuality*, no. 1, September 1994, p. 45.

38 Barton, 'Is the Bible Good News?', p. 54.

39 E. Stuart and A. Thatcher, *People of Passion*, Mowbray, 1997, pp. 249 and 263.

40 J. Webster, *Word and Church*, T&T Clark, 2001, pp. 80–81.

41 J. Calvin, *Institutes* 3.7.1, Eerdmans, 1975, vol. II, p. 7. In similar fashion the Dogmatic Constitution *Dei Verbum* declares from a Roman Catholic perspective:

The obedience of faith (Romans 13.26; see 1.5; 2 Corinthians 10.5-6) is to be given to God who reveals, an obedience by which man commits his whole self freely to God, offering the full submission of intellect and will to God who reveals and freely assenting to the truth revealed by Him. (*Dei Verbum* 5.)

42   Webster, *Word and Church*, p. 82.

chapter 3

1   D. Atkinson, *The Message of Genesis 1–11*, IVP, 1990, p. 73.
2   The Doctrine Commission of the Church of England, *The Mystery of Salvation*, Church House Publishing, 1995, p. 34.
3   *The Mystery of Salvation*, p. 35.
4   L. Houlden (ed.), *Austin Farrer: The Essential Sermons*, SPCK, 1991, pp. 25–6.
5   *The Mystery of Salvation*, p. 43.
6   The Doctrine Commission of the Church of England, *We believe in God*, Church House Publishing, 1987, p. 81.
7   *We believe in God*, pp. 81–2.
8   *We believe in God*, p. 82.
9   J. Keble (ed.), *The Works of Richard Hooker*, vol. II, The Clarendon Press, 1835, p. 606.
10 *St Andrew's Day Statement*, Application I, in T. Bradshaw (ed.), *The Way Forward?*, Hodder & Stoughton, 1997, p. 7. This *Statement* was produced in 1995 by a range of evangelical theologians as a consensus document from that wing of the Church of England, and as a starting point for discussion.
11 A. Richardson, *An Introduction to the Theology of the New Testament*, SCM, 1958, p. 341.
12 Richardson, *An Introduction*, p. 236.
13 J. Calvin, *Epistles of Paul to the Romans and to the Thessalonians*, St Andrew Press, 1961, p. 129.
14 *St Andrew's Day Statement*, p. 9.
15 O'Donovan, *On the Thirty Nine Articles*, p. 44.
16 J. Taylor, *The Whole Works of the Right Revd Jeremy Taylor, DD*, vol. IV, Longmans, Green & Co., 1893, p. 351.
17 See P. Brown, *The Body and Society: Men, Women and Sexual Renunciation in Early Christianity*, Columbia University Press, 1988, Chapter 2, especially pp. 52–3.
18 See for example Romans 15.1-13, Ephesians 5.1 – 6.9, 1 Peter 2.18 – 3.7.
19 J. R. W. Stott, *The Message of Galatians*, IVP, 1988, pp. 100–101.
20 S. Jones, *The Language of the Genes*, cited in D. Alexander, *Rebuilding the Matrix: Science and Faith in the 21st Century*, Lion, 2001, p. 282.
21 M. Hayter, *The New Eve in Christ*, SPCK, 1987, p. 88.
22 B. G. Webb (ed.), *Theological and Pastoral Responses to Homosexuality*, Open Book Publishers, 1994, pp. 69–70.
23 See for example the 1968 Papal encyclical, *Humanae Vitae*, sections 9 and 16.
24 *Familiaris consortio* 11, in *Catechism of the Catholic Church*, Geoffrey Chapman, 1994, p. 499.
25 D. Atkinson, *The Message of Genesis 1–11*, IVP, 1990, p. 73.
26 S. Grenz, *Welcoming but not Affirming*, Westminster John Knox Press, 1998, p. 107.
27 Eucharistic Prayers E, G and H from *Common Worship*, Church House Publishing, 2000.
28 Aelred of Rievaulx, *Spiritual Friendship*, Cistercian Publications, 1977, p. 55.
29 Aelred of Rievaulx, *Spiritual Friendship*, p. 62.
30 Aelred of Rievaulx, *Spiritual Friendship*, p. 63.
31 Aelred of Rievaulx, *Spiritual Friendship*, pp. 74–5. Following the standard mystical interpretation of the Song of Solomon, the 'kiss' referred to here is a metaphor for spiritual union with Christ.
32 Aelred of Rievaulx, *Spiritual Friendship*, pp. 65–6.

33 St Anselm, Epistle 130, quoted in R. W. Southern, *Saint Anselm: A Portrait in a Landscape*, Cambridge University Press, 1990, pp. 145–6.

34 Southern, *Saint Anselm*, p. 150.

35 Southern, *Saint Anselm*, pp. 153–65.

36 E. Storkey, *The Search for Intimacy*, Hodder & Stoughton, 1995, p. 163.

37 See for example J. Boswell, *Same Sex Unions in Premodern Europe*, Villard Books, 1994 and A. Bray, 'Wedded friendships', *The Tablet*, 4 August 2001, pp. 1108–9.

38 See for instance E. Stuart, *Just Good Friends*, Mowbray, 1995; A. Thatcher, *Liberating Sex*, SPCK, 1993, Chapter 11.

39 *The New Oxford Dictionary of English*, Oxford University Press, 1998, p. 1704.

40 Grenz, *Welcoming but not Affirming*, pp. 103–4.

41 Grenz, *Welcoming but not Affirming*, p. 105.

42 As *Issues in Human Sexuality* notes: '. . . firm standards of self-discipline and self-denial are as necessary as they have always been if sexuality is to be channelled within the bounds of God's kind of love for our neighbour'. (*Issues in Human Sexuality*, Church House Publishing, 1991, p. 28.)

43 Bible passages marked 'RSV' are taken from the Revised Standard Version of the Bible, copyright 1946, 1952, © 1971, 1973 by the Division of Christian Education of the National Council of the Churches of Christ in the USA.

44 Hayter, *The New Eve*, Chapter 6.

45 Atkinson, *The Message of Genesis*, p. 71.

46 See for example W. J. Webb, *Slaves, Women and Homosexuals: Exploring the Hermeneutics of Cultural Analysis*, IVP, 2001, pp. 76–81.

47 E. Schillebeeckx, *Marriage: Secular Reality and Saving Mystery* (vol. 1), Sheed & Ward, 1965, p. 46.

48 M. Vasey, *Strangers and Friends*, Hodder & Stoughton, 1995, p. 115.

49 Vasey, *Strangers and Friends*, p. 117.

50 Vasey, *Strangers and Friends*, p. 118.

51 Vasey, *Strangers and Friends*, p. 116.

52 Vasey, *Strangers and Friends*, pp. 116–17.

53 Vasey, *Strangers and Friends*, p. 117.

54 J. P. Haningan, *Homosexuality: The Test Case for Christian Sexual Ethics*, Paulist Press, 1988, p. 77.

55 Grenz, *Welcoming but not Affirming*, p. 108.

56 Grenz, *Welcoming but not Affirming*, p. 106.

57 See for example Exodus 20.14, Matthew 19.3-9, 1 Corinthians 6.9.

58 Atkinson, *The Message of Genesis*, p. 79.

59 Atkinson, *The Message of Genesis*, p. 79.

60 The evidence for this seems clear, but the point that needs to be borne in mind is that the relevant research evidence necessarily deals with what is generally true. This means that, while it is always possible to find examples where children from 'non-traditional' families do better than children from traditional ones, the overall evidence indicates that they are exceptions to the general pattern.

61 *Cohabitation: A Christian Reflection*, The Diocese of Southwark, 2002, p. 115. A similar point was made by *Issues in Human Sexuality* in 1991:

> It is also the marriage committed to loving stability which alone can provide the best home for our children. There is no such thing as a marriage breakdown in which children do not suffer, even if the marriage has been far from perfect. Teachers and social workers alike report that where a child has behavioural problems a home broken or at risk of breakdown is the factor that features in the story more often than any other. The child's tragedy begins with the lack of total commitment to the marriage on behalf of one or both parents. (pp. 21–2.)

62 Thatcher, *Liberating Sex*, pp. 40–41.

63 Barth, *The Humanity of God*, Fontana, 1967, p. 129.
64 *Issues in Human Sexuality*, pp. 29–30.
65 *Issues in Human Sexuality*, p. 25.
66 D. Bonhoeffer, *The Cost of Discipleship*, SCM Press, 1959, p. 79.
67 J. Macquarrie, *Principles of Christian Theology*, 2nd revised edition, SCM Press, 1977, p. 232.
68 S. Coakley, *Powers and Submissions*, Blackwell, 2002, p. 4, referring to D. Hampson, *Theology and Feminism*, Blackwell, 1995, p. 155.
69 Coakley, *Powers and Submissions*, p. 31.
70 Coakley, *Powers and Submissions*, p. 32.
71 Coakley, *Powers and Submissions*, pp. 35–6.
72 N. Pittenger, *Time for Consent*, 2nd revised edition, SCM Press, 1970, p. 46 (italics in the original).
73 Pittenger, *Time for Consent*, p. 47.
74 Pittenger, *Time for Consent*, p. 47.
75 Pittenger, *Time for Consent*, pp. 106–7.
76 Pittenger, *Time for Consent*, p. 107.
77 R. Williams, *Open to Judgement*, Darton, Longman & Todd, 1994, p. 164.
78 R. Williams, *The Body's Grace*, 2nd edition, Lesbian and Gay Christian Movement, 2002, p. 3 (italics in the original).
79 Williams, *The Body's Grace*, p. 3 (italics in the original).
80 Williams, *The Body's Grace*, p. 9.
81 Williams, *The Body's Grace*, p. 11.
82 Williams, *The Body's Grace*, pp. 11–12.
82 E. F. Rogers, *Sexuality and the Christian Body*, Blackwell, 1999.
84 P. Evdokimov, *The Sacrament of Love*, St Vladimir's Seminary Press, 1985.
85 Rogers, *Sexuality*, pp. 72–3.
86 In Chapter 4 we shall look at why he believes that this view is compatible with the teaching of the New Testament.
87 Rogers, *Sexuality*, p. 248.
88 Rogers, *Sexuality*, p. 270.
89 Rogers, *Sexuality*, pp. 207–8.
90 Rogers, *Sexuality*, p. 232.

chapter 4

1 R. Hays, *The Moral Vision of the New Testament*, T&T Clark, 1996, pp. 379–80.
2 M. Hallett, *Out of the Blue*, Hodder & Stoughton, 1996, p. 19.
3 O. M. T. O'Donovan, 'Homosexuality in the Church: Can there be a fruitful theological debate?' in T. Bradshaw (ed.) *The Way Forward?*, Hodder & Stoughton, 1997, p. 28.
4 D. Sherwin Bailey, *Homosexuality and the Western Christian Tradition*, Longman, Green and Co., 1955, p. 5.
5 W. Brueggemann, *Genesis*, John Knox Press, 1982, p. 164.
6 See for example R. Davidson, *Genesis 12–50*, Cambridge University Press, 1979, p. 72; G. Wenham, *Genesis 2*, Word Books, 1994, p. 55; C. Westermann, *Genesis 12–36*, SPCK, 1985, p. 301.
7 V. P. Hamilton, *Genesis 18–50*, Eerdmans, 1995, pp. 34–5.
8 *Issues in Human Sexuality*, Church House Publishing, 1991, p. 10.
9 See R. A. J. Gagnon, *The Bible and Homosexual Practice*, Abingdon Press, 2001, pp. 79–91.
10 See D. J. Wold, *Out of Order: Homosexuality in the Bible and the Ancient Near East*, Baker, 1998, pp. 69–76; Gagnon, *The Bible and Homosexual Practice*, pp. 91–100.
11 B. S. Childs, *Introduction to the Old Testament as Scripture*, SCM Press, 1979, p. 185.
12 R. E. Clements, 'Leviticus' in C. J. Allen (ed.) *Broadman Bible Commentary Vol. 2*, Broadman, 1969–72, p. 47.

Notes

13   See for example G. R. Edwards, *Gay/Lesbian Liberation: A Biblical Perspective*, Pilgrim Press, 1984, pp. 64–9.

14   J. Milgrom, *Leviticus 17–22*, Doubleday, 2000, p. 1568.

15   P. Budd, *Leviticus*, Marshall Pickering, 1995, p. 253.

16   B. G. Webb (ed.), *Theological and Pastoral Responses to Homosexuality*, Open Book Publishers, 1994, p. 79.

17   *Issues in Human Sexuality*, p. 15.

18   See, for example, P. Coleman, *Gay Christians: A Moral Dilemma*, SCM Press, 1989, p. 54; Bailey, *Homosexuality and the Western Christian Tradition*, p. 60; H. D. Lance, 'The Bible and Homosexuality', *American Baptist Quarterly* 8/2, June 1989, p. 145.

19   S. Grenz, *Welcoming but not Affirming*, Westminster John Knox Press, 1998, p. 46.

20   Coleman, *Gay Christians: A Moral Dilemma*, p. 55.

21   Childs, *Introduction to the Old Testament as Scripture*, p. 224.

22   See for example P. C. Craigie, *The Book of Deuteronomy*, Eerdmans, 1976, pp. 301–2; A. D. H. Mayes, *Deuteronomy*, Oliphants, 1979; P. D. Miller, *Deuteronomy*, John Knox Press, 1990, p. 162.

23   As Robert Gagnon comments:

> At different periods of Israelite history, men sometimes had concubines or harems; women never did. It is unlikely that there would have been much of a market in Israel for men to take their barren wives to a local high place to be impregnated by male cult prostitutes, particularly given that paternity would then be held by the male cult prostitute (or Asherah, a female goddess?), not the husband, creating all sorts of problems relating to legitimacy, inheritance rights, and the like. (Gagnon, *The Bible and Homosexual Practice*, p. 104.)

24   See D. Greenberg, *The Construction of Homosexuality*, Chicago University Press, 1988, pp. 94–106.

25   Gagnon, *The Bible and Homosexual Practice*, pp. 108–9 (italics in the original).

26   Gagnon, *The Bible and Homosexual Practice*, p. 109.

27   See for example Exodus 20.14, Deuteronomy 22.13-30, 2 Samuel 11.1 – 12:23, Proverbs 6.20 – 7.27, Amos 2.7.

28   G. J. Wenham, 'The Old Testament Attitude to Homosexuality', *Expository Times* 102, 1990–91, p. 361.

29   Wenham, 'The Old Testament Attitude to Homosexuality', p. 362.

30   See Leviticus 18.1-5.

31   J. D. G. Dunn, 'Romans, Letter to the' in G. F. Hawthorn, R. P. Martin and D. G. Reid (eds), *Dictionary of Paul and his Letters*, IVP, 1993, pp. 840–41.

32   Dunn in Hawthorn et al., p. 844.

33   C. E. B. Cranfield, *Romans Vol. 1*, T&T Clark, 1987, pp. 105–6.

34   C. K. Barrett, *The Epistle to the Romans*, A & C Black, 1971, p. 39.

35   J. A. Fitzmeyer, *Romans*, Doubleday, 1992, p. 276.

36   J. D. G. Dunn, *Romans 1–8*, Word, 1988, p. 74. For other commentators who would take a similar line see Cranfield, *Romans Vol. 1*, pp. 125–7; Paul Achtemeier, *Romans*, John Knox Press, 1985, p. 41; Grenz, *Welcoming but not Affirming*, pp. 48–56.

37   Dunn, *Romans 1–8*, p. 74.

38   Gagnon, *The Bible and Homosexual Practice*, p. 254.

39   Gagnon, *The Bible and Homosexual Practice*, pp. 254–6.

40   Gagnon, *The Bible and Homosexual Practice*, p. 291.

41   G. Fee, *The First Epistle to the Corinthians*, Eerdmans, 1987, p. 242.

42   See Boswell, *Christianity, Social Tolerance and Homosexuality*, Chicago University Press, 1980, pp. 338–53, and Countryman, *Dirt, Greed and Sex*, SCM Press, 1988, pp. 119–20.

43   See for example R. F. Collins, *First Corinthians*, Liturgical Press, 1997, p. 232; Fee, *The First Epistle to the Corinthians*, pp. 242–4; A. C. Thiselton, *The First Epistle to the Corinthians*, Eerdmans, 2000, pp. 599–621.

44 Hays, *The Moral Vision of the New Testament*, pp. 384–5.
45 Thiselton, *The First Epistle to the Corinthians*, pp. 599–611.
46 J. N. D. Kelly, *The Pastoral Epistles*, A & C Black, 1963, p. 48.
47 L. T. Johnson, *The First and Second Letters to Timothy*, Doubleday, 2001, p. 170.
48 I. H. Marshall, *I & II Timothy*, T&T Clark, 1999, p. 380. See also D. F. Wright, 'Homosexuals or Prostitutes?', *Vigilae Christianae* 38, 1984, pp. 125–53.
49 M. Bonington and B. Fyall, *Homosexuality and the Bible*, Grove Books, 1998, pp. 22–3.
50 G. Fee, *1 and 2 Timothy, Titus*, Hendricksen, 1988, pp. 45–6. For a similar argument see Kelly, *The Pastoral Epistles*, pp. 49–50.
51 B. Brooten, *Love Between Women: Early Christian Responses To Female Homoeroticism*, Chicago University Press, 1996, pp. 265–6.
52 Brooten, *Love Between Women,* p. 280.
53 Countryman, *Dirt, Greed and Sex*, 1988, p. 117.
54 R. Scroggs, *New Testament and Homosexuality*, Fortress Press, 1988, p. 126.
55 Scroggs, *New Testament and Homosexuality*, p. 127.
56 See Gagnon, *The Bible and Homosexual Practice*, pp. 361–80.
57 See T. Schmidt, *Straight and Narrow?*, IVP, 1995, pp. 66–85.
58 M. Smith, 'Ancient Bisexuality and the Interpretation of Romans 1.26-27', *Journal of the American Academy of Religion* 64, 1966, pp. 223–54.
59 P. Coleman, *Christian Attitudes to Homosexuality*, SPCK, 1980, p. 101. Even if 1 Timothy is seen as post Pauline this does not affect Coleman's overall point.
60 Hays, *The Moral Vision of the New Testament*, pp. 396–7.
61 Hays, *The Moral Vision of the New Testament*, p. 398.
62 Gagnon, *The Bible and Homosexual Practice*, pp. 191–2.
63 R. Schnackenburg, *The Moral Teaching of the New Testament*, Burns & Oates, 1965, pp. 74–5.
64 Gagnon, *The Bible and Homosexual Practice*, p. 227.
65 See for example D. Wenham, *Paul and Jesus: The True Story*, Eerdmans, 2002 for a detailed argument that St Paul's understanding of Christianity was rooted in his knowledge of the historical Jesus.
66 J. Siker, 'The Bible and Gentile Inclusion' in J. Siker (ed.), *Homosexuality in the Church*, Westminster John Knox Press, 1994, p. 188.
67 For a clear presentation of this argument see Siker, 'The Bible and Gentile Inclusion', pp. 178–94.
68 A. Goddard, *God, Gentiles and Gay Christians*, Grove Books, 2001, p. 19.
69 R. Bauckham, 'James and the Gentiles (Acts 15.13-21)', in B. Witherington (ed.), *History, Literature and Society in the Book of Acts*, Cambridge University Press, 1996, pp. 154–84.
70 See, for example B. Witherington, *The Acts of the Apostles: A Socio-Rhetorical Commentary*, Eerdmans, 1998, p. 461, who argues for a social rather than a textual connection between them.
71 Rogers, *Sexuality and the Christian Body*, Blackwell, 1999, p. 65.
72 Grenz, *Welcoming but not Affirming*, p. 155.
73 M. Doe, *Seeking the Truth in Love*, Darton, Longman & Todd, 2000, pp. 43–5.
74 The headings are taken from Doe.
75 See Article VII of the *Thirty Nine Articles*.
76 J. B. Nelson, 'Are Christianity and Homosexuality Incompatible?' in S. B. Greiss and D. E. Messer (eds), *Caught in the Crossfire: Helping Christians Debate Homosexuality*, Abingdon, 1994, p. 102.
77 Thiselton, *The First Epistle to the Corinthians*, p. 619. See also Grenz, *Welcoming but not Affirming*, pp. 82–6 and Smith, 'Ancient Bisexuality'.
78 Grenz, *Welcoming but not Affirming*, p. 84.
79 G. Comstock, *Gay Theology without Apology*, Pilgrim Press, 1993, pp. 37–8.
80 Comstock, *Gay Theology without Apology*, p. 38.
81 Doe, *Seeking the Truth in Love*, p. 44.

82 *The Lambeth Conference 1958*, Resolution 1.2, SPCK and Seabury Press, 1958, p. 1.33.

83 T. Brown, *Further Reflections on Homosexuality, Christian Faith and the Church*, pp. 4–5.

84 J. Alison, *Faith Beyond Resentment: Fragments Catholic and Gay*, Darton Longman & Todd, 2001, p. 100.

85 Alison, *Faith Beyond Resentment*, pp. 100–101.

86 Alison, *Faith Beyond Resentment*, p. 103.

87 J. Habgood, *The Concept of Nature*, Darton Longman & Todd, 2002, p. 111.

88 Habgood, *The Concept of Nature*, p. 107.

89 J. S. Spong, *Why Christianity Must Change or Die*, Harper & Row, 1998, pp. 161–2.

90 W. Byrne and B. Parsons, 'Human Sexual Orientation', p. 228 cited in S. L. Jones and M. A. Yarhouse, *Homosexuality: The Use of Scientific Research in the Church's Moral Debate*, IVP, 2001, p. 58.

91 Greenberg, *The Construction of Homosexuality*, passim.

92 For a summary of the evidence on this see Gagnon, *The Bible and Homosexual Practice*, pp. 413–20.

93 S. L. Jones, 'Identity in Christ and Sexuality' in T. Bradshaw (ed.), *Grace and Truth in the Secular Age*, Eerdmans, 1998, pp. 91–2.

94 R. Holloway, *Godless Morality*, Canongate Books, 1999, p. 85.

95 *Issues in Human Sexuality*, p. 18.

chapter 5

1 Olympe de Gouges, *The Rights of Woman* (trans. Val Stevenson), Pythia, 1986; Mary Wollestonecraft, *A Vindication of the Rights of Woman* (London, 1792), Penguin, 1986.

2 For a fuller discussion of this point, see Barbara Taylor, *Mary Wollstonecraft and the Feminist Imagination*, Cambridge University Press, 2003.

3 Sarah Grimke, *Letters on the Equality of the Sexes and the Condition of Women*, 1838, quoted in Susan Hill Lindley, *You Have Stept out of Your Place: A History of Women and Religion in America*, Westminster John Knox Press, p. 109.

4 Elizabeth Cady Stanton and the Revising Committee, *The Woman's Bible*, European Publishing Company, 1898.

5 Simone de Beauvoir, *The Second Sex* (trans. H. M. Parshley), Vintage Books, 1974 (first edition 1952).

6 M. Hunt, 'Lovingly Lesbian: Towards a Feminist Theology of Friendship' in J. B. Nelson and S. P. Longfellow (eds), *Sexuality and the Sacred*, Westminster John Knox Press, 1994, p. 172. In recent years, the name 'Stonewall' has been adopted by the British gay, lesbian and bisexual human rights movement that campaigns for full partnership rights for same-sex couples. For more details see their web site at www.stonewall.org.uk.

7 For the spectrum of thinking on this issue, see Saul M. Olyan and Martha C. Nussbaum (eds), *Sexual Orientation and Human Rights in American Religious Discourse*, Oxford University Press, 1998.

8 Thomas W. Laqueur, *Making Sex: Body and Gender from the Greeks to Freud*, Harvard University Press, 1990.

9 See Caroline Walker Bynum, 'The Body of Christ in the Later Middle Ages' in her *Fragmentation and Redemption: Essays on Gender and the Human Body in Medieval Religion*, Zone Books, 1991 and *Jesus as Mother: Studies in Spirituality of the High Middle Ages*, University of California Press, 1982.

10 Londa Schiebinger, *The Mind Has No Sex? Women and the Origins of Modern Science*, Harvard University Press, 1989, p. 215.

11 Cynthia Russet, *Sexual Science: The Victorian Construction of Womanhood*, 1989.

12 Schiebinger, *The Mind Has No Sex?*, p. 216.

13 See, for example, Randolph Trumbach, 'The Birth of the Queen: Sodomy and the Emergence of Gender Equality in Modern Culture 1660–1750' in Martin Bauml Duberman, Martha Vicinus and George Chauncey Jr (eds), *Hidden from History: Reclaiming the Gay and Lesbian Past*, New American Books, 1989.

14 This comment has been made by the eighteenth-century historian, Lisa Cody.

15 Linda Woodhead, 'Sex in a Wider Context' in *Sex these Days: Essays on Theology, Sexuality and Society*,

Sheffield Academic Press, 1997, p. 99.

16 See M. Phillips, *The Ascent of Woman: A History of the Suffragette Movement and the Ideas Behind It*, Little, Brown and Company, 2003.

17 L. Irigaray, 'Sexual Difference' in her *An Ethics of Sexual Difference*, Cornell University Press, 1993, p. 5.

18 de Beauvoir, *The Second Sex*, p. 301.

19 J. Butler, *Gender Trouble: Feminism and the Subversion of Identity*, Routledge, 1990.

20 *St Andrew's Day Statement*, Application I, in T. Bradshaw (ed.), *The Way Forward?*, Hodder & Stoughton, 1997.

21 G. Gutierrez, *A Theology of Liberation*, SCM Press, 1973.

22 R. Goss, *Jesus Acted Up: A Gay and Lesbian Manifesto*, HarperCollins, 1993, pp. 111, 110.

23 Goss, *Jesus Acted Up*, pp. 174–5.

24 See, for example, Stephen D. Moore, *God's Beauty Parlour and Other Queer Spaces In and Around the Bible*, Stanford University Press, 2001, p. 23.

25 This was published in Britain as *The Marriage of Likeness: Same-Sex Unions in Pre-Modern Europe*, HarperCollins, 1995.

26 A. Bray, 'Friendship, the Family and Liturgy: A Rite for Blessing Friendship in Traditional Christianity' in *Theology and Sexuality*, no. 13, September 2000, pp. 16, 31.

27 J. Alison, *Faith Beyond Resentment: Fragments Catholic and Gay*, Darton, Longman & Todd, 2001.

28 Alison, *Faith Beyond Resentment*, p. 26.

29 Alison, *Faith Beyond Resentment*, p. 27.

30 Goss, *Jesus Acted Up*, p. xix.

31 J. Lacan, 'God and the *Jouissance* of The Woman. A Love Letter' in Juliet Mitchell and Jacqueline Rose (eds), *Feminine Sexuality*, W. W. Norton and Co., 1988.

32 M. Doe, *Seeking the Truth in Love*, Darton, Longman & Todd, p. 75.

33 For an account of lesbianism in the Classical world and the Christian response to it see B. Brooten, *Love between Women: Early Christian Responses to Female Homoeroticism*, Chicago University Press, 1996.

34 Hunt, 'Lovingly Lesbian', p. 171.

35 Hunt, 'Lovingly Lesbian', p. 171.

36 Hunt, 'Lovingly Lesbian', p. 171.

37 Hunt, 'Lovingly Lesbian', p. 171.

38 Hunt, 'Lovingly Lesbian', p. 172.

39 Hunt, 'Lovingly Lesbian', p. 172.

40 R. R. Ruether, 'Homophobia, Heterosexism and Pastoral Practice' in Nelson and Longfellow, *Sexuality and the Sacred*, p. 392.

41 M. Wittig, *The Straight Mind and Other Essays*, Beacon Press, 1992, p. 20.

42 Ruether, 'Homophobia, Heterosexism and Pastoral Practice', pp. 392–3.

43 Ruether, 'Homophobia, Heterosexism and Pastoral Practice', p. 393.

44 Ruether, 'Homophobia, Heterosexism and Pastoral Practice', p. 393.

45 Ruether, 'Homophobia, Heterosexism and Pastoral Practice', p. 394.

46 M. May, *A Body Knows: A Theopoetics of Death and Resurrection*, Continuum, 1995, p. 83.

47 Ruether, 'Homophobia, Heterosexism and Pastoral Practice', p. 396.

48 E. Stuart, *Just Good Friends*, Mowbray, 1995, p. 117.

49 Hunt, 'Lovingly Lesbian', p. 179.

50 Hunt, 'Lovingly Lesbian', p. 179.

51 For a more detailed account by Hunt of the significance of friendship see also M. Hunt, *Fierce Tenderness: a Feminist Theology of Friendship*, Crossroad, 1991. See also, Elisabeth Moltmann-Wendel, *Rediscovering Friendship: Awakening to the Promise and Power of Women's Friendships* (translated by John Bowden), Fortress Press, 2000.

52 Hunt, *Fierce Tenderness*, p. 180.

Notes

53 Hunt, *Fierce Tenderness*, p. 181.

54 The plural is used by Stuart to refer to the traditional Christian belief that God exists not as a solitary monad but as a Trinity of Persons in communion.

55 Stuart, *Just Good Friends*, pp. 244–5.

56 Stuart, *Just Good Friends*, p. 245.

57 Stuart, *Just Good Friends*, p. 246.

58 For a discussion of these paradoxes see A. Webster, *Found Wanting: Women,Christianity and Sexuality*, Cassell, 1995.

59 D. A. Austin, 'The Cloistered Closet' in M. Garber and R. L. Walkowitz (eds), *One Nation Under God? Religion and American Culture*, Routledge, 1999, pp. 67–8.

60 Austin, 'The Cloistered Closet', p. 69.

61 Doe, *Seeking the Truth in Love*, pp. 115–17.

62 V. Harrison, 'Male and Female in Cappadocian Theology', *Journal of Theological Studies* 41, 1990, p. 442.

63 V. Harrison, 'Gender, Generation and Virginity in Cappadocian Theology', *Journal of Theological Studies* 47, 1996, p. 66.

64 R. Williams, 'Macrina's Deathbed Revisited: Gregory of Nyssa on Mind and Passion' in L. R. Wickham and C. P. Bammel (eds), *Christian Faith and Greek Philosophy in Late Antiquity: Essays in Tribute to George Christopher Stead*, E. J. Brill, 1993, p. 244.

65 S. Coakley, 'The Eschatological Body: Gender, Transformation and God' in *Powers and Submissions*, pp. 153–67.

66 Williams, 'Macrina's Deathbed Revisited', p. 243.

67 E. Stuart, *Gay and Lesbian Theologies: Repetitions with Critical Difference*, Ashgate, 2003.

68 E. Stuart, *Gay and Lesbian Theologies*, p. 28.

69 E. Stuart, *Gay and Lesbian Theologies*, p. 62.

70 E. Stuart, *Gay and Lesbian Theologies*, p. 63, footnote 4.

71 E. Stuart, *Gay and Lesbian Theologies*, p. 114.

72 E. Stuart, *Gay and Lesbian Theologies*, p. 107.

73 E. Stuart, *Gay and Lesbian Theologies*, p. 107.

74 T. Breidenthal, *Christian Households: The Sanctification of Nearness*, Cowley Publications, 1997, pp. 3, 2. See also the essays in C. Hefling (ed.), *Our Selves, Our Souls and Our Bodies: Sexuality and the Household of God*, Cowley Publications, 1996, for a range of perspectives on this issue.

75 Breidenthal, *Christian Households*, pp. 30–31.

76 Breidenthal, *Christian Households*, p. 92.

77 Breidenthal, *Christian Households*, pp. 90, 81.

78 Breidenthal, *Christian Households*, p. 159.

79 Breidenthal, *Christian Households*, pp. 159–60.

80 *True Union in the Body?* A Paper commissioned by the Most Revd Drexel Gomez, Oxford, 2003, p. 26.

chapter 6

1 E. Stuart and A. Thatcher, *People of Passion*, Mowbray, 1997, p. 269.

2 *Bisexual Lives*, Off Pink Publishing, 1988.

3 Thatcher is referring here to the scale of sexual orientation developed by the American writer Alfred Kinsey, which ran from 0–6 with those on 0 being exclusively heterosexual, those at 6 being exclusively homosexual and those at points 1–5 experiencing varying degrees of heterosexual and homosexual attraction.

4 A. Thatcher, *Liberating Sex*, SPCK, 1993, pp. 155–6.

5 See 1.1.8 and 4.4.51–53.

6 E. O. Laumann, J. H. Gagnon, R. T. Michael and S. Michaels, *The Social Organization of Sexuality*,

Chicago University Press, 1994, p. 289.

7   See for example the discussion in S. Jones and M. Yarhouse, *Homosexuality: The Use of Scientific Research in the Church's Moral Debate*, IVP, 2001, pp. 19–22.

8   Thatcher, *Liberating Sex*, p. 155.

9   *Issues in Human Sexuality*, Church House Publishing, 1991, p. 42.

10 Thatcher, *Liberating Sex*, p. 156.

11 Thatcher, *Liberating Sex*, p. 156.

12 Thatcher, *Liberating Sex*, p. 156.

13 Thatcher, *Liberating Sex*, pp. 156–7.

14 Stuart and Thatcher, *People of* Passion, p. 190.

15 S. George, *Women and Bisexuality*, Scarlet Press, 1993, pp. 165, 182.

16 M. D. Smith, 'Ancient Bisexuality and the Interpretation of Romans 1.26-27', *Journal of the American Academy of Religion* 64, 1966, pp. 243–4. See also E. Cantarella, *Bisexuality in the Ancient World*, Yale University Press, 1992.

17 Smith, 'Ancient Bisexuality', p. 246.

chapter 7

1   *The Storyteller and His Stories*, True Freedom Trust, n.d., p. 136.

2   G. W. Everingham, *Gender Reassignment and the Bible*, G. W. Everingham, 2000, p. 4.

3   *Overcoming Transsexualism: A Christian Testimony*, Parakaleo Ministries, n.d., p. 1.

4   The Home Office, *Report of the Interdepartmental Working Group on Transsexual People*, The Home Office Communications Directorate, 2000, p. 3.

5   The Evangelical Alliance, *Transsexuality*, Paternoster Press, 2001, p. 5.

6   In this chapter 'sex' is going to be used as a shorthand for those characteristics that differentiate people into male and female. In some quotations this is referred to as 'gender'.

7   R. Holder, 'The Ethics of Transsexualism' Part 1, *Crucible*, April–June 1998, p. 90.

8   Holder, 'The Ethics of Transsexualism', pp. 89–90.

9   Holder, 'The Ethics of Transsexualism', p. 94.

10 V. A. Kolakowski, 'Towards a Christian Ethical Response to Transsexual Persons', *Theology and Sexuality*, no. 6, March 1997, p. 12.

11 M. Dainton and K. Tiller, *Ministry to the Gender Confused*, Parakaleo Ministries, n.d., p. 4.

12 Kolakowski, 'Towards a Christian Ethical Response', pp. 12–13.

13 B. L. Hausman, *Changing Sex: Transsexualism, Technology and the Idea of Gender*, Duke University Press, 1995.

14 Evangelical Alliance, *Transsexuality*, p. 13.

15 Evangelical Alliance, *Transsexuality*, p. 13.

16 F. Watts, *Transsexualism and the Church* (unpublished paper), pp. 5–6.

17 J. Money, 'The Concept of Gender Identity Disorder in Childhood and Adolescence after 39 years', *Journal of Sexual and Marital Therapy* 20, no. 32, 1994, pp. 163, 166, cited in Holder, 'The Ethics of Transsexualism', p. 93.

18 Dainton and Tiller, *Ministry to the Gender Confused*, pp. 4–5.

19 Evangelical Alliance, *Transsexuality*, p. 3.

20 See Evangelical Alliance, Transsexuality, p. 28; Holder, 'The Ethics of Transsexualism', pp. 95–8; Kolakowski, 'Towards a Christian Ethical Response', pp. 18–28; D. Horton, *Changing Channels? A Christian Response to the Transvestite and Transsexual*, Grove Books, 1994, pp. 11–12.

21 Evangelical Alliance, Transsexuality, pp. 28–9. See also Holder, 'The Ethics of Transsexualism', p. 95; Horton, *Changing Channels?*, p. 11.

22 Watts, *Transsexualism and the Church*, p. 7.

23 O. M. T. O'Donovan, *Transsexualism and Christian Marriage*, Grove Books, 1982, p. 7.

24 O'Donovan, *Transsexualism and Christian Marriage*, p. 11.
25 O'Donovan, *Transsexualism and Christian Marriage*, pp. 13–14.
26 O'Donovan, *Transsexualism and Christian Marriage*, p. 14.
27 O'Donovan, *Transsexualism and Christian Marriage*, p. 14.
28 O'Donovan, *Transsexualism and Christian Marriage*, p. 16.
29 Evangelical Alliance, *Transsexuality*, pp. 29–30.
30 Evangelical Alliance, *Transsexuality*, p. 47.
31 See for instance Dainton and Tiller, *Ministry to the Gender Confused*, mentioned earlier.
32 Evangelical Alliance, *Transsexuality*, pp. 45–6.
33 R. Holder, 'The Ethics of Transsexualism' Part 2, p. 128.
34 Holder, 'The Ethics of Transsexualism' Part 2, p. 128.
35 Holder, 'The Ethics of Transsexualism' Part 2, p. 129.
36 Kolakowski, 'Towards a Christian Ethical Response', p. 28.
37 Kolakowski, 'Towards a Christian Ethical Response', p. 26.
38 Watts, *Transsexualism and the Church*, p. 8.
39 Watts, *Transsexualism and the Church*, p. 8.
40 Watts, *Transsexualism and the Church*, pp. 8–9.
41 Watts, *Transsexualism and the Church*, p. 9.
42 Watts, *Transsexualism and the Church*, p. 10.
43 Holder, 'The Ethics of Transsexualism' Part 2, p. 133.
44 Holder, 'The Ethics of Transsexualism' Part 2, p. 133.
45 For details see D. Pannick, 'Why Can't a Man be More Like a Woman?', *The Times*, 31 July 2001.
46 European Court of Human Rights, *Case of Christine Goodwin v. The United Kingdom*, paragraphs 94–104.
47 Evangelical Alliance, *Transsexuality*, p. 30. See also O'Donovan, *Transsexualism and Christian Marriage*, passim.
48 G. J. Woodall, *Trans-sexual Persons and Catholic Moral Theology* (unpublished paper), p. 15.
49 Woodall, *Trans-sexual Persons*, p. 15.
50 Woodall, *Trans-sexual Persons*, p. 16.
51 Woodall, *Trans-sexual Persons*, pp. 16–17.
52 Woodall, *Trans-sexual Persons*, p. 17.
53 Holder, 'The Ethics of Transsexualism' Part 2, p. 132.
54 Kolakowski, 'Towards a Christian Ethical Response', p. 29.
55 *Christine Goodwin v. The United Kingdom*, paragraphs 86–93.
56 Evangelical Alliance, *Transsexuality*, p. 48.
57 O'Donovan, *Transsexualism and Christian Marriage*, p. 18.
58 D. Atkinson, *The Message of Genesis 1–11*, IVP, 1990, p. 73.
59 This is the point that is being made by Karl Barth in *Church Dogmatics* III.1, T&T Clark, 1958, pp. 183–206, when he contends that the *imago dei* is seen most clearly in the creation of man and woman together and in their relationship.
60 R. Song, *Human Genetics: Fabricating the Future*, Darton, Longman & Todd, 2002, pp. 67–8.
61 Song, *Human Genetics*, pp. 68–9.
62 Song, *Human Genetics*, p. 69.

chapter 8

1 *Christopher's Story*, True Freedom Trust, n.d., p. 2.
2 *The Storyteller and His Story*, True Freedom Trust, n.d., p. 65.
3 G. W. Everingham, *Gender Reassignment and the Bible*, G. W. Everingham, 2000, p. 25.
4 *Overcoming Transsexualism: A Christian Testimony*, Parakaleo Ministries, pp. 15–16.

5 Studies of the issues faced by homosexual people in the Church, written from contrasting theological perspectives, can be found in the recent report *Christian Homophobia,* Lesbian and Gay Christian Movement, 2000 and in Martin Hallett's book *Out of the Blue,* Hodder & Stoughton, 1996.

6 *Issues in Human Sexuality,* Church House Publishing, 2001, p. 40.

7 *Issues in Human Sexuality,* pp. 40–41.

8 *Issues in Human Sexuality,* p. 41.

9 *Issues in Human Sexuality,* p. 41.

10 *Issues in Human Sexuality,* p. 41.

11 *Issues in Human Sexuality,* p. 41.

12 *Issues in Human Sexuality,* pp. 41–2.

13 *Issues in Human Sexuality,* p. 45.

14 *Issues in Human Sexuality,* p. 45.

15 *Issues in Human Sexuality,* p. 45.

16 *Issues in Human Sexuality,* p. 47. Since the text of this chapter was completed, the Primates of the Anglican Communion have met in Brazil. In their Pastoral Letter they commend for study both *True Union in the Body* and the report on the blessing of same-sex unions by the Theological Committee of the House of Bishops of the Episcopal Church (USA). They also declare:

> The question of public rites for the blessing of same-sex unions is still a cause of potentially divisive controversy. The Archbishop of Canterbury spoke for us all when he said that it is through liturgy that we express what we believe, and that there is no theological consensus about same-sex unions. Therefore, we as a body cannot support the authorisation of such rites.

> This is distinct from the duty of pastoral care that is laid upon all Christians to respond with love and understanding to people of all sexual orientations. As recognised in the booklet 'True Union' it is necessary to maintain a breadth of private response to situations of individual pastoral care.

Pastoral Letter from the Primates of the Anglican Communion text at www.anglicancommunion.org/acns/articles/34/50

17 *Issues in Human Sexuality,* p. vii.

18 S. Vibert, 'Divine Order and Sexual Conduct' in T. Bradshaw (ed.) *The Way Forward?,* Hodder & Stoughton, 1997, p. 124.

19 Vibert, 'Divine Order and Sexual Conduct', p. 124.

20 Vibert, 'Divine Order and Sexual Conduct', p. 124.

21 See for example E. Stuart and A. Thatcher, *People of Passion,* Mowbray, 1997, pp. 185–9.

22 J. John, 'Christian Same-Sex Partnerships' in Bradshaw (ed.), *The Way Forward?,* p. 55.

23 John in Bradshaw, p. 56.

24 M. Vasey, *Strangers and Friends,* Hodder & Stoughton, p. 209.

25 Text in M. L. Soardes, *Scripture and Homosexuality,* Westminster John Knox Press, 1995, p. 77.

26 D. Atkinson, *Pastoral Ethics in Practice,* Monarch, 1989, pp. 87–8.

27 Atkinson, *Pastoral Ethics in Practice,* p. 88.

28 Atkinson, *Pastoral Ethics in Practice,* pp. 85–6.

29 M. Banner, *Christian Ethics and Contemporary Moral Problems,* Cambridge University Press, 1999, p. 267.

30 *Issues in Human Sexuality,* p. 46.

31 See for example Acts 20.28-31, 1 Timothy 3.1-13; 4.12-13; 5.19-20, Titus1.5-9, James 3.1, 1 Peter 5.1-3.

32 T. C. Oden, *First and Second Timothy and Titus,* John Knox Press, 1989, pp. 141–2.

33 H. Thielicke, *The Ethics of Sex,* James Clarke, 1978, p. 285.

34 *Living With Tensions,* The Evangelical Church in Germany, 1998, p. 30.

35 *Living With Tensions,* pp. 44–5.

36 For the arguments for this from two different Christian perspectives see *Marriage and the Church's Task*, CIO, 1978 and J. Stott, *Issues Facing Christians Today*, Marshalls, 1984, Chapter 14.

37 G. Duncan, *Courage to Love*, Darton, Longman & Todd, 2002, p. 287.

38 Duncan, *Courage to Love*, pp. 291–2.

39 T. Brown, *Further Reflections on Homosexuality, Christian Faith and the Church* (unpublished paper), p. 7.

40 J. I. Packer, 'Why I Walked', *Christianity Today*, 21 January 2003.

41 Banner, *Christian Ethics*, p. 266.

42 Those who wish to verify this point should look at the material on pages 286–321 of Duncan, *Courage to Love*.

43 Duncan, *Courage to Love*, p. 126.

44 Martin Hallett, *Sexual Identity and Freedom in Discipleship*, Grove Books, 1997, p. 4.

45 J. Stott, *Same Sex Partnerships?* Marshall Pickering, 1998, p. 39.

46 Packer, 'Why I Walked'.

47 For an account of how one diocese in the Church of England promoted the sort of discussion advocated in the last three bullet points see the Appendix of this report, which gives details of the study days on Issues in Human Sexuality organized by the diocese of Oxford.

48 This is an issue that has been highlighted by the Lesbian and Gay Christian Movement's report on Christian homophobia, referred to in footnote 1 at the beginning of this chapter.

49 Evangelical Alliance, *Transsexuality*, Paternoster Press, 2001, p. 44.

50 Evangelical Alliance, *Transsexuality*, p. 44.

51 'Bishop sanctioning scandal', www.reform.org.uk.

52 G. Woodall, *Trans-Sexual Persons and Catholic Moral Theology* (unpublished paper), pp. 17–18.

53 F. Watts, *Transsexualism and the Church* (unpublished paper), pp. 10–11.

chapter 9

1 The Reform covenant can be found at www.reform.org.uk.

2 The Lesbian and Gay Christian Movement article 'Homosexuality and the Church' can be found at http://www.lgcm.org.uk/useful/church.html.

3 'Homosexuality and the Church'.

4 'Homosexuality and the Church'.

5 As was explained in Chapter 1, the Lambeth resolution does not having binding authority in the churches of the Anglican Communion. Nevertheless, as an expression of the mind of the Communion it can be said to be the 'official' Anglican position on the matter.

6 D. W. Gomez and M. W. Sinclair (eds), *To Mend the Net*, The Ecclesia Society, 2001.

7 *A Response by the Diocese of California to Resolution 1.10.d of Lambeth 1998* at http://www.stpaulsanrafael.org/sermons/taskforce.htm.

8 *A Pastoral Statement to Lesbian and Gay Anglicans from Some Member Bishops of the Lambeth Conference*, text at http://www.justus.anglican.org/resources/Lambeth1998/paststmnt.html.

9 Extracts from *A Final Report from the International Anglican Conversations on Human Sexuality*.

10 For full details of the Cambridge Accord and the names of bishops who signed it, see the web site www.episdivschool.org/abouteds/cambridgeaccord.htm.

11 *True Union in the Body?* a paper commissioned by Most Revd Drexel Gomez, Oxford, 2003, pp. 44–5. The paper also argues that no 'truly representative' Anglican structure would be likely to recommend a change in the position taken at Lambeth 98 because:

> All the evidence is that the overwhelming majority of Anglicans will continue to see the blessing of homosexual practice as 'incompatible with Scripture' and refuse to condone any public recognition of same-sex unions by the Church. (p. 45) <ext ends>

12 Text in E. Stuart and A. Thatcher, *People of Passion*, Mowbray, 1997, pp. 167–8.

13   URC General Assembly 2000, Resolution 14 (a).

14   As was noted in Chapter 1, there are Roman Catholics who dissent from their Church's official teaching.

15   The text of their resolutions can be found in J. S. Siker (ed.), *Homosexuality in the Church: Both Sides of the Debate*, Westminster John Knox Press, 1994, p. 205.

16   See *The Church and Human Sexuality: A Lutheran Perspective*, ELCA Distribution Service, 1993.

17   *Living With Tensions*, The Evangelical Church in Germany, 1998, p. 36.

> It should be noted that strict criteria are laid down to which ordained homosexuals should conform, including the criterion that they should continue to uphold heterosexual marriage as God's ideal in their preaching and explain how their own way of life fits into this ethical framework. The report also concludes that: '. . . there are many arguments against the permitting of single-sex partnerships in pastor's houses'. (p. 40)

18   K. Gergen, *The Saturated Self*, Basic Books, 1991, p. 253. It should be noted, however, that this assertion would be fiercely contended by some 'postmodernist' thinkers: see the recent work of Jacques Derrida, for example.

19   As examples of attempts to engage seriously with the insights of postmodernism from different theological viewpoints see D. Hilborn, *Picking up the Pieces*, Hodder & Stoughton, 1997 and J. R. Middleton and B. J. Walsh, *Truth is Stranger than it Used to Be*, SPCK, 1995.

20   Middleton and Walsh, *Truth is Stranger*, p. 77.

21   N. Rescher, *Objectivity: The Demands of Impersonal Reason*, University of Notre Dame Press, 1997, p. 61.

22   Romans 14.12.

23   1 Corinthians 6.9-10.

24   1 John 4.8-20.

25   *The Porvoo Common Statement*, Council for Christian Unity, 1993, pp. 13–14.

26   ARCIC, *The Gift of Authority*, Catholic Truth Society, 1999, pp. 22–3.

27   Psalm 14.1.

28   1 John 4.2-3.

29   1 Corinthians 15.3.

30   Text in T. Bradshaw (ed.), *Grace and Truth in a Secular Age*, Eerdmans, 1998, p. 309.

31   Leviticus 19.2; Matthew 5.48.

32   M. Doe, *Seeking the Truth in Love*, Darton, Longman & Todd, 2000, pp. 111–12.

33   *Barmen Declaration* 1, in J. H. Leith, *Creeds of the Churches*, Blackwell, 1973, p. 520.

34   K. Barth, *Evangelical Theology*, Fontana, 1969, p. 44.

35   Ephesians 4.15.

36   For these last two points see D. Bonhoeffer, *The Cost of Discipleship*, SCM Press, 1959, pp. 259–60.

37   Bonhoeffer, *The Cost of Discipleship*, p. 36.

38   Rowan Williams, 'Foreword' to James Alison, *Knowing Jesus*, SPCK, 1998, p. ix.

Select bibliography

1. Studies in ethics and biblical interpretation

Atkinson, D., *Pastoral Ethics in Practice*, Monarch, 1989.

Barton, S. C., 'Is the Bible Good News for Human Sexuality? Reflections on Method in Biblical Interpretation', *Theology and Sexuality*, no. 1, September 1994.

Brown, D., *Choices: Ethics and the Christian*, Basil Blackwell, 1983.

Fiorenza, E. Schüssler, *Bread Not Stone: The Challenge of Feminist Biblical Interpretation*, Beacon Press, 1984.

Fowl, S., *Engaging Scripture*, Blackwell, 1998.

Habgood, J. *The Concept of Nature*, Darton, Longman & Todd, 2002.

Hart, T., 'Tradition, Authority and a Christian Approach to the Bible as Scripture' in J. B. Green and M. Turner (eds), *Between Two Horizons*, Eerdmans, 2000, pp. 183–204.

Hays, R., *The Moral Vision of the New Testament*, T&T Clark, 1996.

Jordan, M. D., *The Ethics of Sex*, Blackwell, 2002.

Kelly, Kevin T., *New Directions in Sexual Ethics*, Geoffrey Chapman, 1998.

O'Donovan, O. M. T., *Resurrection and Moral Order*, IVP, 1984.

Stuart, E. and A. Thatcher, *People of Passion*, Mowbray, 1997.

Thiselton, A., *New Horizons in Hermeneutics*, HarperCollins, 1992.

Turner, M., 'Historical Criticism and Theological Hermeneutics of the New Testament' in J. B. Green and M. Turner (eds), *Between Two Horizons*, Eerdmans, 2000, pp. 44–70.

Webb, W. J., *Slaves, Women & Homosexuals*, IVP, 2001.

Webster, J., *Word and Church*, T&T Clark, 2001.

2. Histories and theologies of human sexuality

Alison, J., *Faith Beyond Resentment: Fragments Catholic and Gay*, Darton, Longman & Todd, 2001.

Aquinas, St Thomas, *Summa Theologiae* 1a: Q 98; 3a supplemental Qs 41–68.

Augustine of Hippo, St, *On Marriage and Concupiscence*, Post Nicene Fathers vol. 5, Eerdmans, 1971.

Bailey, D. S. *The Man-Woman Relation in Christian Thought*, Longmans, 1959.

Barth, K., *Church Dogmatics* III/4:54:1, T&T Clark, 1961.

Breidenthal, T. E., *Christian Households: The Sanctification of Nearness*, Cowley Press, 1997.

Brown, P., *The Body and Society: Men, Women and Sexual Renunciation in Early Christianity*, Columbia University Press, 1988.

Calvin, J., *Institutes of the Christian Religion*, Bk II, Ch. VIII: 41–4.

Davies, J.and Gerard Loughlin (eds), *Sex These Days: Essays on Theology, Sexuality and Society*, Sheffield Academic Press, 1997.

Foucault, M., *The History of Sexuality Vol. 1*, Random House, 1980.

Hefling, C. (ed.), *Our Selves, Our Souls and Bodies: Sexuality and the Household of God*, Cowley Press, 1996.

Laqueur, T., *Making Sex: Body and Gender from the Greeks to Freud*, Harvard University Press, 1990.

Rogers, E. F., *Sexuality and the Christian Body*, Blackwell, 1999.

Ruether, R. Radford, *Christianity and the Making of the Modern Family*, SCM Press, 2001.

Schillebeeckx, E., *Marriage: Secular Reality and Saving Mystery*, vols 1–2, Sheed & Ward, 1965.

Storkey, E., *The Search for Intimacy*, Hodder & Stoughton, 1995.

Theology and Sexuality: The Journal for the Centre for the Study of Christianity and Sexuality (published twice a year).

Thielicke, H., *The Ethics of Sex*, James Clark, 1978.

Wesiner-Hanks, M. E., *Christianity and Sexuality in the Early Modern World*, Routledge, 2000.

3. Church of England and Anglican Communion statements on homosexuality

A Final Report from the International Anglican Conversations on Human Sexuality, *Anglican World*, Trinity 2002.

A Pastoral Statement to Lesbian and Gay Anglicans from Some Member Bishops of the Lambeth Conference http://justus.anglican.org/resources/Lambeth 1998/paststmnt.html.

A Response by the Diocese of California to Resolution 1.10.d of Lambeth 1998 at http://www.stpaulsanrafael.org/sermons/taskforce.htm.

General Synod Report of Proceedings vol. 18:3, Church House Publishing, 1987, pp. 913–56.

Gomez, G., A. Goddard and P. Walker (eds), *True Union in the Body?*, Grove Books, 2003.

Homosexual Relationships: a Contribution to Discussion, CIO, 1979.

Issues in Human Sexuality, Church House Publishing, 1991.

The Cambridge Accord: www.episdivschool.edu/abouteds/cambridgeaccord.htm

The Kuala Lumpur Statement on Human Sexuality: http/www.reform.
org.uk.
The Official Report of the Lambeth Conference 1998, Morehouse
Publishing, 1999, pp. 381–2.
The Problem of Homosexuality – An Interim Report, CIO, 1954.

4. Other studies on homosexuality and bisexuality
Balch, D. (ed.), *Homosexuality, Science and the 'Plain Sense' of Scripture*, Eerdmans, 2000.
Bergner, M., *Setting Love in Order: Hope and Healing for the Homosexual*, Monarch 1995.
Bradshaw, T. (ed.), *The Way Forward?*, Hodder & Stoughton, 1997.
Brooten, B., *Love Between Women: Early Christian Responses to Female Homoeroticism*, Chicago University Press, 1996.
Coleman, P., *Christian Attitudes to Homosexuality*, SPCK, 1980.
Coleman, P., *Gay Christians: A Moral Dilemma*, SCM Press, 1989.
Doe, M., *Seeking the Truth in Love*, Darton, Longman & Todd, 2000.
Evangelical Church in Germany, *Living with Tensions*, EKD, 1998.
Gagnon, R., *The Bible and Homosexual Practice*, Abingdon Press, 2001.
George, S., *Women and Bisexuality*, Scarlet Press, 1993.
Goss, R., *Jesus Acted Up: A Gay and Lesbian Manifesto*, HarperCollins, 1993.
Green, T. B. Harrison and J. Innes, *Not for Turning: An Enquiry into the Ex-Gay Movement*, published by the authors, 1996.
Greenberg, D., *The Construction of Homosexuality*, Chicago University Press, 1988.
Grenz, S., *Welcoming but not Affirming*, Westminster John Knox Press, 1998.
Haningan, J. P., *Homosexuality: The Test Case for Christian Sexual Ethics*, Paulist Press, 1988.
John, J., *Permanent, Faithful, Stable*, Darton, Longman & Todd, 1993.
Mason, A. and A. Palmer, *Queer Bashing: A National Survey of Hate Crimes against Lesbians and Gay Men*, Stonewall, 1996.
Olyan, S. M. and M. C. Nussbaum (eds), *Sexual Orientation and Human Rights in American Religious Discourse*, Oxford University Press, 1998.
Ruse, M., *Homosexuality*, Blackwell, 1988.
Schmidt, T., *Straight and Narrow?*, IVP, 1995.
Siker, J. S. (ed.), *Homosexuality in the Church: Both Sides of the Debate*, Westminster John Knox Press, 1994, p. 205.
Smith, M., 'Ancient Bisexuality and the Interpretation of Romans 1.26-27', *Journal of the American Academy of Religion* 64, 1966, pp. 223–54.

Spencer, C., *Homosexuality: A History*, Fourth Estate, 1996.
Stott, J., *Same Sex Partnerships*, Marshall Pickering, 1998.
Stuart, E., *Just Good Friends*, Mowbray, 1995.
Vasey, M., *Strangers and Friends*, Hodder & Stoughton, 1995.
Whitehead, B., *Craving for Love*, Kregel, 2003.

5. Studies in lesbian feminist theology
Daly, M., *Beyond God the Father*, Women's Press, 1986.
Heyward, C., *Touching Our Strength*, HarperCollins, 1989.
Hunt, M., *Fierce Tenderness: a Feminist Theology of Friendship*, Crossroad, 1991.
May, M., *A Body Knows: A Theopoetics of Death and Resurrection*, Continuum, 1995.
Mollenkott, V. R., *Sensuous Spirituality*, Crossroad, 1992.
Rudy, K., *Sex and the Church: Gender, Homosexuality and the Transformation of Christian Ethics*, Beacon Press, 1997.
Webster, A., *Found Wanting: Women, Sexuality and Christianity*, Cassell, 1995.
Wittig, M., *The Straight Mind and Other Essays*, Beacon Press, 1992.

6. Transsexualism
Dainton, M. and K. Tiller, *Ministry to the Gender Confused*, Parakaleo Ministries, n.d.
Evangelical Alliance, *Transsexuality*, Paternoster Press, 2001.
Hausman, B. L., *Changing Sex: Transsexuality, Technology and the Idea of Gender*, Duke University Press, 1995.
Holder, R., 'The Ethics of Transsexualism', *Crucible*, April–June 1998, pp. 89–99, and July–September 1998, pp. 125–36.
Home Office, *Report of the Interdepartmental Working Group on Transsexual People*, The Home Office Communications Directorate, 2000.
Horton, D., *Changing Channels? A Christian Response to the Transvestite and Transsexual*, Grove Books, 1994.
Kolakowski, V., 'Towards a Christian Ethical Response to Transsexual Persons', *Theology and Sexuality*, no.6, March 1997, pp. 10–23.
O'Donovan, O. M. T., *Transsexualism and Christian Marriage*, Grove Books, 1982.

General index

General index

Index of biblical references